ROUTLEDGE LIBRARY EDITIONS:
DEVELOPMENT

PROLETARIANISATION IN THE THIRD WORLD

PROLETARIANISATION IN THE THIRD WORLD

Studies in the Creation of a Labour Force Under Dependent Capitalism

Edited by
B. MUNSLOW
and
H. FINCH

Volume 93

Routledge
Taylor & Francis Group

LONDON AND NEW YORK

First published in 1984

This edition first published in 2011
by Routledge
2 Park Square, Milton Park, Abingdon, Oxon, OX14 4RN

Simultaneously published in the USA and Canada
by Routledge
711 Third Avenue, New York, NY 10017

Routledge is an imprint of the Taylor & Francis Group, an informa business

First issued in paperback 2013

British Library Cataloguing in Publication Data
A catalogue record for this book is available from the British Library

ISBN 13: 978-0-415-58414-2 (Set)
eISBN 13: 978-0-203-84035-1 (Set)
ISBN 13: 978-0-415-60192-4 (Volume 93)
ISBN 13: 978-0-415-85019-3 (Volume 93 pbk)
eISBN 13: 978-0-203-83551-7 (Volume 93)

Publisher's Note
The publisher has gone to great lengths to ensure the quality of this reprint but
points out that some imperfections in the original copies may be apparent.

Disclaimer
The publisher has made every effort to trace copyright holders and welcomes
correspondence from those they have been unable to contact.

PROLETARIANISATION IN THE THIRD WORLD

Studies in the Creation of a Labour Force
Under Dependent Capitalism

Edited by B. Munslow and H. Finch

CROOM HELM
London • Sydney • Dover, New Hampshire

©1984 B. Munslow and B. Finch
Croom Helm Ltd, Provident House, Burrell Row,
Beckenham, Kent BR3 1AT

Croom Helm Australia Pty Ltd, First Floor, 139 King St.,
Sydney, NSW 2001, Australia

Croom Helm, 51 Washington Street, Dover,
New Hampshire 03820, USA

British Library Cataloguing in Publication Data

Munslow, Barry
    Proletarianisation in the third world.
    1. Labor supply—Developing countries—
    History
    I. Title   II. Finch, H.
    331.12'09172'4   HD5852

    ISBN 0-7099-1764-3

Library of Congress Cataloguing in Publication Data

Main entry under title:
Proletarianism in the Third World.
        Bibliography: p.
        Includes index.
        1. Labor and laboring classes – Developing countries.
    2. Labor supply – Developing countries. 3. Poor –
    Developing countries. 4. Proletariat. I. Munslow,
    Barry. II. Finch, M.H.J. (Martin Henry John)
    HD8943.P76   1984   305.5'62'091724   84-12739

    ISBN 0-7099-1764-3

CONTENTS

Contents

TABLES AND FIGURES

Tables

Figures

CONTRIBUTORS

Bill Albert is Lecturer in Economic and Social History,
University of East Anglia

Jeff Crisp is with the Research and Information Division,
British Refugee Council, and Labour Correspondent of
African Business

Manuel Fernández was until recently Research Fellow, University
of Glasgow, and is currently teaching at the United World
College of the Adriatic, Trieste

Henry Finch is Lecturer in Economic History, University of
Liverpool

David Goodman is Lecturer in Economics, Department of Political
Economy, University College London, and Institute of Latin
American Studies, University of London

Nigel Haworth is Lecturer in Industrial Relations, University
of Strathclyde

Ronaldo Munck is Lecturer in Sociology, Ulster Polytechnic

Barry Munslow is Lecturer in Political Theory and Institutions,
University of Liverpool

Martin J. Murray is Associate Professor, Department of
Sociology, State University of New York at Binghamton

Richard Newman is Lecturer in Social History, Department of
Economic History, University College of Swansea

Jay O'Brien is Assistant Professor, Department of Anthropology
and Sociology, Lawrence University, Wisconsin

Contributors

Phil O'Keefe is at the Beijer Institute, Royal Swedish Academy of Sciences

Bernardo Sorj is a political sociologist at the Instituto de Relações Internacionais, Pontífica Universidade Católica do Rio de Janeiro

Elizabeth Taylor's research in Egypt and at the Department of Sociology, University of Manchester, is funded by the Population Council

John Wilkinson teaches rural sociology at the Universidade Federal Rural do Rio de Janeiro

PREFACE

Five of the chapters in this book were presented at the SSRC/ Third World Economic History and Development Group conference held at Liverpool in September 1982. We wish to thank the Social Science (now Economic and Social) Research Council, and the Faculty of Social and Environmental Studies of the University of Liverpool, for their financial support of the conference. We also thank Rory Miller who helped to organise the meeting. We wish to make it clear that responsibility for the opinions and conclusions expressed in this book rests with the editors and authors, not with the ESRC. In the preparation of the book, Diane Elson and Jeffrey Carroll gave valuable help. Our greatest debts of gratitude are owed to Phil O'Keefe, for his immense generosity in placing production facilities at our disposal; to the Research Fund of the University of Liverpool for financial assistance; and to June Summers, who gave up her spare time for months on end to see this project through to completion. We cannot praise her too highly, or thank her enough.

Chapter One

INTRODUCTION

It may seem odd to begin this Introduction with a confession of uncertainty. Nonetheless, it is as well to acknowledge at the outset that proletarianisation in the Third World is not a clearly-defined and unambiguous phenomenon. Essentially this book is concerned with the emergence of a free wage-labour force in a range of low-income countries. But the experience of the Third World has not been, on the whole, simply a replication of the kind of proletarianisation that occurred in Britain and the other advanced capitalist countries, with the creation of a large-scale permanent proletariat, divorced from ownership of the means of production and thus totally dependent on the sale of its labour power for survival. This is the sense in which a proletariat is understood in this book. However, the process of proletarianisation, in the way it has occurred in the Third World, has not conformed either to the model of the advanced countries or to a new general pattern. On the contrary, perhaps one of the most important conclusions which may be drawn from this collection of studies is that Third World proletarianisation has been an immensely varied and complex set of processes.

What these processes have in common is their origin in the impact of capitalism on dependent or peripheral social systems.(1) Their variety is due to a host of interrelated factors, amongst which the nature of the imperialist relationship, the indigenous social structure, and the work process itself have all clearly been of importance. But the most significant factor has been the varying nature of the supply of labour that capitalism encountered in the Third World. For capital to be accumulated a labour force must be created in order that the process of surplus extraction may occur. This took place in widely-varying conditions of labour scarcity, with the result that solutions to the labour supply problem had to be tailored to the specific circumstances of each society.

Accordingly, although under the capitalist mode of production the sale of labour is generally assumed to occur in

1

a free market, one of the most striking features of the various case-studies collected here is the importance of non-free market mechanisms or extra-economic coercion in the early stages of proletarianisation. Such practices frequently carried the approval of colonial governments, although the state itself had a labour requirement which might bring it into competition with private capital. In many cases labour shortage dictated a process of partial proletarianisation based on migrant labour.(2) An additional feature of these studies is the evidence they provide on the way in which the labour process and the specific working conditions in particular sectors of agriculture, mining, manufacturing or transport may affect the nature of the labour force which is formed in those sectors. In some cases they contributed to divisions and weakness in the working class, implanting structural and ideological limitations on the development of working class consciousness. An important measure of such factors is the intensity of working class organisation and struggle, and most of the authors in this volume have assessed the capacity for working class resistance. Indeed, it constitutes a major theme of the last three chapters. But in the main we have chosen not to focus attention here, placing more emphasis on the creation of Third World proletariats.(3)

It would be idle to claim that the studies contained in this book define or even adequately represent the range of problems associated with the emergence of wage labour in the Third World, but the coverage is nonetheless comprehensive both geographically and in terms of time-span. Four chapters concentrate on the late nineteenth century, examining the formation of labour forces in the nitrate industry in Chile, in gold mining in the Gold Coast (Ghana), on the sugar plantations of Peru, and in the urban and rural sectors in Argentina. O'Brien's study of agricultural proletarianisation examines the period 1920-50 in Sudan, a decisive phase in the creation of a labour supply for cotton production. The chapters on Brazil and Kenya focus on the complex changes occurring in the agricultural sector in recent years. Four chapters present a broader historical overview of proletarianisation in Egypt, Indochina, Mozambique and Peru. Finally, and in contrast, Newman gives a detailed analysis of events in Shanghai and Bombay during 1927-9, two of the most significant proletarian upsurges to have occurred on the global periphery. Given the diverse nature of the material which it was felt desirable to include in order to demonstrate the range of experience, there were obvious problems of how best to arrange the sequence of chapters. Almost any mode of organising the material would serve to highlight certain features, but this would inevitably be at the expense of others. Because of this we have opted to avoid a rigid division of the book into sections, preferring instead to order the chapters according to certain of the major themes that emerge from them.

The first four studies of gold mining in Ghana, nitrate production in Chile, the transport sector in Mozambique and the sugar plantations in Peru reflect the particular common character of early capitalist development in the Third World, that of the export of primary products to the advanced industrialising economies of the north. Each also highlights our central theme of the preoccupation of capital with the supply of workers, the so-called 'labour question'. Labour supply conditions could be drastically different from one case to the next, and the process of proletarianisation was one of accommodating the level of labour scarcity. In the general case, securing and maintaining a labour supply depended in part on the relative attraction to workers of remaining in the peasant economy. Studies in this volume on Egypt, Bombay and Sudan, as well as Ghana, illustrate how the rural refuge might be employed, either as a way of escape from wage labour or as a bargaining counter in industrial disputes. The export economy had either to recruit its labour from the area surrounding the location of production, or a workforce had to be - often quite literally - shipped in.

The process by which capitalism creates a surplus population eligible for proletarianisation was analysed by Marx in terms of three component parts: the latent, floating and stagnant surplus. The first of these refers to that part of the agricultural labour force which is surplus to agriculture's needs, resulting in a continuous flow of labour to the urban sector. The floating surplus population is fully proletarianised and 'free' labour, existing in the industrial centres. It is employed, or unemployed, according to the fluctuating level of activity in the economy. The third category is the stagnant component, which forms a part of the active labour army but has extremely irregular employment in the 'decaying branches of industry', and lives in the most miserable conditions. As surplus value is extracted from the working class and a part is reinvested, a change in the organic composition of capital occurs with constant capital (machinery) growing at the expense of variable capital (labour). 'The labouring population therefore produces, along with the accumulation of capital produced by it, the means by which itself is made relatively superfluous, is turned into a relative surplus-population; and it does this to an always increasing extent'.(4) This surplus population is needed, according to Marx, both to act as a dampener on wage levels but also to permit ready response or take-up in production in the upturns within the regular cyclical fluctuations of capitalism. Although at a certain stage of development these processes create their own surplus labour from within the urban areas, in the early period capital is reliant on creating the surplus in the rural sector.

In Ghana, labour was locally scarce as people had other options in agriculture or prospecting on their own account.

Introduction

Mine owners were sometimes obliged to use traditional holders
of authority, the chiefs, as an avenue for recruitment. This
use of intermediaries is very much in evidence in Peru also.
Under the enganche system, traders or contractors would most
commonly forward loans to individuals who then had to pay these
off through the sale of their labour power. Attempts at
recruitment were concentrated in periods when seasonal work in
peasant agriculture was reduced. Owners of haciendas, using a
system of labour services, would also sell these to plantation
owners. Although a similar system was used in Chile,
recruitment for the nitrate mining industry was simpler in that
peasants had in many cases already left the rural economy. An
initial separation from the land had occurred with the building
of the railways and via recruitment into the army.

In some cases the problem of securing labour supplies
remained an on-going one, with employers being obliged to
experiment with a variety of possible remedies. In the case of
Ghana, successive devices included mechanisation to substitute
for labour, subcontracting to African entrepreneurs, payment by
task was substituted for a daily wage, and intensified
managerial and supervisory discipline was employed. But the
gold mines of Ghana never managed to achieve the level of
efficiency and organisation associated with the recruiting
system of the South African mines although they tried to
emulate this.(5) There, a successful monopsonisation occurred.
Throughout Africa and lasting for varying periods of time,
forced labour was employed as one very obvious answer to the
problem of securing a labour supply.(6) In the British colonies
this ended in the 1920s, the 'prestation' system in the French
territories ceased only at the end of the Second World War,
whilst forced labour in the Portuguese colonies continued until
1961. Contemporary accounts, such as that of Nevinson's visit
to the Portuguese colony of Angola in 1904, reveal the harsh
reality of forced labour.(7) Munslow's chapter on Mozambique
describes the different forms it could take, and provides a
fragment of the oral record of those who suffered under it.

The first four case-studies all demonstrate the other
option open to employers, that of bringing in immigrant labour.
In the case of Ghana, Kroo labourers from Liberia were
employed. Chinese labour was imported to work on the Peruvian
sugar plantations and on the Mozambique railways, and in the
first decade of this century up to 60,000 were imported to work
in the South African gold mines when the Boer War disrupted the
existing regional supply system.(8) This option was considered
for Ghana also, but was rejected because of the outcry that
accompanied charges of slave 'coolie' labour being used within
South Africa. Indian labour also was employed both in east and
in southern Africa. Pressure of population on land in parts of
the Asian continent was such as to provide a ready-made reserve
at the disposal of the imperial powers for employment in the
more open frontier continents of Africa and Latin America. But

4

even within Europe an increasingly impoverished peasantry from Ireland and southern Europe in particular helped constitute a part of the Third World proletariat. There was seasonal migration across the Atlantic, for example, of Italian labourers working in Argentina.

The following four chapters focus on the transformation of rural relations of production. Capitalist development in Sudan has been overwhelmingly concerned with cotton production, another raw material export commodity. After much experimentation the British colonial regime opted for a tenancy scheme with a fixed percentage of returns from the crop being distributed between the family, a private company entrusted with its overall management, and the colonial state. Familial labour was not sufficient to meet the need for hands at the busy times of the agricultural cycle and a pattern of seasonal migration emerged. A process of semi-proletarianisation took place, drawing labour from local Sudanese peasants and West African immigrants. O'Brien's study is important in that it corrects an interpretation of capitalist development on the periphery which sees the role of those peoples as being purely passive. The Sudan study shows the wide range of possible responses contingent upon the local situation and the internal characteristics of the various communities.

Capital accumulation on the global periphery frequently involved not the complete destruction of pre-capitalist communities but their articulation with the capitalist mode.(9) The latter benefitted by having the reproduction and social welfare costs of labour borne by the pre-capitalist mode. Hence there was not a total divorce of the wage labourer from the means of production. To this extent the most common form of wage labour found in the Third World did not correspond to the completed proletarianisation process of the advanced industrialised societies. A conceptual problem has emerged, therefore, of how to characterise this group of migrant workers. One way is offered by O'Brien's designation of a semi-proletariat, others have preferred the term 'worker peasants',(10) with perhaps the most colourful conceptual addition coming from Robin Cohen - the 'peasantariat'(11). Whatever the term used, the underlying notion is one of partial proletarianisation based on migrant labourers who have not necessarily ceased to own means of production, principally in the form of land. Such a situation can be inherently unstable over the long term as land availability for the peasantry is reduced with an expansion of capitalist farming. In those areas where labour reserves were strictly institutionalised, notably in southern Africa, population pressure on severely restricted and increasingly eroded areas of generally infertile land is gradually reducing the capability of the reserves to fulfil their original role. In South Africa, Lesotho and Zimbabwe, for example, a reverse dependency of food imports into the reserves has become increasingly apparent.

Introduction

Whilst many of the contributions have concentrated on a study of the emerging working class at the point of production, the chapter on Kenya explores the effects on the rural areas of this partial form of proletarianisation. With the development of capitalism on the one hand and the limits to the physical environment on the other, the rural population finds itself trapped between the two. Much of the rural poverty thereby engendered is shown to result from a familial labour shortage caused by male outmigration, which leads to increased soil erosion, diminishing yields and growing hunger. The partial proletarianisation process is shown to contribute to the lack of labour militancy in the urban areas. The current recession in the Kenyan economy, coupled with high population growth, has resulted in increased unemployment. Given the extensive linkages between the two, when the urban working class is thus affected in a situation of labour migrancy, a crisis in peasant family production inevitably follows as rural survival so much depends on off-farm income generation.

Elizabeth Taylor's chapter signals a warning to those who see an inevitable process of global social change occurring, in which proletarianisation proceeds apace with the expanding accumulation of capital, inexorably swallowing up the peasantry in its train. The process may be reversible, at least in the short term. In Egypt, indeed, we find an expansion of the peasant farming sector at the expense of wage-labour employing capitalist agriculture - peasantisation is replacing proletarianisation! Undoubtedly a group of landless workers existed in the rural areas but these found jobs either as foreign migrants in the oil-rich Arab states or in the domestic construction industry. Instead of a surplus labour situation emerging in the rural areas as a result of the agglomeration of land holdings, there has been a rural labour shortage. Hired non-household labour at certain seasons of the year has been the norm for many peasant families. An expansion of migrant labour abroad and to the towns has absorbed agricultural labour and even the returning migrants do not replenish the rural labour force. But it is the capitalist rather than the peasant farmer who has experienced the brunt of the burden, as a result of the particular labour market situation that exists. The peasant agricultural labourer can be both a buyer and a seller of labour at different stages of either the production process or the life of the household. Instead of transactions occurring within the context of a totally free and open labour market, the tendency is for the creation of specific exchange relations between people. Because the capitalist farmer is unable to offer his own labour in exchange, therefore, he is the one to suffer the effects of rural labour shortage. As a result, peasant farming is expanding at the expense of capitalist farming.

Goodman, Sorj and Wilkinson provide a comprehensive overview of the recent complex debates on the transformation of

Brazilian agriculture and offer their own particular contribution, which seeks to get away from the former static and reductionist analysis of agro-industry. Rather they see agro-industrial capitals as the protagonists of an unstable and shifting alliance between rural and capitalist industrial production processes with the latter continually advancing at the former's expense. But agro-industrial expansion is proceeding without the need to impose a homogenising pattern on the social division of labour. Four basic structures are characterised, corresponding with particular geographical regions of Brazil: agro-industry and large properties in the Centre-South; the modernised family farm in the South; the North is much more diversified but with the strong influence of a modernised form of the latifundio system called pecuarização, existing alongside huge numbers of impoverished family labour producers on minifundia; and in Amazonia, the initial frontier occupation by peasant settlers exploited by merchant capital is being transformed as modern capital takes control of the settlement process. Instead of identifying a single dominant tendency, Goodman et al. show how state modernisation policies and agro-industrial expansion may not only maintain but even accentuate the diversity of rural social relations.

The final four chapters address the issue of proletarianisation from a national or regional rather than sectoral perspective, emphasising in particular the political dimensions of the process. Nonetheless, the dominance of primary production for export as a factor in the creation of wage labour is again evident. Murray on Indochina and Haworth on Peru place great emphasis on the world market as the conditioning factor in explaining each country's specific proletarianisation process. They examine the progressive incorporation of the countries into the global capitalist system. In the case of Peru, these origins are traced back to the time of the Spanish Conquest. During the nineteenth century Peru was engaged at various times in the export of guano, nitrates, cotton and sugar. Extraction of guano and nitrates was not suited to the traditional labour tribute systems and required the formation of a stable labour force. Thus a proletariat grew up as a function of export enclave development, but only modestly before 1890. Early efforts to develop a sound base for national capital were thwarted and Peru's integration into the world market proceeded apace. Agromineral extraction was a similar feature in Indochina, though here a migrant labour system was a much more dominant feature. Murray warns of the problems encountered in trying to compile accurate statistics on the growth of the proletariat, a problem facing all of those working in this field. In the case of Indochina, official employment figures omitted many groups of workers, including those employed by local businessmen, and the landless casual rural workers.

Introduction

     It is in this last group of cases that the capacity of
workers for resistance receives most prominence. The question
is bound -up with the subject of class consciousness, a
particularly vexing problem with much of the discussion cast in
Marx's terms of emerging classes an sich and established
classes für sich. Like proletarianisation itself, it has to be
understood as a process. Initially it is the response by
individuals rather than by the workforce as a whole to the
newly-found work situation which is the most striking feature
of resistance. Cohen has produced an important article (12)
building upon van Onselen's earlier work,(13) drawing a
distinction between hidden and overt forms of resistance. The
former appear to dominate in the early period and
characteristic workers' responses might include desertion,
target-working, sabotage, thefts, accidents and sickness and
drug use. These hidden forms may also include non-individual
responses such as community withdrawal or revolt, task,
efficiency and time bargaining, and the creation of a
'work-culture'. The evidence from Crisp's study of Ghana would
also add physical assault and personal abuse to this list. Some
of the historical incidents connected with desertion were
tragic. At the end of the last century Mary Kingsley related
the tale of how labour was obtained from all parts of the West
Coast to work on the island plantations of São Tomé and
Fernando Po. One group, known as the Krumen, refused to work on
the plantations because some years earlier the employers had
continually delayed the shipping back of workers following
completion of their two-year contract. 'At last the home-sick
men, in despair of ever getting free, started off secretly in
ones and twos to try and get to 'we country' across hundreds of
miles of the storm-haunted Atlantic in small canoes, and with
next to no provisions. The result was a tragedy...'(14) And as
Fernández notes, Chinese indentured labourers imported to work
in Peru committed suicide by throwing themselves from the
cliffs of the guano islands.
     In examining the propensity for the development of more
overt forms of resistance, the cultural dimensions of class
solidarity and action are clearly important, with the level of
literacy a most significant factor. The proletariats of
different countries are also the bearers of different political
cultures which may take anarcho-syndicalist, communist,
socialist or reformist organisational expressions. Most common,
however, are a combination of these, or even the complete
absence of working class political parties. Argentina, for
example, is for the most part a nation of immigrants. Until
recent times its development was comparable to that of Canada
or Australia. A crucial feature of the Argentine case is that
part of the working class was brought in already formed,
importing with it the left political groupings and attendant
rivalries that had bedeviled the working class movements in
Europe. The capitalist class in Latin America was not alone in

blaming labour unrest on outside agitators. It was correct in doing so to the extent that political agitation came from abroad but wrong in that it rapidly found indigenous roots. It is of interest to compare overt forms of working class action amongst railway workers in Argentina and those in Mozambique - two totally contrasting situations. Amongst black railway workers, in Mozambique at least, not only were political parties banned but so too were trade unions, hence parochial divisions in the labour process at work could not be overcome to permit a broader working class consciousness to emerge. In Argentina, at the other extreme, the strikes of 1917 and 1918, including a general strike, exposed the division between the syndicalist-led La Fraternidad of the footplatemen and the workshop personnel's Federación Obrera Ferroviaria. Hence both ends of the spectrum of levels of political and union organisation could produce divisions and hamper the working class unity necessary if the whole social order was to be challenged - as it was by the working class movement in Chile with the inauguration of the Allende government at the beginning of the 1970s. The chapter on Argentina shows how political reformist movements may neutralise working class consciousness and divert it from radical paths. It also demonstrates the extent of divisions which may exist within a working class composed of immigrants from peasant backgrounds, artisan craftsmen, established local workers and internal rural immigrants. Not the least of the differences were those of language and traditions.

The comparative study of Shanghai and Bombay by Newman shows the potential which does exist from time to time for a much more vigorous display of united working class action, which may indeed threaten and even overturn existing authority. However, the context in which this occurred in the Chinese case was of civil war between rival armies, with the nationalists attempting to defeat the warlords and establish a united sovereign state. The insurrection's success, however shortlived, was intimately bound up with the context of war. No less, it should be observed, was the October Revolution in Russia in 1917. The Shanghai insurrection was put down by the combination of a counter-revolutionary thrust by the Green Gang secret society and Chiang Kai-shek's army. There are many examples of such right-wing militia-style units being employed to crush left-wing workers' insurrections, and not only in the Third World, as events in Europe in the closing years of the second decade of this century remind us. The brutality with which the insurrection was put down provides a savage reminder of the fragility and reversibility of working-class gains, and indeed, of the vanguard party whose political work did so much to initiate that process. As Newman writes, 'The communist position was completely destroyed in the very city where the industrial structure and the development of working class organisations offered China's best hope of a proletarian revolution'. The subsequent major rethink of strategy by the Chinese Communist Party (CCP) led to a turn away from the proletariat to find instead a base amongst the peasantry. The CCP was to fight a protracted people's war in the rural areas rather than risk another aborted urban workers' insurrection. This move was to have ramifications well beyond the Chinese frontiers. The reverberations, even today, echo in the inner debates of Third World revolutionary movements.

The events of the Bombay strike of 1928 were also of great importance, lasting for six months, involving 140,000 workers and propelling the role of the Indian Communist Party to the fore. Arrests of union leaders in the following year promoted a further strike but the lack of experienced direction plus the weariness engendered by industrial action led to eventual collapse. The defeat of the trade union movement was not as great as in Shanghai but was serious nontheless. In both cases, working class organisations were bound up with the nationalist movement. There was much to divide each internally and as is so frequently the case, too much energy was diverted into internal squabbling. The emerging trade unions in India had to compete and treat with the jobbers for influence over the workers. In Shanghai and elsewhere, tame 'guilds' etc were set up by employers to preempt trade unionism. The institutional mechanisms of working class organisation and expression provide an important area for study.

In analysing the growth of working class organisation, it is as well to remember that a worker is never just a worker. He or she is generally parent, provider, member of the community and of special groups within that community. This interpenetration has to be understood if the complex and contradictory process of consciousness formation associated with proletarianisation is to be properly dealt with. As Newman writes, 'the industrial labour force was not a discrete entity and its organisation inside the workplace could not be started without involving the various networks that operated across the workers' lives'. Too little research has been done on this dimension of the Third World's proletariat, and we have nothing approaching the comprehensive account provided in E.P. Thompson's case-study, The Making of the English Working Class.(15) However, exceptions do exist, notably with van Onselen's recent work on the social and economic history of the Witwatersrand.(16)

Various attempts have been made to categorise the degree of working class consciousness since the pioneering contribution of Engels.(17) Sandbrook and Cohen have proposed a classification of three levels.(18) The first is a simple acceptance by a group of workers of their common identity related to the production process. Secondly there is the recognition of common economic interests as a class and the need to collectively organise to defend these against the claims of opposing classes. Finally there is the conviction of

an irreconcilable antagonism between labour and capital and the
need to replace the system. The authors go on to warn,
correctly in our view, of the 'temptation to see them as part
of an incremental chain, a logical progression to a
more-and-more expansive and pervasive consciousness'.(19) The
paradox in the development of a group consciousness such as
that associated with the Ghanaian gold workers or Mozambican
dockworkers is that it may be a step towards the formation of a
higher class consciousness or, as in these two cases and
doubtless thousands more besides, it may be an impediment to
its development. A sense of 'occupational community' may be so
strong that it becomes impossible to identify with other
sections of the working class.

Haworth's chapter attempts to provide a systematised
framework for analysing the divisions existing within the
working class. He notes first of all possible fragmentation
along ideological, sectoral, spatial, organisational and
temporal lines. Furthermore he identifies various distinct
levels of operation: nation, region, sector, community and
plant. As he says, 'It is not impossible for a worker to be
represented at all of these levels, but at each to find a
different complex of political processes and tendencies in
motion'. In addition to these multiple sources of potential
divisions we also find ethnic and clientelistic solidarities
existing, which normally promote conservative rather than
radical politics.(20) The Mozambican study shows how different
occupations have a different labour process and how this plays
an important role in determining consciousness; a general
hypothesis which it suggests is that the more basic the
production process, utilising undifferentiated and unskilled
labour, the more militant will be the workers' resistance.

One of the most neglected dimensions of division within
the labour force is gender. In particular, the female working
class of the Third World has been almost completely ignored as
an area of study. Only now and in a halting manner is research
being carried out. A particular impetus is provided by the
establishment by multinational enterprise of manufacturing
operations employing cheap labour in the Third World, which
rely heavily on female workers.(21) Patriarchal methods are
frequently used as a control mechanism in the workplace.
However, it is only in certain parts of the Third World that a
growing proletarianisation amongst women is obvious. In Africa,
for example, with the exception of Swaziland and Tunisia, women
account for less than ten per cent of the labour force in
manufacturing.(22) In Africa the role of women has become much
more that of covering the costs of the reproduction of a male
migrant working class, with their own labour expended in
peasant farming. In Mexico, by way of contrast, in the early
years of this century women were providing about one third of
the labour force in manufacturing, according to the
censuses.(23) Women workers appear to be particularly

11

vulnerable to extremes of exploitation as rates of unionisation are frequently low, with a high labour turnover because of the requirements of child-birth and child-rearing which are not accommodated by employers. An additional problem in terms of the unionisation of women is the lack of free time, given the domestic shift which a woman is also expected to work. There are some notable exceptions, however, where women have organised themselves into unions and fought successful struggles against employers.(24) But in the prevailing ideology, a woman's wage is generally not seen to be as 'important' as a man's, and sexism within trade unions themselves frequently acts as a barrier to extending the unionisation of women workers.

A recurring theme throughout this collection is the role of the state in accelerating the proletarianisation process, for example by land annexation, taxation or the introduction of forced labour obligations. In some cases, the state can be found organising the migrant labour system, whilst more generally it is active in policing labour resistance. However, in many of the countries on the global periphery there is no equivalent to the all-powerful capitalist state exercising a monopoly of violence or asserting a ruling class hegemony over society. We find instead sections of capital exercising their own direct forms of coercion. In the case of Ghana, and this is not unique, the colonial state is in fact in competition with private capital for labour. The precise forms of intervention made by the state will clearly vary from one context to the next. We find it encouraging the formation of an organised labour movement in Bombay whilst actively discouraging it in the most violent manner in Shanghai. The state may be called upon to try to reconcile the conflicting interests of different fractions of capital, such as mining, manufacturing and agriculture, whose need for labour will vary and possibly conflict. With manufacturing capital being more mobile than mining capital, especially in the era of the multinational corporation, mining capital may be obliged to rely more readily on overt state coercion whereas manufacturing capital can exercise control simply by changing or threatening to change location to find a more servile labour force elsewhere. A variety of different means for disciplining the labour force are demonstrated in the case studies - including 'kangaroo' courts in Peru, corporal punishment in Mozambique (with the state taking over the task from the railway administration only in 1962), and in Ghana, workers were handed over to the traditional courts. But increasingly the most important mechanism of control was that exercised by the capitalist production process itself.

Marx drew a distinction between 'formal' and 'real' control by the capitalist over wage labour.(25) In the early phase of manufacture, 'formal' control was exercised solely through the ownership of the means of production; although the division of labour was a central characteristic - Adam Smith observed its importance in the 1770s - the technical base of manufacturing still lay in handicraft. As Gareth Stedman Jones has pointed out, the power of the skilled journeyman remained, to exercise considerable control over the content and pace of the labour process. This was only to be broken with the introduction of the new machine technology,(26) which revolutionised the labour process, leading to the 'real' as opposed to the 'formal' subordination of labour to capital over an extended period of time. The key to the process was the breaking of labour's control over the production process to the extent that human labour became an appendage to the machine. This process has been most graphically described by Max Weber:

> the mechanization and discipline of the plant, and the psycho-physical apparatus of man is completely adjusted to the demands of the outer world, the tools, the machines - in short, to an individual function. The individual is shorn of his natural rhythm as determined by the structure of his organism; his psycho-physical apparatus is atuned to a new rhythm through a methodical specialisation of separately functioning muscles and an optimal economy of forces is established corresponding to the conditions of work.(27)

The development of manufacturing sectors has been extremely uneven in the Third World. Variations in the patterns of industrial development are evident from one continent to the next and even between neighbouring countries. Extremely rapid contemporary industrialisation in the free production zones and world market factories of Hong Kong, Taiwan, Singapore and South Korea, reflecting a new division of labour,(28) contrasts markedly with the slow growth of small light industries in Latin America up to the 1930s depression, after which the production of consumer goods received a boost under the impetus of import substitution industrialisation, to be followed by steady infrastructural development and heavy industrial growth from the late 1950s.(29) The size of Latin America's industrial sector and its growth compares most favourably with that of Africa however. As a recent United Nations report concluded, 'Africa remains by far the least industrialised region in the world'.(30) These variations are reflected in the proportion of the labour force employed in industry at the end of the 1970s. In 36 countries having the lowest per capita GNP, the average proportion was 14 per cent (with none higher than 20 per cent). For 60 middle-income countries, the proportion averaged 23 per cent; while 18 high-income countries had an average of 38 per cent of the labour force in industry.(31) In addition, it is estimated that up to a half or more of the Third World workforce is employed in small establishments of less than ten workers, generally in appalling conditions.(32) Ghosh describes in detail such establishments in Calcutta:

> Dirty and narrow alleys branching out from the main road,
> which itself is little more than a narrow street; open
> stinking and choked drains; tottering sheds
> unsystematically huddled together in miserable clusters of
> a few turning shops; a precision grinding works is almost
> choked with the heat and smoke of the surrounding forging
> units... Working conditions in those workshops are simply
> horrifying. In a dark and smoky shed measuring 20ft x 15ft
> there are likely to be up to ten lathes and capstans with
> hardly any space for a person to move between them. All
> the machines are linked by a primitive device to a
> rotating shaft overhead which in its turn is driven by an
> electric motor. The workers move about in between and
> underneath the whirling belts with perfect ease,
> apparently unconcerned about the dreadful consequence of
> even the slightest error in their movements.(33)

Even today a permanent proletariat in manufacturing
represents only a small section of the wage labour force in the
Third World. As was noted at the very beginning of the
Introduction, much more common has been an incomplete
proletarianisation process based on the use of migrant labour.
We have explored a number of the central themes emerging from
studies of proletarianisation around the globe, the various
different mechanisms employed to obtain a labour force, to
divide it and ensure its weakness, the diverse forms of worker
resistance, with varying patterns of state intervention. The
picture that emerges is a complex one which defies any attempt
to encapsulate it in a single phrase. The comparative study of
proletarianisation in the Third World remains as yet in its
infancy, still fighting to break down the barriers between the
subject disciplines of social and economic history, sociology,
geography, economics, politics and development studies. It
faces further impediments in the form of area specialisms. This
volume is offered as a contribution to the effort to overcome
such problems. We have deliberately eschewed an approach
apparent in a certain current in the literature, that asserts a
claim for the development of a proletariat and working class
consciousness beyond that which has actually been attained in
the Third World. By so doing, we do not intend to downgrade the
importance of worker resistance against frequently atrocious
conditions and high levels of exploitation. Rather we see the
need for a more realistic assessment of the barriers to the
development of working class resistance as being a necessary
stage in the process of overcoming them.

NOTES
    1.   An influential analysis of the global capitalist
system and the concepts of core and periphery is developed in
I. Wallerstein, _The Capitalist World-Economy_, (Cambridge

University Press, Cambridge, 1979). For a powerful critique of Wallerstein's conceptualisation of the role of free wage labour in the periphery, see R. Brenner, 'The Origins of Capitalist Development: A Critique of Neo-Smithian Marxism', New Left Review, no. 104 (1977). The use of the term 'Third World' in this volume is simply a short-hand expression for the low and middle-income countries of Africa, Latin America, Asia and the Middle East, and does not necessarily imply approval of the term in any other sense.

2.   The growing use of temporary migrant labour also in advanced capitalist countries is a notable development. See S. Castles and G. Kosack, Immigrant Workers and Class Structure in Western Europe (Oxford University Press, London, 1973).

3.   For studies of working class organisation and action in the Third World, see R. Cohen, P. C.W. Gutkind and P. Brazier, Peasants and Proletarians: The Struggles of Third World Workers (Hutchinson, London. 1979).

4.   K. Marx, Capital, vol. 1 (Lawrence and Wishart, London, 1970), p. 631.

5.   F.A. Johnson, Class, Race and Gold: A Study of Class Relations and Racial Discrimination in South Africa, (Routledge and Kegan Paul, London, 1976); A. Jeeves, 'The Control of Migratory Labour on the South African Gold Mines in the Era of Kruger and Milner', Journal of Southern African Studies, vol. 2,no.1, (1975) pp. 3-29; F. Wilson, Labour in the South African Gold Mines, 1911-1969, (Cambridge University Press, Cambridge, 1972).

6.   A.T. Nzula, I.I. Potekhin, A.Z. Zusmanovich, Forced Labour in Colonial Africa, (Zed Press, London, 1979).

7.   H.W. Nevinson, A Modern Slavery, (The Daimon Press, Essex, 1963).

8.   P. Richardson, Chinese Mine Labour in Transvaal, (Macmillan, London, 1982).

9.   For a theoretical discussion of these processes see H. Wolpe (ed.), The Articulation of Modes of Production (Routledge and Kegan Paul, London, 1980); J.G. Taylor, From Modernisation to Modes of Production (Macmillan, London, 1979); L. Cliffe, 'The Agrarian Question and the 'Mode of Production' Debate in Africa', in H. Alavi, A.G. Frank and K.H. Harris (eds.), Relations of Production In Indian Agriculture, forthcoming.

10.   R. First, Black Gold: The Mozambican Miner, Proletarian and Peasant, (Harvester Press, Brighton, 1983), part iv.

11.   R. Cohen, 'Workers in Developing Societies', in H. Alavi and T. Shanin (eds.), Introduction to the Sociology of 'Developing Societies' (Macmillan, London, 1982), p. 282.

12.   R. Cohen, 'Resistance and Hidden Forms of Consciousness Amongst African Workers', Review of African Political Economy, no. 19 (1980).

13.   C. van Onselen, Chibaro. African Mine Labour in
Southern Rhodesia 1900-1933. (Pluto Press, London, 1976).
    14. M. Kingsley, Travels in West Africa (1897, re-issued
Virago Press, London, 1982), p. 49.
    15.   E.P. Thompson, The Making of the English Working
Class, (Penguin, Harmondsworth, 1963).
        16.   C. van Onselen, Studies in the Social and Economic
History of the Witwatersrand Vol 1: New Babylon, Vol 2: New
Ninevah, (Longman, London, 1982).
        17. F. Engels, The Condition of the Working Class in
England in W.O.Henderson,(ed.) Engels: Selected Writings
(Penguin, Hardmondsworth, 1967), pp 55-93.
    18.   R. Sandbrook and R. Cohen, (eds.) The Development of
an African Working Class (Longman, London, 1975), p.8.
    19. Ibid, p.313.
    20. R. Sandbrook, The Politics of Basic Needs (Heinemann,
London, 1982), Ch. 6.
    21.   D. Elson and R. Pearson, 'The Subordination of Women
and the Internationalisation of Factory Production', in K.
Young, C. Wolkowitz and R. McCullagh (eds.), Of Marriage and
the Market, (CSE Books, London, 1981,), pp 144-66, and by the
same authors, 'Nimble Fingers Make Cheap Workers: An Analysis
of Women's Employment in Third World Export Manufacturing',
Feminist Review, no. 7 (1981); K. Young (ed.), Just One Big
Happy Family (forthcoming); A. Fuenter and B. Ehrenreich, Women
in the Global Factory (Institute for New Communications, New
York, 1983); L.G. Arrigo, 'The Industrial Workforce of Young
Women in Taiwan', Bulletin of Concerned Asian Scholars vol. 12,
no. 2, (1980); UNIDO, Women in the Redeployment of
Manufacturing Industry to Developing Countries (UNIDO Working
Paper on Structural Changes, No. 18, 1980); W. Chapkis and C.
Enloe (eds., Of Common Cloth: Women in the Global Textile
Industry (Transnational Institute, New York and Amsterdam,
1983); J. Salaff, Working Daughters of Hong Kong (Cambridge
University Press, Cambridge, 1981).
    22.   J.M. Bujra, 'Urging Women to Redouble their
Efforts...: Class, Gender and Capitalist Transformation in
Africa', (paper given to the African Studies Seminar,
University of Liverpool, December 1983, p. 6).
    23.   R.D. Anderson. Outcasts in their Own Land: Mexican
Industrial Workers 1906-1911 (Northern Illinois University
Press, DeKalb, 1976), ch. 2.
    24.   See for example, B. du Toit, Ukubamba Amadolo:
Workers' Struggles in the South African Textile Industry (Onyx
Press, London, 1978).
    25. Marx, Capital, vol. 1. (Lawrence and Wishart, London.
1971, p. 510).
    26.   G. Stedman Jones, Languages of Class. Studies in
English Working Class History 1832-1982, (Cambridge University
Press, Cambridge, 1983), p. 46.

27.   H.H. Gerth and C. Wright Mills (eds.), From Max Weber: Essays in Sociology (Routledge and Kegan Paul, London, 1964.), pp. 261-2.

28.   F. Frobel, J. Heinrichs, O. Kreye, The New International Division of Labour (Cambridge University Press, Cambridge, 1980).

29.   This threefold periodisation of Latin America's industrialisation is provided by P. Rains, 'The Workers and the State in Latin America: Patterns of Dominance and Subordination', Civilisations, vol. 29, nos. 1-2, (1979).

30.   United Nations Economic Commission for Africa, Survey of Economic and Social Conditions in Africa, 1979-1980. Part One   (UN.E/CN. 14/802, New York, 1981), p. 11. Comparing the share of the less developed countries in world manufacturing value added between 1960 and 1980, Africa accounts for only 0.9 per cent, Latin America for 6 per cent, South and East Asia for 2.6 per cent and West Asia for 0.7 per cent. UNIDO, World Industry in 1980 (U.N. Biennial Industrial Development Survey, New York, 1981), p. 31.

31.   The World Bank, World Development Report, 1981. (Oxford University Press, London, 1981). Table 19.

32.   I. Roxborough, Theories of Underdevelopment, (Macmillan, London, 1979), p. 80.

33.   M.P. Ghosh, 'Small Engineering Workshops in Howrah (India)', in H. Johnson and H. Bernstein (eds.), Third World Lives of Struggle, (Heinemann, London, 1982), p. 126.

Chapter Two

THE LABOUR QUESTION IN THE GOLD COAST, 1870-1906

Jeff Crisp

> The native himself seems to be the only person who can
> stand the climate and who should do the work, but the
> question is, how is he to be induced to do it in order
> that it shall be profitable to those who invest their
> capital?

George MacDonald, The Gold Coast Past and Present, 1898

In 1471 Portuguese explorers first reached the Gold Coast in
search of the precious metal which gave the area its name. For
the next four hundred years they and other Europeans made
repeated attempts to take control of gold production in the
area, but they enjoyed no success. Although indigenous rulers
were happy to trade in gold, they refused to reveal the
location of their mines and continued to control production
either directly, through the use of slave labour, or
indirectly, through the tribute system. It was not until the
last quarter of the nineteenth century, when Britain 'pacified'
and annexed the Gold Coast hinterland, that European
entrepreneurs finally gained direct access to the colony's
mineral deposits.

The establishment of a capitalist gold mining industry in
the Gold Coast between approximately 1870 and 1910 proved to be
a very risky enterprise, and many investors saw their capital
wasted on mines that failed to produce a single ounce of gold.
A number of obstacles confronted the early mining
entrepreneurs. As a result of the lack of infrastructural
development in the colony at this time, the establishment of a
new mine was invariably a very long and expensive process.
Political instability and the absence of concession legislation
prolonged this process further, and wasted the scarce capital
resources of the many speculative mining companies formed
during the 'jungle boom' of the 1880s. Such enterprises were
further weakened by climatic and health conditions on the
coast, which took a severe toll of expatriate mining personnel
and discouraged experienced mining engineers from working in
the colony.

The most important obstacle to the development of modern mining, and the central concern of this chapter, was what became known amongst British entrepreneurs and investors as the 'labour question'. Thomas Haughton, for example, writing to the Mining Journal from the coast in 1883, complained that 'the labour question is undoubtedly one of the greatest troubles'. Twelve years later Edwin Cade reported to the shareholders of the Cote d'Or mine that 'labour is the most difficult of the local questions'.(1)

What exactly was the 'labour question'? The answer is provided in another statement by Haughton. 'The greatest consideration', he wrote, 'is that the mines ... have a constant supply of first class labour, and that at a cheap rate'.(2) In other words, the mines wanted three things: a regular and adequate supply of native workers, a labour force that was efficient and reliable, and a labour force that was willing to accept low wages. These three demands, and the failure of the mining industry to satisfy them, constituted the 'labour question' in the period 1870 to 1906.

ORIGINS OF THE LABOUR QUESTION, 1870-1900

Expatriates on the coast had no doubt that the labour question had its origins in the inherent laziness of the local population. As Burton and Cameron suggested in 'The Labour Question in Western Africa', 'their beau idéal is to do nothing for six days in the week and to rest on the seventh'.(3) While this explanation had the virtue of simplicity, it had the defect of totally ignoring the real origins of the labour question, which were to be found firstly in the socio-economic structure of the societies inhabiting the gold producing areas of south-western Ghana, and secondly in the conditions of work offered to them by the new expatriate mining companies.

As Hopkins has stated, in pre-colonial West Africa 'there was more land available than there was labour to cultivate it'.(4) This statement was certainly true of the Gold Coast's mining areas. Skertchly, for example, noted that 'like all the West Coast, Wassaw is but sparsely peopled ... one vast forest with meagre villages of a dozen huts or so scattered at long intervals along the roads'.(5) There was, therefore, no real demographic pressure forcing the local population off the land and into paid employment.

This situation was not altered by the emancipation of the colony's slaves in 1874. In theory, the colonial administration wanted the slave population to be turned into wage labourers or cash-crop farmers, thereby boosting the colony's economy. In practice, the government's fears of unrest amongst the slave-owning Asante ensured that the Anti-Slavery Ordinance was never enforced very rigorously. Moreover, as a member of the Basel Mission predicted:

No breadless proletariat will develop, because the ex-slaves can either farm land belonging to someone else for a small proportion of their yearly product, or can go and farm the uninhabited tracts. The majority... have remained with their masters either because they are well handled, and are part of the family, or because they fear to be independent.(6)

In a situation where even the poorest members of society could subsist without selling their labour power, some financial incentive was obviously needed to mobilise a labour force. The incentive which the early mining companies offered, a daily wage of under one shilling and six pence for unskilled workers, was not sufficiently attractive to achieve that objective. Inspired by the notion that local labourers would only work long enough to save a fixed cash target, the mining companies refused to increase wage levels, and instead merely petitioned the administration with indignant complaints about the supply and price of labour. The government, however, tended to have little sympathy for the mines, since it could rely on the use of compulsory and imported labour to satisfy its own demand for labour. Indeed, by using coercive methods of recruitment and brutal methods of labour control, the government simultaneously depleted the reservoir of local labourers available to the mines, and reinforced the indigenous population's reluctance to work for expatriate employers. As Edwin Cade of Ashanti Goldfields complained, when government troops descended on local market places to recruit carriers, there was a 'tremendous stampede' of men out of the mines and mining areas.(7)

Low wages were not the only unattractive feature of the work offered by the mines. The tasks assigned to native workers were invariably the most arduous, dirty, and dangerous, and quite unlike the agricultural labour in which most local men and women were engaged. Moreover, in those areas where mining was traditionally the work of slaves, free men were understandably very reluctant to offer their services to the new mining companies.

Finally, the methods of supervision and management employed by the mines acted as a further disincentive to prospective wage labourers. Expatriate entrepreneurs constantly bemoaned the indigenous attitude towards work, complaining that the local labourer 'requires that you should be continually watching him, otherwise he is sitting down, praying for night and the whistle to blow'.(8) There was, however, a solution to this problem. As John Daw explained, 'provided efficient white foremen of sterling character be available... then the greater number of men from any of the districts will do a fair day's work'.(9) Inevitably though, the workers' perception of what constituted a 'fair day's work' was very different to that of the white supervisor. Thus in Skertchly's words, 'when carrying for themselves a hundredweight is not overweight, but when working for a white man anything over 30 pounds is "too much"'.(10)

It was the function of European supervisors to overcome such objections and to replace the worker's norms with those of the Victorian capitalist: 'We freely admit that we do impose conditions which an uncivilized nation may deem to be hard and exacting. We insist on punctuality, on rigid temperance, on morality and on diligence'.(11) In practice, the imposition of such virtues was not merely 'hard and exacting', but depended on the use of overt physical coercion. One former supervisor, for example, admitted in his memoirs that in order to teach a worker a new task it was necessary to give him 'a good hiding'. 'Lagos boys', he complained, were unsuitable workers 'because they object to being hit without good reason and hit back', whereas the Fanti worker 'can be hit with or without cause and does not worry'.(12)

There is no doubt that supervisory violence was a common feature of life in the mines at this time. The trading firm of Swanzy's and the Basel Mission both complained to the colonial administration about the harsh treatment of native mine workers, informing the Governor that the mining companies would quite happily have seized the land from the local population and forced men to work in the mines without wages. Not surprisingly, 'seething discontent' was reported to be the prevailing mood amongst the workers: 'The causes of such discontent are not far to find. The native employees have been brutally treated, kicked about and often had revolvers pointed at their heads when they demanded their wages'.(13)

LABOUR PROTEST AND THE LABOUR QUESTION, 1870-1900

Even in this first phase of capitalist gold mining, when the Gold Coast lacked a true wage-labouring class, the activities of workers and potential workers clearly contradicted the interests and objectives of mining capital. People in the mining areas refused to work for the low wages offered to them, or alternatively used their bargaining power to push wages up to more acceptable levels. They refused to perform most tasks within the mines except for the more familiar ones such as carrying and bush clearing, and resisted the efforts of supervisors to increase their work-rate. Workers would not agree to sign the six or nine-month contracts which managers introduced in an attempt to resolve the labour question, and in this way they retained their mobility within the colony's embryonic labour market. Consequently mining companies which paid particularly low wages or treated their workers exceptionally badly soon lost their employees to other mines or to other sectors of the economy.

Although the withholding and withdrawal of labour was the dominant mode of protest in the mines prior to 1900 it was by no means the only one. From the very beginning of modern mining, workers supplemented their wage by stealing gold, candles, nails and explosives from their employers. As one mine manager acutely observed: 'You must remember that they do not think they are taking that which does not belong to them. They look upon us as robbing them, hence in this direction their conscience is unlimited in its flexibility'.(14) Workers also expressed their discontent in the way they behaved towards European mining personnel. This mode of protest usually took the form of 'refractory behaviour', abusive language, and the deliberate misunderstanding of instructions, but on occasions it could assume much more serious proportions. In one incident, for example, a worker stabbed an accountant to death in protest against his dismissal, and in another, two workers were arrested for attempting to poison European staff. At the Ashanti Goldfields Corporation a white supervisor disappeared in mysterious circumstances and was publicly said to have fallen down an abandoned shaft. Privately, though, both the company and the government suspected that he had been murdered by friends of a worker who had been tortured by European supervisors.

In a more sophisticated form of protest, workers also exercised their ability to restrict and disrupt production. The reaction of workers to a delay in wage payments at one mine was described in this way:

> An unsteadiness and indifference as to whether or not they continued to improve in learning how to work as miners commenced to appear among them. When railed for their faults the reply would invariably be 'we get no pay'. I countered this with the only means at my disposal i.e. persuasion and starvation, but this could not prevent many pieces of work being done in a slovenly, indifferent fashion.(15)

Finally, strikes were not entirely unknown in the mines prior to 1900. In December 1898 Edwin Cade told Ashanti Goldfields' shareholders that 'among the hundreds - nay even thousands we have employed, we have not met with a single one who has brought against us or our method of government a single word of complaint'.(16) Evidently Cade had a short memory, for just five months earlier he had told the same group of people that 'we have already gone through one or two costly experiments and met with strikes and disturbances which we have dealt with to the best of our ability'.(17) Unfortunately only one of these strikes is documented in the company's records. In January 1898 six West Indian carpenters stopped work because 'the native food, discipline, and hard work did not agree with them'.(18) The men were dismissed and replacements brought from

Kumasi. Other mines were also affected by this form of protest. McCarthy reported that at a mine in Tarkwa wage payments to Kroo workers were delayed by a shortage of coinage. 'One day about 3 p.m. the Kroos struck work and came up all armed with machetes... and demanded to be paid off'.(19) Kroo workers were also involved in a strike at Pierre Bonnat's alluvial mine. Bonnat trained the Kroos to dive for gold, but before they would start work they went on strike to demand more pay.

It would appear from this fragmentary evidence that the early strikes in the mines were confined to small, ethnically homogenous groups of workers who had some degree of skill and therefore greater bargaining power than their unskilled colleagues. Nevertheless, ordinary workers quickly learned the power of collective protest. In 1892 between 300 and 500 workers at the Gie Appantoo mine organised a demonstration to express their 'great dissatisfaction' over delays in wage payments and poor food. The <u>Mining Journal</u> reported that 'the feeling against [the mine manager] was so strong that it was evident a radical alteration was necessary'.(20) The manager was subsequently dismissed and replaced by a man who was instructed to be more understanding in his treatment of the workers.

ORIGINS OF THE LABOUR FORCE, 1870-1900

Despite the mining industry's failure to attract the regular supply of cheap, passive, and efficient workers which it required, it did manage to survive a thirty-year period of erratic development between 1870 and 1900. Where then, did the early mining labour force come from? To a large extent, it came from outside the gold producing areas. In 1903 under 68 per cent of the industry's labour force came from the Gold Coast, but of the Gold Coast contingent, 16 per cent came from outside the mining areas of the south-west. Local workers therefore constituted only 55 per cent of the total labour force. Significantly, the majority of these were hired not to perform the most important task of underground mining, but the ancillary tasks of carrying, bush clearing, woodcutting and farming.(21)

The Kroos of the Liberian coast were numerically the most important group of foreign workers, providing 14 per cent of the labour force in 1903. The Kroos had a number of advantages for the mines. They had a long tradition of employment with expatriate masters, and were described as 'docile, tractable, and not fastidious as to their surroundings'.(22) They had no objection to working underground, and were 'in a position to give continuous labour', usually contracting to work for a period of twelve months.(23)

It also seems likely that some of the locally-recruited workers were members of the large population of gold winners in the south-west of the colony.(24) They were not, however, particularly keen to join the mines as wage labourers, since they could earn more by mining independently than they could by working for a European master, especially if they used explosives to blast gold-bearing rock.(25) Some entrepreneurs, both Europeans and coastal Africans, attempted to deal with the problem of finding gold winners on their concession land by incorporating the traditional tribute system into their modern mining operations. Under this arrangement, the gold winners were left to mine and pan independently, on condition that a fixed proportion of their output (often one third) was paid to the concession holder as a form of rent. The more ambitious mining pioneers and managers were, however, less tolerant of a system of labour utilisation where 'of supervision there was none', and where 'the miners seem to have worked at their own sweet will in whatever place or direction they liked'.(26) Cade, for example, had no time for this 'absurd system of sharing', and was determined to see the gold winners either expelled from his concession or turned into wage labourers. By December 1897 he was able to report that 'all bother with native miners had passed away' and so there was 'no need to resort to those acts of gentle persuasion that we had in view'.(27) It is impossible to estimate how many gold winners became mine workers and how many chose to find an alternative means of subsistence, but it would appear that a substantial number did pursue the former option. Thus in 1909 a mining engineer with many years experience on the coast noted that the gold winners had been 'finally eliminated.... by a process of gradual absorption'.(28)

The early mining companies were also able to secure some labour through arrangements with the local chiefs who had leased their land for modern mining operations. Such arrangements were highly desirable, since they allowed the mines to negotiate a fixed, and usually low, wage for the workers supplied. Thus Cade reported: 'For bush work I arranged with the King for one shilling per day, thinking that one shilling and threepence would be paid, although I insisted on one shilling in the agreement'.(29)

Finally, the employment of women as carriers, rock sorters, and washers in this first phase of mining development should not be overlooked. No information is available on the wages paid to female workers, but it does seem that they were often assigned the most arduous tasks:

> As for the poor wretched carriers, I can only say 'God help them', for some of their loads must have often proved a fearful burden to them. Many women, each with little babies, some a few weeks old only strapped on their backs, have taken 70, 80, 90 and 100 lb loads over this very hilly road of 120 miles. It strikes me as almost incredible.(30)

THE IMPENDING LABOUR CRISIS, 1900-1906

By the turn of the century the modern mining industry on the Gold Coast had survived, somewhat precariously, for almost thirty years. The labour question had not been resolved, but the erratic pace of mining development and the availability of imported labour had averted any serious labour crisis.

After 1900 three factors threatened to precipitate that crisis. First, as a result of the pacification of Asante, the closure of the South African mines during the Boer War, and the construction of the Sekondi-Kumasi railway, the colony experienced a speculative gold rush in the period 1900-1. A hard core of 40 mines survived the collapse of the boom and took delivery of the machinery required for deep-level mining, creating a heavy new demand for the few workers who were prepared to perform underground labour. Second, the period after 1900 saw the appearance of new competitors in the Gold Coast labour market. The defeat of the Asante, the subsequent programme of road and rail construction promoted by Governor Nathan, and above all, the spectacular growth of the cocoa industry, all created new income-earning opportunities, many of them more attractive than work in the mines. Third, and perhaps most seriously, the 'foreign solution' hitherto adopted by the mines in response to the labour question was becoming increasingly unsatisfactory. French expansion on the Liberian coast made Kroo labourers more scarce and more expensive, and mine managers expressed a growing unease about the Kroos' refusal to work for more than one twelve-month contract.

The mining companies' initial response to the impending labour crisis was to look further afield for supplies of foreign labour. The mining lobby in London pressed the Colonial Office to allow a free interchange of labour between the British West African colonies, but the governors of the Gambia, Sierra Leone, and Southern Nigeria were not prepared to see their own scarce labour resources being drained away into the Gold Coast. The mines then turned their attention to Asia. As early as 1873 Brackenbury had advocated the employment of Chinese coolies in the Gold Coast mines, hoping that they would 'breed in with the natives and infuse some energy into the Fanti races'.(31) This proposal fell on deaf ears in London and Accra. Missionaries and educated Africans were strongly opposed to such a scheme, and a disastrous experiment with the importation of 18 Chinese prospectors in 1897 had already convinced the Gold Coast government that such a proposal should be rejected. At the Colonial Office, the political scandal which followed accusations that Chinese 'slave labour' was being used in the South African mines ensured that no further experiments with the 'coolie solution' would be allowed. Much to their regret, therefore, the mining companies began to look for a local solution to the problem of finding the 'supply of cheap and reliable labour' which was still 'the most important factor in facilitating the rapid development of the mining industry of the Gold Coast'.(32) The remainder of this chapter describes the three principal strategies employed by the mines in seeking to avert the impending labour crisis, and analyses the reasons for their failure.

Labour Utilisation

In the speculative era of mining between 1870 and 1900, the numerous, hurriedly-formed mining companies on the Gold Coast had given almost no systematic attention to the problems of labour utilisation and productivity. After 1900, with the shortage of labour growing steadily more serious and investors clamouring for profit, the mines became much more aware 'that every nigger costs £50 a year, and that every one saved means £50 towards the dividend'.(33)

In their attempt to save labour and improve productivity, the mines adopted a number of strategies. First, using the recently completed Sekondi-Kumasi railway, they installed much heavier and more efficient machinery than they had been able to use when all the equipment had to be head-loaded from the coast. Second, the mine managers experimented with new forms of work organisation. For example, many ancillary tasks in the mines were sub-contracted to competing African entrepreneurs from the coast, and payment per task was introduced in place of the fixed daily wage on the assumption that it would 'substitute the hope of gain for the drudgery given under a master'.(34)

These innovations were successful, and reduced working costs by up to 40 per cent, but they failed to achieve the kind of improvements in productivity that the mine managers sought, and they offered no lasting solution to the problem of labour shortages. If those objectives were to be achieved, then the mines recognised that they would have to find a means of ensuring that their employees worked harder, more efficiently, and more consistently than they were normally prepared to. There appeared to be only one means of attaining that end, and that was to intensify managerial and supervisory discipline and authority within the mining workplace.

Significantly it was precisely at this time that an influx of South African mining capital and personnel into the Gold Coast took place. South African attitudes towards and expectations of native workers were much more rigorous than those of other expatriates on the coast. Consequently, the new campaign for better labour utilisation and higher productivity came to depend on increasingly punitive and coercive managerial and supervisory techniques. Almost immediately, the Government Transport Officer began to complain of the South African's 'anti-negro prejudices' and 'inability to see things from the native point of view'.(35) 'I regret to say', he told the Colonial Secretary, 'that from what I have up to the present seen of mining men from South Africa they are not as a rule to be trusted to deal fairly with employees'.(36)

In 1903 the government made an attempt to put an end to the ill-treatment of native workers through the appointment of a Mines Inspectorate, but its members did little to mitigate the impact of the new systematically authoritarian style of management in the mines. According to one of the more enlightened members of the Mines Department: 'The plain truth about an Inspector of Mines' work is that he has a duty to defend all employees in the mines, and particularly of course the predominating native employees in a colony from the greed of the financial interests in London'. This, however, was virtually impossible, given the close social links between most Mines Inspectors and mine managers: 'In fact, my chief was on far too friendly terms with these managers ... If an Inspector's chief is in the habit of wining, dining and card playing with those he is supposed to control, then his lot - like that of a policeman - can hardly be a happy one'.(37)

Ironically, the quest for improved productivity after 1900, which was intended to offset the acute shortage of local labour in the colony, actually perpetuated the problem of labour supply. By intensifying supervision and discipline and allowing the maltreatment of workers, managers simply deterred prospective workers from joining the mines and encouraged existing mine workers to leave for less onerous forms of employment. Governor Rodger had no doubt about the contradictory nature of the mining companies' strategy:

> I have been informed on more than one occasion that their people were ready and willing to do mining work provided they were paid their wages regularly and were treated fairly, but felt they would not work for companies where their wages were withheld or where they were fined on every possible pretext.(38)

Labour Stabilisation

The second response of the mines to the impending labour crisis was to introduce a policy of labour stabilisation. In pursuit of this objective the larger mines spent substantial sums of money building new and more attractive villages for their workers. Long service awards were introduced to foster a commitment to mine work, and with the help of the colonial administration vigorous efforts were made to solve the long-standing problem of food shortages and high food prices in the mining areas.

These innovations had a limited success. In July 1904 for example, the Ashanti Goldfields Chairman noted: 'The Ashantis are beginning to realize that there is some value and pleasure in work, and they are beginning to get amusements on which they can spend their money. As we go on these will be still further provided in order to give them greater inducement to earn money'.(39)

However, only skilled workers such as carpenters and mechanics showed any inclination to provide the regular, dependable labour demanded by the mines. The mass of unskilled labourers continued to work for short periods, to move from mine to mine, and to move in and out of wage employment.

Why, then, did the mining industry fail to stabilise the unskilled labour force, and thereby solve the labour question? First, this was a period of rapid economic expansion in the Gold Coast, which allowed workers and prospective workers to choose from a range of other, more attractive means of securing a cash income. Second, despite the improvements initiated by the mining companies, living conditions in the mining towns continued to be extremely unattractive. Food supplies remained inadequate, and all efforts at price fixing in local markets met with stern resistance from traders. Workers agreed to a proposal that they should grow their own food on land provided by the mines, but demanded time off to do so, thereby defeating the whole object of the scheme. The newly-constructed mining villages were usually sited some distance from the pit-head in low-lying, damp, and malarial locations 'which no ingenuity could convert into really desirable building sites'.(40) After the collapse of the 1900-1 mining boom many of the villages got out of control, sanitation standards dropped, and rooms became crowded with men who rarely, if ever, worked in the mines. As one mining company complained, 'natives in the Gold Coast simply squat in [the company's] villages and come to work when they feel inclined to do so'.(41)

The third reason for the failure of the mining companies' labour stabilisation strategy once again demonstrates the self-contradictory nature of the industry's objectives. As described in the previous section, the intensive nature of supervision in the mines after 1900 made an inherently unpleasant occupation even less attractive. Similarly, although the mines wanted to foster the growth of settled, stabilised communities of workers, they also insisted on maintaining very strict social control within those communities. Consequently, the authoritarian nature of the mining workplace was replicated in the authoritarian nature of the mining community, reinforcing the 'labour repulsive' character of work in the mines.

The obsession of mining capital and the colonial state with the maintenance of law and order in the mining districts of the Gold Coast was quite understandable. Following the unsuccessful Asante rising of 1900, when one European mine had been captured and ransacked, expatriates feared that in any subsequent unrest the Asante would avoid a conflict with government troops, preferring to 'drop unexpectedly on the isolated mining camps and chop all whites'.(42) The diversity of ethnic groups now living within the mining areas also gave cause for concern. In the words of one District Commissioner:

> The mushroom growth of Obuasi and the petty fights and
> squabbles amongst the conglomeration of natives from
> almost every tribe on the West Coast of Africa... may
> constitute a danger of a riot breaking out here, which if
> we had not sufficient force to cope with it, might turn
> into a very serious affair.(43)

Fears of disorder in the mining towns also stemmed from the
observation that their inhabitants were 'more prone to commit
breaches of peace than natives of the country'. Ever since the
beginning of modern mining, 'renegades from the coast' had
flocked to towns such as Tarkwa and Obuasi, and by 1906 such
towns contained 'a large crowd of determined wastrels living
more or less on crime'.(44)

Finally, discontent amongst the mine workers was perceived
as a threat to law and order. As a later section will show,
after 1900 workers in the mines began to engage regularly in
collective, and at times violent, forms of protest. With many
mines closing down and unable to pay wages, and with
intermittent food shortages still occurring, the possibility of
large-scale labour unrest was by no means remote.

In response to these perceived threats to civil order,
mine management and the colonial administration introduced four
forms of social control. First, large numbers of policemen and
soldiers were stationed in the principal mining towns. At
Obuasi, for example, up to 200 native soldiers were stationed
at the railway sidings, equipped with an armoured train that
could move quickly to the heart of the town. In 1902 a Mines
Police Force was formed especially and solely for the purpose
of preserving law and order in different mining centres, and
these official units were supplemented by the expatriate Gold
Coast Mines Volunteer Force.

Second, the judicial system acted as an instrument of
social control. Extremely harsh sentences, such as three
months' imprisonment with hard labour for the theft of one
candle, were used to deter potential law breakers, as was the
custom of having 'criminals wearing prison clothing and eating
prison food paraded daily before their families'.(45)

In addition to these official forms of social control, the
mining companies also used their extensive legal rights to
control most forms of social and economic activity within their
concession areas. At Obuasi, the Ashanti Goldfields Corporation
established a twelve-man Village Council to hear petty criminal
cases and to pass on offenders to the Mine Superintendent for
an appropriate punishment. The company's enthusiasm for the
council, however, was not shared by local administrators. The
first two Village Council presidents were dismissed for
blackmail and rape, and the council as a whole soon assumed
juridical powers to which it was not entitled. Eventually, the
District Commissioner abrogated the council on the grounds that
the mine manager 'thought a great deal more of the mines and

the production of gold than the village or the welfare of the people'.(46) A similar conclusion could also be drawn from the mine managers' obsessive determination to deprive their native workers of alcoholic drinks. Having failed to impose total prohibition on the mining concessions, the mines opened their own spirit shops and were given the power to veto all applications for spirit licences from native traders in the area. In this way the mines were able to deprive 'troublemakers' of alcohol, and to withdraw the sale of intoxicating liquor completely in times of unrest.

Finally, after 1900 the mining companies made a far more determined effort to prevent and detect the theft of gold. Black detectives were employed to work 'undercover' in the mining towns, while the government was persistently encouraged to impose stricter controls over local goldsmiths, the main receivers of stolen gold. Fencing was erected around parts of the mine where theft was most common, and 'unauthorised loafers' were expelled from the area. Such precautions inevitably led to further restrictions within the workplace:

> As an essential part of a 'security system' it would be necessary to provide a change house where the natives will be obliged to leave their working clothes on quitting work, and such convenience should be provided inside the enclosure as this will deprive them of any excuse for going outside during working hours.(47)

Although these four strategies of social control were far less coercive than those being used at this time in the compounds of South Africa and Southern Rhodesia, in the socio-economic and political context of the Gold Coast they could only serve to contradict the mining companies' attempt to resolve the labour question through a programme of labour stabilisation. Very few individuals in the Gold Coast had been forced into the labour market by this time, and with the economy expanding, the demand for wage labourers inevitably exceeded the supply. It was a seller's market, and very few of the men and women who wished to sell their labour power were prepared to accept the restrictive kind of living and working environment which the mining industry was seeking to impose on them. As one colonial official remarked, 'in bringing order to these districts we have not attracted the working native... The mining towns are full - not of the industrious men the mines require, but of those who have no regard for the law'.(48) Thus the labour question remained unanswered and mining capital was forced to look for an alternative solution.

Monopsonisation of the Labour Market

In the first decade of the twentieth century the gold mines of South Africa and Southern Rhodesia, like the mines of the Gold

Coast, were confronted with a shortage of labour and rising working costs. Short term solutions to this crisis were found in the use of forced labour (in Southern Rhodesia) and indentured Chinese labour (in South Africa), but the long term answer was found in the creation of what Berg has called a 'monopsonistic regional labour market'.(49) The key feature of this labour market was an agreement between the principal (white) employers of labour to avoid the competitive recruitment of scarce labour supplies, and to use the absence of competition in the labour market as a means of forcing down wage rates.

Prior to 1900 the Gold Coast mining companies had not been oblivious to the advantages which could be gained from the elimination of competition from the labour market. Burton and Cameron, for example, had predicted in 1883 that labour shortages would push up wages, and had suggested that only by acting together could the mines stabilise wages and introduce longer contracts.(50) The following year, Haughton had stressed the need for 'unanimity between the various companies... for controlling or regulating the labour supply'.(51) In 1901, when the labour question had become more serious, Dupont argued the case for monopsonisation at greater length: 'When the demand for labour becomes greater, recruitment and the fixing of wage levels will be assisted by the fact that the whole area is under the control of the same people. In this way we will avoid the competition for labour which was the main reason for the great rise in wages on the Transvaal'.(52)

Given the new influence of South African capital and personnel within the Gold Coast mines, it was not surprising that the mine managers should move to put an end to the 'warfare between large employers of labour' which had now broken out, and that they should do so by attempting to establish a monopsonistic regional labour market.(53)

In May 1901 a group of mining companies under the guidance of Percy Tarbutt and A.L. Jones submitted proposals to the Colonial Office for the creation of a 'West Coast of Africa Labour Bureau'. This non-profit-making company would undertake 'the duty of collecting and segregating labour in properly supervised and effectively managed depots, from which labour would be supplied as required to different undertakings'. The Bureau, Tarbutt explained to shareholders in the mines, would create 'a monopoly of labour engagement', and would receive the assistance of the British Foreign Office.(54) This optimism proved unfounded, for neither metropolitan nor colonial administrations were prepared to grant the Bureau the substantial powers which the scheme demanded. Seven months later the New Gold Coast Agency, a subsidiary of Consolidated Gold Fields of South Africa, made another proposal to the Colonial Office, recommending the creation of a recruitment agency which would be free to engage foreign and local labourers. This proposal, and a plan for the compulsory registration of all workers, was also rejected.

Having failed to establish an autonomous labour bureau with monopsonistic powers, the mines now turned to less formal approaches to the problem. In South Africa competitive recruitment amongst the mines had been eliminated by the creation of a powerful central organisation, the Transvaal Chamber of Mines, which could impose financial penalties on mines which contravened commonly-agreed policies. In 1902 the Gold Coast mines moved in a similar direction, establishing the Mine Managers' Association, followed in 1905 by the West African Chamber of Mines.(55)

Like its South African counterpart, the Mine Manager's Association attempted to reduce and stabilise wage rates for mine labourers. In June 1903 a 'no poaching' agreement was drawn up and wages were fixed at one shilling and threepence for surface workers and one shilling and ninepence for underground workers. The unanimity of the mine managers very quickly proved illusory. Within weeks (or according to one manager, hours) of the agreement being signed, some mines began to offer higher than the agreed rates, and sent out recruiting agents to lure workers away from other mines with promises of better wages and living conditions.(56)

Simultaneously, the Gold Coast government was making its own attempts to establish a monopsonistic labour market in the colony. Operating on a very limited budget, the government's plans for extensive infrastructural development were being obstructed by the scarcity and high price of labour. In 1902 Governor Nathan established the Transport Department, whose principal function was to act as a labour bureau with monopsonistic powers. All natives seeking work as labourers or carriers were to register with the Department, which would allocate them to expatriate employers in return for a capitation fee. The Department would make a daily subsistence payment to each man, and the remainder of his wages were not to be paid until he had completed a twelve-month contract. Using its monopsonistic powers, the Department would gradually reduce wages to an 'acceptable' level.(57)

In practice the Transport Department enjoyed little success in its attempts to control the labour market. In 1904 only 793 of the mines' 17,044 workers were supplied by the Department, and by 1906 the number had declined to 487. The Department did succeed in supplying the government's own labour requirements, and marginally reduced the daily wage rate for carriers, but in the mining areas the gold mines persistently outbid the Department for unskilled labour.

Why did the Mine Managers' Association and the Transport Department fail to eliminate competition in the labour market? In the next two sections it is proposed that the failure can be explained at two levels. First, at a superficial level, the failure of monopsonisation derived from the inability of the mining companies and government to take united action on the labour problem. Second, and more fundamentally, the failure of monopsonisation stemmed from the successful resistance of workers and prospective workers to this strategy of labour control.

Capital and State: the Failure to Unite. The structure of mining capital in the Gold Coast was not conducive to the formulation of a coherent strategy of monopsonisation. After the collapse of the 'jungle boom', many small mines were competitively struggling for survival without the backing of the large, interlocking mining groups which had made the South African mining industry such a powerful economic and political force. The most important mine, Ashanti Goldfields, refused to join the Mine Managers' Association since its high level of profitability allowed the mine to outbid others in the labour market, while its 100 square-mile concession ensured that it faced far less competition in its labour catchment area than the closely spaced mines on the Tarkwa-Prestea gold field. Consequently, the Ashanti Goldfields mine manager was able to adopt a distinctly superior tone in describing his counterparts:

> You know the difficulty of getting into cooperation with the Tarkwa managers. The Mine Managers' Association, if it had been properly conducted, was a place where these things could have been discussed and finally settled, but as you know, when they did meet and fix upon any decided action, one or other of the managers immediately contravened the general views and until they make the Mine Managers' Association on the same footing as that in Johannesburg and inflict a fine for the contravention of rules I am afraid it will never do any good.(58)

The problem of cooperation also appeared to be at the root of the inability of the mining industry and colonial government to take joint action over the labour question. In theory, the Transport Department scheme had several advantages for the mines, providing long-term workers on written contracts for a capitation fee which was considerably lower than the cost of recruiting a Kroo or other foreign worker. In practice, the mining industry could only see the disadvantages of the scheme, believing that it would undermine managerial authority over the workers, and prevent supervisors from using the disciplinary measures which were thought to be essential if productivity were to improve. As the Transport Officer explained, expatriates in the mines 'prefer to do as they please without anyone questioning their acts or punishments'.(59)

Cooperation between the government and the mining industry was limited by two other factors. First, the Transport Department scheme was opposed by coastal merchants such as Miller Brothers, who enjoyed a profitable business supplying carriers to the mines. They formed a ring to outbid the

Transport Department in the labour market, and persuaded the mining companies to withhold cooperation from the official scheme. Second, the abortive attempts to monopsonise the labour market in this period took place against a background of deteriorating relations between the government and mining industry. The government was constructing railways and roads, many of them to aid the expansion of gold mining, and yet the mining companies merely complained that such projects were exacerbating the shortage of labour. Moreover, in deciding to raise revenue by taxing the mines rather than the politically volatile population of the colony, the Governor simultaneously reduced the industry's profit levels and rejected the one certain method of forcing the local inhabitants into the wage labour market.

LABOUR PROTEST AND THE FAILURE OF MONOPSONISATION

The failure of monopsonisation in the Gold Coast was not simply a result of disunity amongst the mining companies and the administration, but also stemmed from a major contradiction inherent in this strategy of labour control. As an earlier section of this chapter has described, prior to 1900 workers and prospective workers in the mining areas withheld or withdrew their labour in protest against the low wages and hard work offered by the mines. Local men could subsist without access to a cash income, and those who did wish to acquire money could do so through the production of cash crops or by entering other, more attractive forms of wage employment. This situation had not changed by the time the government and the mines began to think of monopsonising the labour market. Consequently when unilateral wage reductions were made, workers and prospective workers simply refused to work. As F.W. Migeod explained, 'Whilst it remained possible to obtain many undersized men, men of poor physique and boys for that rate in considerable numbers, it was found that able-bodied men would not do a full days work for one shilling and six pence per working day'.(60) Moreover, workers who had developed a commitment to work in the mines did not accept wage reductions passively. As the following list demonstrates, between 1900 and 1906 there was a growing tendency for discontent amongst the mine workers to be manifested in the form of overt and collective resistance.

    1. In July 1903, carriers on the Bekwai-Obuasi route were taking twice the allotted time and the Transport Officer reported that 'neither persuasion nor threats have been able to reduce the time taken by natives'. In an attempt to remedy the situation one group of carriers was fined. They all deserted and after this incident all other groups of carriers refused to work on this route. The Transport Officer lamented, 'We have no means of compelling the carriers to work against their will. I have fined them, but apparently they do not mind this'.(61)

2.   In September 1903, 400 labourers at Anfargah mine went on strike. They returned the following day and proceeded to commit 'acts of open violence', breaking into the lock-up where some of their colleagues had been detained the previous day. The workers clashed with European staff and six labourers were injured in the fighting.(62)

3.   In February 1904, 80 workers at Akrokerri (Ashanti) mine went on strike after wages had been raised at the nearby mine of Ashanti Goldfields. Workers demanded parity with the Ashanti Goldfields labour force and claimed that their work was too hard. The mine manager stated that the strike was 'another attempt to squeeze the white man in a situation of labour shortage', and the stoppage ended after the intervention of the local District Commissioner.(63)

4.   In March 1904, Ashanti Goldfields reduced the wages of skilled labourers and introduced full day Saturday shifts. A group of carpenters, whose wages had been reduced by up to two shillings, sent a telegram of protest to the District Commissioner. A group of bricklayers wrote to the District Commissioner with similar complaints.(64)

5.   In July 1904, a Lagos man took out a summons against the Head Wood Contractor at Akrokerri on behalf of 60 other woodcutters. They charged the contractor with failing to pay their wages.(65)

6.   In January 1905, Ashanti Goldfields announced its intention to reduce basic wages by threepence. The mine managers reported rumours that all men affected by the reduction threatened to go on strike and destroy the mine by fire.(66)

7.   In July 1905, all firewood cutters at Ashanti Goldfields went on strike to demand higher wages. The mine manager asked the District Commissioner to come to the mine and give the men 'a good talking to'.(67)

8.   In August 1905, labourers at Sansu mine became restless after management failed to pay wages for two months. The Governor wrote to the Colonial Office: 'It is not impossible that in consequence of the non-payment of the labourers, disturbances such as a raid on the local markets for the purpose of obtaining food, or even an attack on the mine property itself, may occur'.(68) The following month, he reported: 'An outbreak, which may have had serious consequences, was only averted by the distribution of ready money and by the personal influence of the Commissioner and the local manager'.(69)

Incidents such as these (which almost certainly represent only a small proportion of mine workers' strikes in this period),(70) had a profound impact on the attitude of mine managers towards the strategy of monopsonisation. While they agreed in principle with the idea of reducing wages unilaterally, in practice they recognised that to do so would provoke at best a drift of labour away from the mines, and at worst strikes, demonstrations and other manifestations of collective resistance. For example, in January 1904 the Governor asked the mine manager of Prestea Mines for his assistance in cutting wage rates. The manager replied that while he welcomed the proposal, he could not cut wages without 'risking a paralysis of mining operations'.(71) The mine manager at Obuasi made the same point even more clearly. Replying to a proposal from the Gold Coast Railway that the mine should 'cooperate in a summary reduction of wages to one shilling per day', the manager reluctantly declined the invitation: 'In case we should make a wholesale reduction in the price we pay our ordinary labour, we should have to face the possibility of an equally wholesale strike, and this we do not, at present anyhow, care to risk'.(72)

CONCLUSION

The strikes of 1900 to 1906 represented an important turning point in the historical struggle between labour and capital in the Ghanaian gold mines. A cross-ethnic, occupational, and perhaps even a class consciousness was beginning to emerge amongst the mine workers. They now recognised the power of collective action, and were prepared to use that power to thwart the strategies of labour control employed by mining capital and the colonial state. Within three years Ashanti Goldfields, the largest and most profitable mine in the colony, was to experience its first general strike, and the mine manager accurately predicted that 'the natives, year by year as they are becoming more educated will, I think, give us further trouble in this direction'.(73) Recognising this problem, after 1906 the mining industry, with the intermittent assistance of the colonial governor, began to look for a new way of securing a cheap, productive, and passive labour force.

The experience of the South African mining industries had already demonstrated that in order to reduce wages without endangering the supply of labour or provoking collective resistance, it was necessary to satisfy four basic preconditions. First, there had to be complete and enforceable unanimity between the principal employers of labour. Second, it was necessary to develop economic and political mechanisms designed to regulate a flow of migrant labour out of undeveloped peripheries and into the centres of urban and industrial growth. Thirdly, the mobility of labour within those urban and industrial centres had to be severely restricted. Finally, it was necessary to eliminate the workers' ability to participate in both individual and collective forms of protest by introducing more intensive and punitive forms of social and workplace control.

Taking note of the South African experience, in the period after 1906 the mining industry made a determined, but ultimately unsuccessful effort to introduce a fully-fledged, 'labour-coercive' model of labour mobilisation and control in the Gold Coast. Observing this process at first hand, in 1909 the Government Transport Officer made an incisive assessment of this new attempt to resolve the labour question: 'The ultimate aim of the mine managers is forced labour in fact, if not in name'.

NOTES
Author's note: this chapter is adapted from J.Crisp, The Story of an African Working Class: Ghanaian Miners' Struggles. 1870-1980 (Zed Press, London, 1984).

The following archival abbreviations are employed:
AGCI   Ashanti Goldfields Corporation Inward Correspondence (Mine Manager to Company Secretary), Guildhall Library, London.
AGCO   Ashanti Goldfields Corporation Outward Correspondence (Company Secretary To Mine Manager), Guildhall Library, London.
BM   Basel Mission Archive (typescript translation), Centre of West African Studies, University of Birmingham.
CP   Cade Papers, University of Birmingham Library.
CHP   Chamberlain Papers, University of Birmingham Library.
GNA   Ghana National Archive, Accra.
GNAK   Ghana National Archive, Kumasi.
GNAT   Ghana National Archive, Tamale.
LT   Lonrho (Technical) Archive, Roman House, London.
MP   Migeod Papers, Royal Commonwealth Society, London.
NP   Nathan Papers, Rhodes House, Oxford.
PRO   Public Records Office, Kew.

1.   T. Haughton, The Mining Journal, 8 May 1884, p. 575; CP, 'Report on Obbuassie Gold Mine Estate', August 1895, p. 31.
2.   T. Haughton, The Mining Journal, 8 May 1884, p. 575.
3.   R. Burton and V. Cameron, To the Gold Coast for Gold, (2 vols., Chatto and Windus, London, 1883), vol. 2, p. 328.
4.   A. Hopkins, An Economic History of West Africa, (Longman, London, 1973), p. 15.
5.   J. Skertchley, 'A Visit to the Goldfields of Wassaw, West Africa', Journal of the Royal Geographical Society, no. 48 (1878), p. 281.
6.   BM, Fritz to Basel dd. Christiansborg, 28 July 1875.
7.   CP, E. Cade to A.G.C Directors, 10 December 1897. For a typical official response to the mining companies' complaints see PRO, CO96/487/14471, Antrobus Minute, 22 May 1909: 'We get periodically complaints that there is a "general scarcity of labour", but on the Gold Coast it generally turns out that there are plenty of labourers to be had by employers who pay adequate wages and treat their men well'.
8.   T. Haughton, The Mining Journal, 8 May 1884, p. 575.

9.   LT, 'Minutes of an Extraordinary General Meeting of the Ashanti Goldfields Corporation', 10 December 1898.
10.   Skertchley, 'A Visit to the Goldfields of Wassaw', p. 275.
11.   LT, 'Minutes of an Extraordinary General Meeting of the Ashanti Goldfields Corporation', 10 December 1898.
12.   D. Foster, 'Labour and Superintendence on the Gold Coast', Mining and Scientific Press, 3 February 1912.
13.   Further Correspondence Regarding Affairs of the Gold Coast, Colonial Office African No. 249, Secretary, Aborigines' Protection Society, to Colonial Office, 2 April 1882.
14.   AGCI, 26 February 1902.
15.   The Mining Journal, 16 May 1885, p. 551.
16.   LT, 'Minutes of an Extraordinary General Meeting of the Ashanti Goldfields Corporation', 12 December 1898.
17.   LT, 'Minutes of an Extraordinary General Meeting of the Ashanti Goldfields Corporation', 12 December 1898.
18.   CHP, JC9/5/2/2, J. Daw to A.G.C. Directors, 10 December 1898.
19.   E. McCarthy, Incidents in the Life of a Mining Engineer, (George Routledge, London, 1918), pp. 77-8.
20.   The Mining Journal, 23 July 1892, p. 817.
21.   Annual Report on the Mines Department, 1904.
22.   CP, 'Report from Obuasi', 1895, p. 6.
23.   Annual Report on the Gold Coast, 1894, p. 9.
24.   The exact size of this population is impossible to estimate because of discrepancies in the accounts of expatriate observers. For example, in 1878 Skertchley reported 6,000 gold winners in Tarkwa, whereas Harvey's report of the same year put the figure at 1,000. The Civil Commissioner in Tarkwa wrote, 'It is impossible to give any accurate estimate of the number of inhabitants in Tarkwa as the native miners gravitate at various intervals towards the richest and most recently discovered gold deposit'. O. Whitelaw, The Geological and Mining Features of the Tarkwa-Abosso Goldfield, (Gold Coast Geological Survey Memoir No. 1., Government Printer, Accra, 1929), p. 5; Further Correspondence Regarding Affairs of the Gold Coast, Parliamentary Paper C3687, Civil Commissioner, Tarkwa, to Colonial Secretary, 31 August 1881.
25.   Gold winners earned between 1 shilling and 2 shillings a day. Cameron noted that gold winners using explosives 'make more money for themselves than by working for wages'. V. Cameron 'The Goldfields of West Africa', Journal of the Society of Arts, June (1882), p. 281. Skertchley reported that a gold strike by native minders was usually celebrated by 'a general debauch among the lucky finders and their friends'. Skertchley,' A Visit to the Goldfields of Wassaw', p. 281.
26.   G. Eaton-Turner, A Short History of Ashanti Goldfields Corporation,(A.G.C., London, 1947), p. 3.
27.   CP, E. Cade to A.G.C. Directors, 25 February 1897.

28. E. McCarthy, 'Early Days on the Gold Coast', The Mining Magazine, vol. 1, no. 4 (1909), p. 293.

29. CP, 'Report from Obuasi', 1895, p. 6. The Commissioner at Tarkwa stated that 'these Chiefs (or Kings) claim to rule the districts in which the land is situated. But they are commonly in the hands of one or more of the European managers who by costly presents keep them in their pay'. Further Correspondence Regarding Affairs of the Gold Coast, Parliamentary Paper C3687, 1883, Civil Commissioner, Tarkwa, to Colonial Secretary, 31 December 1881. The acquisition of labour in this way provides a good example of how pre-capitalist and 'unfree' forms of labour are readily accommodated within the capitalist mode of production.

30. CP, E. Cade to A.G.C. Directors, 25 December 1897. It seems doubtful that this sight caused Cade too many sleepless nights, since he admitted that he was 'not a believer in driving philanthropy and business with the same pair of reins'. LT, 'Minutes of an Extraordinary General Meeting of the Ashanti Goldfields Corporation', 12 December 1898.

31. Quoted by Burton and Cameron, To the Gold Coast, p. 176.

32. L. Bowler to Colonial Office, 10 July 1901, quoted by L. Walker, 'The Gold Mining Industry in Ghana', unpublished PhD thesis, University of Edinburgh, 1971.

33. AGCI, 18 October 1902.

34. AGCI, 26 March 1903.

35. GNA, BP228, Transport Officer to Colonial Secretary, 25 March 1902.

36. GNA, BP228, Transport Officer to Colonial Secretary, 11 October 1903.

37. A. Vivian, 'A Man of Metal: The Autobiography of A.C. Vivian', n.d., Rhodes House, Oxford, Ms., pp. 63-4. The mining companies were certainly not short of influential allies. Ashanti Goldfields predictably enjoyed the best network of influence in the metropolis. In the mine manager's words: 'The Corporation is one of the very strongest in London, and consequently in the world. The King of England is one of our largest shareholders, 400 Members of Parliament are on the stockholders list, the Directory is composed of some of the wealthiest noblemen and merchants of England, and altogether it is a chance that does not often come to a mining man, to ally himself with a most influential set of people'. AGCI, 18 May 1905.

38, AGCI, 20 May 1904.

39. AGCI, 16 July 1904.

40. Lieutenant-Colonel Giles, Sanitation and Anti-Malarial Measures in Sekondi, The Goldfields, and Kumasi, (Liverpool School of Tropical Medicine Memoir No. 15, Liverpool, 1905), p. 17.

41.   PRO, C096/370/33643, Gold Coast Amalgamated Mines to Colonial Office, 1 November 1910.

42.   GNA, ADM12/5/112, West African Hinterlands Concessions Ltd. to Colonial Secretary, 4 April 1902.

43.   GNA, ADM53/1/1, District Commissioner, Obuasi, to Commissioner of Police, 25 September 1904.

44.   Annual Report on Ashanti, p. 17; Further Correspondence Regarding Affairs of the Gold Coast, Parliamentary Paper C3687, 1883, Civil Commissioner, Tarkwa to Colonial Secretary, 31 December 1881; GNA, ADM53/1/1, District Commissioner, Obuasi, to Commissioner of Police, 25 September 1904.

45.   AGCI, 14 November 1903.

46.   AGCI, 7 November 1903.

47.   LT, 'Report of W.R. Feldtmann', 15 July 1905.

48.   GNA, ADM53/1/3, District Commissioner, Obuasi, to Colonial Secretary, 3 November 1904.

49.   E. Berg, 'The Development of a Labour Force in Sub-Saharan Africa', Economic Development and Cultural Change, no. 13, (1965).

50.   Burton and Cameron, To the Gold Coast, p. 333.

51.   T. Haughton, The Mining Journal, 8 May 1884, p. 575.

52.   H. Dupont, Les Gisements Aurifières de la Côte d'Or d'Afrique, Dupont et Banquiers, Paris, 1901), p. 36.

53.   GNA, BP228, Transport Officer to Colonial Secretary, 21 January 1904.

54.   PRO, C096/389/18670, West Coast of Africa Labour Bureau to Colonial Office, 29 May 1901; Dupont, Les Gisements Aurifieres, p. 31. Tarbutt was Consultant Engineer for Consolidated Gold Fields of South Africa, and a director of 25 South and West African mining companies.

55.   The Mine Managers' Association brought together the managers on the Tarkwa-Prestea gold field, while the Chamber of Mines represented the interests of directors and investors in the metropolis. The first Chairman of the Chamber was none other than Lord Harris, former Governor of Bombay, Chairman of Consolidated Gold Fields from 1899 to 1929, and a central figure in the 'Chinese slavery' controversy. In his spare time he played cricket for England.

56.   GNA, BP228, Mine Manager, Prestea Mines, to Governor, 6 January 1904; AGCI, 8 October 1907.

57.   Migeod, the Transport Officer, began his campaign to solve the labour question in a very optimistic mood: 'The Colonial Government should make a virtual monopoly of transport.... there would be a fixed rate of pay and carriers would know that refusing it, they would have little prospect of work elsewhere. As soon as they recognised that they must take the Government wage or none at all, they must perforce yield'. MP, Transport Officer to Colonial Secretary, 19 January 1901.

58.   AGCI, 3 September 1907.

59.   GNAT, ADM1/24, Transport Officer to Colonial Secretary, 13 December 1903.

60. Quoted by D. Greenstreet, 'The Transport Department - the First Two Decades (1901-1920)', Economic Bulletin of Ghana, vol. 10, no. 3 (1966), p. 36.

61.   MP, Transport Officer to Colonial Secretary, 6 July 1903.

62.   MP, Transport Officer to Colonial Secretary, 28 September 1903.

63.   GNAK, 17/20/1907, Mine Manager, Akrokerri Mine, to Commissioner, Southern District Ashanti, 24 February 1904.

64. GNAK, 17/20/1907, A.G.C. Bricklayers to Commissioner, Southern District Ashanti, n.d.

65.   GNA, ADM53/1/1, District Commissioner, Obuasi, to Mine Manager, Akrokerri Mine, 1 July 1904.

66. AGCO, 25 January 1905.

67.   GNAK, 17/20/1907, Mine Manager, Ashanti Goldfields Corporation, to Commissioner, Southern District Ashanti, 25 July 1905.

68. PRO, CO96/432/31746, Governor to Secretary of State, 8 August 1905.

69. PRO, CO96/432/33924, Governor to Secretary of State, 1 September 1905.

70.   It has not been possible to trace any documents describing strikes on the Tarkwa-Prestea gold field in this period.

71. GNA, BP228, Mine Manager, Prestea Mines, to Governor, 6 January 1904.

72. AGCI, 25 July 1903 and 27 July 1903.

73. AGCI, 25 January 1909.

Chapter Three

BRITISH NITRATE COMPANIES AND THE EMERGENCE OF CHILE'S PROLETARIAT, 1880-1914

Manuel A. Fernández

Within the traditional, sluggish social development of Latin America, Chile, together with Brazil and Argentina, stand out as exceptions. In all three countries full-scale labour movements had already developed before 1914.(1) Indeed, the complex social phenomenon of Popular Unity during the early 1970s, in which organised workers played a significant role, cannot be explained without referring to the strong historical roots of the working class movement in Chile. The case of nitrate production in Chile in the late nineteenth century offers a classic example of the formation of a new class which can properly be called a proletariat in spite of the fact that it developed within a national context where old forms of production and labour relations still prevailed, particularly in the countryside. It is classic in the sense that the recruitment of the labour force employed in the nitrate districts, formerly a desert both in human and in geographical terms, entailed a rupture with the traditional economic and social system that prevailed in other parts of Chile. Although the nitrate sector - owned mainly by British companies with inputs supplied from abroad and the output marketed in Europe - was bound to become a foreign enclave with respect to the Chilean economy, the development of labour organisation and action in the nitrate establishments was crucially important in the emergence of Chile's proletariat as a whole.(2) This chapter sets out to describe two basic aspects of the process of proletarianisation in the nitrate enterprises: the origins of the labour force and its living and working conditions. It also touches upon the development of class consciousness among nitrate workers within the general context of the Chilean labour movement as a whole.

THE FORMATION OF NITRATE ENTERPRISES

Nitrates (salitre), used both as a fertiliser and as raw material for the production of gun powder, had become an international commodity by the early 1830s. Large scale production, however, began in the 1860s and continued to grow at a rate similar to that by which guano production was declining. The first deposits to be exploited were located in the then Peruvian province of Tarapacá. British, Peruvian and Chilean enterprises were the major producers responsible for an impressive upsurge in nitrate exports. During the late 1860s annual production averaged around 100,000 tons, and this figure more than doubled during the 1870s. The Peruvian government, with the hindsight of the guano experience which, in the view of one observer during the 1880s had constituted a 'financial orgy', aimed at a tight control over the production and marketing of nitrates and embarked upon a process of nationalisation which involved the expropriation of most nitrate enterprises during the second half of the 1870s.(3) This process was interrupted in 1879 when the War of the Pacific broke out between Chile and the alliance of Peru and Bolivia.

Chile, victorious on the battlefields, took over as spoils of war the provinces of Antofagasta (formerly Bolivian) and Tarapacá (formerly Peruvian). The Chilean government, enthralled by the doctrines of 'laissez faire', reversed the nationalisation process and handed back the nitrate fields to private companies. In the spate of new company formation that ensued when the war was over, it was not only Peruvian interests that were affected. Chilean enterprises were also taken over by British interests which, by 1890, were in control of nearly 70 per cent of the nitrate industry.(4) Nevertheless, there still remained a sizeable sector owned by Chileans, Germans, and investors of other nationalities.

The final exhaustion of the most important guano deposits during the late 1870s increased world demand for alternative fertilisers and, consequently, opened up new prospects for nitrate producers. The old-fashioned technology in use, however, was a hindrance to the enlargement of output. Traditionally, the extensive stratum of nitrate-bearing ores was extracted by open-cast mining in a costly labour-intensive operation. The ores were then diluted in small tanks and the nitrate was obtained by applying heat in order to achieve the decantation of the substance once the solution had cooled down. The process was slow, expensive and only applicable to ores of the highest grade. By the late 1870s it had become clear that in order to meet the increased demand it was necessary either to recruit considerably more labour or to improve dramatically the method of producing nitrate. The technological bottleneck was eased in 1878 with the introduction of the Shanks system which increased output to levels not previously imagined. The new method involved the enlargement of the plants using a chain of tanks operating simultaneously with hot water circulating within the system. This led to considerable fuel savings with the added advantage that the new system was also suitable to treat low-grade ores.(5) Productivity increased dramatically. The 200,000 tons per annum produced during the 1870s trebled during the 1880s, and by the end of the nineteenth century annual output rose to 1.25 million tons.(6) It was the predominant British sector which was largely responsible for this increased output. Before the War of the Pacific, most British interests operated as direct investments, that is, as enterprises fully based in the nitrate districts. During the 1880s, the British enterprises were organised as joint-stock companies registered on the London Stock Exchange. In 1885 there were only two such companies but this number increased to 19 in 1890, 24 in 1900 and 39 in 1910. There were in addition a number of other nitrate-related undertakings including seven railway companies, a bank, a waterworks company, a steamship company and a nitrate provision supply company.(7)

FORMATION OF THE LABOUR FORCE IN THE NITRATE DISTRICTS

The fact that the nitrate fields were located in the middle of a desert was obviously a hindrance to the easy establishment of viable commercial enterprise. The main problem, however, was not a labour scarcity localised in the nitrate districts alone but one that involved the whole west coast of South America, at least during the first two-thirds of the nineteenth century. Labour was at that time so scarce that mine-owners and merchants on the west coast resorted to all known forms of labour ranging from slaves to wage labourers. British and French contractors exploiting the guano deposits in Peru in 1842 turned to the Peruvian government to get assistance in recruiting hands for the new enterprises. The government declared guano districts as penal areas and sent convicts and army deserters to work in the extraction of guano. This workforce was supplemented with wage-labour introduced from Chile.(8) The situation was similar in the coast of Bolivia where in 1842 'the prisoners from all the jails in the Republic' were sent to work for the guano deposits of Cobija.(9) When the House of Gibbs became the sole consigner of guano in Peru in 1849, the limited labour supply had to be supplemented with slave labour from the Far East. Taking advantage of an Immigration Law that granted a subsidy of 30 soles per 'colonist' imported into the country, Peruvian contractors engaged thousands of Chinese coolies to work in sugar plantations and in the extraction of guano. It is estimated that between 1849 and 1875 about 90,000 coolies survived the voyage to Peru. British Hong Kong and Portuguese Macao played the most important role in this traffic of mainly Cantonese coolies.(10) This indented labour also reached Chilean shores, though in very limited numbers because the labour scarcity there was less pressing than on the Bolivian and Peruvian coast.(11) Moreover, coolies were not the only source of indented labour. In 1862 around one-third of the inhabitants of Easter Island were forcefully taken to the guano fields.(12) Nonetheless, indented labour and convicts did not provide the solution to the labour shortages. Coolies in particular never adapted themselves to the harsh labour conditions prevailing on the west coast, and the degree of their rejection frequently assumed a dramatic character. Indeed, the tendency to commit suicide among coolies is widely documented by eye-witness accounts and official reports.(13) Besides, the fact that coolies were also in demand in other parts of the world contributed to increased costs and affected the supply of such labour. These problems led the guano contractors to look for alternative sources of labour.

Historically, central Chile was the principal region to provide a steady supply of labour for all non-agricultural enterprises on the west coast. An intermittent flow of emigrants from that region can be traced back to the 1830s, mainly connected with mining-related ventures, whether silver or guano in Peru or gold in California.(14) This emigration began as early as 1830 when an unknown number of Chilean workers sailed to Arequipa, in southern Peru, hired as miners. This early flow of emigrants has to be construed as crucially important in the formation of the proletariat in the nitrate region, because it entailed the full transformation of a rural-based labour force into a modern working class. Such a process of dissolution of all traditional rural ties began in central Chile itself. The diversification of the social and economic structure in Chile had started with an early, albeit limited, industrial expansion during the 1860s.(15) In the countryside, the traditional hacienda or manor was still predominant and the labour force was substantially tied to the land by means of the inquilinaje system which basically consisted of inquilinos or peasants who were alloted a plot of land and who paid their rent with labour, working on the lands of the hacendado.(16) The inquilinaje system, however, could not function without a mass of afuerinos or outsiders, the landless rural population living on the fringes of the haciendas and labouring on them at times of harvests. This floating population has been associated with the all too frequent cases of brigandage and rustling in the rural areas. Salazar characterises the afuerinos during the nineteenth century as a 'sub-proletariat... constantly subject to forced conscription, either to join the ranks of the army or a revolutionary faction of the elites...'.(17)

By the mid-nineteenth century, when arable land became scarce in central Chile due to increased exports of wheat and barley mainly to the British market, the landowners further developed the inquilinaje system by multiplying the numbers of plots alloted to new inquilinos and by abolishing the common land and reducing the land resources available to the individual inquilinos.(18) This sort of 'second serfdom'

45

contributed to the impoverishment of the inquilinos and to the reduction in seasonal openings for the afuerinos who were, therefore, pushed toward the emerging urban areas in Santiago and Valparaíso (central Chile) and also toward the coastal mining fields of Peru.

It is evident that the majority of these former peasants (whether inquilinos or afuerinos) moved to urban environments within Chile itself, attracted by the new light industries and the construction of railways which began in Chile in the late 1840s, and only a minority migrated to the Peruvian coast. But there is an important element which has to be remarked upon; a significant number of former peasants and new settlers in the urban areas of central Chile did not lose their links with the countryside, because they managed to return there for the harvests. For instance, when the railroad from Santiago to Valparaíso was being built during the 1850s and 1860s, the contractors faced a substantial reduction in the workforce during the harvest months (December to February) so that for many years the work was either slowed down or stopped altogether during two or three months. This reflects the former peon's attachment to the countryside where, after all, his friends and family still remained. Economic incentives were rarely behind the urban workers' decision to return to the countryside for the harvest. Very often the harvest pay was lower than the wage in the towns. It was rather a sense of belonging to the old community, which gathered during the harvest in traditional festivals and ceremonies, which pulled the emigrants back 'home'.(19) On the other hand, those who left for foreign shores were less likely to return to their old rural homes. The decision to go abroad, therefore, involved a stronger element of rupture with the traditional productive system and made the migrant peon more prone to a process of proletarianisation.

It should also be emphasised that many of the future proletarians in the nitrate fields had previously undergone a process of semi-proletarianisation within Chile itself. The metamorphosis from rural peon to industrial labourer went through various stages: first, the peons were pushed from the countryside to the urban areas within Chile; then, they emigrated to the mining settlements in Peru; and finally, they ended up as recruits in the expanding oficinas (nitrate establishments) in the provinces of Tarapacá and Antofagasta. The clearest example of this is the case of the workers employed by the contractor Henry Meiggs, who having built the most important railroads in Chile during the 1860s and 1870s, moved to Peru to do the same, always employing Chilean workers. By 1871 it was estimated that around 20,000 Chilean workers had gone to Peru and only 3,000 of them returned to Chile after the completion of the lines.(20)

The emigration of workers from Chile's rural areas to Peru, in addition to the labour requirements of increased

public works and military expansion during the last third of
the nineteenth century, made the Chilean landowners uneasy and
led them to seek official support to stop the outflow of their
former reserve of cheap seasonal labour. A leading figure in
the Sociedad Nacional de Agricultura, the association of
Chilean landowners, suggested in 1871 that in order to halt
emigration from the rural areas 'it seems opportune to extend
the inquilinaje system to a scale much wider than at present'
so that the peons would still be somewhat bound to the
land.(21) During the same year, a bill prohibiting emigration
to Peru was discussed at the Chilean Congress but did not get
the support of a majority.(22)

It is, therefore, not surprising that even before the War
of the Pacific the proportion of Chilean inhabitants in the
nitrate provinces of Tarapacá (Peru) and Antofagasta (Bolivia)
was so large. According to the Peruvian census of 1876, 9,664
out of 38,226 inhabitants were Chileans in the province of
Tarapacá, and in the nitrate fields there, the majority of the
miners were Chileans. In the Bolivian province of Antofagasta,
a census taken in 1875 gave a total population of 5,384 of whom
4,530 were Chileans.(23) On the eve of the war the total number
of inhabitants in both nitrate provinces, which later were
called the Norte Grande region, was around 45,000, a third of
whom were Chilean.

The war itself brought about considerable disruption to
the nitrate fields. This was acute during its early stages
(1879-80) when all the main battles were fought in the two
provinces where the nitrate fields were located. As soon as the
Chileans took over those provinces, the new authorities
encouraged the resumption of production and export. Obviously,
with forced conscription during the war, nitrate oficinas found
it hard to procure a sufficient number of labourers to re-start
production. Some oficinas, such as Sacramento, were forced to
close down 'for want of peons' while most of the others
complained that 'the number of men is barely sufficient to make
200,000 quintals [11,200 tons]'.(24) On the other hand, when
the battles in the Norte Grande were over, the war itself
contributed to alleviate the shortage of hands. In May 1880,
the Chilean forces defeated the allied army in the decisive
battle of Campo de la Alianza, near Tacna. It was a savage
battle in which nearly 3,000 of the 12,000 strong allied army
were killed in combat and many more were wounded. A large
proportion of the remainder dispersed into territories not far
distant from the nitrate fields. Some companies took advantage
of the situation and gave these wandering soldiers employment
in the labour-starved oficinas. The House of Gibbs in London,
for example, was informed that by July 1880, 'some hundreds of
Bolivian workmen had been brought into the province (Tarapacá)
from Tacna'.(25)

After the war, with the nitrate fields now under Chilean
administration, the supply of labourers was further increased

Chile

by a significant number of ex-combatants who remained in the
Norte Grande. Even while the war was still going on, a number
of Chilean soldiers deserted and went to work at the
oficinas.(26) This flow of Chilean soldiers increased further
in the aftermath of the war. A newspaper published in Iquique
(the main nitrate port) reported in 1885:

> Nowadays, the Pampa del Tamarugal is crossed in various
> directions by several caravans of Chilean peons, many of
> whom are ex-combatants from the last war ... the
> victorious soldiers of yesterday, now destitute labourers,
> cross the sandy grounds dressed in rags under the blazing
> sun, thirsty, humbly pleading for work so that they need
> not die.(27)

Another source of labour became available when the
old-established copper mines in the Norte Chico region of Chile
began to decline. In 1888 the British Consul General in
Valparaíso informed the Foreign Office that the significant
expansion in copper production in previous decades had given
'full employment to a large number of labourers ... (but now)
... the breaking down of the copper syndicate ... has released
many miners, and labour in the nitrate districts is plentiful
and cheaper than for a long time previous'.(28)
    During the 1880s and 1890s the nitrate industry
experienced an impressive expansion which, occasionally,
provoked a temporary labour shortage. On such occasions, when
labour was scarce, mine owners resorted to agents who were sent
to central Chile to hire workers. These expeditions were called
enganches (literally 'hooking') and were carried out by
enganchadores who became very professional in their work.
Meiggs himself had used them to recruit workers for his railway
schemes. The system lent itself to many abuses. As Monteón has
described it, the future nitrate labourer 'was promised a paid
voyage north, a great salary, good housing, low-cost food, a
great 'patron', anything to get him into the boat. What he
discovered upon landing in the desert was his own problem'.(29)
In 1907, the Nitrate Producers Association itself recommended
that recruiters should be discouraged from making false
promises.
    Until 1901 each nitrate company made its own arrangements
to recruit labour in central Chile. In that year, the
Association agreed to set up a common recruitment agency
financed by a small levy paid by each member company. The
Chilean government offered to pay free passage to any Chilean
wishing to go north. The producers refused this aid mainly
because they preferred to select the type of labour they wanted
instead of indiscriminately importing peons who might either be
inexperienced in mining work or still too attached to the
land.(30) As did Meiggs in previous decades, nitrate producers
rejected the peasants and preferred 'the bold type, willing to

travel the length of Chile, or to Peru, Panama, or California in search of opportunity, for justice, beans and pay'.(31) This type of landless, semi-urban labourer was therefore transported to the Norte Grande there to complete the process of proletarianisation.

The common recruiting agency was on the whole very successful in relieving the labour shortages. The agency not only recruited workers in southern Chile but also in Peru, which reversed the flow of labour existing before 1880. So successful were the recruiting drives undertaken by the agency that during the first half of 1908, in the aftermath of the formidable Santa María strike of December 1907, more than 5,000 new workers were brought to the pampa, a number more than sufficient to replace the miners killed during the strike and those whose frustration had led them to leave the district.(32) Despite this, producers never ceased to complain publicly of the 'shortage of hands' in the nitrate sector. This has led some historians to believe that labour scarcity was a structural problem in the nitrate region which helped to improve the bargaining position of the miners. It is more likely that labour shortages were brief and far between and that complaints regarding labour scarcity had more to do with the need to keep a sizeable reserve of unemployed. Stickell has pointed out that not only the cynic contended that the 'scarcity of labour' was, in fact, a 'scarcity of wages'.(33)

When the producers in 1884 agreed to form a combination with the purpose of restricting output, their main goal was, of course, to prop up the price of nitrate in the international market. A subsidiary purpose was to keep the labour force under control. The allotment of production quotas was effected using a time factor, that is, nitrate oficinas were allowed to produce at full capacity for a certain period of the year, after which they had to close.(34) During the shut-down periods, large numbers of workers were made redundant. Since the combinations became an almost permanent feature in the history of nitrates, the majority of workers never had the security of permanent employment. It was only in those periods of either lack of agreement among producers or increased demand in the world markets that full production was resumed, producing temporary labour shortages. They were only temporary because, as noted above, the common recruiting agency proved very effective from 1901 onward. When cutbacks in output were resumed, many labourers again were made redundant and, at times, the government had to intervene by reversing the flow of workers and relocating them in agricultural areas of central Chile, although without much success.(35)

Table 3.1 shows a consistent increase in the total number of workers in the industry, with a tendency also for the number of miners per oficina to increase. This steady supply of labour was one of the factors that hindered technological development in the nitrate industry which, for most of the period, remained

Chile

Table 3.1: Chile: Labour in the Nitrate Industry (five-year averages)

	Oficinas in Operation	No. of Workers	Average Per Oficina
1880-84	n.a.	5,492	n.a.
1885-89	n.a.	7,382	n.a.
1890-94	46	14,215	309
1895-99	48	18,685	389
1900-04	69	22,661	328
1905-09	102	36,774	360
1910-14	118	46,470	393

n.a. = not available
Source: Chile, Oficina Central de Estadística, Sinópsis Estadística, 1916 (Santiago, 1918), p. 98

Table 3.2: Estimates of Output and Labour in Chilean Nitrate Oficinas, 1908

Total output in 1908	2,327,495 tons
Total number of nitrate workers	40,825
No. of oficinas in operation	131
Average annual output per worker	57 tons
Average no. of workers per oficina	311
No. of workers in smallest oficina	28
No. of workers in largest oficina	1,309

	No. of Oficinas	Share of Total Output (%)
Oficinas with more than 500 workers	20	33.9
Oficinas with 300-500 workers	39	36.2
Oficinas with less than 300 workers	72	29.9
Total	131	100

Source: Derived from data in Domingo Silva Narro, Guía Administrativa, Industrial y Comercial de Tarapacá y Antofagasta, (Santiago, 1908), pp. 99-103.

stagnant.(36) The purpose of having a permanent reserve of unemployed is explicitly mentioned in the correspondence of the House of Gibbs. In a letter from the head office to the branch in Valparaíso in 1908, Herbert Gibbs wrote:

> The present effective supply of labour is 20,000 men, after allowing for the permanent floating stock of unemployed, then it is clear that if the production quotas were reduced to a total of 35,000,000 quintals (1.6 million tons), there would theoretically be a surplus of some 300 men which would probably suffice before long to enable salitreros to resume control over the labour market.(37)

WORKING CONDITIONS IN THE NITRATE FIELDS

'At the oficinas', wrote Monteón, 'the life of the nitrate worker was nasty and short. It was also brutish because even the easiest chores were made difficult by the environment'.(38) However, working conditions during the nitrate era, appreciated from the distance at which many contemporary observers kept themselves, were usually seen as reasonable if only because miners' wages were above the national average. Some authors have contended that the purchasing power of the miners was sufficiently high to constitute a decisive factor in the expansion of Chilean agriculture and industry, but it is rarely noted that, in terms of the cost of living and consumption per head, the condition of nitrate labourers inexorably deteriorated as years went by and, in most respects, they were worse off than their southern counterparts.(39)

The poor conditions prevailing in the nitrate area constituted another factor that helped to develop a considerable degree of consciousness and organisation among labourers which was remarkable in so isolated a social and geographical environment. Uprooted from the countryside and set down in the middle of nowhere, in a desert which was the subject of disputed national claims, in which workers of different nationalities were concentrated, the condition of the nitrate workers resembled that prevailing in the contemporary coalmines of Upper Silesia (then under German control) where there was 'a specific entanglement of class and national antagonism'. The analogy between the Upper Silesian region and Chile's nitrate region is suggested by the fact that in the former there was a labour force from Poland, Austria and Russia subject to an industrial model imposed by German administrators. Likewise, in the nitrate region there were Chilean, Bolivian, Peruvian and Argentine miners under the management of British administrators.(40)

The contemporary impression that nitrate miners were comfortably off had no better counterargument than a visit to the nitrate establishments themselves. The dreariness of the setting was the first sign noted by the visitor. A British journalist who toured the nitrate district in 1905 commented:

> Profitable though the working of nitrates may be, it is a deadly dull occupation ... There is nothing more depressing or gloomy in appearance than a nitrate field, the whole country in which it is situated being of the most dreary nature - sand, sand, sand everywhere, except where the bare, brown, cruel-looking mountains intervene. Most people who go up to the nitrate fields feel at first the greatest depression of spirit, and invariably look forward to the time when they are to be released from their voluntary but trying imprisonment.(41)

The situation was not improved by the deficiencies of the Chilean state which greatly benefitted from nitrate wealth but hardly provided any services for those areas which were the source of public income. A lone Chilean deputy complained in the lower Chamber in 1907 that although 'the nitrate workers have amassed, by the sweat of their brows, the fortunes of many national and foreign millionaires', very little had returned to the Norte Grande in the form of public services.(42) The nitrate producers themselves, when faced with petitions and accusations of being exploiters of the labour force, retorted that the Chilean state was also to blame because of the 'clear deficiency in those services which more effectively influence the moral and material improvement of the people, such as primary education, religion, administration of justice and health services'.(43)

Housing in the Norte Grande

The nitrate oficinas were numerous and scattered over a wide area. Their size varied considerably, but on average there were over 300 workers per establishment plus 30 to 40 foremen, administrative and technical personnel and management, and their respective families. Table 3.2 shows the disparity in sizes of nitrate settlements. The table also shows that 70 per cent of the total output was produced by 59 oficinas and the remaining 72 oficinas produced only 30 per cent of the output. This indicates that the smaller oficinas were more numerous and less productive and it can be safely assumed that generally living conditions were worst in the most inefficient fields.(44)

The first nitrate settlements were until the 1890s quite primitive. The provision of accommodation for the workers was almost non-existent and they had to make their dwellings with whatever material they could lay their hands on. The situation was similar in the ports where nitrates were shipped. Labourers there 'lived in hovels outside the main city. Their housing was made of wood or corrugated iron and zinc'.(45) Corrugated zinc, or calaminas, became common by the end of the century and although in desert conditions such dwellings became extremely hot during the day and cold during the night, they were a significant improvement. Adobe walls and calamina roofs were the main features of the nitrate campamentos by the 1900s, but, with neither toilets nor other sanitary services, conditions remained extremely poor. Even in 1904 workers complained that their houses were 'filthy, insanitary, disease-prone, and mended with old sacks, tin cans, old tubing and refuse'.(46)

By 1909, the general layout of the oficinas was made up of three basic structures. One was the plant itself where the nitrate ores were processed. The second was the administrative section and the houses for managers, engineers and other mainly British personnel. The third section, at a distance of about one hundred metres from the main buildings, was the campamento for the workers made of rows of houses 'built in such simple and rudimentary fashion that by comparison, the wigwam of an Indian was a prodigy of comfort'.(47) There were rows of single rooms for unmarried men and rows of two-roomed houses for families. The area of the rooms ranged from 15 to 20 square metres. Men slept three or four to a room. The houses for families had a small backyard which they used as kitchen and pen. The flooring of all dwellings was the rough nitrate-bearing soil, and the houses had neither windows nor running water.(48) In the larger and more modern oficinas there was a central square surrounded by the pulpería (the company's grocery shop), a school, a chapel and the houses of the management. The latter houses had exclusive access to a 'country club' with a shooting range and swimming pool.(49)

Since the campamentos were the private property of the companies, the miner was a tenant in a very vulnerable position. Eviction was the immediate consequence of losing one's job. When the Parliamentary Commission of 1904 arrived in Iquique, a delegation of miner's representatives handed them a petition which had a lengthy point devoted to the poor housing conditions prevailing in the Pampa. The most dramatic point referred to the frequent eviction of miners:

> The eviction is carried out by placing a mule-cart at the door of their dwelling and, using armed force in case of resistance, the cart is loaded with all their belongings, the family group is also loaded on top and they are expelled to the middle of the Pampa, left to their own resources and providing a spectacle of horror which can break the soul of the most hard-hearted mortal. Such a via crucis of daily occurrence usually takes the whole day and sometimes the next, so that those families have to spend the night with no other roof over their heads but the dark vault of heaven.(50)

Wages and Cost of Living

Two main difficulties preclude the proper assessment of wages in the nitrate fields. The first has to do with the fact that the majority of miners, those involved in the excavation of caliche (the nitrate-bearing ores), were paid on a piece-work basis. Teams of six to eight miners (particulares) were dispersed over the extensive fields, with each team allotted a barretero. The barretero made all the preparations to blast a large area of the surface and the particulares had to gather the ores and load them into mule-carts which carried them to the plant. Whereas the barretero was paid a set daily wage, the particulares received their pay according to both the quality (grade) and quantity of the caliche collected. Therefore, rates of earnings are difficult to ascertain because of the many variables involved: for example, hours, assessment of grade by the foreman, charges for tools and transports. Cases were reported where the site allotted to a team of particulares was either without nitrate or at the grade below the lower limit acceptable, and workers actually lost money during such occurrences. In other cases, the caliche was assessed as having a grade below the limit and the whole cart load was rejected and dumped in the waste grounds, only to be recovered later by the company once the particulares had left the field.(51) On the other hand, the Chilean Minister of the Interior argued in 1907 that the particulares also made attempts to exaggerate the grade of their caliches by concealing low-grade ores in their deliveries.(52)

The second difficulty in establishing rates of earnings lies in the fact that, for most of the nitrate era, workers were not paid in legal currency but in tokens called fichas which were issued by the employers. The ficha system combined aspects of the truck system and the tommy shops.(53) As in Britain, the truck system had also been abolished in Chile by a decree of 1852, but in fact its use persisted, particularly in mining districts.(54) The nitrate companies argued that, strictly speaking, settlements of wages were made once a month in legal currency but, due to the workers' 'squandering and improvidence', the companies were forced to help them out by issuing fichas that would enable the workers to get groceries from the pulperia. Money was neither needed - they claimed - nor was it readily available due to the 'inherent dangers of handling and holding large sums in the offices surrounded by large masses of heterogeneous population'.(55) When the Minister of the Interior was challenged in Congress to explain why a system abolished by the legislation of England, United States, Germany and, indeed, Chile, was still permitted in the Norte Grande, he replied that it was a practical system because through the fichas the workers would get all they needed at the pulperia and leave the balance resulting at the end of the month as savings.(56)

The ficha system, however, was wholeheartedly resisted by the nitrate miners. They claimed that fichas were in fact the only currency in circulation and when they wanted to exchange the tokens for cash, they could only do so by accepting a discount of 30 per cent.(57) In 1907, the directors of the Association of Producers issued a circular to all member companies advising them to stop the 'surcharge on exchange of fichas for pesos because the practice could incense the workers to interrupt the tranquility of pampa operations'.(58) Obviously, the advice went unheeded because another Parliamentary Commission sent to the nitrate districts in 1919 still confirmed that

> beyond any doubt, the majority of companies refuse to exchange fichas for money at par value ... instead, they exchange them for bills or promissory notes at 90 or 180 days sight payable by the relevant company's agency at the port. In this way, the interested parties are forced to resort to intermediaries who have established the large-scale business of exchanging fichas for money discounting a considerable proportion of their nominal value.(59)

The ficha system, therefore, makes meaningless the exercise of comparing wage rates between the nitrate districts and the rest of Chile. In other non-agricultural sectors the workers were at least paid in legal currency. Unaware of the mechanisms involved in the ficha system, and far from the remote desert where nitrates were produced, it is understandable that public opinion in other parts of Chile, assisted by the preaching of enganchadores and the publicity of the producers themselves, would have been led to believe that high wages were paid in the nitrate fields. By simply glancing at the average rates of wages published in Chile's official statistics - with the nitrate workers at the top of the scale - it was difficult to grasp the reason for the greediness of so handsomely-paid workers. The poverty of their living conditions was attributed to negligence and drunkeness, lack of knowledge about how to live and unwillingness to save. For some, higher wages could only mean 'a temptation rather than a benefit'.(60) J.R.Brown cites the case of the American consul in Iquique who

> denied that the workers had legitimate complaints, stating that there was no need for wage increases. His reasons for holding this opinion were as follows: the workers were improvident; their houses were small and had little furniture; their clothing was cheap; the climate made heating unnecessary. Thus, since the workers had relatively nothing, they didn't require much in wages to live on! (61)

The ficha system was not the only problem facing the miners. Real wages were further reduced by the high prices ruling in basic consumer goods. The British consul in Iquique reported to the Foreign Office in January 1914:

> The cost of living in Iquique is at least double that of the United Kingdom. It is cheaper to purchase clothes, groceries, etc., at retail prices in the United Kingdom, pay freights and duty, etc. - which together often amount to as much as the cost price of the goods in the United Kingdom - than to purchase them in Iquique.(62)

The fact that the nitrate fields were located in a barren and isolated region, more than a thousand miles from the source of agricultural provisions in central Chile, was bound to have an effect on the retail prices of consumer goods sold at the oficinas. Articles of consumption sometimes taken for granted, such as water, were scarce and had to be bought at high prices.(63)

The companies monopolised the retail trade through their pulperías where groceries could be bought with the fichas. In the survey made by Semper and Mitchels in 1902-3 of 80 oficinas, they reported the following on retail sales:

> Through the pulperías, every oficina endeavours to recoup the money paid in wages and make every effort to exclude competition in this field. Since mineowners can ban pedlars and traders from entering their properties, at every oficina they are free from competition and ready to increase prices at will.(64)

For their part, the companies alleged that they had to establish the pulperías 'by force of circumstances ... to provide the workers with consumer goods and clothing which they could not get anywhere else'.(65) They also argued - as the Minister of the Interior declared in Congress - that pulperías were the source of 'enormous losses' for the oficinas. When the Minister was asked why was it not possible to diversify the supply of goods and establish free trade, he replied that such an attempt would constitute an 'ill-bred onslaught against the right of property'.(66)

It is probably true that at times of temporary labour shortages some companies offered reasonable prices at their pulperías in order to attract more workers, but the evidence tends in general to substantiate the impression conveyed in Semper and Mitchels' report. Freedom of trade was a major point in all workers' petitions and pulperías were attacked in workers' publications for overcharging and swindling with weights and measurements. The possibility that producers suffered losses in the running of the pulperías is contradicted by the fact that in their own cost calculations there was an item headed 'General management and housekeeping expenses for staff, after deducting profits in pulpería'.(67) Semper and Mitchels, again, calculated that the cost of producing one quintal of nitrate (of which, on average, more than 45,000,000 were produced annually during the 1900s) was reduced by 0.2 pence because of the profits from the pulperías.(68)

Another indication of the high prices ruling at the pulperías is given by the success of the black market established on the fringes of the oficina. The workers from Tocopilla reported in 1904 that pulperías

> overcharge the price of groceries and clothing in a proportion which almost doubles the normal price and this has no plausible justification because travelling salesmen and pedlars ... despite the fact that they have to get their own supplies at retail prices in the port and have to carry them to the Pampa with great effort and danger to themselves, still sell the same articles 60 to 80 per cent cheaper than the mine owners who are wholesale purchasers ... with large capital and unlimited credit.(69)

Further evidence was provided by the shrewd critic who wrote in 1910: 'The salitreros, with shocking impudence, brand the workers as ungrateful in view of the losses, they say, the companies incur in running the pulperías, but it is worth mentioning that none of these generous benefactors has so far agreed to close down this kind of business'.(70)

Data on wages for the period is scanty but Table 3.3 provides an indication for 1911-12. In view of the discussion on abuses in wage payments, the apparent superiority of the nitrate workers would certainly disappear and would probably leave them worse off than workers in some of the other sectors included in Table 3.3. The real wages of nitrate miners further deteriorate if it is borne in mind that, for some part of the year, they received no wages during closures forced by the combination of producers. Moreover, there is good evidence that the cost of living was higher in northern Chile. An official survey carried out in 1912-14 of the price of a 'basket' of 13 articles of basic daily consumption for a family of seven members apparently assessed market retail prices in established grocery shops. It seems likely that pulperías were not included. The average basket price for those years was 4.7 pesos in the Norte Grande region, 4.0 pesos in the urban area of central Chile (Santiago and Valparaíso) and 3.9 pesos in central and southern Chile.(71)

Clearly, there is a paucity of data available on comparative real wages in Chile during 1880-1914. Nonetheless it seems that nitrate workers were by no means a labour aristocracy but, on the contrary, a deprived sector whose nominally higher wages were eroded by a significantly higher cost of living. Even the 1904 Parliamentary Commission remarked

Table 3.3:   Average Daily Wages in Chile, 1911-12 (pesos)

Mining		Manufacturing		Other	
Nitrate	$5	Food processing	$4	State railways	$5
Salt	5	Leather	5	Agriculture	1
Borax	5	Garment industry	4		
Sulphur	5	Lumber	5		
Coal	4	Metallurgical			
Silver	5	industry	6		
Iron	3	Paper & printing	5		
Copper	4	Beverages	3		
		Pharmaceuticals	5		
		Textiles	5		
		Other manufacturing			
		(average)	3		

Source: Report of the Parliamentary Commission of 1913 (quoted in A.L. Stickell, 'Migration and Mining in Northern Chile in the Nitrate Era, 1880-1930', unpublished PhD dissertation, Indiana University, 1979, p. 264).

Table 3.4:   Major Strikes in Chile, 1884-9, 1901-8

	Norte Grande	Chile		Norte Grande	Chile
1884	2	2	1901	3	5
1885	4	4	1902	4	21
1886	1	1	1903	6	17
1887	4	5	1904	7	11
1888	6	24	1905	17	23
1889	8	23	1906	20	48
			1907	31	80
			1908	3	15

Source: H.Ramírez Necochea, Historia del Movimiento Obrero en Chile (Austral, Santiago, 1956) pp. 282-5; M. Barrera, 'Perspectiva Histórica de la Huelga Obrera en Chile', CEREN No. 9, September 1971, p. 125; and P. De Shazo, 'Urban Workers and Labor Unions in Chile, 1902-1927', unpublished PhD dissertation, University of Wisconsin, Madison, 1977, p. 212.

on the fact that most of the high wages paid in the nitrate region were received back by the employers through the pulperías and other deductions that considerably reduced the miners' incomes. The Commission cited the case of six oficinas whose combined annual wages bill was 5.7 million pesos, of which the workers spent 4.34 million pesos at the pulpería during the same year, leaving a net balance of 1.35 million pesos which, to a large extent, was spent at the canteen, the open market and the railways, all of them also run by the nitrate owners.(72) De Shazo has noted that the apparent advantage of higher wages paid in the Norte Grande was offset by the 'harshness of life in those regions and their tremendously high cost of living'.(73) Other factors, such as working hours, safety and lack of health services, contributed to the discontent of nitrate miners.

THE EMERGENCE OF A CONSCIOUS PROLETARIAT

The first organisations in which Chilean manual workers were involved had emerged by the mid-nineteenth century. They were the Sociedades Mutualistas (mutual-aid or friendly societies) organised by artisans and skilled workers with the help of some liberals influenced by the 1848 social movements in Europe. Their main aims were of a practical nature: helping their members with sickness and accident pay, a 'dignified' burial, death benefits to dependents and, in some cases, a modest retirement pension.(74) Their meetings were also frequented by emerging social democrats, free-thinkers, utopian socialists, marxists and anarchists and their small libraries contained works by Proudhon, Saint Simon, Bakunin, Kropotkin and many other non-orthodox thinkers.(75) The mutualist movement, however, as Jobet has pointed out, did not have a significant bearing upon the improvement in living conditions of the working class as a whole: 'The labouring classes continued to suffer almost incredible conditions of exploitation and they continued to be a passive mass which was only occasionally active and then, only as the bandwagon of the liberal bourgeoisie and its representatives'.(76)

By the end of the nineteenth century, however, an independent working class was already apparent and developed in two main strands, anarchism and socialism. The anarchists were not very strong until 1902. Attempts to organise an anarchist movement during the early 1890s failed and only in 1898 was a more stable group formed which managed to publish a number of periodicals.(77) The anarchists read Kropotkin as well as Marx. Like anarchists in other parts of the world, their ideal consisted in the achievement of absolute freedom 'without other limits than the impossibilities of Nature and the wants of our neighbours'.(78) As a matter of principle, they rejected all established authority and government. In practical terms, they supported direct action by workers and favoured the idea that power would be attained by a general strike. Chilean anarchists developed strong links with their counterparts in Argentina, Uruguay, Brazil, Europe and, in particular, the United States.

The socialist current, on the other hand, was made up of an array of groups the most important of which was the leftist tendency within the Partido Democratico, a party organised in 1887 by dissidents from the old Radical Party and intended to represent the interests of the middle sectors, artisans and workers. In many respects, this was the offspring of the mutualist tradition.(79)

Although anarchists and socialists generally joined forces to further the success of strikes and demonstrations, the two groups were divided in their long-term objectives. Whereas the anarchists aimed for an absolute rupture with the establishment, the socialists sought 'a place in the sun', trying to achieve respectability and a voice that could be heard in Congress and in public opinion. In the early years, until 1905, the anarchist sociedades de resistencia were the more successful in organising public protests and strikes in Central Chile. Some anarchist leaders managed to organise important movements which can properly be called 'national strikes'. One example was the 1903 dockers' strike in Valparaíso and another the 1905 protests against the rise in meat prices in Santiago.(80) However, the failure to secure the conscious support of the masses transformed these protests, however heroic, into spontaneous movements and riots which were suppressed by the government.

The situation in the Norte Grande was somewhat different. The nitrate districts had also experienced sudden upsurges of popular protest such as the important strike in 1890, but the development of the workers' organisations followed a different path. The most obvious difference is that nitrate workers, insofar as they were linked together by a single and easy-to-identify antagonist - the nitrate company - found it relatively easy to join forces. In the process, socialists became more radical and anarchists more reflective. The nitrate workers, having experienced an independent social development, were neither burdened by an immediate rural inheritance of submission, nor affected by the purely riotous and spontaneous behaviour of anarchist followers. Nor indeed were they susceptible to the appeal of a purely mutualist movement devoid of social protest. All these hindrances to class formation prevailed in central Chile rather than in the Norte Grande. The ideological conflict between socialists and anarchists, although it did exist in the nitrate region, was subordinated in the struggle against the oppression of a common opponent.

One of the main factors which favoured the development of class consciousness among workers in the nitrate region was the clear-cut division between employers and employees in terms of social identity. The members of the 1904 Parliamentary

Commission were quick to notice that the conditions of nitrate workers were different from those of workers in other parts of the country, whether in industry, agriculture or urban workers in general, 'due to the absence of effective moderating factors arising from natural agents, culture, ... property distributed among many ... in sum, the satisfactions brought about by common education and morality'.(81) For the nitrate workers, the class divide was a simple matter of 'us' and 'them' which even had separate geographical and national representation. 'His Excellence knows', wrote the commissioners in their report to the President, 'that both the owners and the managers of the nitrate oficinas are almost all foreigners and the majority of the labourers are Chileans (and) this inexorably contributes to the lack of bonds between bosses, managers and higher personnel, on one side, and the vast mass of workers on the other'.(82) The contrast was apparent in language, housing, recreational and other facilities, most of which were non-existent for the workers.(83) Stickell has remarked on this fact by noting that

> managerial ideologies current in the developed countries of the North Atlantic attributed moral and intellectual superiority to persons who had achieved the higher levels of industry. The English, in particular, brought these attitudes with them to Chile where they were reinforced by the division of labour along national lines. Most foreign-owned oficinas were staffed by men of foreign birth while most physical labour was performed by a work force of local origin. Although all companies accepted Spanish as their official language, customs, status, and authority created a wide gulf between management and labour.(84)

Another factor which reinforced the sense of identity among workers and stimulated them to organise themselves, was the fact that mine owners had set up their own Association of Nitrate Producers designed mainly to form the combinations aimed at restricting output and improving nitrate prices. From 1884 onwards the Association appointed a Permanent Nitrate Committee based in London with a subsidiary Comité Salitrero based in Iquique. The producers' organisation was called in Chile La Combinación Salitrera. The nitrate workers, together with other unions in the ports, viewed the combinations as the source of unemployment and in 1900 decided to set up their own counterpart which they called the Combinación Mancomunal de Obreros. Their main objective was 'the defence of labour'. The Combinación Mancomunal was formed by the unions of dock workers, longshoremen, nitrate miners and workers from other trades. Only active manual workers qualified for membership and foremen, white collar workers, industrialists, merchants, proprietors and rentiers were expressly prevented by the Statutes from joining the Combinación Mancomunal.(85)

The workers' Combinacion Mancomunal was the culmination of a process that had begun immediately after the War of the Pacific. The development of large scale production resulted in an active process of division of labour that facilitated the organisation of the resulting trades. Stevedores, longshoremen and dock workers in general were pioneers in the organisation of the first labour unions. Indeed it was ironic that in the aftermath of the war the Chilean government itself promoted the organisation of dock workers in the early 1880s. Having restored private property in the nitrate fields, and not wishing to interfere with the day to day running of the nitrate establishment, the government viewed the dock workers' unions as a useful tool in indirectly controlling the payment of export duties by the companies. Such control assumed a degree of docility on the part of the dock workers' unions so that government officials would have access to the union records in order to assess the volume of nitrate handled by the workers which should match with the exports declared by nitrate owners.(86) The expected degree of docility, however, was not forthcoming and, on the contrary, the increasing militancy of the workers changed the basic assumptions of the government. Instead of a submissive semi-official union movement, dock workers developed into a formidable threat to normal production and export of nitrate when they began to strike for better conditions. In the event, and from the late 1880s onwards, the government definitely took sides with the nitrate companies by sending troops either to load nitrate during the strikes or to restore order at any price.(87)

A remarkable feature of the dock workers' organisation is that from the beginning of their struggles they realised the importance of developing links with workers in all Chilean ports and also, in their particular struggles in the nitrate sector, they linked their movement with the emerging unions in the nitrate oficinas. It is the development of this sense of common struggle that explains the magnitude of the nitrate strikes, particularly those of 1890 and 1907. The maturity of the workers organisation was a fact that made a strong impression on the members of the Parliamentary Commission that visited the nitrate districts in 1904. The following is a sample of their opinions regarding the organisation of the nitrate workers:

> Now that they are organised and in their own ranks they have intelligent men, we think that things are bound to change, if not radically, at least to a substantial degree ... Obviously, we were impressed by their articulate speech, the clarity of their exposition and the amazing knowledge they had regarding the workers' needs, their forms of labour, the irregularities of contracts, the abuses committed by employers, etc ... It is our impression that the Mancomunal is a powerful association

because it involves all unions of workers and its scope of action covers the country almost from one end to the other.(88)

The nitrate workers were at the heart of the Combinación Mancomunal. After the visit of the first Parliamentary Commission in 1904, nitrate workers felt frustrated by the report prepared by the commissioners, which they considered biased in favour of the nitrate producers, and they convened a National Conference of Workers which challenged the findings of the Commission. The Conference was the first attempt at organising workers on a national scale and the majority of the participants were delegates from the nitrate districts.(89)

Although the percentage varied widely, a large proportion of the most important strikes between 1884 and 1908 took place in the nitrate region (Table 3.4). The extent of industrial unrest and workers' response acquires more relevance if we bear in mind that the Norte Grande never had more than eight per cent of Chile's total population. This did not only take the form of strike action; there are other indicators that also point towards a relatively higher level of activity and participation in workers' organisations in the Norte Grande. In his survey of the popular press at the turn of the century, Arias Escobedo has shown that, in relative terms, workers' publications were more numerous and lasted longer in the Norte Grande than in the urban areas of Central Chile.(90) Even the traditional mutual aid societies had a more extensive development in the Norte Grande. The Chilean Labour Office reported in 1910 that there were 130 societies with 12,800 members in the Norte Grande whereas the more populated urban areas of Valparaíso and Santiago had only 84 with 10,800 members and 72 with 12,000 members respectively.(91)

The higher level of activity and organisation among workers in the nitrate region was their response to the progressive isolation into which they were pushed both by the nitrate companies and the government, and was also the product of persistently appalling living conditions prevailing in the area. A comparison of the major strikes that took place in the nitrate region before 1914 reveals that despite the enormous wealth accruing to mine owners and to the government, living conditions basically remained unchanged and the sources of conflict were the same in 1890 and in 1907 (Table 3.5). Both of the strikes are remarkable examples of organisation and mobilisation of thousands of nitrate workers from all the oficinas scattered over an extensive area with deficient communications and poor means of transport. They are also remarkable because the movement spread to other parts of Chile and posed a threat to the government which resorted to extreme repression, killing hundreds of workers in order to restore order.

63

Table 3.5: Chile: Workers' Demands in Two Major Strikes, 1890 and 1907

1890 Strike	1907 Strike
1. End of the ficha system or conversion of fichas at par value.	1. End of the ficha system. Fines against companies refusing conversion at par value.
2. End of pulperia monopoly and free access to outside merchants and pedlars.	2. End of pulperia monopoly. Each pulperia to have a scale and a yardstick at the door for checking weights and measurements.
3. Wages to be fixed in gold or silver-related currency.	3. Wages to be fixed using standard pesos equivalent to 18 pence sterling.
4. End of arbitrary fines and discounts in wages.	4. Prevent the companies from processing the ores that have been rejected for not complying with the minimum grade required.
5. Safety in working conditions. Protective shields to be installed in nitrate boiling tanks.	5. Safety in working conditions. Fines to be paid by companies and compensation to injured workmen.
6. Right to petition and assembly.	6. Job security for those involved in current strike. In future, fix a minimum 15 days' notice for dismissals.
7. Establishment of a primary school at each oficina.	7. Provision of rent-free premises to set up evening schools for workers.
8. Prohibition of drink, gambling and prostitution.	
9. End charges for drinking water.	
10. End companies' control over workers' correspondence.	

Source: Chile, Sesiones Ordinarias de la Cámara de Diputados, Session of 10 January 1908; H.Ramírez Necochea, Historia del Movimiento Obrero (Austral, Santiago, 1956), p.296; M.Segall, El Desarrollo del Capitalismo en Chile (Santiago, 1953), pp. 228-233; and M. Monteón, 'The Nitrate Miners and the Origins of the Chilean Left', unpublished PhD dissertation, Harvard University, 1974, pp. 53-4.

The strikes are also illustrative of the way in which the nitrate companies and the Chilean government combined forces in order to check the development of workers' organisations and to isolate the labour force from the union movement in the rest of the country. The community of interests between the state and the nitrate companies was a logical consequence of the way in which the industry had been established after the War of the Pacific. As explained elsewhere, the Chilean state never became involved in the actual productive process, and instead chose to intervene only at the circulation stage of the final commodity by charging an export duty per volume of nitrate exported. Since the nitrate duty provided more than 50 per cent of the fiscal revenues, the various governments were interested in preserving law and order at all costs to prevent disruptions to the productive process. To the same end, they granted the mine owners a free hand in the running of their companies in exchange for the nitrate duties, which spared the ruling classes the payment of either direct or indirect taxation.(92) The social unrest in the nitrate fields, therefore, bears no relation to other conflicts such as the strike of 1912 against British railway companies in Buenos Aires, in which the Argentine government acted as mediator and gave way to public support for the strike by helping the workers to obtain some concessions from the companies.(93) In the case of the Chilean government, it always took sides with the nitrate companies to the extent that most of the strikes in the area were bloodily terminated.(94)

For the nitrate producers, the social conflict, as such, did not exist. The only problem was the disruptive action of 'agitators' and the lack of appropriate policing in the nitrate districts. They were even prepared to contribute financially to strengthen the police force in the mines.(95) The Association of Nitrate Producers claimed in 1904: 'There is not a labour conflict as such, but elements alien to the nitrate industry trying to upset the tranquility according to ends far removed from the interests of the labouring people'.(96) So extreme was the position of the mine owners that it is possible to discern a different attitude among British diplomats and consuls, except, of course, when a consul had his own axe to grind in the nitrate business.(97) The case of the 1907 strike is a clear instance of differing views between nitrate producers and British diplomats in Chile. Visiting the nitrate districts only weeks before the workers struck, the British minister in Santiago acknowledged that 'the sudden recent drop in exchange (of the Chilean currency) and consequent rise of price in imported commodities may, not without reason, cause a demand for some advance in wages'.(98) To the mine owners, however, the workers' claims were groundless. 'Even at the present low rate of exchange', said one producer during the 1907 strike, 'the rate of wages paid to the workmen is very high and they have absolutely no ground of complaint; the present

difficulties   being   due   entirely   to   the   action   of
agitators'.(99)

In practice, the 1907 strike developed into a test of
stubborness between workers and employers. From the beginning
of the strike the Nitrate Producers Association put strong
pressure upon the Foreign Office to get British warships sent
to Iquique, the focus of the conflict.(100) However, the
Admiralty was reluctant to become involved in the dispute and
stated that

> should a man-of-war happen to be present at a large
> Chilean port on the occasion of serious riots ... My Lords
> would strongly demur to her landing men or otherwise
> taking part in actual measures of police; and they would
> suggest that in any case, the proper course to pursue for
> the protection of British subjects, if their life or
> liberty is in any way endangered, would be for the British
> consul to employ the British merchant shipping in the port
> for accommodation of refugees ... On the evidence before
> them, however, My Lords do not anticipate any need for
> such measures.(101)

Having failed to persuade the Foreign Office and the
Admiralty to intervene by force in the nitrate region, the
Producers Association had no problem in enlisting the support
of the Chilean government to end the dispute with decisive use
of force. The magnitude of the strike, which involved the
marching into Iquique of around 12,000 miners, plus the support
of local workers from the port and the town together with
expressions of solidarity from workers throughout the coast to
Valparaíso, made the government initially amenable to a
negotiated settlement, first by proposing arbitration and then
by offering the producers 50 per cent of the expense involved
in meeting the miners' claims. However, the Nitrate Producers
Association bluntly refused to enter into any negotiation
unless the workers either returned voluntarily or were returned
by force to the oficinas. Indeed a committee formed by three
lawyers and the Bishop of the Catholic Church had been
appointed by the provincial authorities to mediate in the
dispute, and although it was accepted by the strikers, it was
rejected by the employers on the grounds that a negotiated
settlement would indicate that 'either the Authorities were
showing considerable weakness in dealing with the situation, or
were laying undue stress on its dangers, with a view to
inducing the Directorate of the Nitrate [Producers] Association
to make some declaration that the men could construe into a
victory for them'.(102) In the end, the course of action taken
by the government was a drastic repression, the extent of which
crippled the labour movement for a number of years.

CONCLUSIONS

At the point in history when nitrate became a commodity of major importance in European markets, British companies took over and organised the largest proportion of nitrate enterprises together with nitrate railways, waterworks, shipping and other related services. The labour attracted to the nitrate Pampa, either through spontaneous migration or by means of organised recruitment, was mainly a segment of the Chilean society that had already undergone an initial process of proletarianisation either in Chile's urban centres or in Peru's mining and railway works. Detached from their former rural environment and engaged in activities that were partly extractive and partly manufacturing, they became a labour force that was likely to develop into a modern proletariat. Additional factors contributed to the process of proletarianisation. One was the persistence of what the Parliamentary Commission called 'effective and real causes of unrest' derived from poor housing and working conditions and the high cost of living.

Most importantly, the common interests of employers and the Chilean state in sharing the surplus generated from nitrate enterprises led to the isolation of the workers and fostered their union and class solidarity as their only viable response to the hostile world that surrounded them. This isolation from the state, however, was counterbalanced by the strong commitment towards unity with the rest of the Chilean workers. The experience of the Mancomunal shows that, although originally it was a nitrate-based organisation, one of its most significant endeavours was the development of links with other sister organisations in the rest of Chile.

The higher level of organisation, both in terms of workers' participation and in the relatively larger number of unions, societies, publications, leaders and strikes in the Norte Grande, when compared with other regions of Chile, supports the idea that the nitrate region contained the nucleus of a modern working class which was about to emerge during the first decade of the twentieth century. Despite its attempts to develop links with workers in other parts of the country, the organisation of nitrate workers was a localised phenomenon. As such, it failed to reach a stage of development whereby it could achieve a revolutionary impetus that would transform the basis of Chilean society. Also, whether within the existing political spectrum or whether as an independent movement, it failed to develop as a political force capable of challenging the prevailing structure of state power.

Unable and unprepared to deal with the formidable force and violence that inevitably confronted them at critical points in their struggle, the nitrate workers suffered recurrent setbacks that disabled their organisation for years at a time. The violence of the repression they had to endure was in parallel with the increasing degree of organisation that they were achieving during the first decade of the twentieth century. The repression they suffered in the 1907 strike was unprecedented in its violence. Hundreds of workers were killed, thousands emigrated from the Norte Grande and were replaced by a more docile contingent of workers. The First World War brought about a serious crisis in the nitrate sector and combined to worsen the conditions of the workers' organisation. A second and more mature stage of development in the process of proletarianisation developed in later decades. However, the emergence of working class parties and political organisations that added consistency to the process was built upon the experience of pre-1914 labour movements in the nitrate region.

NOTES
1. Herbert A. Spalding, Organised Labor in Latin America, (Harper & Row, New York, 1977), p.1.
2. On the nitrate sector, treated as an economic enclave, see M.A. Fernández, 'El Enclave Salitrero y la Economía Chilena' in Nueva Historia, vol.1 no.3, 1981. The other major 'embryo' in the formation of Chile's proletariat is obviously the urban sector in central Chile. The most complete analysis is found in Peter DeShazo, 'Urban Workers and Labor Unions in Chile, 1902-1907', unpublished PhD dissertation, University of Wisconsin, Madison, 1977.
3. See J.A. Marquez, La Orgía Financiera del Peru, Salitre y Guano (Santiago, 1904). For the nationalisation of nitrates by Peru see Oscar Bermúdez, Historia del Salitre desde los Origenes hasta la Guerra del Pacífico (Edit. Universitaria, Santiago, 1963). Also Robert Greenhill and Rory Miller, 'The Peruvian Government and the Nitrate Trade, 1973-79', Journal of Latin American Studies, vol. 5, (1973).
4. See Thomas O'Brien, 'British Investors and the Decline of the Chilean Nitrate Entrepreneur, 1870-1890', unpublished PhD dissertation, University of Connecticut, 1976. In his recently published book, O'Brien has reinforced his point that Chilean nitrate interests had begun to flounder already in the 1870s, and most of the nitrate industry was taken over by European companies in the 1880s: The Nitrate Industry and Chile's Crucial Transition: 1870-1891 (New York University Press, New York, 1982) pp. 63-76. See also M.A.Fernández, 'The Chilean Economy and its British Connections, 1895-1914', unpublished PhD dissertation, University of Glasgow, 1978, chap.V.
5. On the introduction of the Shanks system see M.A.Fernández, 'Technology and British Nitrate Enterprises in Chile, 1880-1914', Occasional Papers No. 34, Institute of Latin American Studies, University of Glasgow, 1981.
6. Ibid., Table II, p. 5.
7. A complete account of British portfolio investment in Chile can be found in M.A.Fernández, 'British-Chilean Economic Relations, 1870-1914. Statistical tables and guide to sources',

unpublished typescript, University of Glasgow, 1981.

8. Jonathan Levin, The Export Economies (Cambridge, Mass, Harvard University Press, 1960), p. 86.

9. Roberto Querejazu Calvo, Guano, Salitre, Sangre. Historia de la Guerra del Pacífico (Amigos del Libro, La Paz, 1979), p. 28.

10. Ibid, pp. 87-8. See also Watt Stewart, Chinese Bondage in Peru (Durham, North Carolina, Duke University Press, 1951).

11. See Marcelo Segall, 'Biografía Social de la Ficha-Salario', Mapocho, vol. II, no. 2 (1964), pp.325-69. See also Hernán Ramírez Necochea, Historia del Movimiento Obrero en Chile (Austral, Santiago, 1956), pp. 70-2.

12. Levin, Export Economies, p. 89.

13. A Peruvian government survey carried out in 1853 stated that during 1852-3 alone 'about sixty Chinese labourers succeeded in eluding their guards and throwing themselves over the cliffs to their death ... hardly a day went by without an attempted suicide'. (Cited in Levin, Export Economies, p. 89)

14. On Chilean emigration to California see Enrique Bunster, Chilenos en California (Zig-Zag, Santiago, 1965); V. Pérez Rosales, Recuerdos del Pasado (Zig-Zag, Santiago, 1943), partially translated into English as Californian Adventure (San Francisco, 1947), and Jay Monagham, Chile, Peru, and the California Gold Rush of 1849 (University of California Press, Berkeley, California, 1973).

15. See Luis Ortega, 'Acerca de los Orígenes de la Industrialización Chilena, 1860-1879', Nueva Historia, vol.I no.2 (1981); also his unpublished PhD dissertation, 'Change and Crisis in Chile's Economy and Society, 1865-1879', University of London, 1979.

16. On inquilinaje see Mario Góngora, Origen de los Inquilinos de Chile Central (Edit. Universitaria, Santiago, 1960). Also Cristóbal Kay, 'Comparative Development of the European Manorial System and the Latin American Hacienda System', unpublished PhD dissertation, University of Sussex, 1971.

17. Gabriel Salazar, 'El Movimiento Teórico sobre Desarrollo y Dependencia en Chile, 1950-1975', Nueva Historia, vol. I, no.4 (1982).

18. Cristóbal Kay, El Sistema Señorial Europeo y la Hacienda Latinoamericana (Ediciones Era, Mexico, 1980), p. 44.

19. Robert B. Oppenheimer, 'Chilean Transportation Development: the Railroad and Socioeconomic Change in the Central Valley, 1840-1885', unpublished Phd dissertation, University of California, 1976, pp. 220-3.

20. The Santiago-Valparaíso railway was completed in 1868, whereupon Meiggs moved to Peru, followed by his workers, to build Peru's most important lines. It is estimated that in the Lima-Oroya line alone Meiggs employed more than 5,000 Chileans. See Horacio Aranguiz, 'La Situación de los Obreros Agrícolas en el Siglo XIX', Estudios de Historia de las Instituciones Políticas y Sociales, vol.I no.2 (1967), pp. 28-9. See also

Watt Stewart, 'El Trabajador Chileno y los Ferrocarriles del Peru', Revista Chilena de Historia y Geografía, vol. 85 (1938), pp. 128-71: and Henry Meiggs. Un Pizarro Yanqui (Editorial Universitaria, Santiago, 1954).

21. Cited in Aranguiz, 'Situación de los Obreros', p.28.

22. Bermúdez, Historia del Salitre, pp. 367-8.

23. Ibid, p. 368.

24. Oficina Limeña to A. Gibbs & Sons, 30 June 1880, cited by Arthur L. Stickell, 'Migration and Mining in Northern Chile in the Nitrate Era, 1880-1930', unpublished PhD dissertation, Indiana University, 1979, p. 47.

25. Cited in ibid, p. 69.

26. Ibid., p.69.

27. La Industria, 30 September 1885, quoted by Ramírez, Historia del Movimiento Obrero, p. 279.

28. Consular report from Valparaíso for year 1888. Parliamentary Papers, Miscellaneous Series No. 142, (C. 5896). See also Joanne F. Przeworski, 'The Decline of Copper Industry in Chile and the Entrance of North American Capital, 1870-1916', unpublished PhD dissertation, University of Washington, 1979, passim.

29. Michael Monteón, 'The Nitrate Miners and the Origins of the Chilean Left, 1880-1925', unpublished PhD dissertation, Harvard University, 1974, p. 82. Monteón has collected a number of colourful descriptions of 'enganches' (see pp. 79-84).

30. Stickell, 'Migration and Mining', p. 71.

31. In Roberto Hernández Cortez, El Roto Chileno (Valparaíso, 1929), pp. 78-9. Cited in Stickell, 'Migration and Mining', p. 54.

32. Stickell, 'Migration and Mining', p. 50.

33. Stickell, 'Migration and Mining', p. 63. Also, the petition submitted by the nitrate workers to the 1904 Parliamentary Commission read: 'Chile is crowded up with labour, Your Excellency. Whenever they say that there is a shortage of workers in a district or province, it is only because they intend to produce a superabundance of hands in order to cheapen their price'. Cited in Manuel Salas Lavaqui, Trabajos y Antecedentes Presentados al Supremo Gobierno de Chile por la Comisión Consultiva del Norte (Imprenta Cervantes, Santiago, 1908), p. 560.

34. J. Robert Brown, 'Nitrate Crises, Combinations, and the Chilean Government in the Nitrate Age', Hispanic American Historical Review, vol. 43 (1963), p. 236. See also Fernández, 'The Chilean Economy, pp. 248-75.

35. South American Journal, vol XLI, 19 September 1896, p. 307.

36. This is discussed in Fernández, 'Technology', passim.

37. Head Office to Valparaíso, 3 January 1908, Antony Gibbs & Sons Ms. 11,471, vol. 78. Herbert Gibbs had made the same point in his Chairman's Report to the A.G.M. of the Pan de Azúcar Nitrate Co. on 15 November 1907: 'If we had the power of

reducing production, and consequently reducing the excessive demand for labour, we should have the power of resuming control over the labour market'. (The Economist, 16 November 1907, p.1995).

38. Monteón, 'Nitrate Miners', p. 110.

39. See Fernández, 'El Enclave Salitrero', pp. 2-17.

40. See Andrzej Brozek, 'Industrial Labour Force in a Politically Divided Area. The Upper Silesian Example, 1870-1938', Proceedings of the 7th International Economic History Congress, (Edinburgh, 1978), p. 452.

41. Percy F Martin, Through Five Republics of South America, (Heinemann, London, 1906), p. 342. Cited by J.R.Brown, 'The Chilean Nitrate Industry in the Nineteenth Century', unpublished PhD dissertation, Louisiana State University, 1954, p. 199. The dreariness of the environment also affected the British expatriate community and sometimes called for 'strong medicine', as the Englishwoman visiting the region in 1911 found out when she asked a Scot how he could stand living in such a desolate place. The firm reply was: 'It is not bad out there, when you get used to it... There are cafes, and an English Club, and we just sit there, a lot of us, and see who can drink the most whisky'. On a more serious note, observing the conditions of life the nitrate workers had to endure, the same traveller commented: 'Life in these flat-topped hovels under a cloudless glare, soon sends the men stationed here to the whisky-bottle, the cemetery, or home leave. It is a pity that the so-called nitrate kings of the Stock Exchange do not pay an annual visit to their subjects, for never was wealth won under more arduous conditions'. (Charlotte Cameron, A Woman's Winter in South America (London, 1911), pp.148 and 153.

42. Deputy Bonifacio Veas, Chilean Congress, Sesiones Ordinarias de la Cámara de Diputados (hereafter called SOCD), Session of 27 December 1907. Deputy Veas, a member of the Partido Democrático, was the only manual worker in the Chamber of Deputies in 1907.

43. 'Observaciones hechas por los patrones a la petición de los obreros' in Salas Lavaqui, Trabajos y Antecedentes, p. 610.

44. The distinction between low and high cost production oficinas is discussed in Fernández, 'The Chilean Economy', pp. 254-61.

45. Monteón, 'Nitrate Miners', pp. 108-9.

46. In Salas Lavaqui, Trabajos y Antecedentes, p. 539. Semper and Mitchels also confirmed that miners lived in 'miserable hovels made from old sacks, pieces of corrugated iron and chunks of pressed soil strata' (E.Semper and E.Mitchels, La Industria del Salitre en Chile, (Santiago, 1908), p. 103).

47. Baldomero Lillo, 'El Obrero Chileno en la Pampa Salitrera', Obras Completas (Santiago, 1961), p. 406.

48. Ibid. See also Stickell, 'Migration and Mining', pp. 185-6.

49. Monteón, 'Nitrate Miners', p. 121.

50. 'Presentación del Comité de Obreros presentada al Señor Ministro del Interior y Miembros del Congreso Nacional', in Salas Lavaqui, Trabajos y Antecedentes, p. 575.

51. The abuses to which particulares were subjected are mentioned in several sources. See SOCD, speech by Deputy Malaquías Concha, session of 30 December 1907. See also 'Presentación del Comité de Obreros in Salas Lavaqui, Trabajos y Antecedentes, pp. 575-6.

52. Speech by Rafael Sotomayor, Minister of the Interior, SOCD, Session of 2 January 1908.

53. E.P.Thompson, The Making of the English Working Class (Penguin, Harmondsworth, 1970), p. 270. See also G.W.Hilton, The Truck System (Heffer, Cambridge, 1960).

54. In the case of Chile, the truck system also prevailed in parts of the countryside where landowners issued their own promissory notes and tokens instead of using legal currency. Sometimes peons had their wages settled only twice a year and during the intermediate time they bought on credit at the landowners' pulperias with the frequent result that when the settlement was done, they became debtors and the amounts due were carried forward to the next period. See Paul Treutler, Andanzas de un Alemán en Chile (Santiago, 1950), pp. 529-30 and George McBride, Chile: Land and Society (New York, 1936).

55. 'Observaciones de los industriales al proyecto sobre pago de salarios', in Salas Lavaqui, Trabajos y Antecedentes, p. 635.

56. SOCD, session of 30 December 1907.

57. Ibid.

58. Association of Nitrate Producers, Circular Semestral no. 42, 1907. (Quoted by Stickell, 'Migration and Mining', p. 279).

59. Cited by Enrique Reyes, El Desarrollo de la Conciencia Proletaria en Chile. El Ciclo Salitrero (Orbe, Santiago, 1973), p. 100.

60. South American Journal, XXXVI, 13 January 1894. (Cited by J.R. Brown, 'The Chilean Nitrate Industry', pp. 200-1.

61. Consul J.W. Merriam to Department of State, No. 507, 23 July 1890. (Quoted by J.R.Brown, 'The Chilean Nitrate Industry', p.204.

62. Consul Hudson to F.O., 30 January 1914. FO 368/944.

63. See Monteón, 'Nitrate Miners', p. 111.

64. Semper and Mitchels, La Industria del Salitre, p. 102.

65. 'Nuevas observaciones hechas por los salitreros al Proyecto de Ley' in Salas Lavaqui, Trabajos y Antecedentes, pp. 641-2.

66. SOCD, session of 30 December 1907.

67. The Economist, 30 June 1894, p. 805.

68. Semper and Mitchels, La Industria del Salitre, p.85.

69. 'Informe pasado a la Municipalidad de Tocopilla' March 1904, in Salas Lavaqui, Trabajos y Antecedentes, p. 550. Semper and Mitchels also confirmed the success of the black market and gave an indication of the scale of illicit trade in the pampa: 'At the centre and north of Tarapacá ... there are small villages almost exclusively with shops, gambling houses and brothels which are suitable places for smugglers of spirits and groceries ... to prevent this competition, the oficinas indirectly force workers to get the largest portion of their wages in 'fichas' ...' (Semper and Mitchels, La Industria del Salitre, p. 102).

70. J.Valdes Cange, Sinceridad, Chile Intimo en 1910 (Santiago, 1910), p. 209.

71. Stickell, 'Migration and Mining', p. 265.

72. See Salas Lavaqui, Trabajos y Antecedentes, p. 895. On the other hand, Stickell's view that, on account of their high nominal wages, nitrate workers enjoyed a standard of living higher than that of Chilean workers in other regions should be criticised because it fails to take full account of the higher cost of living in the nitrate region. Also, Stickell overestimates the validity of claims and data found in the reports of the Parliamentary Commissions. For instance, his contention that the diet of nitrate workers was better than that of southern workers ('Migration and Mining', pp. 319-20) is based on the Report of the 1913 Commission which stated that daily meals in the Pampa were the following:

Breakfast :	Beef-steak, eggs, potatoes, onion, coffee and bread
Lunch :	Choice from two meat stews 'in abundant quantities', second course of beans and bread
Early Tea :	Same as breakfast but chicha (cider) or wine instead of coffee
Dinner :	Same as lunch

Such data cannot be taken seriously and probably represents the meals served during the Commission's visit. The assumption that such diet was representative for all nitrate workers would lead to the absurd conclusion that, considering the quantity of meat available in the region during 1913, yearly meat consumption per capita in the Norte Grande was 182 kg among miners and only 10.7 kg among the remaining non-mining population in the area. Stickell's contention is hard to sustain because in terms of meat consumption, the nitrate region was much worse off than the rest of Chile. For instance, the official statistics on yearly meat consumption per capita for 1915 were the following:

Norte Grande   36 kg

Santiago	71 kg
Valparaíso	59 kg
national average	40 kg

(Source: Chile, Sinopsis Estadística, 1915 (Santiago, 1916), p. 132).

73. DeShazo, 'Urban Workers', p. 54.
74. Julio C.Jobet, Luis Emilio Recabarren. Los orígenes del movimiento obrero y del socialismo chileno (Edit. PLA, Santiago, 1955) p. 112.
75. DeShazo, 'Urban Workers', p. 189.
76. Jobet, Luis Emilio Recabarren, p. 84.
77. The following publications are mentioned for the late 1890s: La Voz del Pueblo (1896), El Proletario (1898), El Rebelde (1898), La Tromba (1898), all of them in Santiago plus La Campana, El Acrata, La Agitación and several others in provinces. See F. Casanueva and M.A. Fernández, El Partido Socialista y la Lucha de Clases en Chile (Quimantu, Santiago, 1973), p. 52.
78. Thomas Kirkup, A History of Socialism (A. & C. Black, London, 1892), p. 191.
79. On the Partido Democrático, see Casanueva and Fernández, El Partido Socialista, pp. 48-9.
80. The background to the 1905 strike is discussed in R.C. Wright, 'The Politics of Inflation in Chile', Hispanic American Historical Review, vol. 53 (1973).
81. 'Informe pasado por la Comisión Consultiva al Presidente de la República', in Salas Lavaqui, Trabajos y Antecedentes, pp. 5-6.
82. Ibid., p. 6.
83. The Guía Administrativa, Industrial y Comercial de Tarapacá y Antofagasta, compiled by Víctor Domingo Silva, (Iquique, 1908) carried interesting photographs showing the luxury of well carpeted and lavishly furnished buildings of the administrators in contrast with the appalling conditions prevailing in the workers' campamentos.
84. Stickell, 'Migration and Mining', p. 243. Monteón makes a similar point by stating that 'the British, in particular, tended to trust only each other in important positions'. (See Monteón, 'Nitrate Miners', pp. 124-5).
85. Jorge Barría, El Movimiento Obrero en Chile (Edit. Universidad Técnica del Estado, Santiago, 1971), pp. 26-7.
86. See O'Brien, The Nitrate Industry, p. 91.
87. Ibid., pp. 93 and 121.
88. Salas Lavaqui, Trabajos y Antecedentes, p. 876.
89. Barría, El Movimiento Obrero, pp. 26-7.
90. Osvaldo Arias Escobedo, La Prensa Obrera en Chile (Edit. PLA, Santiago, 1970), passim. Luis Emilio Recabarren, one of the most outstanding labour leaders both in the Norte Grande and nationally, has left a recollection of the way in which his career as a leader was changed dramatically in 1903.

In that year, Recabarren left his high position in the bureaucracy of the Partido Democrático and went north to work hand in hand with the nitrate miners. His decision to move to the nitrate region was to a large extent prompted by the following episode, as related by Recabarren himself: 'I always remember with emotion the occasion when a group of workers from Tocopilla arrived in Valparaíso and came to tell me "Compañero, we have brought two thousand pesos with us to buy a press. The Tocopilla Workers' Federation (then called Mancomunal) has managed to raise this money and we want you to accompany us to choose a press". "And what are you going to do with it?" I enquired. "Publish a paper", was the reply. "And who is going to write it up?" (I asked again). "Well", they said, "We have no one to compose it and we want you to help us find a typesetter". Finally, they said: "In fact, we expect you yourself to go to Tocopilla and take care of the paper".' After this meeting, Recabarren moved to the nitrate region and from 1903 to 1906 he became either editor or contributor to El Defensor de la Clase Proletaria and El Pueblo Obrero, published in Iquique, La Voz del Pueblo, published in Taltal, El Proletario and El Trabajo, published in Tocopilla, and other similar publications. See Luis Emilio Recabarren, Obras Escogidas (Edit. Recabarren, Santiago, 1965), pp. 52-3.

91. Cited by Michael Monteón, Chile in the Nitrate Era (University of Wisconsin Press, Madison, 1982), p. 87.

92. See Fernández, 'El Enclave Salitrero', pp. 17-21.

93. See Spalding, Organised Labor in Latin America, p. 13.

94. One of the most remarkable features in the development of the northern proletariat is the fact that, despite the scale of repression facing them, workers persistently continued to build up their organisation. It is difficult to find a parallel elsewhere to the numbers of workers killed in northern Chile. They were counted by the hundred. The 1907 strike alone ended with over 1000 casualties. Julio Valdes Cange, who visited the Pampa after the strike, wrote that nitrate workers 'are not surprised at being exploited by the English because they have not pitched their tents in such desolate grounds to practice philanthropy. But ... to see the leaders of their own fatherland, those called upon to defend and look after their welfare, sending cannons and machine guns handled by brothers in misery and blood, to cowardly murder them in order to please the potentate, that is something the miners cannot forgive'. (J. Valdes Cange, Chile Intimo, p. 210).

95. See Reyes, Desarrollo de la Conciencia Proletaria, p. 198.

96. Ibid., p. 192.

97. Consul C. Noel Clarke is a case in point. He was British consul in Iquique during the disturbances in December 1907, and his reports to the Foreign Office, unlike other reports sent by the British Minister in Chile, expressed a partisan view against the nitrate miners. Although factually

correct, his reports frequently used derogatory terms for the Chilean workers. (See, for instance, C. Noel Clarke to F.O., 3 January 1908. F.O. 368/176). Later, in 1910, heavily indebted to the nitrate owners, Clarke abandoned his creditors, much to the embarrassment of the Board of Trade which had to deal with the requests for payment. (See Board of Trade to F.O., 13 May 1910, F.O. 368/280).

98. E. Rennie to Sir Edward Grey, confidential, 7 December 1907, F.O. 369/127. The fall in the rate of exchange benefitted the nitrate companies greatly because it reduced labour costs in the same proportion that the Chilean peso depreciated. For instance, on the eve of the 1907 strike, the chairman of Pan de Azúcar Nitrate Co. greeted as good news the drop in value of the Chilean peso and stated: 'The important effect on us of a fall in exchange is that it counterbalances ... the rise in the (Chilean) dollar price of labour, that is to say, when we find that we are paying more dollars for wages, it is a great advantage to be able to get those dollars at a reduced price'. The Economist, 16 November 1907, p. 1995.

99. A.Gibbs & Sons to Sir E. Grey, 23 December 1907, F.O. 368/94.

100. See Permanent Nitrate Committee to Sir E.Grey, 19 December 1907, F.O. 368/94; A.Gibbs & Sons to Sir E. Grey, 19 December 1907, F.O. 368/94 and W. & C. Lockett to F.O., 24 December 1907, F.O. 368/176.

101. Admiralty to F.O., 20 December 1907, F.O. 368/94. Despite the reluctant reply of the Admiralty Office, as a precautionary measure HMS Sappho was despatched at full speed to Iquique. It arrived 15 days after the strike had been brutally suppressed, but still in time for Commander Hodges to congratulate the Chilean General Silva Renard on his success in dealing with the strikers and rioters with a firm hand. The general, in turn, expressed his 'regret that there was not always a British Man-of-War in Chilean waters, to remind his countrymen of their best friends'. (See N.Clarke to F.O., 13 January 1908, F.O. 132/99 and Commander M.H.Hodges to Admiralty, 20 January 1908, F.O. 368/176).

102. N.Clarke to F.O., 3 January 1908, F.O. 368/176. On the offer made by the Chilean government to cover 50 per cent of the workers' claim, see SOCD, session of 10 January 1908.

Chapter Four

PROLETARIANISATION IN MOZAMBIQUE

Barry Munslow

A study of the emerging working class in Mozambique is
essentially an exercise in explaining why this class has been
so constrained in its growth: limited in its size, restricted
in the formation of its own organisations, and with only a
minimal development of class consciousness. The latter may
perhaps appear surprising, given that Mozambique is one of the
few countries on the global periphery to experience a
revolution, producing a government seriously undertaking a
development strategy based on a socialist option. This chapter
will begin by trying to explain the peculiar nature of working
class formation in Mozambique in overall perspective, before
focusing more specifically on the ports and railways, to
produce an argument which challenges certain conventional
wisdoms concerning proletarianisation and the development of
class consciousness.

THE CONTEXT OF WORKING CLASS FORMATION

Classes are formed by people entering into particular
relationships of production, and with the penetration of
colonial capitalism a process of rapid social and economic
change was experienced on the periphery. The direction of
change in a social formation is always determined by the
dominant mode of production within that formation, and in the
case of Mozambique processes of proletarianisation and
semi-proletarianisation began with capitalism's penetration of
Southern Africa from the nineteenth century onwards.
Pre-capitalist modes of production were articulated with the
capitalist mode, eventually producing a regional sub-system
dominated by the process of capital accumulation at the
peripheral centre, South Africa. Southern Rhodesia soon came to
perform the role of a secondary peripheral centre.
    The case of Mozambique is particularly interesting as it
provides us with an example of proletarianisation by proxy.
Portugal was a sub-metropolitan colonial power on the periphery

of Europe, exporting raw materials and importing finished products, but maintaining, at the same time, its own periphery of empire in Africa. Without the capital to exploit its colonies directly, Portugal acted as an intermediary for foreign capital's exploitation of Mozambican labour. Given the weakness of the sub-metropolitan economy, Mozambique's dependency took a very particular form.(1) Within the whole southern African region South Africa was dominant and the neighbouring states were to a greater or lesser extent brought under its influence. Their economies were subordinated to the rapid process of capital accumulation which took place in that country, resulting in a grossly unbalanced pattern of regional development. The economic dependency of Mozambique took three main forms: at the level of the labour force, contracts were made to furnish Mozambican workers to Rhodesia and South Africa; at the level of investments, there was the installation of privileged monopoly companies dominated by foreign capital; at the level of infrastructure, there was the construction of railways and ports to serve the needs of Nyasaland, Rhodesia and principally, of course, South Africa. These three features were established in the early colonial period (1880-1930). Portugal, without the necessary capital to directly extract surplus value from the Mozambican labour force, was obliged to rent it out in two different ways. South of parallel 22^0 it hired the labour to the Transvaal. North of that line, it invited in foreign companies to use the labour and pay a rent for so doing. Portugal's own direct exploitation of the colony only began later with the widespread introduction of forced cash crop cultivation after Oliveira Salazar took power in 1930.

In the period 1930 to 1955, there was a slow-down in the rate of foreign investment in accordance with Salazar's nationalist policies, and forced cash crop production was intensified to produce low-cost raw materials for Portugal's developing industries. Industrial development, widespread settler immigration, and the growth of the two major cities, began only in the final period of colonialism, from 1955 to 1974. Under the impetus of the armed nationalist struggles breaking out in the 1960s in its three major African colonies, Portugal was obliged to open up once again its territories to foreign investment, which largely accounted for this expansion.

The capitalist penetration of Mozambique was essentially carried out through the agencies of the chartered companies, the mines, and the ports and railways. Chartered companies accelerated the process of creating a petty commodity-producing peasantry as distinct from a pre-colonial peasantry. The former produced cash crops for the metropolitan and sub-metropolitan markets, whilst the latter produced only for use.(2)

When examining proletarianisation, a careful distinction needs to be made between the 'external' and the 'internal' proletariat. By the 'external' proletariat, we mean those workers of Mozambican nationality whose point of production is outside the territorial boundaries of the state, while the 'internal' proletariat refers to those working inside the geographical boundaries of Mozambique. In this chapter we will be focusing on the latter, who thus far have been much neglected in the literature.(3) South African and Southern Rhodesian mines created a migrating proletariat with its point of production external to the national boundaries, but it was the ports and railways built to service the interests of these same two countries which acted to create the core of an internal Mozambican working class.

According to the classical model the most important feature of the proletariat is that it has lost all ownership of the means of production and is forced to sell its only remaining asset, labour power. However, capitalism on the periphery produces a proletariat within a specific (peripheral) social context. This differs from the process of proletarianisation in the industrial countries in three major ways: the slow pace, the partial character of its development, and the racial divisions existing within it. Proletarianisation refers to the increasingly necessary character of indigenous participation in the labour market and the closing off over time of alternatives. It also involves increases in the numbers of wage earners, the length of time spent in employment and the percentage of total income derived from wages. With the creation of new wants a further impetus towards proletarianisation develops. But in Mozambique there were several constraints in operation preventing a full and rapid proletarianisation. First, the primary sector (mines and plantations) operated a migrant labour system creating a class of worker-peasants rather than a permanent proletariat. Secondly, there were those features of the country's political economy that Mozambique shared with other countries on the periphery: it was a raw materials exporter to the industries of the sub-metropolis and the metropoles; hence its own secondary sector was tiny, and the need for a manufacturing working class was therefore small. Thirdly, Portuguese private capital and the state were unable to compete for Mozambique's labour on an open market; hence a chibalo or forced labour system was employed. The ability to call on labour for a compulsory and fixed period each year arrested tendencies towards a more permanent and widespread proletarianisation. This clearly affected the development of workers' organisations and the growth of a class consciousness, in particular when coupled with the quasi-military control exercised on the mine compounds where non-forced labour was used. Given the major impact of forced labour in retarding the proletarianisation process we must first turn to examine how this system worked.

Forced Labour

When Salazar came to power there was a serious attempt to make the administration of the colonies and the utilisation of the labour force more effective, and the Regulamento do Trabalho dos Indígenas of 1930 was introduced to achieve this end.(4) This law led on from the Native Labour Code of 1928. It was a comprehensive piece of legislation covering every aspect of employment. With few exceptions, all able-bodied African men were expected to work for six months in every year for a wage, either for a private employer or for the state. This was the so-called contract labour. The only exceptions covered: those Africans given assimilado status (the equivalent to the evolués in the French colonies), the 'civilised' black Portuguese, of whom only 4353 were recorded in the census of 1950; those Africans in permanent wage employment; rich peasants; and finally those doing migrant labour abroad. Three other forms of forced labour were also to be found, but these were of lesser importance. The first was obligatory labour, levied by the government for public works projects. Correctional labour, punishment for breaking the Labour or Criminal Code or failing to pay taxes, was a lucrative alternative to the expense of keeping idle prisoners. A colonial judge, Fernando O. Gouveia da Veiga, expressed the rationale thus: 'Pursuing the general policy of attempting the readjustment of the offenders to community standards, the emphasis in the prison system has been placed on work as the medium through which this is to be achieved'.(5) Voluntary labour referred to a contract between employer and employee without the mediation of the state. But the latter was something of a misnomer, as the threat of contract labour took much of the volition out of voluntary labour.

A system of close collaboration developed between the administration and employers. Indeed, increasing administrative efficiency and a more intensive use of African labour went hand in hand. The district administrator and chefe de posto would collect men together for the private recruiters. Field research conducted over many different parts of the country revealed forced labour to be ubiquitous and the closest collaboration to exist between the colonial administration and private employers. Duart João reported on his experience in Zambezia province:

> Those contracted were paid 100 escudos per month. They worked on the tea plantations in Vila Junqueiro near to Alto Molocue from 5.00 am to 5.00 pm. Only the men - but all the men except assimilados - worked on the plantations. People worked for six months. They were bound and forced to work. For running away from the plantations people were beaten and imprisoned.(6)

Saraiva Gomes, working in the same area on the Cha Luso tea plantation, reported that the chiefs and regulos organised the people to go to the plantations: 'Those who recruited people to work received gifts from the white settlers. The recrutadores and chiefs received their gifts at the end of the year, in the final month, so that they would work harder at getting labour for the plantations'.(7) Arrangatoni Mikiras, an agricultural worker, had lived and worked in the province of Tete. He gave his experience and explanation of the contract labour system as follows:

People were put in chains and obliged to work - it was forced labour. It started when boys were fourteen or fifteen years old. They had to go every year. Some were sent to one place and others to another. The administrator sent cipaios (police) to get the people and bind them, and after they would be brought to the administration. Then the recrutador would ask them if they wanted to go with him - and they were standing in front of him in chains! People were paid 100 escudos per month.(8)

He added finally, 'I have many sufferings in my heart and it would take a long time to explain all of them'.(9)

Contract labour was employed to work on the plantations and roads, as well as in railway and port construction in the urban areas. One informant reported his experience with a recruitment company in the south called Empresa de Transportes de Gaza (The Gaza Transport Company). The company brought young boys from the rural areas to the capital and 'sold' them to various enterprises. The informant, Albino Sitoe of Chibuto, Gaza province, was 'sold' to the Padaria Aliança (a bakery) in 1953.(10) During his first two months' work the recruit received no wages; instead the money was used to pay for the cost of having him transported to the city. Jorge Coelho, Director of the Government Stevedoring Agency (EMAP), confirmed in another interview that the same practice was carried out if there was a shortage of stevedores on the docks.(11) Henrique Galvão presented evidence of forced labour and widespread abuses of African labour to Portugal's National Assembly in his famous report of 1948, but there were no improvements made.(12) One effect of this forced labour was to fuel the flow of migrants abroad to the neighbouring states, which ran at several hundred thousands annually throughout the first three quarters of the twentieth century. They tended to work on the mines, plantations and farms, and in domestic service.

The administration profited greatly from its role in the recruitment system. Recruiters had to buy a licence and pay a fee for each man they received. The legal wage in force was also closely related to the tax: under the Regulamento of 1930, a certain ratio was maintained between the two. Frequently, after working a contract a man would have barely sufficient to pay his imposto (tax). Forced labour was generally employed for public works and on the plantations although, as we have seen, it was also used albeit in a more limited fashion in industry. Given Mozambique's role in the global division of labour, necessarily the manufacturing sector would be small, but nevertheless a working class did emerge. In the following section we briefly analyse its major structural characteristics.

Workers in Manufacturing

From the 1950s onwards, under the stimuli of a larger settler presence, Portugal's own belated industrialisation, South Africa's outward expansion, and the opening up of the sub-metropole and colonies to foreign investment, Mozambique's manufacturing sector grew from 8.6 per cent of the total workforce in 1950 to 14.9 per cent in 1966.(13) The Mozambican manufacturing working class had essentially five structural characteristics. First there was little stability and much fluctuation in its membership, as a result of the chibalo (forced labour) and internal migrant labour systems. A study made of the urban African population arrived at the following conclusion:

> The age distribution of the African population of Lourenço Marques in 1957 demonstrated the abnormality in age structure which can be expected for urban Africans where migrant labourers spend only a contract period in areas controlled by Europeans, where semi-migrant workers live on urban outskirts for the greater part of their productive years and where only a small proportion of Africans settle permanently in the cities and towns while the majority return in their declining years to homes in rural areas.(14)

A further factor accounting for the high fluctuation rate relates specifically to the cashew-processing industry where many young women were employed. With pregnancy and marriage there was a very high labour turnover, given the complete absence of maternity-leave provision or crèche facilities. In addition, working conditions were so bad that the deteriorating health of women workers seriously contributed to the rapid turnover.(15) A second characteristic was the racial division of the working class, with whites occupying the well-paid skilled and semi-skilled jobs and blacks the low-paid unskilled jobs. Thirdly, industry tended also to be labour intensive, with a low level of technology and, therefore, little need for a large and skilled workforce. A fourth feature was the small scale of the manufacturing enterprises: the 1973 statistics indicate that three-quarters of them employed 49 workers or less.(16) This contrasts markedly with the large concentration of workers in the transit sector. Finally, there was a massive regional distortion, with Lourenço Marques province accounting for 40.5 per cent of the manufacturing working class and three provinces alone accounting for 73.6 per cent.

In addition to these five structural characteristics which acted to constrain the development of the manufacturing sector of the internal working class, there was a further feature of great importance - the illegality of free trade unions and political organisations for black workers. Writers studying the British colonies, for example, often see the growth of African trade unions after the Second World War as marking a new period in the history of resistance; some trade union movements made a major contribution to the success of their nationalist struggles.(17) African trade union organisation was absent in the Mozambican experience, but, as we will demonstrate, workers' struggles were not.

Colonial development policies did not significantly improve the conditions of the working class, hence there was much to protest about. Sutcliffe has argued from a study of Rhodesia that the local spread effects of industrial expansion did not appreciably extend living standards from the white to the black sector.(18) The African population in fact was beginning to feel the adverse consequences of the rapid changes and the index of retail prices in Lourenço Marques (baseline 1956/7 = 100) shot up from 115 in 1969 to 163 in the first half of 1972.(19) That same year the provincial government of Mozambique launched its four year action programme which aimed to encourage local and foreign capital to invest in the manufacturing sector.(20) A balance of payments crisis with the sub-metropole meant that the development of local import substitution industries took on a renewed importance.(21) Overall, however, the developments in manufacturing did not produce an increased wealth for the mass of the African population which might have induced them to lessen their support for the nationalist struggle.

PROLETARIANISATION AND RESISTANCE: THE PORTS AND RAILWAYS

The Emergence of the Port and Railway System, 1880-1930
The extensive external migrant labour flow created internal problems of labour shortage. Labour was urgently required to construct the railway lines and ports to enable the Portuguese government to take further advantage of the growth of mines and plantations in South Africa and Southern Rhodesia by providing transit facilities for their export and import requirements.(22) It was for this reason that the first widespread introduction of forced labour occurred. But when the construction of the first rail line began in the 1880s, the south of the country still remained to be pacified and so the Portuguese were unable to secure sufficient African labour. Several thousand Cantonese workers were imported in 1887 to make up the shortfall.(23)

The railway line linking the Transvaal to the port of
Lourenço Marques, begun in the 1880s, was finally completed in
1894. When the line was being built, the Boers still controlled
the Transvaal Republic. Lourenço Marques was the natural sea
outlet for the Transvaal but, in addition, the Boers had a
clear preference for a line passing through the Portuguese
colony rather than the British-controlled port of Cape
Town.(24) The railway ran in deficit only for the first few
years, then it began to make a mounting profit as it carried
South Africa's raw material exports and its imports. The line
was intimately connected with the port of Lourenço Marques.
There was a doubling of the railway's profits in 1902,
coinciding with the opening of the Gorjão wharf which permitted
steamers to pull directly alongside to unload their cargoes.
Total tonnage handled in the port increased from a quarter of a
million tons at the turn of the century to one million tons by
the beginning of the First World War.(25) The bulk of South
African exports was coal (over half a million tons) providing
receipts of £57,000, in comparison with £7,686 for passenger
fares.(26) The railway also served to transport labour quickly
and efficiently to the Transvaal mines.
    South Africa's influence was so great that it could force
the Portuguese government to nationalise the port and railway
in January 1929. This was done in an attempt to improve the
functioning and efficiency of the system. However, South Africa
was not strong enough to take over full control of the port and
railways itself.(27) These nationalisations did not include the
stevedoring and freight handling companies, however, many of
which were South African-owned. Undoubtedly, in the early part
of the century the railways did not run at the height of
efficiency. The system of padrinho (patron-client relations)
ensured promotion on the basis of who a person knew and what he
was prepared to pay.(28) In the annual report of the port and
railways for 1923 there was a proposal to 'methodically reduce
the staff, increase the number of salaried employees and pay
them in conformity with their merits'.(29) The report continued
in a sarcastic vein to say: 'Whosoever has no qualities to
recommend them is almost guaranteed a place around the payments
table'.(30)
    Further to the north, Cecil Rhodes had a railway built
linking Rhodesia to the port of Beira; this was completed in
1899. The port of Beira was constructed with the financial
backing of the British South Africa Company. As with Lourenço
Marques, the function of this port was to serve the
non-Portuguese hinterland. Fully 90 per cent of the 682,000
tons of cargo handled in Beira in 1928 came from, or was going
to, non-Portuguese areas.(31)
    A railway from Nyasaland to Beira was completed in
1922.(32) The British were hoping to further their interests in
the area through their proxy, the Mozambique Company. Any
concern about the actual development of Mozambique was

completely subordinated to more powerful interests elsewhere. At the end of the 1920s the construction of a bridge over the Zambezi was approved to replace the existing ferry service. But the main motivation for this step appears to have been the desire to increase orders for the British steel industry which was stagnating at this time on the eve of the Great Depression. Exploiting the coal resources of the Moatize mine in Tete province could have made the rail and bridge project financially viable, but this was prevented through fear of creating competition with the Welsh coal industry. Finance for this railway came from the Nyasaland governmental budget.

Mozambique had a 'transit' rather than a 'transport' system. Rail lines ran from east to west and even today the best route from south of the Zambezi River to the north lies through Malawi. The three main rail lines linked Mozambique with South Africa, Southern Rhodesia and Nyasaland. The transport services provided for the neighbouring countries had a three-fold impact upon the political economy: they were a major source of foreign exchange, the principal reason for the growth of the country's two major cities, and finally, a small working class grew up around the ports and railways of the cities of Lourenço Marques and Beira.

Working Class Resistance Before 1930

In the pre-Salazar period, the greatest organised militancy was expressed by the white workers. With the onset of the Republican period in Portugal (1910-26), there was a broad upsurge of workers' struggles in the sub-metropole and these were reflected amongst the white workers in the colonies. Anarchism and syndicalism were powerful political forces in the Iberian peninsula, and sometimes political leaders found themselves in forced, or self-imposed, exile in the colonies. By the beginning of 1917, the Portuguese economy was entering into crisis and a huge increase in the number of strikes occurred. On 6 June 1917, a general strike of all European personnel in the port and railways was called in Lourenço Marques.(33) A rise was demanded to compensate for a wage reduction when the management stopped payment for Sunday work. Tram drivers struck in sympathy, and a state of siege was declared in the city by the governor's assistant. This strike took place in a crucial year of the First World War, when troops were fighting Germans in the north of the colony. Very soon the military moved in, workers were arrested and 22 were sent to the prison island of Xefina in the bay of Lourenço Marques. In response, the workers issued a proclamation on 8 June demanding the release of prisoners, freedom of assembly, and a reply by the governor to their requests. The Governor-General, Dr.Alvaro de Castro, returned from the war front in the north (where fighting against German Tanganyika was occurring) and soon brought the situation back under control.

85

But Portugal's economic crisis continued to worsen, with rampant inflation in the sub-metropole severely affecting real wages in the colonies. The escudo, worth 20p in 1917, had fallen to 14p in 1918, and by 1922 was worth 1p.(34) In January 1919, there was a further stoppage at the port by European workers, this time because changes in the exchange rate had led to a de facto reduction in the real wage.(35) The next major strike of white workers happened in 1925 and lasted from 11 November of that year to 15 March 1926. According to the official history of the port and railway, it grew out of a desire to clean up the administration initiated by Eng. Avelar Ruas.(36) From oral data collected, it seems that the strike mainly affected train drivers and crane operators.(37) From the published monthly statistics of employees, it appears that the strike had a considerable impact.(38) All traffic was far from being halted but movement on the railway was severely interrupted. The strike was particularly bitter and included the sabotage of a mainline train in January 1926, resulting in a derailment. The strike was not a success, but it cost the railways a considerable amount of money, with monthly receipts falling from £41,193 in October 1925, to £25,448 in November, and only rising slowly again thereafter.(39) Severe repression was used to crush the strike. After the derailment, a group of the workers' leaders were bound and placed in a carriage attached at the front of a 'phantom' train, as a severe warning against further acts of sabotage.(40) Wives of striking workers carrying black (anarchist?) flags held a hunger march which was violently dispersed by mounted troops and police.(41) As a result of the tension and city-wide ill-feeling generated by the strike, Eng. Avelar Ruas was removed.(42) This strike had a similar importance to that of the white miners on the Rand a few years earlier. Whether intended or not, when Salazar came to power repression of all workers increased, but the privileges of white workers over black workers were consolidated in the colonies.

With the overthrow of the Republican government in 1926, workers' rights to organise and strike were severely curtailed. State-organised sindicatos replaced trade unions. It is significant to note that during this early period there was not one major combined struggle of white and black workers. Despite colonial mystique to the contrary, a very real racial division existed in the workplace, mirroring that of the colonial society at large. White workers monopolised the skilled jobs, had rights to organise which were never conceded to blacks, and under the stimulus of radical political movements in the sub-metropole they entered into co-ordinated and extended periods of industrial action. Even so, African workers were not entirely quiescent and there are several instances of them taking strike action.

Amongst black workers, many forms of resistance appeared: crime, desertions, avoidance and even strikes. A clear example of avoidance of the worse-paid jobs and choice of the better paid was the labour shortage in Lourenço Marques at the end of the first decade of the century.(43) Men were going to the mines of South Africa rather than work for an absolute pittance in the city. The first recorded incident of a strike took place on 18 January 1904, not in the port and railways but amongst African labourers in the Lingham Timber and Trading Company in Lourenço Marques.(44) At issue was a cut in wages; the strikers managed to win and the former wage was regained. Again it was a cut in wages which prompted a work stoppage on the wharf on 11 July 1910, but this time it was unsuccessful. The following year, wagon drivers in the capital won the confrontation in a strike over a small wage rise. Even outside the capital there were examples of overt and organised workers' resistance, with a walkout at the Incomati Quarry over beatings and poor food (March 1904) and a commercial work stoppage in Chai Chai (April 1908).

The upsurge of strikes amongst white workers provided an example for Africans of the power of combined workers' action. Following the stoppage in the port by European workers in January 1919, black workers on the wharf attempted a strike in May to secure for themselves the 20 to 30 per cent wage increase being demanded by whites. But the Administration was keen to discourage such a trend and three of the strike leaders were sentenced to forced labour. Given the increasing economic chaos, and in particular massive inflation, African workers were obliged to press ahead with their claims for more money if only to halt the tremendous decline in their real wages. These actions were mainly defensive therefore. It was decidedly the port which was the scene of the most active workers' resistance. In January 1920, there was a work stoppage at the port and in June, stevedores struck for higher wages and demanded that these be paid in gold standard currency rather than in the increasingly worthless paper escudos. The Câmara do Comércio (Chamber of Commerce) was sufficiently worried by the 'unrest' on the wharfs to carry out an investigation. In July of that same year, names of ringleaders were handed over to the Department of Native Affairs for action to be taken. This still did not prevent a work stoppage by chibalo labourers from Nampula province, working on the port and railways, on 25 November 1920. Further strikes by stevedores were recorded in 1921 and 1925. In all, there were 27 recorded incidents over the first 25 years of the century involving white or black workers, but never both together.

1930 to 1955

The vulnerability of dependent countries on the periphery is particularly evident in times of economic crisis. The Great Depression had an important impact upon the transit trade and this can be well illustrated with evidence from the port of

Lourenço Marques. As previously mentioned, the port's most important cargo was coal. The vulnerability is all too obvious of a country strongly dependent on transit earnings, with a substantial amount of these based on one commodity from a single foreign country. When India opened new coal mines, South Africa lost one of her principal buyers and this coincided with the Depression. In the first four months of 1929, the port handled 167,000 tons of coal. A mere 65,000 tons were handled during the equivalent period in 1932.(45) Unemployment, a reduction in wages, a large surplus capacity in the port, and no possibility of finding alternative cargoes were just some of the consequences of the transport system's dependence on South Africa. The entire growth of the port continued to be determined by South Africa's requirements. Later in the 1930s, for example, early mechanisation of South African agriculture increased that country's food exports and refrigeration plants had to be built in the port of Lourenço Marques to handle this new cargo. However, minerals continued to provide the bulk of the Transvaal's exports. In 1950, for example, coal accounted for 73 per cent and chrome a further 22 per cent of the total tonnage coming from South Africa.(46) Throughout the 1930s between 80 per cent and 90 per cent of the total cargo handled in the port came from or went to the Transvaal. After the Second World War, although the Transvaal's percentage of traffic was somewhat reduced it still represented more than two-thirds of the total.

In the late 1930s Salazar undertook a series of minor development plans to strengthen the colonial economy. They were mainly concerned with expanding port facilities and transport systems; over £10 million was spent on Mozambique.(47) In 1937 the port was handling just over two million tons of cargo and by the following year 1,200 Africans were regularly employed in the docks of Lourenço Marques.(48) Then the Second World War caused a stagnation in the port. The number of blacks employed in the entire transport sector in the capital fell from 5,500 to under 2,000 (from 1937 to 1941). It is a measure of the discrimination practised in the workplace that the number of white employees remained constant over the same period. The work of the port picked up at the end of the war, remaining at or below four million tons per annum of cargo handled until the mid-1950s. The Portuguese government only took over the management of the port of Beira from the Mozambique Company in 1948.

A slow, discontinuous mechanisation had taken place but the work of the ports remained heavily reliant on the black, unskilled labour force. On the docks and railways a small but significant working class was growing up. With the consolidation of the corporate state, repression and control in the workplace increased. During the height of the Depression in the early 1930s, the ports and railways cut Africans' pay from 12.5 escudos to 12 escudos per day and the workers decided to strike. But police soon arrested all the strikers and forced them to return to work.(49) Informers were present in the workplace, enabling most 'agitation' to be prevented at an early stage. Racial barriers were strictly applied, entrenching white workers in their privileged and supervisory position over blacks. The continuing and reinforced racial division amongst the workers successfully prevented the development of combined struggles between white and black workers.

At the end of the Second World War there was evidence of increasing discontent amongst African workers, eventually building up to a major strike wave around the capital in 1947. It is possible to measure the 'passive' resistance of the workers in the years immediately preceding the strike by examining productivity indicators. If we look at the statistics for the average number of tons unloaded per day by each worker on the Lourenço Marques docks, then a marked decline is apparent. The evidence must be treated with caution, however, as other factors could influence the figures. The average fell from ten tons per indígena per day in 1944, to 6.9 tons in 1945 and 5.7 tons in 1946.(50) Even taking into account the expansion in numbers employed on the docks, producing a less skilled workforce overall, the statistics could provide an indicator of the build-up of resentment and resistance expressed in work slow-downs, which finally culminated in the strike. Not only the dock workers in the Lourenço Marques area went on strike but also those on the plantations.(51) Following the strike, in 1948, there was an abortive rising in the capital of which little is known; but, according to one account, as a result of the rising more than 500 were exiled to the coffee plantations of São Tomé.(52)

In 1956 there was a further revolt on the docks, exacerbated in part by the increased need for labour as a result of growing South African trade and the opening up of the Rhodesia link-line to the port of Lourenço Marques. Stevedores were employed on a casual basis; they gathered each morning at the gates of the port and the numbers required for the day were then chosen. The exact numbers needed were never known beforehand, as the work of the port varied greatly from day to day. By maintaining a large pool of labour, wage rates could easily be depressed. To ensure that there was always the large pool of labour necessary, each stevedore had a card which was supposed to be stamped every day at the dock gates, whether a man worked or not. To meet the extra labour needs of 1956, one morning the police swooped and arrested all those stevedores who had no stamp for the previous day.(53) They were then obliged to do three months' forced labour on the docks and were housed in the pousada (the boarding house) of the railways. Those stevedores not arrested were encouraged by this incident to make an appearance every day at the docks. Chibalo labour was also brought in from the north (Macuas from Nampula), which was an unusual practice.(54) There was a large scale riot over

89

poor food served in the pousada and a demand for improvements. The cook in the pousada at the time explained in an interview that the cause of the riot was bad flour, brought in from a different supplier.(55) Police and dogs were used to break up the disturbance and many chibalos were injured.(56) One author cites 49 deaths as a result, but this is impossible to verify.(57) There were also reports of fighting between the chibalo labourers from the north and those from the south.(58)

Although workers in the port had the longest and most dynamic history of resistance amongst the blossoming Mozambican proletariat, other workers also made their protest felt. In 1957, nurses from the Lourenço Marques hospital struck for better wages, and the leaders of the strike had their hands beaten with the palmatória (59) (a heavy wooden bat with holes, which drew blood when applied). Samora Machel, later to become the President of independent Mozambique, was a nurse in Lourenço Marques province throughout the 1950s, and could not fail to be influenced by the strike. Not all workers' responses took the more spectacular form of strike action. Moreira has produced the following statistics for the number of small craft brotherhoods or guilds existing in the capital at this time: merchants (380), bootmakers (36), carpenters (117), barbers (53), tailors (52), launderers (99), porters (115), and waiters (86).(60) These guilds, displaying a defensive and organisational character, looked after their members in times of distress. Mutual assistance organisations existed over many parts of the country, in Beira and Chai Chai, as well as in the capital; they too provided many future leaders of Frelimo (the Front for the Liberation of Mozambique, which eventually defeated the colonial power).(61)

Comparative Observations on the Port and Railway Workers
Hemson, in his study of the Durban dock workers in South Africa, has similarly found that they have a long history of resistance.(62) He suggests that this is because the dock workers played an instrumental role in the labour process; they were central to all work operations in comparison with African workers in manufacturing, who performed service roles or were unskilled or low-skilled workers in a tight pattern of skilled/operative/labour relationships.(63) Port workers, we would argue, even though they were the most advanced sector of the internal working class, never developed beyond a sense of group consciousness to one of collective class consciousness. As Iliffe has shown in his study of the Dar es Salaam dockworkers, the former is a necessary step towards the latter.(64) However, it is important to recognise that the necessity of a prior sense of group consciousness does not imply the inevitability of a progression on to class consciousness. Class formation is a slow process; it is the ever-increasing unity of organisation in defence of common interest. This interest has as its base a common relationship

to the means of production.

An examination of the labour process is crucial for an understanding of the formation of group and class consciousness. The organisation of the labour process creates a technical and occupational division within the working class and can promote or impede the development of class consciousness, as can the system of labour control, which has similarly to be examined. The labour processes within the ports and railways were very different, and this was a major contributing factor to the differential development of group consciousness and its overt expression in the form of strike action. An analysis of the labour processes and systems of labour control helps explain why the most militant workers were the stevedores, followed by the dockers and finally the railwaymen. The railways were organised in a number of different and separated sections. Within each section there was a strict and highly differentiated work hierarchy.(65) In the secção do movimento, for example, there were 27 separate grades of workers. Ten of these (the lowest ten) were reserved for blacks. Occupational differentiation did not correspond with the technical division of labour; for example, there would be first, second and third class firemen, station auxiliaries and servants.(66) Different rates of pay, authority and prestige were attached to the different job categories. Hence workers in the railway were not only divided into clearly demarcated sections, but they were also hierarchically divided within each section, making unity very difficult. Loyalty tended to be towards the section, and did not promote group consciousness among workers as railwaymen. Voluntary self-help associations, for example, were organised on a section by section basis.(67) In addition, promotion resulted from long and faithful service as well as from the padrinho system, and anyone wishing for promotion would be wary of being seen to be organising his fellow workers.

The strict hierarchy within the railways reached almost military proportions. Heads of sections were treated like gods and the slightest criticism of superiors met with immediate reproof.(68) As a punishment, Europeans were fined and Africans were frequently beaten with the palmatória. As a more serious punishment, they were immediately dismissed. One of the changes induced by the existence of the nationalist movement, was that (after 1962) workers would be handed over to the police for corporal punishment to be administered. The greatest form of control was exercised structurally through the presence of the reserve army of labour. A worker knew that he could easily be replaced, especially because the railways provided permanent, full-time positions with the state as the employer and they were highly prized. As one informant put it: 'An employer dies and you are left without work, but the state never dies'.(69)

Permanent employment has always been assumed to be one of the important objective criteria for developing a militant worker's consciousness. In fact this was not the case in the

Portuguese colonial context. African dock workers were recruited on a casual basis from a registered pool. Their history of militancy under Portuguese colonial conditions indicates that they felt they had less to lose by taking militant action than the more quiescent railway workers. The black railway worker had the possibility of minor promotion with an extra few escudos in earnings per week. Port workers had no such promotion prospects.

In the port as with the railway, a strict racial division existed in the occupational hierarchy. Within the African workforce, a clear distinction has to be made between those working on the quay (dockers) and those who go onto the ship (stevedores). The highest level of militancy was found amongst the stevedores. Chibalo workers were employed in large numbers on the quay as well as casual dockers, but they were not used on the ships; hence the stevedores did not have the permanent threat of chibalos being able to take over their jobs always hanging over them. Chibalo labour was strictly controlled, not only at the point of production but also at the pousada where they were housed. However, control over the casual dock workers could not be as tightly exercised as in the railways. There were no strict compartmental divisions, with workers being permanently placed in different sections. Neither was there a massive and complex hierarchy of job categories. Most of the black workers were carregadores (carriers) and arrumadores (stowers), and every day they would have different workmates. This enabled a certain group consciousness to emerge, but militancy was diluted, as already indicated, by the presence of large numbers of chibalo workers.

Stevedores congregated at the port gates every morning and the numbers required for the day were chosen. They worked in gangs with a membership varying from day to day, in stark contrast to the compartmentalised sections in the railways. Working under appalling conditions in the holds of the ships, a close solidarity developed. Only a minimum technical division of labour existed within a gang, and this was not complicated by an occupational hierarachy as on the railways.(70) Possibilities of promotion for Africans were virtually non-existent. The labour process and absence of occupational hierarchy helped cement the growth of a group consciousness undiluted by fear of chibalo labourers replacing them. This group consciousness was reinforced by a certain ethnic and regional unity. A 20 per cent sample taken of registered stevedores indicated that 48 per cent came from Lourenço Marques and 45 per cent from Gaza province.(71) Within Lourenço Marques province, 38 per cent of the stevedores came from one district alone, and 78 per cent from only three districts. There was a similar concentration in Gaza province: 35 per cent came from one district and 90 per cent from only four districts. A further sense of group solidarity was reinforced (with certain limitations to be mentioned later) by the method of recruitment. All the stevedores met together each morning at the gates of the port. No such group congregation occurred on the railways.

The entire history of strikes in the port and railway in the twentieth century demonstrates that the stevedores were involved in the most militant actions, followed by the dockers. The mechanisms of daily control were harsh. Each morning when the workers gathered at the dock gates to try to obtain work, there was a contingent of cipaios present. A strong police presence was 'required' to maintain order, given the arbitrary and anarchic system of work distribution. Police would stand behind the throng of stevedores and beat workers in the general mêlée which ensued as the work tickets were distributed.(72) Police used a carval marinho, (a heavy whip), which the South Africans call a sjambok. If any of the workers questioned why they were beaten, they sometimes were driven thirty kilometres out of town, their money was confiscated and they were forced to report to the Administration in the city that same day. The general competition for work caused fighting amongst the men, with those at the back of the crowd pushing towards the front. This inter-worker conflict was probably viewed positively by the private stevedoring companies. The sheer physical struggle in the crowd was to the disadvantage of the old and weak. Not infrequently men were severely injured when they fell and were trampled by the throng. Such a system of recruitment was dehumanising and brutalising and was itself an aspect of control in its intention of breaking the collective spirit of the workers. Nevertheless, this strategy did not entirely succeed.

The stevedores working on the ships naturally made contact with sailors and the news of the better wages and working conditions abroad, as well as the successful independence struggles in many African countries, could not fail to have been transmitted by word of mouth. In August 1963, the stevedores of Lourenço Marques went on strike yet again and those of Beira and Nacala followed suit. These were to be the most significant strikes of all, not for what they achieved but for what they did not achieve. More than 60 strikers were arrested in Lourenço Marques and both police and troops were called out. The first issue of the Frelimo publication, Mozambique Revolution, which came out soon after the strike, made an appeal not to waste more time striking as the time had come for workers to join the nationalist movement.(73) Mondlane wrote later of the strike action, saying: 'Its failure and the brutal repression which followed in every instance have temporarily discouraged both the masses and the leadership from considering strike action as a possible effective political weapon in the context of Mozambique'.(74) That same bitter lesson had been learnt in Portuguese Guinea after the dock workers strike in Bissau, when 49 dockers were massacred in 1959.(75)   In the Mozambican context there were severe

Mozambique

limitations to the potential for strike action and working class organisation, arising from the limited growth of the working class and class consciousness, leaving an important legacy for the attempted socialist transition after independence. Nonetheless, the experience of workers resistance did provide a vital thread in the weaving of the nationalist tapestry.

NOTES
1. For the full development of this argument see B. Munslow, Mozambique: The Revolution and Its Origins (Longman, London, 1983).
2. See S. Stichter, 'The Formation of a Working Class in Kenya' in R.Sandbrook & R. Cohen (eds.), The Development of an African Working Class (Longman, London, 1975), p.22.
3. A detailed study of migrant labour to South Africa was carried out collectively by a number of us working under Ruth First at the Centro de Estudos Africanas, Universidade Eduardo Mondlane, Mozambique, in the 1970s, and is published under the title Black Gold (Harvester Press, Brighton, 1983).
4. Regulamento do Trabalho dos Indígenas na Colônia de Moçambique, 2nd edn (Imprensa Nacional de Moçambique, Lourenço Marques, 1947).
5. See A. Milner (ed.), African Penal Systems (Routledge & Kegan Paul, London, 1969), p.222.
6. Interview with Duarte João, a textile factory worker and teacher in an evening class, Vila Pery, Manica and Sofala province, 28 April 1975. (One pound sterling = 55 escudos)
7. Interview with Saraiva Gomas, a textile factory worker and teacher in an evening class, Vila Pery, Manica and Sofala province, 28 April 1975.
8. Interview with Arangatoni Mikiras, Sussendenga, Manica and Sofala province, 1 May 1975.
9. Ibid.
10. Interview with Albino Sitoi, a dock worker, Maputo, 2 March 1978.
11. Interview with Jorge Quelho, Director of the Government Stevedoring Agency, EMAP, Maputo, 21 March 1978.
12. See H. Galvão, Santa Maria: My Crusade for Portugal (Weidenfeld and Nicolson, London, 1961), pp. 57-71 for excerpts of the report.
13. Terceiro Plano de Fomento, part 1, vol. 3.
14. H.F. Mitchell, Aspects of Urbanisation and Age Structure in Lourenço Marques (1957), p.21.
15. Unpublished survey of the labour history of women workers in the cashew industry (1978), archive of the Centro de Estudos Africanos, Universidade Eduardo Mondlane, Maputo.
16. Quoted in Centro de Estudos Africanos, Projecto de Investigação: Desenvolvimento histórico e situação actual da classe operária nos sectores de indústria e transporte na região de Maputo, mimeo, (Universidade Eduardo Mondlane, Maputo, 1977).

17. See, for example, Stichter, 'Formation of Working Class in Kenya'.

18. R.B.Sutcliffe, 'Stagnation and Inequality in Rhodesia 1946-68', Bulletin of the Oxford Institute of Economics and Statistics, vol. XXXIII, no.1 (1971), p.35.

19. Economist Intelligence Unit, Quarterly Economic Review, Portugal and Overseas Provinces, Annual Supplement, 1973, p.29.

20. 'Programa de Acção Governativa para o Quadriénio, 1972/75'. A summary of the main points appeared in Actualidade Econômica em Moçambique, ano VII, no. 354, (22 June 1972), pp. 23-24.

21. See J.M. Brum, Manufacturing Industries in Mozambique: Some Aspects, mimeo, (Universidade Eduardo Mondlane, Maputo 1976).

22. It is of interest to note that in Kenya and parts of West Africa, railways were constructed in order to make colonial exploitation possible. But in Southern Africa, they followed the establishment of capitalist enterprises.

23. Informação Econômica Sôbre O Império. IV Volume. Moçambique (Edições Da Exposição Colonial Portuguesa, Porto, 1934), p. xvi.

24. D.M. Abshire and M.A. Samuels (eds.), Portuguese Africa: A Handbook (Pall Mall Press, London, 1969), p.330.

25. Relatório, Propóstas e Orçamentos do Pôrto e Caminho de Ferro de Lourenço Marques, 1915 a 1923 (Lourenço Marques, 1924).

26. J.L.S. Rufino, Lourenço Marques. Edifícios Públicos, Pôrto, Caminhos de Ferro etc. (Album No.2, Broschek & Co., 1929), p.vi.

27. See the argument of S. Katzenellenbogen, South Africa and Southern Mozambique (Manchester University Press, Manchester, 1982).

28. Africans would pay chickens or money to their boss, whilst whites could pay up to 15 or 20 contos (one conto = one thousand escudos) to rise up one category in the job hierarchy. (Interview with Marrulane P. Mondjane, contramarca first class of the Lourenço Marques port, Maputo, 2 March 1978).

29. Relatórios, Propóstas e Orçamentos do Pôrto e CFLM 1915-1923, pp.15-16.

30. Ibid.

31. B. Neil-Tomlinson and L. Vail, 'Discussion: The Mozambique Company', Journal of African History, vol. XVIII, no. 2 (1977), p.285.

32. The history of the railway and its hinterland can be found in L. Vail, 'The Making of an Imperial Slum: Nyasaland and its Railways, 1895-1935', Journal of African History, vol. XVI, no.1 (1976), pp. 80-112; and L. Vail, 'Railway Development and Colonial Underdevelopment: The Nyasaland Case', in R.Palmer and N. Parsons (eds.), The Roots of Rural Poverty in Central and Southern Africa (Heinemann, London, 1977).

33. See A.P. de Lima, História dos Caminhos de Ferro de Moçambique, Vol. 1, (Edição da Administração dos Pôrtos, Caminhos de Ferro e Transportes de Moçambique, Lourenço Marques, 1971), p.231.

34. W.C.Atkinson, A History of Spain and Portugal (Penguin, Harmondsworth, 1960), p.338. (The English currency equivalent has been translated from shillings to new pence).

35. O Brado Africano, Lourenço Marques, 24 January 1919.

36. de Lima, História dos Caminhos de Ferro, p.231.

37. Interview with Joaquim da Costa, Robert Tembe and Guilherme de Brito, Maputo, 5 July 1977. (Contained in the Jeanne Penvenne Collection, deposited in the archive of the Centro de Estudos Africanas, Universidade Eduardo Mondlane, Mozambique. Interviews used from this source are indicated as Jeanne Penvenne Collection).

38. Conselho de Administração do Pôrto e dos C.F.L.M., Relatório da Direcção 1926-27, (Lourenço Marques, 1928), p.109.

39. Ibid., p. 42.

40. de Lima, História dos Caminhos de Ferro, p.231.

41. Interview with Gilberto Varegilão, Carlos Sousa Coelho, José Francisco Madeira, Nassone Mulate, Suleimane E. Juma, Farinha Lopes, Benjamin Wilson and Abdul Magid Hassangy, all senior officials of the railway, Maputo, 1 March 1978. See also interview with Joaquim da Costa, et al.

42. de Lima, História dos Caminhos de Ferro, p.232.

43. Direcção do Pôrto e Caminho de Ferro de Lourenço Marques, Relatório Anual dos Serviços da Exploração, 1909, p. xxxi.

44. See J. Penvenne, Preliminary Chronology of Labor Resistance. Lourenço Marques, mimeo, 21 April 1977. The following analysis is based on the 'raw' data provided in this chronology. Jeanne Penvenne's highly detailed study of labour in the capital city is contained in 'A History of African Labour in Lourenço Marques, Mozambique, 1877 to 1950', unpublished PhD dissertation, Department of History, Boston University, 1982.

45. Relatório Anual de Administração dos Serviços Dos Portos, Caminhos de Ferro e Transportes da Colônia de Moçambique, (Lourenço Marques, 1932).

46. Relatório Anual, (Lourenço Marques, 1950).

47. J. Duffy, Portuguese Africa (Harvard University Press, Cambridge, Mass., 1959), p. 193.

48. These and the following statistics are taken from the relevant years of the Relatório Anual.

49. Interview with Jose Mandulane Cossa, Maputo, 10 June 1977, Jeanne Penvenne Collection.

50. Taken from the Relatório Anual for the years 1944, 1945 and 1946.

51. E. Mondlane, The Struggle for Mozambique (Penguin, Harmondsworth, 1970), p.115.

52.   D.J.Mabunda and J.Sakupwanya, 'Brief History of Moçambique' in R.H. Chilcote (ed), Emerging Nationalism in Portuguese Africa: Documents (Hoover Institution Press, Stanford University, 1972), p. 388.

53.   Interview with thirteen long-serving stevedores, Maputo, 28 March 1978. Corroboration of this incident may be found in Chilcote (ed), Emerging Nationalism, p. 389.

54.   Interview with Mondjane.

55.   Interview with Roberto Tembe, Maputo, 15 June 1977, Jeanne Penvenne Collection.

56.   Interview with Joaquim de Costa, contramarca, Maputo, 11 November 1977, Jeanne Penvenne Collection.

57.   R.H. Chilcote, 'Mozambique: The African Nationalist Response to Portuguese Imperialism and Underdevelopment' in C.B. Potholm and R. Dale (eds), Southern Africa in Perspective (The Free Press, New York, 1972), p. 189.

58.   Interview with Mondjane. After 1956 there was an increasing mechanisation of the ports, no doubt spurred on by the troubles of that year.

59.   (Report of the) United Nations Special Committee, 'The Situation in the Territories Under Portuguese Administration Since January 1961', Présence Africaine, vol. 17, no. 45 (1st Quarter, 1963), p. 184.

60.   A. Moreira, 'African Elites', International Social Science Bulletin, vol. VIII, no. 3 (1956), p. 477.

61.   Mondlane, Struggle for Mozambique, pp. 119-20.

62.   D.Hemson, 'Dock Workers, Labour Circulation and Class Struggles in Durban 1940-1959', Collected Seminar Papers No. 21, The Societies of Southern Africa in the Nineteenth and Twentieth Centuries vol. 7, (University of London, Institute of Commonwealth Studies, 1977).

63.   Ibid., p. 197.

64.   J. Iliffe, 'A History of the Dock Workers of Dar es Salaam', Journal of the Tanzania Society, no. 71 (1970), p. 120.

65.   Interview with Gilberto Varegilão and Carlos Sousa, Secção do Movimento, Maputo, 1 March 1978.

66.   The rigidity in the occupational hierarchy did not correspond with that of the technical division of labour. Black workers, employed and paid at a given category, were frequently obliged to perform work that was theoretically reserved for whites (interview with Nassone Mulate, Caminhos de Ferro de Moçambique, Maputo, 3 March 1978).

67.   Interview with Nassone Mulate, Manuel B. Cossa and Marcelo Caetano, three of the oldest serving African railway workers, Maputo, 3 March 1978.

68.   Interview with Varegilão, et al.

69.   Interview with Mondjane.

70.   Each gang had an induna (foreman), guincheiro (who gave signals to direct the crane driver) and carregadores (carriers) who were in the vast majority. The induna came from

the carregadores, and the guincheiro would tend to be one of the older or infirm stevedores who no longer had the strength to be a carregador.

71.   The sample was taken from the record cards of the Sindicato Nacional dos Profissionais de Estiva do Pôrto de Maputo. Every fifth card was recorded between numbers 505 and 4225. Seven hundred and twenty seven workers figured in the sample. (The author wishes to acknowledge the work of Kurt Habermeier on the sample).

72.   Interview with thirteen long-serving stevedores.

73.   Mozambique Revolution, (organ of Frelimo), no.1 (December 1963). See also Boletim Informativo, no.2 (1963).

74.   Mondlane Struggle for Mozambique, p. 116.

75.   See A. Cabral, Obras Escolhidas de Amilcar Cabral. A Arma De Teoria. Unidade e Luta I, (Seara Nova, 1976), p. 74.

Chapter Five

THE CREATION OF A PROLETARIAT ON PERU'S COASTAL SUGAR
PLANTATIONS: 1880-1920

Bill Albert

INTRODUCTION

In many parts of Latin America by the First World War the urban
proletariat, although still small in size, had begun to make
its collective voice heard through unions and political
parties, as well as by various forms of direct action.(1) But,
the voice of the vast majority who laboured on the land, while
frequently raised in revolt, generally remained muted (with the
major exception of Mexico), because of rural isolation, the
predominance of sharecropping or other forms of non-wage labour
exploitation, and the overriding authority of the landed
elites. Workers on Peru's coastal sugar estates suffered many
of the same problems as other rural labourers, but during and
immediately after the First World War, in a series of bitter
strikes, they organised and fought the estate owners for higher
wages and better conditions. In doing so they began to define
themselves as proletarians. The complex process by which this
took place is explored here. A brief account of the particular
conditions affecting both sugar production and the Peruvian
coast is followed by a consideration of how labour was
recruited for the estates and the nature of productive
relations. In the final section the causes and significance of
growing labour unrest is detailed.

THE SETTING

Peru's Sugar Industry
The Peruvian coast along almost its entire length is completely
arid, all agriculture being confined to about 40 river valleys
fed from the Andes which cut green ribbons of varying widths
through the desert to the sea. From colonial times estate
owners here faced two essential problems: assuring themselves
sufficient water for irrigation and sufficient labour for
production. Labour was difficult to find partly because the
bulk of the country's population (about 80 per cent in 1876)
remained in the sierra (mountains).(2) More important was the
fact that the coastal dwellers were extremely reluctant to

submit themselves to the harsh, slave-like regime of the sugar estates,(3) and despite their considerable political and economic power the hacendados (plantation owners) were unable to force much labour out of the subsistence or petty commodity sectors on the coast and were too far away to set the requisite forces in motion which would have pushed or pulled labour from the sierra. But before the 1880s this did not pose too serious a problem, for after the abolition of slavery in 1854 the hacendados were able to bring in yet another group of captive workers - indentured Chinese coolies, 90,000 of whom came to Peru between 1849 and 1874.(4) Although free and re-contracted Chinese continued to work on the coast after the trade ended, their numbers declined steadily. The hacendados were, therefore, soon forced to seek alternative sources of labour.

Besides the need to find new sources of labour, from the 1880s sugar planters faced a number of other major difficulties. Many estates were devastated by the Chilean army during the War of the Pacific and the subsequent occupation (1879-1884), and most hacendados were heavily in debt because of the extensive modernisation carried out in the two decades before 1879, a period which saw sugar exports rise from 820 to 83,500 metric tons.(5) To make matters worse, the increased production and export of subsidised beet sugar from Europe contributed to a major collapse in the world price for sugar in 1884, a collapse from which there was no recovery before 1914.(6) However, the same process of capitalist advance which fostered the development of the European beet sugar industry also continued to provide a flood of technical innovations which by revolutionising the system of cane sugar production made it possible for some cane growing regions to compete effectively within the rapidly changing world market. For Peruvian planters this meant essentially adopting the new processes or going out of production. Many were forced out, the number of ingenios (mills) falling from 68 in 1895 to 38 in 1913 to only 27 by 1928 (Table 5.1). Over the same period production rose substantially, as did the average size of the mills.(7)

The Impact of Technical Change

To understand more clearly the nature of the labour supply problem it is important to consider the general impact of technical change on the sugar plantations. With some important exceptions (e.g. the steam plough, improved cultivation tools, movable rail lines, etc.), most of the major innovations were made in the mill and factory, not in the field. This occurred for two principal reasons. Technical change in cane fabrication led to the production of a substantially different product - centrifugal sugar. If producers wanted to remain in the increasingly competitive world market they had more or less to adopt the new technology completely. Secondly, this technology

Table 5.1: Peruvian Sugar 1885-1928

	No. of Mills	Area in Cane (000 hectares)	Production (000 metric tons)	Exports (000 metric tons)	Share of total export value (%)	No. of Workers
1885	-	-	-	46	37	-
1890	-	-	-	39	28	-
1895	68	-	-	59	35	-
1900	-	-	-	112	32	-
1905	-	-	162	134	35	-
1910	-	-	-	123	21	-
1913	38	40	184	143	15	20,942
1918	33	50	287	198	21	25,081
1922	33	51	319	274	24	28,034
1928	27	53	362	306	12	30,151

Sources: Albert, Peruvian Sugar, pp. 13a-14a, 26a, 28a, 30a, 128a. Peru, Ministerio de Fomento, Estadística de la Industria Azucarera en el Peru(Lima, 1929).

was derived in the main from European refining and beet sugar industries in which relative factor costs tended to favour labour-saving innovation. This was not the case in the cane fields, where despite widespread complaints of labour shortage, somewhat paradoxically relatively cheap labour continued to be found. Partly because of this, new field techniques were less revolutionary, were borrowed from a more general pool of agricultural innovations, and harvesting (the process which demanded the greatest labour input) was left virtually untouched. As technical change was biased toward increasingly large processing plants requiring a much greater volume of cane, there was, therefore, a substantial increase in the demand for field hands. This may explain, in part at least, why at a time of extremely rapid technological transformation many plantation owners were anxious to retain servile labour. In short, even though sugar was the first tropical crop to be 'modernised', because of the uneven nature of technical change as between factory and field, modernisation required relatively few skilled workers and a mass of unskilled, often temporary, labour.(8)

The preceding considerations were particularly relevant in the Peruvian case. Because all cane is grown on irrigated land there is a need to control rigorously planting, cane maturation, cutting and delivery in order to maintain an uninterrupted supply of high quality cane to the mills. This and the general shortage of water in the valleys made the growers want to control as much land as possible and in turn led to the development of extensive integrated estates which both grew and processed cane.(9) These so-called agro-industrial estates employed increasingly large numbers of workers. By about 1914, for example, the medium-sized estates of Cayaltí and Santa Barbara employed 1000 and 1250 workers respectively, while the larger plantations in the Chicama valley had more than twice this number of workers.(10)

THE RECRUITMENT OF LABOUR

Conditions in the Sierra
Before the War of the Pacific there had been little effort made by the coastal hacendados to tap the relatively large sierra population, mainly because of the availability of non-free labour on the coast. There were also formidable problems of communication, and the fact that, at least in the northern sierra, the conditions were not such as to compel highland peasants to seek work on the coast. Lewis Taylor writes of Cajamarca between 1850 and 1880:

> the household economy in the highlands at this time was as yet only weakly integrated into capitalist exchange, did

not suffer from a serious reproduction squeeze, and (that) the differentiation of the peasantry, with the appearance of a pool of rural proletarians, was only weakly developed.(11)

From the 1880s, changes in both the hacendados' labour situation and conditions in the sierra provided the basis for the full development of labour contracting. Before considering in more detail the historical evolution of this method of recruitment, it is necessary to consider the changes in the sierra which made it possible for the hacendados to entice peasants down to the coast. It is impossible to generalise about the entire Peruvian sierra, and the following discussion centres on the department of Cajamarca in the northern sierra, the principal recruitment area for the Lambayeque and La Libertad haciendas, and the most significant region in terms of the coastal sugar industry (together [1911-13] producing 70 per cent of the country's sugar exports). It would seem that the principal push factor here was rapid population growth and the greater fragmentation of peasant landholding.(12) Cajamarca's population almost doubled between the mid-1830s and 1876, and by 1940 it had doubled once again. To this was added the effects of the post-War of the Pacific economic depression which hit Cajamarca as it did the rest of the country, until the 1890s. This led to landowners in the sierra attempting to increase their direct control of land, to raise rents and extract increased labour services. These forces were given further impetus from the 1890s by the growing demand for foodstuffs from the expanding coastal economy. Taylor contends that the sierra peasants 'looked to the sale of labour power in the capitalist sector as a means of restoring equilibrium to the family's labour-consumer balance'.(13) They also preferred wage labour on the coast to similar work in the sierra. This was because the former was short-term, could be entered into during slack periods in the sierra's agricultural year, and provided them with money immediately (in the form of an advance). Work on the sierra haciendas, on the other hand, would have meant falling under the more or less permanent control of the semi-feudal sierra hacendados. 'Seen in this light', Taylor writes, 'migration to the coast, itself a manifestation of the appearance of peasant proletarianization became at one and the same time a vehicle for resisting proletarianization and shoring up the independence of the "free" peasant economy in Cajamarca'.(14) These conclusions are similar to those of Henri Favre, who argues that in the central sierra region of Huancavelica, 'turning to wage labour constitutes a means of maintaining the traditional social order at a time when that order is no longer viable'.(15) Both Taylor's and Favre's arguments are persuasive and, as will be discussed below, cast doubt on the widely accepted idea that labour contracting was essentially a semi-feudal system of debt-bondage dependent on extra-economic coercion.

The Mechanisms of Labour Contracting

From the 1880s conditions for drawing wage labour from the
sierra were improving, but there was no existing mechanism by
which recruitment could be easily accomplished. The serranos
(peasants from the mountains) may have wanted to work, but
there was undoubtedly a reluctance to make the long journey to
an unknown labour market on the disease ridden coast.
Consequently the sugar and cotton growers adopted and adapted
the system of enganche (hooking),(16) a form of contracting in
widespread use throughout Peru as well as other Andean
countries. Over its history, from the 1880s to the early 1960s,
enganche changed as conditions in the sierra and on the coast
altered. At any point in time the methods used varied, as each
hacienda employed its own particular variant of the system.
Essentially, however, enganche was organised in the following
manner; the coastal estate entered into an agreement with a
local merchant or small estate owner in the sierra, who was
also often a cattle dealer supplying the hacienda with beef
cattle, to provide a given number of workers for a given length
of time or number of tareas (tasks). In the early years many
estates used the services of what was known as a 'real'
contratista (contractor), who could send men down to the coast
with his own man who would supervise their work. The hacendado
paid a lump sum to the contratista who would in turn pay his
workers. Because of the many abuses associated with this and
the unrest among the workers which resulted, by World War I
many estates were phasing it out and either using salaried
recruiting agents or making contracts with independent
enganchadores (contractors). The latter would find and contract
workers who were then employed directly by the haciendas. These
men were generally advanced money by the haciendas to make the
loans necessary to get labour contracts signed, and they were
paid either a flat rate per worker delivered and/or a
commission on each tarea worked. The enganchadores generally
worked for one hacienda, although it was not unknown for them
to work for several. It was also common for them to be assigned
a particular recruitment area in the sierra so as not to foster
competition among an estate's agents. In the case of Casa
Grande, the largest estate in the country, a recruiting agency
was established in Cajamarca to co-ordinate the activities of
enganchadores.

The period of most active recruiting was immediately after
harvest, planting, or religious festivals in the sierra, when
the serrano's need for ready cash was greatest and he was
temporarily free from his own agricultural tasks. In return for
a cash advance a contract was signed to work for a specified
period on the coast. This was generally for 90 days or the time
needed to repay the initial advance. While on the estate he
received a very small sum in cash, a daily ration (meat and
rice), accommodation of a primitive kind, and the balance (the
largest part of the wage) went to amortise the original loan
and pay the recruiting agent's commission. A sample wage

breakdown is given below:

Daily Wage of Contracted Worker on Cayaltí, March 1919

Amortisation of loan	.50 soles
Commission to contractor	.12½
Cash wage	.15
Ration (1lb meat, 1½lb rice)	.40
	————
	1.17½

Source: Cartas Administrativas, Cayaltí-Lima,
          13 March 1919. Cayaltí Mss. Archivo del
          Fuero Agrario (AFA), Lima.

Conditions of Contracted Workers

Enganche was open to a great many abuses as the serranos,
generally unable to read or fully understand the contracts they
signed, were at the mercy of contratistas or enganchadores, a
group of men not known for their honesty or kind-heartedness.
All kinds of tricks were used in signing up workers and
prolonging their stay on the coast, the latter including not
properly discounting loans, overcharging at contratista-run
stores on the estates, imposing fines, underpaying wages, etc.
These and other abuses were particularly prevalent in the late
nineteenth and early twentieth centuries when the system was
being developed, and were blamed by some for the failure of
migratory labour from the sierra to solve the problem of
chronic labour shortage on the coast. For example, a report in
1902, prepared by leading sugar producers on the crisis in the
industry, claimed that the serranos were discouraged from
coming to the coast because they were unfairly treated under
the unregulated system of enganche.(17) Complaints such as this
can be easily multiplied. It is clear that although enganche in
coastal Peru did not lead to the kind of horrific abuses
reported by Turner in pre-revolutionary Mexico, or those so
dramatically portrayed in the novels of B. Traven,(18)
nonetheless, conditions were bad enough to provoke complaints
not only, as might be expected, from those who championed the
Indian cause,(19) but also from the hacendados themselves and
those who shared their concern with increasing agricultural
output. This suggests that even though enganche may have relied
more on material incentives than extra-economic coercion, the
two were by no means mutually exclusive. This is not
particularly surprising when it is remembered that the
hacendados had been long accustomed to the use of servile
labour and generally felt that the serrano was racially and
culturally inferior.

Changes in the Enganche System

It was probably due to a growing realisation by hacendados that it was against their own interests to allow contratistas to cheat and mistreat their workers that during the first decades of the century many estates began to get rid of the independent contratistas and replace them with employees or agents.(20) Using the latter arrangement, they could exercise a far greater direct control over the size of advances, the contracts, and wages and conditions. By taking over the payment of wages and the distribution of rations, and on many estates refusing to allow the contratistas to run stores, they could also ensure that the workers received what was due to them. The need for these reforms became more apparent as the market for labour in the sierra developed and competition was stepped up, not only from other estates but also from the mines, government projects, road building and the army. This concern is reflected in the Cayaltí correspondence which shows a continued preoccupation with improving conditions on the estate and lowering food prices, mainly at times of high sugar prices, so as to keep workers contented and attract more from the sierra.(21) There was also a great deal of discussion on how best to meet the competition of other estates, with attention given to the most attractive pay schemes, (i.e. how much to loan, the rate of repayment, the amount to be given in cash, and the quantity of the ration), and repeated admonitions to make sure the contratistas were not mistreating workers.

The replacement of independent contratistas seems also to have been part of a general desire on behalf of the hacendados to limit their dependence on enganche. Some thought they could do this by purchasing haciendas in the sierra, thereby gaining a captive reservoir of labour and a source of foodstuffs for their workforce. (Cattle, cereals, dairy products, etc. from the sierra found a ready market on the coast). This policy was pursued in the early decades of the century by a number of estates, but the results were not particularly satisfactory.(22) During the 1920s and 1930s some enterprises sought to contract labour directly, hoping in this way to reduce the large amounts of capital tied up with enganchadores. There were also attempts to increase the number of non-contracted workers by improving conditions and offering to make estate loans once the enganchado had worked off his original socorro (loan).(23) These measures had a reasonable degree of success from the mid-1920s as roads into the sierra were improved, the possibilities of work on the coast became more widely known and the overall demand for labour declined.

How successful were the hacendados in lessening their dependence on contracted migrant labour? Klarén argues that the migrant serranos settled on the coast and became full-time wage labourers, but is not very clear as to the timing of this.(24) Gonzales' study of Cayaltí shows that by the 1920s the proportion of contracted workers had fallen considerably - from

88 per cent of the workforce in 1905 to 44 per cent in 1924.(25) He quotes Ismael Aspillaga, one of the family who owned the estate, who wrote in 1926: 'the peon invariably tends to become "free" by the payment of the debts of his contract to establish himself in the agricultural region of the coast, where he works, raising a family, making it, as such, his home and only returning to the sierra infrequently'.(26) A similar comment was made by the administrator of San Jacinto in 1931: 'there are a growing number of contracted workers who after a series of renewed contracts have cancelled their debts (papelitas) and have been on the hacienda for many years ... some of them have been working for 10 to 15 years'.(27)

In Casa Grande there was a marked reduction in labour turnover between the 1920s and the 1940s.(28) This strongly points to the growth over these years of a large permanent workforce, although there is no easy way to gauge its size or the exact timing of its formation.

Enganche clearly played a transitional role in the formation of a rural proletariat on the coast, and it continued to be important in providing labour for most estates well into the 1950s. One reason for its continuing importance was that hacendados did derive a number of important advantages from the use of temporary migrant labour. They were more easily able to reduce their labour force during mill shutdowns (about two months each year) or to meet other contingencies. Having temporary workers also made union organisation more difficult on the plantations. Finally, many migrant workers were not entirely wage-dependent, maintaining their links with the peasant subsistence sector in the sierra. It was, therefore, possible for the hacendados to pay the enganchados (contracted workers) a wage below that needed to reproduce their labour (a 'single wage').(29) While this may have been offset to some degree by the costs of recruitment and competition for labour, Taylor presents a convincing argument that 'By making it possible for the sugar owners to hold down real wages, the smallholdings belonging to the peasant migrants from Cajamarca were assisting the process of capital accumulation on the coastal sugar haciendas'.(30)

Another major reason why enganche remained important was that the contracted workers who settled on the coast, as well as the local workers, did not necessarily continue to work on the sugar estates. For example, on San Jacinto the proportion of contracted workers fell throughout the 1930s but rose again in the 1940s. In January 1941 only 7 per cent of the workforce was contracted (although many 'free' workers were migrants from the sierra who came down without being contracted), but by March 1945 this proportion had risen to 37 per cent. It was claimed that this change came about because of the steady decline in the number of free workers:

> With the outbreak of hostilities in Europe and the
> initiation of other industries and public works in the
> country, the free labourers, having a more adventurous and
> noverero spirit, began to flow to those centres where
> better wages were offered than by the Sugar Industry ...
> Work in the fields is considered too crude, and the
> diversions and life of the city, freedom from regulation
> as well as facilities for the secondary education of their
> children, offer a greater attraction. ... Apparently there
> are no possible means of attracting these people once
> again to agricultural work, no matter how good the
> conditions they are offered.(31)

It is not clear to what extent this movement from the land was
representative of conditions in other coastal valleys. But,
assuming it was, it provides one important reason why enganche
continued to be necessary for most estates until the 1950s,
when a combination of population growth, increased migration
from the sierra and labour-displacing technical change in the
cane fields resulted in a surfeit of labour in most coastal
valleys.(32)

The Nature of Labour Shortage

Although enganche allowed coastal hacendados to tap the
reserves of labour in the sierra, why until the 1950s did they
continue to complain of not being able to get enough workers?
As stated above, the migration of coastal agricultural workers
to the cities was a constant drain. Secondly, the labour
scarcity that the hacendados complained of was fluctuating
rather than constant. When the industry was expanding rapidly,
as during the two world wars, hacendados did find it difficult
to get enough workers, but when the industry was depressed, as
during much of the inter-war period, there were few complaints
about labour supply. It remains the case, however, that in the
years before World War I, and subsequently at times of rapid
expansion, the industry as a whole seems to have been unable
fully to meet its labour needs. There were a number of reasons
for this, and they changed over time.

In the earlier years, it was felt by many hacendados that,
in the words of Felipe de Osma, 'our plebe, singularly the
Indian, has no more necessities than primitive man'.(33) They
failed to work the entire week because 'Working three or four
days they make enough to satisfy their needs for seven'. To
raise wages in order to attract more workers could, therefore,
only lead, at least in the short run, to a higher labour
turnover or more absenteeism as higher wages would reduce the
time needed by the contracted workers to repay their advances.
In 1919 it was said of the workers in Cayaltí, 'it is beyond
doubt that the more money the more laziness', and that the more
they earned per tarea the less tareas were performed.(34) This
type of complaint - that there was in effect a backward-bending

supply curve for labour (35) - is similar to that made by the factory masters in the early stages of the British industrial revolution, (36) and suggests that the Peruvian hacendados were faced with a similar situation of a labour force which retained pre-capitalist attitudes toward work, and beyond a certain point was not responsive to material incentives. While this may have been a problem for the hacendados in the early decades of the century, as the sierra peasants became more integrated into the coastal labour market it became less important. (37)

Perhaps the most important reason why enganche could not always deliver the number of workers required was because for most migratory workers coastal employment was supplementary to working their own land. This meant that during the sowing or harvesting season in the sierra it was difficult to recruit labour. Evidence for this was found throughout the years under review. In December 1896 Luis Alba, one of San Jacinto's contratistas, wrote that he could not send many workers as planting was in progress. (38) In 1911 it was observed on the same estate that more workers were being contracted, not because of any increased material inducements, but because the sierra harvest had failed. (39) Similar comments appear throughout the inter-war years in Casa Grande's monthly reports, and in 1952 one of the enganchadores reported that it was difficult to recruit peons because 'at this time of year people prefer to earn grain and not money'. (40) The seasonality of labour and an associated high level of labour turnover were the principle features of the 'labour scarcity' which periodically affected the sugar estates until the 1950s.

The Relations of Production

The preceding analysis raises a number of important questions as to the nature of both the wage labour market, especially for harvest labour, and the relations of production on the sugar estates. José Carlos Mariátegui, Peru's foremost Marxist writer, argued that enganche represented '(the) feudal methods which persist in coastal agriculture'. (41) By employing this method of recruitment,

> the large proprietors block the appearance of free-wage contracting, a functional necessity of a liberal and capitalist economy. Indenture (enganche), which prevents the labourer from disposing of his person and his labour until he satisfies the obligations he has contracted with the landlord, is unmistakably descended from the semi-slave traffic in coolies. Coastal agriculture has evolved rather rapidly toward a capitalist procedure in farming and in the processing and sale of crops. But it has made little progress in its attitude and conduct as regards labour. Unless forced to by circumstances, the colonial latifundium has not renounced its feudal treatment of the worker. (42)

109

His arguments both restate earlier attacks on the system and are echoed in most subsequent analyses. Was he correct? Was enganche semi-feudal? And if so, what did this mean in terms of the social relations of production on the coastal haciendas?

Firstly, in the hacendado-enganchado relationship surplus labour was not extracted through traditional or land-based servile obligations, as in a feudal system, but through a wage relation. This was true despite the fact that part of the wage was paid in advance and that rations, basic housing and other non-monetary benefits were offered. Moreover, as Taylor has argued,(43) it was expressly to avoid having to become a quit-rent or labour service tenant in the sierra that many peasants opted to migrate temporarily to the coast. Another important determinant of wage labour is a market for its sale, and it is clear that from a very early period such a market did exist in the sierra. The hacendados' correspondence attests to the intense competition for labour, and although, particularly in the early years, unfair recruiting practices were undoubtedly used, the serrano was normally free to choose to whom he sold his labour. Finally, as Taylor and Favre have shown, enganche was essentially a voluntary system which relied more on material incentives than extra-economic coercion.(44)

However, while the methods by which the surplus was appropriated and the character of the market are indicative of capitalist relations, there were other factors which were not. In the first place, all sugar workers, whether contracted or 'free', suffered under a system of pervasive and unrelenting paternalism on the haciendas, which were in the case of the larger estates fairly self-contained company towns. Housing was owned by the estates, medical services and educational and recreational facilities were provided. The other face of paternalism was represented by a strict system of internal control, including summary justice, corporal punishment (in the early years), curfews and the firm, sometimes violent, suppression of any attempt to organise the workers. Certain of these conditions can be seen as hangovers from the time of slave and coolie labour, and although they do not in themselves affect the essence of the productive relations on the estates, they definitely affected the character of these relations.

A more serious problem is posed by the question of whether the contracted workers were 'free', in the sense of free from the ownership of the mean of production. Many continued to have smallholdings in the sierra and worked on the coastal estates to obtain a 'target' income so as to be better able to maintain their position as independent peasants. For those who eventually settled on the coast enganche served a transitional role, but many of the contracted workers remained essentially migrant peasants who worked only part-time as wage labourers. A somewhat similar situation has been observed in Jamaica, where 'The plantation worker who is also a peasant appears to be straddling two kinds of sociocultural adaptions, and may represent a cultural type which is not necessarily transitional but in a kind of flux equilibrium'.(45)

The preceding distinctions are of considerable importance. To quote Mintz once again, 'the nature of productive relations is crucial in determining the character of rural proletarians as a class; and the behaviour that accompanies their class position is in some measure informed by that position'.(46) An appreciation of the particular characteristics of the social relations of production associated with the contracted field workers is, therefore, important when in the final section the development of class conflict on the coast is considered. For example, although the serranos could be quick to show their anger over wages or conditions, because they were on the coast for only a short period of time, the formation of strong, stable unions was difficult. This was well understood by the estate owners, as witnessed by the following remark from an administrator arguing for shorter contracts with Japanese contract workers:

> In these days of more wages and intelligent workers precedents will be less easily established and any temporary measures taken to keep work people contented would be more easily obliterated. The constant and frequent replacing of men and women would avoid to a great extent the possibility of cliques and consequent ruses for the betterment of conditions. With short contracts they would have no time to study matters properly.(47)

LABOUR STRUGGLES ON THE ESTATES

Bauer has argued that enganche in Peru took place in 'a world of mutual adjustment and accommodation'.(48) Although this was largely true it must be remembered that, as Genovese has shown,(49) so did slavery in the southern United States. What Bauer plays down is the pervasive socio-economic and political system of domination and deference under which 'adjustment and accommodation' took place. The neo-classical assumptions about the allocative rationality of the market which seem to underly Bauer's analysis leave little room for questions of social class or economic power. Perhaps this is why he can dismiss labour unrest on the coastal estates as of little significance. However, as will be argued, these struggles were of central importance. It was through them that the sugar workers began to forge a distinctive class consciousness.

Important as it is, an account of the causes and results of strikes and unrest gives little more than a one-dimensional view of the process of class formation. Much more needs to be known about the participants, the relationship between different groups of workers, about the cultural and social milieu on the estates and in the nearby towns, about how and why working and living conditions varied between estates and valleys and over time. Class, as E.P.Thompson has observed, is not a thing but an historical relationship:

111

> class happens when some men, as a result of common experiences (inherited or shared), feel and articulate the identity of their interests as between themselves, and as against other men whose interests are different from (and usually opposed to) theirs. The class experience is largely determined by the productive relations into which men are born - or enter involuntarily. Class-consciousness is the way in which these experiences are handled in cultural terms: embodied in traditions, value-systems, ideas, and institutional forms.(50)

The analysis presented here deals almost entirely with certain aspects of the 'experience' and with the external pressures brought to bear on the estates and their workers. The intricate problem of consciousness demands a far more detailed treatment.

The First Modern Strike

During the era of slavery and through the years when the Chinese laboured on the coast there were periodic uprisings on the haciendas. But it was not until the first decades of the present century that 'modern' manifestations of unrest began to occur. The most significant of these erupted in 1912 on estates in the Chicama and Santa Catalina valleys.(51) For some months the Gildemeisters, owners of Casa Grande, had been replacing Peruvian employees with technicians brought from Germany. They were also trying to get rid of the independent contratistas in order to hire workers directly. These moves had given rise to a great deal of resentment, and when an attempt was made to increase the amount of the tarea almost the entire workforce came out on strike, occupied the factory, and began to sack the hacienda's stores. The unrest quickly spread to the Gildemeisters' Sausal estate and the neighbouring haciendas of Cartavio, Chiquitoy and Laredo. Demands for higher wages, reduced tareas and better conditions were common as were violent clashes between workers and the authorities. The strikes were suppressed only after local police and militia joined by soldiers sent from Lima had killed an estimated 150 workers. After a short return to work Casa Grande's workers again came out on strike. This time there was no violence. A strike committee was formed and a formal agreement negotiated which gave the workers many of the improvements which they sought. As Gonzales observes, this strike was significant in that it was the first time organised action had been taken by the Peruvian sugar workers and a good degree of success achieved.(52)

These events were unprecedented in their scale and violence and caused considerable alarm among hacendados in other valleys. Their disquiet was no doubt exacerbated by the fact that these strikes occurred against a background of growing worker unrest throughout the country. There had been a general strike in Lima in 1911,(53) and a few months after the

112

Chicama troubles Antero Aspillaga (one of the owners of Cayaltí), the Civilista presidential candidate, was defeated in the elections by Guillermo Billinghurst, a populist leader, who came to power through the direct intervention of the Lima workers.(54) In 1913 the workers pressed their claims with increasing force, and in Callao the dockers won the eight-hour day. It was an uneasy time for Peru's capitalists. In an editorial on the Chicama strikes the West Coast Leader commented:

> The entire industrial world is being shaken to its foundations in the struggle between capital and labour, and the West Coast will have its share unless some concessions are voluntarily made before they are secured by strikes with the possible loss of life. It must be remembered that it is no longer possible to import coolies or Chinese in large numbers, and that even unskilled labour is rightly or wrongly raising its head nowadays. We are not special pleaders for the proletariat, but in the interests of capital and for its self-protection we strongly urge that our employers and labour accept the new and coming conditions and remember the well-known axiom - that well-paid and well-fed labour will give ample returns for the increased wage total.(55)

However, it would seem that on the whole the hacendados were unwilling to accept the 'new and coming conditions'. They believed that class conflict was something that might occur in other countries, at worst in other parts of Peru, but definitely not on their estates. Unrest, if and when it broke out, was for them the work of the ubiquitous, but elusive, 'outside agitator', who infected their otherwise peaceful, contented workers. The most frequent response was to call in government troops.

Reasons for Unrest

Much as they would have preferred to, the Peruvian sugar producers could not avoid the increasingly bitter confrontations with their workers. This was a complex process, which can be traced in the main to the industry's capitalist transformation and the way in which this transformation was conditioned by external factors. Firstly, there was a steady growth in the use of wage labour, and because of what can reasonably be seen as an externally imposed need to adopt more and more sophisticated technology, a significant minority of the labour force became permanent skilled workers. It was from this group, who were generally more literate and informed than the migrant field workers and who tended to resist in a more purposeful way the harsher aspects of plantation life, that union leaders emerged. Also, although the hacendados' claims of

113

outside agitation were deliberaly exaggerated, workers on the sugar estates, in common with other workers in the country, were strongly influenced from the early decades of the century by anarchist ideas. These provided them with a framework within which to more clearly understand their position and fight against their exploitation.(56)

Finally, it can be argued (albeit tentatively) that Peru's relatively weak position (lower level of development of forces of production) within the world capitalist system made class conflict here that much more intractable and potentially violent. On the one hand, hacendados generally tried to offset price falls by lowering wages or increasing the tarea. This was a constant source of conflict. Moreover, because of the generally lower levels of productivity in Peru and the fact that wage goods, particularly food, were drawn directly and indirectly from Peru to the metropolitan countries, it took longer for labour to reproduce itself (higher ratio of necessary to surplus labour). With this limitation on the rate of exploitation, and the fact that so large a proportion of the work on the estates, particularly harvesting, resisted mechanisation until the 1960s, the hacendados were faced with the need to increase the level of exploitation by extending the working day or increasing the intensity of work.

Kay is correct in suggesting (57) that workers in countries such as Peru are exploited to a lesser extent than those in the metropolitan countries, and this was one reason why Peruvian capitalists were forced to drive their workers harder and conditions tended to be much more unpleasant (this unpleasantness being wrongly labelled as over-exploitation). The hidden extraction of relative surplus value was denied them. Together with the fact that on the Peruvian sugar estates many of the workers were in the process of being socialised as wage labourers, with all the attendant coercion this involved, and that the hacendados were accustomed from the years of slavery and coolie labour to treating their workers harshly, a very explosive situation was created. The spark to set off this volatile mixture was provided by the extreme fall in real wages brought about by World War I.(58)

Strikes 1914-21

The extent and severity of rural labour unrest during and immediately after the war was unprecedented. As Blanchard has shown,(59) this was part of the heightening of the class struggle throughout the country, with strikes affecting the ports, railways, northern oilfields and mines as well as the coastal sugar and cotton estates. Higher wages were a common demand in every strike, and this is hardly surprising in a period of rapid inflation and falling real wages. But no strike was concerned solely with wages, and demands for shorter hours, reduced tareas, improved working conditions, better housing and

education, and freedom to form unions, all denote more than a
simple spasmodic reaction to falling living standards. This
more coherent, organised response by the rural workers owed
much to the militant example of, and in some cases the direct
assistance from, an increasingly self-aware and organised urban
working class - especially the anarchist-inspired groups.
During these years strikes on estates creased to be isolated
affairs.(60) They spread quickly from hacienda to hacienda,
from valley to valley, and as this happened the alarm among the
property-owning class grew.

In the Cayaltí correspondence every strike is discussed in
detail and suggestions made for preventing trouble on the
hacienda.(61) An indication of the way in which conditions were
changing is given by Antero Aspillaga, who commented in August
1916 that it was necessary to treat workers with great care as
'the working class of today is not as before'.(62) A year
earlier estate administrator Ronald Gordon had observed that
'native workers day by day are becoming more careful of their
rights'.(63) Despite this, and the fact that workers were able
to extract some concessions on wages and conditions, the
hacendados, fully backed by the government of fellow sugar
producer José Pardo, were able to maintain tight control by
calling on troops to put down strikes. Time and again this
tactic was used. It was seen by the hacendados as important,
not only in terms of smashing individual groups of workers, but
also in that displays of force intimidated workers generally.
For example, the Aspillagas were pleased when seven workers
were killed by troops on the neighbouring estates of Pomalca in
July 1917. They felt this would dissuade their own workers from
coming out on strike.(64)

The historic victory of the Lima workers in winning the
eight-hour day in January 1919 signalled the beginning of a
short period when the fortunes of the working class seemed to
be in the ascendant.(65) While of limited direct value to the
mass of sugar workers who laboured by the tarea, the eight-hour
movement was of great importance in giving confidence to the
workers and impetus to their struggle for better conditions.
From the early months of 1919, workers on the sugar estates
were continually on the offensive, striking for and winning, in
most cases against only minimal opposition (possibly because
sugar prices were so abnormally high at the time), increased
wages and improved conditions.(66) This run of success came to
an end in 1921, when with sugar prices falling precipitously,
hacendados in the Chicama valley tried to roll back the
workers' wage gains. This led to a mass mobilisation of workers
in the region, the establishment of the first sindicatos
(unions) on some estates, and a bitter and prolonged series of
strikes in the valley. These were finally brought to a violent
climax when the government sent in troops to crush the strikes,
disband the unions and arrest the strike leaders.(67)

CONCLUSION

In common with most other sugar producers in the nineteenth century, in order to survive in the increasingly competitive world market Peru's coastal hacendados had to transform their industry completely in terms of technology, scale and structure of production and relations of production. It was the last change which proved to be the most difficult for all concerned. Although many planters were willing to embrace new techniques, they were extremely reluctant to abandon forms of exploitation, such as slavery or indentured labour, which gave them absolute control over their workers. When they were eventually forced to contract labour from the sierra they tried to maintain this control, but the cruder forms of coercion which it required proved counterproductive as competition for labour increased. While certain coercive and paternalist methods were retained, the hacendados were obliged to depend increasingly on wages and other material incentives to recruit and hold labour. This new basis for the hacendado-worker relationship when combined with the other changes in the sugar industry and Peruvian society generally became a potent source of conflict.

Pre-war labour troubles had given a warning of the new mood among the sugar workers, but the war and post-war years saw them emerge more forcefully from their legacy of slavery and indentured labour to challenge both the archaic, paternalist framework within which they laboured and the capitalists by whom they were exploited. The sugar workers and the hacendados were joined together in a social system characterised by the dominance of wage relations combined with an overlay of paternalist controls. The hacendados tried to maintain this inherently unstable structure not only because paternalism had proven an effective means of class domination, but also because many saw themselves as both capitalists and patrons. However, paternalism rests on a degree of mutual obligation and the acceptance by the servant of the authority of the master. What vestiges of this there may have been on the sugar plantations(68) were steadily undermined by the harsh realities of capitalist wage relations, as well as the constraints imposed on the hacendados by their relatively weak position within the world capitalist system. These internal contradictions and external pressures proved too great to be contained, and in the period 1914-21 the country was shaken again and again by waves of labour unrest. Although the capitalists emerged victorious from this battle, the events of these years served to define more clearly the nature of class conflict on Peru's coastal sugar estates. The struggle between labour and capital had been firmly joined. This struggle was to be taken up once again in the early 1930s when it assumed national significance, the sugar estates of the Chicama and Santa Catalina valleys providing vital working class support for Haya de la Torre's radical APRA movement. Subsequently, the fortunes of APRA (Alianza Popular Revolucionaria Americana) and the sugar workers were to be closely intertwined.

NOTES
1.   Hobart A.Spalding, Jr., Organized Labor in Latin America. Historical Case Studies of Workers in Dependent Societies (Harper & Row, New York, 1977), pp. 1-39.
2.   George Kubler, The Indian Caste of Peru, 1795-1940; a Population Study Based on Tax Records and Census Reports (Smithsonian Institution, Washington D.C., 1952), pp. 31, 35.
3.   Pablo Macera, Las Plantaciones Azucareras en el Peru, 1821-1875 (Biblioteca Andina, Lima, 1974), pp. lxxviii-cviii.
4.   Ibid., pp. cix-cxxi. Watt Stewart, Chinese Bondage in Peru. A History of the Chinese Coolie in Peru, 1849-1874 (Duke University Press, Durham, N.C., 1951), passim.
5.   Bill Albert, An Essay on the Peruvian Sugar Industry 1880-1920 and the Letters of Ronald Gordon, Administrator of the British Sugar Company in Canete, 1914-1920 (School of Social Studies, University of East Anglia, Norwich, 1976), p. 13a.
6.   Noel Deerr, The History of Sugar (2 vols., Chapham and Hall, London, 1950), vol. 2, p. 531.
7.   Albert, Peruvian Sugar, p. 110a.
8.   Ibid., p. 162a. In Peru (1915-22) about 84 per cent of the labour force was engaged in field work.
9.   Peter F. Klarén, Modernization, Dislocation and Aprismo: Origins of the Peruvian Aprista Party, 1870-1932 (University of Texas Press, Austin, 1973), chaps. 1-3.
10.   Michael J. Gonzales, 'Cayaltí: The Formation of a Rural Proletariat on a Peruvian Sugar Plantation, 1875-1933', unpublished PhD thesis, University of California at Berkeley, 1978, p. 212. Albert, Peruvian Sugar, p. 211.
11.   Lewis Taylor, 'Main Trends in Agrarian Capitalist Development: Cajamarca, Peru, 1880-1976', unpublished PhD thesis, University of Liverpool, 1979, p. 64.
12.   This section is based primarily on Taylor, 'Main Trends', chapters 2 and 3.
13.   Ibid., p. 89.
14.   Ibid., p. 92.
15.   Henri Favre, 'The Dynamics of Indian Peasant Society and the Migration to Coastal Plantations in Central Peru', in K. Duncan and I. Rutledge (eds.), Land and Labour in Latin America. Essays on the Development of Agrarian Capitalism in the Nineteenth and Twentieth Centuries (Cambridge University Press, Cambridge, 1977), p. 255.
16.   Recent works on Peruvian enganche include Albert, Peruvian Sugar, pp. 89a-102a; Gonzales, 'Cayaltí', chapter 7; Michael J. Gonzales, 'Capitalist Agriculture and Labour Contracting in Northern Peru, 1880-1905', Journal of Latin American Studies, vol. 12, no. 2 (1980), pp. 291-315; Klarén, Modernization, pp. 26-32; Peter Blanchard, 'The Recruitment of Workers in the Peruvian Sierra at the Turn of the Century: the Enganche System', Inter-American Economic Affairs, vol. 33, no.

3 (1980), pp. 63-83; C. D. Scott, 'Peasants, Proletarianisation and the Articulation of Modes of Production: The Case of Sugar-Cane Cutters in Northern Peru, 1940-69', The Journal of Peasant Studies, vol. 3, no. 3 (1976), pp. 321-42. A general comparative survey is given in Arnold J. Bauer, 'Rural Workers in Spanish America: Problems of Peonage and Oppression', Hispanic American Historical Review, vol. 59, no. 1 (1979), pp. 34-63.

17.   Peru, Ministerio de Fomento, La Crisis de Azúcar: Informe de la Comisión Oficial (Torres Aguirre, Lima, 1902), pp. 9-10. The producers were not against enganche but wanted to see it more closely regulated.

18.   John Kenneth Turner, Barbarous Mexico. An Indictment of a Cruel and Corrupt System (Cassell and Co., London, 1911); B. Traven, March to Caobaland (Penguin Books, London, 1971); and The Rebellion of the Hanged (Penguin Books, 1970).

19.   Blanchard, 'Recruitment of Workers', p. 80. The most important organisation was the Asociación Pro-Indígena established in Lima in 1909.

20.   Albert, Peruvian Sugar, p. 106a. Gonzales, 'Cayalti', pp. 318-18a.

21.   Albert, Peruvian Sugar, p. 94a.

22.   Taylor, 'Main Trends', pp. 138-43.

23.   Gonzales, 'Cayaltí', pp. 243-7.

24.   Klarén, Modernization, pp. 31-2.

25.   Gonzales, 'Cayaltí', p. 245.

26.   Ibid., p. 246.

27.   Correspondence, 8 April 1931, San Jacinto Mss., Archivo del Fuero Agrario (AFA), Lima.

28.   Monthly and Annual Administrative Reports, Casa Grande Mss., AFA.

29.   Taylor, 'Main Trends', pp. 164-7.

30.   Ibid., p. 165.

31.   All information for this section from 'Informe: Mano de Obra', 25 May 1945, San Jacinto Mss., AFA.

32.   Scott, 'Peasants', p. 334.

33.   Felipe de Osma, Informe sobre las Huelgas del Norte (Biblioteca Peruana de Historia Económica, Lima, 1972), p. 21.

34.   Cayaltí Mss., Cartas Administrativas, Cayaltí-Lima, 3 September 1919, 3 December 1919 (AFA).

35.   E. J. Berg, 'Backward Sloping Supply Function in Dual Economies - The African Case', Quarterly Journal of Economics, vol 75 (1961).

36.   S. Pollard, The Genesis of Modern Management (Penguin Books, London, 1968), chapter 5.

37.   Scott, 'Peasants', p. 332. Gonzales, 'Cayaltí', pp. 316-17.

38.   Correspondence Alba-San Jacinto, 5 December 1896, San Jacinto Mss., AFA.

39. Ibid., Lima-San Jacinto, 28 October 1911.
40. C. D. Scott, Machetes, Machines and Agrarian Reform: The Political Economy of Technical Choice in the Peruvian Sugar Industry, 1954-74 (School of Development Studies, University of East Anglia, Norwich, 1979), p. 333.
41. José Carlos Mariátegui, Seven Interpretive Essays on Peruvian Reality (University of Texas Press, Austin, 1971), p. 63.
42. Ibid., pp. 62-3.
43. Taylor, 'Main Trends', p. 160.
44. See above.
45. Sidney Mintz, 'The Rural Proletariat and the Problem of Rural Proletarian Consciousness', The Journal of Peasant Studies, vol. 1, no. 3 (1974), p. 321.
46. Ibid., p. 300.
47. Albert, Peruvian Sugar, p. 163. Between 1899 and 1923 about 17,000 Japanese contract workers were brought into Peru. They worked mainly on the cotton and sugar estates in the central valleys, rather than the main sugar valleys of the north. See Ibid., pp. 102a-5a, 271-5.
48. Bauer, 'Rural Workers', p. 38.
49. Eugene D. Genovese, Roll, Jordan, Roll. The World the Slaves Made (Vintage Books, New York, 1976), pp. 3-7.
50. E. P. Thompson, The Making of the English Working Class (Penguin Books, London, 1968), pp. 9-10.
51. Details of the strike from Klarén, Modernization, pp. 33-7. Osma, Informe, passim. Joaquín Diaz Ahumada, Historia de las Luchas Sindicales en el Valle de Chicama (Editorial Bolivariana, Trujillo, 1962), passim.
52. Gonzales, 'Cayaltí', pp. 345-6.
53. Peter Blanchard, The Origins of the Peruvian Labor Movement, 1883-1919 (University of Pittsburgh Press, Pittsburgh, 1982), pp. 81-3.
54. Ibid., pp. 84-101.
55. The West Coast Leader, 15 May 1912.
56. On anarchism in Peru see Blanchard, Origins, pp. 47-64.
57. Geoffrey Kay, Development and Underdevelopment: A Marxist Analysis (Macmillan, London, 1975), p. 116.
58. Albert, Peruvian Sugar, pp. 163a-74a. The real wages of male field workers fell from 100 in 1913 to a low point of 60.5 in 1920. This was all the more remarkable as the hacendados profits soared during the same period. Ibid., pp. 126a-7a.
59. Blanchard, Origins, chapters 7 and 8.
60. Albert, Peruvian Sugar, pp. 180a-218a.
61. Ibid., pp. 182a-4a, 189a-90a.
62. Cartas Reservadas, Lima-Cayaltí, 18 August 1916, Cayaltí Mss., AFA.
63. Albert, Peruvian Sugar, p. 47.

64.   Cartas Reservadas, Lima-Cayaltí, 12 July and 17 July 1917, Cayaltí Mss., AFA.
65.   Blanchard, Origins, pp. 148-59.
66.   Albert, Peruvian Sugar, pp. 197a-8a.
67.   Ibid., pp. 206a-18a.
68.   Some estates did retain a more paternalist framework well into the 1960s: C. D. Scott, 'The Labour Process, Class Conflict and Politics in the Peruvian Sugar Industry', Development and Change, vol. 10 (1979), pp. 63-5.

Chapter Six

THE POLITICAL ECONOMY OF SEMI-PROLETARIANISATION UNDER COLONIALISM: SUDAN 1925-50

Jay O'Brien

The history of colonial capitalist development in Sudan is the history of the development of cotton production, primarily in the vast irrigated Gezira Scheme. This history is in turn largely the history of the formation of a cheap and malleable agricultural labour force, composed of tenant cultivators and seasonal wage labourers. This paper examines the colonial policies involved in promoting such a labour force and the impact that incorporation into the capitalist system had on peasants and pastoralists.(1) Capitalist penetration brought these people into expanding colonial markets as producers but largely excluded them from markets for major consumption goods. The result was that the dominant pattern of the colonial labour force was semi-proletarianisation.

THE DEVELOPMENT OF IRRIGATED COTTON PRODUCTION: THE GEZIRA SCHEME

British interest in Sudan's potential for producing cotton dates at least from 1839, and became increasingly keen toward the end of the nineteenth century as Lancashire's declining competitive position in world textile markets forced the industry to shift production toward the fine end of the trade. This was dependent on Egyptian-style long staple cotton, for the production of which Sudanese conditions appeared to be ideal.(2) Four years after the British conquest of Sudan in 1898, the British Cotton Growing Association (BCGA) was formed, and this organisation soon began to press for the development of long staple cotton production in Sudan.

The first experiments with cotton growing in Sudan began in 1906. However, it was not until the Sennar Dam on the Blue Nile River was completed in 1925, initially watering 240,000 feddans (1 feddan = 1.038 acres), that large-scale production was undertaken. The early years of experimentation with cotton cultivation had less to do with testing technical conditions than with testing social and economic arrangements. The latter concerns derived from the combination of the need to irrigate in arid Sudanese conditions with the absence of a significant labour market in Sudan. On the one hand, the government wanted to avoid the entrenchment of any substantial economic interest which might weaken its ability to act decisively in Sudan in accordance with its strategic interests in Egypt. This meant that the development of a strong indigenous class of large landowners was unacceptable to the British. It also meant that the regime could not provide sufficient guarantees of profitability and permanence to attract substantial foreign investment in irrigational infrastructure and land. Yet a huge investment and a correspondingly large central management were clearly necessary.(3)

On the other hand, the substantial wage labour force needed for a direct labour plantation was absent and the government wished to avoid the political volatility of a large class of landless labourers. Furthermore, the British feared the consequences of the use of such devices as heavy taxation, normally used in the African colonies to stimulate the spread of cash needs and wage labour, as this had been a focal point for the successful mobilisation of the population in the Mahdist revolt against the Turko-Egyptian regime in 1881-5.(4)

The period of experimentation provided a viable way out of these twin dilemmas. It was quickly established that even a small plantation could not attract sufficient labour to operate profitably, even by importing labour.(5) Some form of tenancy arrangement with cultivators appeared more promising, but the initial rate-paying form of tenancy had the serious drawback that management simply could not collect the rates from tenants in years of poor harvest. Ultimately, the traditional form of share-cropping in waterwheel-irrigated cultivation along the Niles provided the key to solving not only the problem of the form of association of the tenants with the enterprise, but also the relationship of the state and private capital to it as well. Traditionally, each contributor of land, labour, equipment or oxen was entitled to a conventionally fixed share of the harvest of an irrigated unit. The proportions of the traditional shares worked out at 40 per cent to labour and 60 per cent to other inputs defined by the British as 'capital'.

This discovery pleased the authorities, who converted the experimental farms to this arrangement in order to work out a suitable system of sharing. Ultimately, they allocated to the tenants, whose contribution was defined as labour, a 40 per cent share in the net revenues of their cotton crops. Government assumed the role of landowner and made the investment in irrigation works in return for 40 per cent of the cotton revenues. A London-based company, the Sudan Plantations Syndicate (SPS), assumed the management functions in return for the remaining 20 per cent.(6) Thus was born the tripartite 'partnership' model of agricultural development in Sudan, later extolled as a model for non-communist development in the Third World in Arthur Gaitskell's Gezira: A Story of Development in the Sudan.

The British were also enthusiastic about the tenant model devised for the Gezira Scheme as promoting the emergence of a self-sufficient 'prosperous peasantry' along the lines of the fabled English yeomanry. To this end, they allocated to tenants irrigated plots, for the cultivation of sorghum for household consumption and fodder for their animals. These crops were to belong exclusively to the tenants without shares or charges. The standard tenancy thus became (after modifications in the early years) 40 feddans, of which 10 were under cotton, 5 each under sorghum and fodder, and 20 fallow each year. Tenancies were allocated on the basis of previous landownership in the area, with some large landowners obtaining several tenancies each while smaller landowners obtained half-tenancies.(7) All land incorporated into the scheme was either purchased by the government or compulsorily leased to the government at low and permanently fixed rents.

The idea of the Gezira tenancy was, then, that it would be worked entirely by the tenant's family and dependents, supplemented by some hired labour for cotton picking. The tenant's reward would be secure subsistence and fodder crops, plus a modest cash income from the cotton crop. The self-sufficient peasantry which the British thereby hoped to create would not only obviate the necessity for a permanent large wage labour force and keep demand for seasonal labour at manageable levels, but would also become a complacent body of Sudanese grateful to and supportive of the colonial order.

The actual performance of the scheme during the 25-year SPS concession period certainly could not have disappointed the two senior 'partners'. Despite the very low cotton prices during the depression and a series of disastrous crop failures due to disease in the early years, the SPS paid annual dividends to its shareholders which averaged 15 per cent over the full concession period. At liquidation in 1950 they enjoyed a further capital profit of 25 shillings on every 20 invested. Meanwhile, the government of Sudan amassed a cumulative surplus after debt service of over LE 16 million (Egyptian pounds, fixed at a rate of LE = £1.0s.6d. sterling during this period) on its direct Gezira share - not counting additional revenues from related taxes and freight charges. Moreover, from 1925 to 1956 cotton exports from Gezira accounted for about 60 per cent of Sudan's export earnings and the direct government share provided about 50 per cent of total government revenues.(8)

Meanwhile, payments to the tenants for their cotton shares (out of which they had to meet any out-of-pocket expenses, such as for wages paid to cotton pickers) averaged LE 30 per standard tenancy between 1925 and 1946 and LE 175 for the last four years of the concession period, when cotton prices rose sharply on the world market. In three of the depression years, average payments due to tenants fell short of the charges they owed on account.(9)

THE SUPPLY OF WAGE LABOUR TO THE GEZIRA SCHEME, 1925-50

From the start the successful cultivation of the cotton crop depended much more heavily on wage labour than the planners had anticipated, not only in cotton picking, but in other operations as well, especially weeding. Economic incentives for tenants to devote family labour to cotton cultivation, particularly when in competition with the two crops wholly owned by the tenants, were not overwhelming. Moreover, the average family (about six persons) could have fielded a work team large enough to do all the work even in non-picking operations for only a brief period in its life cycle.(10) It was to meet this demand for seasonal labour in the Gezira Scheme that the British regime adopted policies to stimulate a large supply of cheap labour beginning in the 1920s.(11)

The supply of wage labour to the Gezira Scheme, both seasonal and settled, was ample from the beginning and included large numbers of immigrants. An intelligence report of 1928 estimated that there were 80,000 West African immigrants settled in Sudan, of whom 55,000 were permanent settlers and the other 25,000 were described as 'floating'. The report further estimated that 3,000 new West African immigrants settled in Sudan each year.(12) Many of these settled in and around the Gezira area and worked for wages in the scheme. The Takari,(13) together with immigrants from French Equatorial Africa (later Chad) and from Sudan's western provinces, formed the core of the Gezira labour force.

The coincidence of the opening of the Gezira Scheme with the widespread severe drought and famine conditions throughout Sudan in 1925/6 and 1926/7 played an important role in stimulating the supply of seasonal migrants to the scheme and established a pattern of migration which dominated seasonal labour supply to the scheme for 50 years. Peasants whose crops failed in those years and herders whose animals died responded in droves to the propaganda efforts of local government officials extolling the merits of the Gezira Scheme as a source of money and food.(14)

Recruitment of pickers was concentrated in the Blue Nile Province itself, Kassala Province, and the parts of central Kordofan which lay along the railway line from Kosti to el Obeid. These areas have continued to supply the largest number of cotton pickers to the Gezira Scheme ever since, though their numbers have varied greatly from year to year. The fluctuation in supply of seasonal labour from these sources was due mainly to annual variations in the crop yields of rainland peasants due to fluctuations in rainfall, incidence of locusts, and so forth, and to variations in animal prices. When rainfall was low (or locusts plentiful) and rainland crops were consequently small, large numbers of peasant farmers would go to the Gezira in search of employment. When their crops were good, many of them stayed home through the dry season. Similarly with herders; when animal prices were low many more went to the

Gezira for seasonal wage labour than when prices were high.(15)

A number of policies were implemented, beginning in the 1920s, by government in concert with the SPS to cope with this instability of labour supply. The Powers of Nomad Sheikhs Ordinance of 1922, and its replacement in 1927 by the broader Powers of Sheikhs Ordinance, defined the general administrative structure within which these policies operated. A permanent Labour Board was formed by the government in 1920 to cope with a labour crisis in that year. Demand for wage labour had abruptly increased for new projects - especially work on the construction of the Sennar Dam to irrigate Gezira - following removal of the restrictions imposed during the war years. The immediate problem was one of different employers bidding up wages to attract labour. In his Annual Report for 1923, the Governor-General noted that there had been no problems demanding the attention of the Board since the original crisis and described its aims as follows:

> Its general policy has been to secure as much uniformity as possible in the scale of wages paid to unskilled labour by different employers, to prevent indiscriminate or competitive recruitment of labour, especially in certain areas but otherwise to interfere as little as possible with the flow of labour. (16)

This policy seems to have been remarkably successful, for the average daily rate of pay to unskilled labour of 4 to 6 pt (100 pt=LE 1) reported by the Governor-General in 1922 (17) remained basically unchanged until the years following World War II, when wage levels rose slightly to an average of 5 to 8 pt per day.(18)

Upward pressures on wage rates were experienced during the war, but regulations fixing wage rates were issued to control the situation. Thus, the Governor of Blue Nile Province issued a circular dated 4 November 1940 in which he set ceilings on wages by types of labour as follows:

1. Completely unskilled labour normally accustomed to light agricultural work only: not normally to exceed 4 P.T. (pt) a day.
2. Slightly skilled casual labour to be used on manual work: not normally to exceed 6 P.T. a day.
3. Semi-skilled casual labour, to be used for porterage, and other forms of hard manual labour: not normally to exceed 8-10 P.T. a day. In rare cases, where work is extremely hard a 12 P.T. rate may be paid.(19)

These rates were binding on all government and military units, but were intended to apply to all employers, as explained by the Governor: 'The object is, of course, to prevent undue competition in the local labour market, and it is hoped that private employers of labour will fall into line without compulsion'.(20)

Except for wage contracts and controls during the war years and general policies of keeping track of labour supply and wage rates throughout the country (using the Labour Board to police competition among employers for labour), the British preferred to let market forces regulate labour supply. Nevertheless, the government did intervene decisively in one other crucial area, the encouragement of the settlement of immigrants in and around the Gezira Scheme.

The Settlement of Immigrants

The history of West African immigration to Sudan, and the position of Takari settlers in the Sudanese labour force, have long been surrounded by misunderstanding in both academic and official writings as well as in the public conception.(21) Fortunately, the matter has been substantially clarified through the recent important work done by Duffield on Takari settlement in Sudan and the role of the Takari in the agricultural labour force.(22) West African immigration to Sudan is a phenomenon of long standing,(23) and Takari settlers in Sudan, particularly religious figures, played prominent roles in the Mahdist rebellion both for and against the Mahdists, and were involved in the affairs of the Mahdist state.

Many of these early settlers came to Sudan on the pilgrimage to Mecca or on their return from the Hejaz. Some stayed only a short time, while others settled permanently. Most prominent among them were a number of respected religious teachers and healers. The popular conception of Takari settlement was formed by this pattern, but this pattern has changed substantially since the British conquest of Sudan and Nigeria.

In the twentieth century Takari immigration to Sudan increased significantly and its nature altered.(24) The goal of the pilgrimage came to play a very minor role, as the bulk of the immigrants comprised poor Hausa peasants seeking to escape the oppression of the Fulani aristocracy in Nigeria. Their settlement in Sudan was encouraged by the British authorities from an early date, but not without some ambivalence due to the Mahdism of some.(25)

The Fulani Sultan Mai Wurno settled with 2,000 followers in Sheikh Talha, across the Blue Nile from Sennar in 1906. The British Inspector in Sennar later induced Mai Wurno to move to a new location on the west bank, just south of Sennar, in an area in which labour was in short supply, and where in 1915 the government granted him 3,000 feddans of rainland. This settlement, called Maiurno, came to be the focal point of Takari movements and the colonial administration of them.

As the importance of the Takari as a supply of casual wage labour rapidly came to be felt by the British, more measures were adopted to encourage their settlement and to woo the support of Mai Wurno. In 1908 Governor-General Wingate recommended the formation of 'Fellata' (i.e. West African immigrant) colonies on the Rahad and Dinder rivers, which areas had been abandoned by cultivators during the Mahdia and the early years of British rule. Land and tax concessions were made available to the settlers, and this area subsequently became one of heavy West African settlement. In 1911 the Governor-General extended the area of preferential settlement to include any available land between Sennar and Sinja.(26) In 1917 B.R.J. Hussey, Inspector at Sennar, made a formal suggestion to the government that the 'Fellata' and Mai Wurno as their leader could help alleviate the anticipated labour shortage that threatened the planned Gezira Scheme.(27)

Mai Wurno enthusiastically concurred with this suggestion, writing: 'As long as I am well treated, and I am in my present position, there is no fear of not getting enough labourers'.(28) Mai Wurno was given the presidency of a Sheikh's Court according to the Powers of Sheikhs Ordinance of 1927, and his general influence over all West Africans in Sudan was reduced in 1931 to a concrete form, when he was granted his own dar (29) in the regions of Takari settlement on the Blue Nile south of Sennar and to the east in the Rahad/Dinder area. In his dar he enjoyed the rights accorded to Native Sheikhs in the 1927 Ordinance, including the right to keep 10 per cent of the taxes collected and to receive labour service. The Governor of the Blue Nile Province, in proposing the latter step to the Civil Secretary in a letter dated 13 February 1930, summed up its benefits in the following terms: '...besides having made this corner of Sudan safe for autocracy, we should have an assured and not inconsiderable source of the labour so badly needed in the Gezira Scheme, where I believe the Fellata are the most valued labour of all'.(30)

Mai Wurno for his part seems to have conscientiously applied his energies to supplying labour to the Gezira Scheme, not only as sheikh of what amounted to a labour reserve, but also as an active direct recruiting agent. References to his activities in this regard can be found in the files of the SPS, where it is recorded, for example, that in December 1935 he hired a lorry to transport Takari labour from the Rahad area to the Gezira Scheme to pick cotton.(31) The costs were refunded by the SPS and charged against the joint cotton account. In return, the SPS made a judicious practice of sending frequent 'presents' to Mai Wurno.(32)

Takari labour was not only recruited for cotton picking. Indeed, its strategic importance from the beginning lay in another area. The failure of tenant families to supply large amounts of labour affected other operations as well as the harvest, particularly the critical weedings of the cotton plots during the rainy season, when peasant cultivators were generally busy in their own fields and the transport of labour into the area was seriously inhibited by the rains. An additional problem in weeding operations lay in the fact that traditional northern rainland tools and methods of weeding were inadequate for the heavy weeding that was required for cotton in the Gezira, especially in areas to the south of the scheme. The indigenous practice involved light surface weeding using a long-handled hoe (malod), an operation which could only be carried out after the soil had dried out significantly. In contrast, the Takari used a heavy, broad-bladed, short-handled hoe (kadanka) which was more suited to the heavy weeding demanded in wet conditions.(33)

From the beginning then, Takari and other Westerners (34) were encouraged to settle in the Gezira Scheme in permanent labour camps. The pattern of recruitment and settlement of permanent labour camps was haphazard in the early years. Sometimes the sheikh of a tenant village would make contact with a prominent Westerner - perhaps granting him a tenancy as a personal incentive - who then would recruit followers, relatives and friends to settle with him near a tenant village, where they would supply a perennial source of labour. Such settlement gained great impetus after 1929 as many Westerners were recruited in the depression and blights.

By 1933 the financial insecurity of the Gezira Scheme, due to the depression, had led the SPS to pressure the government to adopt measures which would secure an abundant labour supply at low wages, and avoid any possibilities of a crisis of labour shortage which could further exacerbate the situation. In particular, the SPS complained (as it would repeatedly in later years when such measures were imposed) that the Sudan Medical Service's practice of holding immigrants from the west in quarantine at Kosti (to combat the spread of bilharzia, or schistosomiasis, and relapsing fever) seriously inhibited the flow of immigrant labour to the scheme. In October 1933 the Commissioner of the Gezira Area wrote to the Manager of the SPS announcing that the government was about to lift the Kosti quarantine of immigrants in order to increase the flow of labour to the Gezira Scheme and that, since a resulting rise in the incidence of bilharzia was anticipated, he asked that all settlement of Westerners in the scheme should be undertaken only after written consent had been obtained from the District Commissioner.(35) In the following month the Senior Medical Inspector for Blue Nile Province began a survey of existing and proposed sites of settler villages.(36) There followed a period of reorganisation of settler villages and intensified recruitment of new settler groups. As a measure to control the spread of malaria and bilharzia, the requirement was imposed that all settler villages had to be located a minimum of 300 metres from the nearest canal, with an optimum distance of 500 metres, and that all proposed sites should first be approved by the Senior Medical Inspector.(37)

Cash subsidies, building materials and free transport were promised to new settlers, and settlers whose villages were moved to new sites were given compensation for their homes in the old villages. Sites were chosen for the availability on or near them of land for the cultivation by the settlers of small plots of sorghum, some of which were irrigated, and sources of wood for fuel and building materials. Some of the settler village lands and sorghum plots were in areas removed from the main crop rotation. In March 1934 the Financial Secretary approved the rental of 400 feddans of additional land outside the irrigated area for labour settlement sites.(38)

A census of existing labour settlements carried out in November 1933, at the beginning of this reorganisation and intensification of the settlement programme, counted a total of 7,791 'workers' including 2,000 Westerner tenants, scattered in numerous settlements throughout the scheme.(39) Working children were not included in the count, and it is unclear from the figures whether women were always counted. Ethnic identifications were not given in all cases, and where given were sometimes ambiguous,(40) but Takari clearly predominated. There were also substantial numbers of Borgu, while smaller numbers were counted of Fur, Masalit, Salamat, and a few other western Sudanese groups, particularly in South Block. In 1954 a village survey counted 59,000 people settled in labour villages, of whom 2,500 were tenants.(41)

Takari workers were especially in demand, as they were widely reputed to be particularly hard-working. Field Inspectors especially preferred them in areas of heavy weed-growth because of their use of the kadanka. For example, in his report on existing labour settlements and the need for additional settlements in his inspectorate, the Meselemiya Group Inspector wrote as follows about the labour needs of Abdel Rahman Block: 'This is one of the blocks where fellata labour is most necessary as there is always a large area of 'Said' grass, which is most easily dealt with by Kadankas. Kobor and Gabana ought to be fellata villages, while any type of labour will do for Abdel Rahman'.(42)

Tenant Attitudes Toward Labour Settlement

The attitude of the tenants toward the settlement of immigrant labour in the Gezira Scheme seems, from the comments of inspectors, to have been on the whole positive. The sheikhs of many tenant villages helped select sites for settlement and often took charge of building houses for the settlers. However, a number of Halaween tenant villages refused to accept any settlers at all in their areas. Thus, at the time of the November 1933 census of labour settlements, there were no such settlements in the heavily Halaween blocks of Dolga and Istrahma.(43) According to Abdel Hamid, this attitude stems from the fact that the Halaween, who have a long history of settled cultivation, made extensive use of family labour, including that of women, in their fields.(44) The men objected to the presence of foreign men in the same fields with their wives and daughters. It should be noted that among other groups of tenants this same objection to women mixing with foreigners and men from other Sudanese groups is given as the reason for withholding the labour of women from work in the tenancies.(45)

In the following years, tenant attitudes toward the Takari settlers in their midst became intensely ambivalent. On the one hand, Takari labour was indispensable to the successful cultivation of the tenancies. On the other hand, however, the tenants viewed the Takari as the main drain on their financial resources and therefore as at least partly responsible for the smallness of their incomes.(46) Moreover, the Takari represented a pool of cheap labour that helped by its presence to keep wages down in other sectors as well. Tenant irritation with settled Takari labour was exacerbated by several factors. One of the most prominent of these was the fact that the Takari tended to act collectively, usually through their village sheikhs. They would gather in groups before taking work and agree that all would ask for the particular rate of pay they judged they could command and that no one in the group would accept to work for a wage below an agreed minimum.

Another factor in the scheme that led to the development of ill-feeling between tenants and settled labour was the institution of tulba, still used today. If a management-employed inspector (exclusively British before 1950) is dissatisfied with the standard or timeliness of a tenant's execution of any operation in his cotton plot, the inspector unilaterally may recruit labour to do the work at a higher wage, which is then billed to the tenant's account.(47) Settled labour is of course most frequently recruited for this purpose.

In the context of such hostilities, another factor grew in importance as the scheme recovered financially in the 1940s from the ravages of the depression and blight. When a number of Sudanese tenants had abandoned their tenancies in the crisis, many of them had been replaced by Takari and French Equatorial African settlers. These groups accounted for 2,000 or 13 per cent of the scheme's tenants in 1933/4 and 3,000, but still 13 per cent, in 1944/5.(48) In the meantime, the improved economic performance of the scheme had led to greatly increased numbers of applications from local Sudanese for tenancies, and the older tenants were beginning to feel the problem of not being able to pass on tenancies to all their children. In this context, the occupation of tenancies by Takari and other groups of foreign origin began to be a focal point of tenant resentment and a matter for general public debate.(49)

As an outgrowth of this and related debates during the 1940s, the Sudanese Nationality Act of 1948, which was part of the process of paving the way for Sudanese self-government and eventual independence, adopted a very restricted definition of Sudanese nationality which essentially excluded the Takari and other western immigrants, even, not uncommonly, those who had been born in Sudan.(50) Desirable jobs in government, Gezira Scheme tenancies, trading licenses and access to a number of social services were restricted to Sudanese nationals. The effect was thus to restrict Takari social mobility severely, isolating them socially and culturally, and freezing them to a great extent in unskilled occupations lacking job security and other benefits.

Other Policies Affecting Seasonal Labour Supply

While the settlement of western immigrants in and around the Gezira Scheme provided the stable core of the agricultural wage labour force during the colonial period, a number of other colonial policies stimulated key additional flows of seasonal labour from indigenous sources. These policies included: taxation; suppression of slavery; suppression of traditional textile production; marketing of key consumption goods; labour conscription; and recruitment and propaganda.

Taxation. During the early 1920s a series of basic tax laws was promulgated which represented a break with the low taxation policies of the martial law period. New taxes were introduced and existing ones raised.(51) The agricultural taxes involved have remained basically unaltered since that time.(52) The main taxes affecting peasants and herders were a crop tax, a poll tax, a house tax, animal taxes, and, in the Northern Province, a tax on date palms.(53) These taxes were introduced in different mixes in various regions.

Increased taxation was effective in stimulating cash needs, as indicated by the Governor-General's comments on experiments with encouraging cultivation of cotton in the southern districts of Blue Nile Province: 'The cultivation of American cotton as a rain or flood crop is being encouraged and is popular. In districts where this is possible the amount realised from the crop should eventually be sufficient to pay for the ushur ('tithe') tax on the dura (sorghum) crop'.(54)

Slavery. Also in the 1920s, the British regime began to act against slavery for the first time, in ways that went beyond arresting individuals caught trading captives. British policy regarding slavery in Sudan remained informal, being based on Kitchener's Memorandum to Mudirs, in which he stated that the government did not recognise slavery in Sudan but did not at the time find it expedient to take any steps against it, except where specific complaints of maltreatment were raised.

With the country securely pacified and the demand for labour in the Gezira Scheme rising, the government finally found it 'expedient' to suppress slavery in the 1920s. This was accomplished in a variety of ways in different regions, none of them however involving public announcements. In the Gezira itself, a number of slaves were given tenancies and became independent in this way. According to older informants in villages in central Kordofan, the British District Commissioner simply arrived in the villages in the mid-1920s and told the slaves that they were free to go, which they promptly did.(55) During the 1920s Mai Wurno and other Fulani aristocrats in Blue Nile villages found their slaves suddenly deserting.(56) Abdel Ghaffar dates the end of slavery in the Rufa'a el Hoi nazirate from the 1920s, after which time the Rufa'a el Hoi lost their ability to meet their needs for grain internally and many were forced to seek wage labour to obtain the cash with which to purchase it.(57)

Suppression of Indigenous Textile Production. Experiments with the cultivation by peasants of short staple cotton in Blue Nile Province in the early 1920s were abandoned after the opening of the Gezira Scheme, and the cultivation of cotton in Blue Nile Province and adjacent areas was banned by law. This was officially attributed to the terms of the SPS concession which barred competition with the cotton production of the Gezira Scheme, but this argument was manifestly lame, for short staple cotton was in no way competitive as a commodity with the long staple cotton grown in the scheme. Moreover, beginning in 1924 the cultivation of short staple cotton by peasants was actually encouraged in the Nuba Mountains, located a safe distance away from the scheme and not regarded as a labour supply area for Gezira.

Older informants in villages on the Rahad River in eastern Blue Nile Province recounted stories of how their cultivation of small amounts of cotton to meet their personal needs for clothing, donkey saddles and sacks was suppressed by the District Commissioner in the late 1920s. Anyone caught cultivating cotton would have his crop confiscated and a fine levied on pain of arrest. In this area, the traditional ganja cloth was tougher and remained cheaper than Manchester damuria, and local production continued in competition with imports. After the banning of cotton cultivation, cotton was moved inside compound fences, which the police nevertheless penetrated; and eventually they managed to suppress cultivation. In central Kordofan traditional cotton cultivation was not suppressed administratively as it was in Blue Nile Province. Informants there reported simply that cotton cultivation and local spinning and weaving abruptly ceased in response to the appearance in local markets of cheaper, higher quality cotton goods imported from Lancashire.(58) In each case, however, the result was the same. A new cash need was introduced, driving people to search for opportunities to earn money, and a traditional handicraft was undermined, thereby weakening the self-sufficiency of peasant productive systems.

Marketing of Consumption Goods. The British pursued from the start a policy of aggressively marketing sugar, tea and coffee in addition to manufactured cotton cloth for common consumption in rural areas. A discussion recorded in the minutes of the Eighth Meeting of the Labour Board illuminates the manner in which the manipulation of the supply of consumer goods was used to influence flows of labour.(59) The meeting, held in August 1943, had as its main subject for discussion the shortage of labour which had occurred in the Gezira Scheme during the previous picking season. One important reason given for the shortage was that the rains had been heavy and peasant crops had been good, bringing prosperity to a prime labour supply area for the Gezira, which consequently did not send much labour to the scheme that year.

When the discussion turned to ways and means of avoiding future repetition of such shortages, some members suggested, among other devices, the possibility of increasing the supply in the scheme area of consumer goods in high demand. It was noted that the principle already existed of allotting increased supplies of such goods in 'producing areas', and that 60 tons of sugar and 350 bales of cotton cloth had been allotted to the Gezira and distributed through the scheme's block offices. But it had been necessary to deprive other provinces of their normal supplies to do this, since wartime supplies to Sudan were tight. At this point in the discussion the comments of the SPS manager were minuted as follows:

> Mr. Archdale considered that cloth issues have the greatest effect in stimulating work and the Board noted that the War Supply Board were considering adjustment to give a permanent higher quota of goods to producing areas in order to maintain production, and in order to become known to potential labour supply areas, rather than irregular issues which did not produce the required effect.(60)

He also went on to make a plea for increased supplies of sugar and to say that the supply of coffee was crucial, stating that a failure of the supply of this item would be 'fatal'.

Labour Conscription. The Labour Board also explored and rejected another traditional colonial policy option, that of conscripting labour. The Chair introduced the question of conscription by stating that it was

> universally agreed that it would be impossible owing to lack of staff and other facilities. Mr. Archdale agreed with this view which was confirmed by the Board. It was noted that certain methods of local coercion could legally be used e.g. the Local Government Ordinance permitted

> compulsory labour on works of public utility up to a maximum of ten days a year and this method had been applied to one scheme in Northern Province in order to avoid the necessity of importing labour which might have been otherwise employed e.g. in the Gezira. It was also noted that an order... had been promulgated which permitted the Governors to move surplus labour out of their provinces.(61)

This passage illustrates the general position of labour conscription in northern Sudan during the colonial period. Conscription was used, according to the Local Government Ordinance, for road building and repair and for construction and maintenance of government buildings in rural areas, as well as supplying small amounts of labour services to Native Administration sheikhs.

In the south, as mentioned earlier, conscript labour remained the primary form of wage labour in the region, augmented from time to time for major works by contract labour imported from the north. The use of conscript labour in the southern provinces was so extensive that government practice in Equatoria at least frequently violated Article 12 on Forced Labour of the International Labour Convention, which limited the period any individual could be forced to work on 'public' works to 60 days in any year.(62) The question of the use of conscript labour in northern Sudan, as in the south, was not decided on the basis of principle, nor yet by the existence of the International Labour Convention, but explicitly on the sole basis of expediency. In the Gezira Scheme during the early years of the depression, conscripted labour was tried out in cotton picking, but the tenants were unhappy about taking such labourers and, except for some Westerners brought in this way, conscripts generally proved unsatisfactory due to their high propensity to escape, and the low standard of their work when they did stay.(63) After the disappointing results of the experiments with conscripts in the 1931/2 season, the health quarantine on immigrant labour was lifted at the beginning of the 1933/4 season and the reorganised and intensified programme of settling immigrant labour in the scheme area was pushed ahead with more success.

Recruitment and Propaganda. The 1932/3 season in the Gezira saw a return to the propaganda efforts on behalf of the scheme by the government in cooperation with the SPS, which had been so successful in stimulating an initial cheap labour supply in the mid-1920s. Thus, in December 1932 the Manager of the SPS submitted to the Governor of the Blue Nile Province a request for the assistance of government officials in labour supply areas 'to advertise and popularise the conditions of work in cotton picking in the Gezira among the local population and organise entrainment at the nearest railway station'.(64) In response, the Governor sent out a circular to the District Commissioners at el Obeid, Nahud, and Um Ruwaba in Kordofan, at Sennar and Sinja in Blue Nile, and at Gedaref and Kassala in Kassala Province.(65) In it, he requested local officials to assist in broadcasting information on cotton picking conditions in the Gezira, including the fact that the piece-rate had been raised from 2 pt per standard guffa (basket) of 35 rotls (1 rotl = 0.99 lb) the previous year to 2.5 pt per guffa in the current season. They were also to spread the word that weighing machines had been issued to the tenants, so there would be no more arguments over wages due. Although people were to be told that they ought to be able to earn 5 pt per day at these rates (an exaggerated claim), they were also to be informed that there would be no more work at daily rates. Potential pickers were also to be informed that housing would be provided and reduced rail fares would be available to those travelling to Gezira stations.(66) The same circular authorised District Commissioners to sign railway warrants for picking labour and requested them to try to send pickers in parties under the leadership of a responsible sheikh or headman.

The fact that the principal strategy for recruiting labour to the Gezira Scheme shifted from conscription to persuasion does not mean that the use or threat of force and subtler forms of coercion in semi-official and unofficial guises were totally absent. Many tenants in the Gezira recount stories of being beaten and otherwise coerced by British Field Inspectors to get them to work diligently in their own fields.(67) One of the items in a list of 'do's and don'ts' drawn up by experienced inspectors for new recruits reported by Gaitskell is suggestive of the nature of this problem: 'Patience pays. Don't lose your temper. Don't swear at tenants or labourers. Never strike anyone'.(68)

Furthermore, small numbers of conscripted labourers were brought to the Gezira under cover of various legal euphemisms, such as 'draftees' and 'imported labour', (69) during the crisis years (1929-1945). Beyond this, parties of seasonal labourers, recruited in outlying areas and transported at reduced fares paid by the SPS, were accompanied on their journeys by armed police to prevent them from escaping en route or getting off at the wrong station by mistake.(70)

Impact on Labour Supply of Agricultural Policies. A specific agricultural policy decision taken in the mid-1930s also had important implications for labour supply to the Gezira Scheme. Originally, lubia had been included in the Gezira rotation as a legume complementary to cotton. In the early 1930s, however, it was discovered that the common failure of tenants to keep their lubia plots sufficiently clean of weed and cotton debris contributed to the spread of the diseases which were

devastating the cotton crops.(71) Consequently, lubia was
entirely eliminated from the rotation for two years during the
campaign to eradicate the diseases, and there was a very strong
feeling among the field staff and agricultural researchers that
lubia was more of a liability than an asset and should
therefore be permanently dropped from the rotation. Intense
pressure from tenants to retain the lubia crop eventually
prevailed, as they insisted that the availability of lubia for
grazing at the time of the cotton harvest was essential to
attract herders from the White Nile areas and the east bank of
the Blue Nile. Large numbers of tenants, particularly in the
northern and western blocks of the scheme, depended on these
pastoralists for their main source of picking labour.(72)
Hence, lubia remained in the primary Gezira rotation
principally because of its role in attracting labour to the
scheme.

More generally, British policy during this period strove
to prevent economic developments - agricultural and otherwise -
which might create damaging competition for cheap labour with
the Gezira and other cotton producing areas. Thus, in 1928 an
application by the SPS for a license to produce sesame in Blue
Nile Province south of the Gezira was rejected on the basis of
worries about its potential for disrupting the secure supply of
cheap labour to the Gezira Scheme.(73) Again, during World War
II when the government required increased supplies of grain to
feed the Sudan Defense Force and Allied troops stationed in
North Africa, it initially tried to produce the required grain
through complete mechanisation in order to avoid drawing labour
away from the Gezira.(74)

The Impact of Seasonal Wage Labour on Peasants and Pastoralists
The agricultural labour force which took shape after 1925 in
response to these policies had a core - or rather several cores
- of regular participants and a periphery of irregular migrants
who sought seasonal wage labour in some years but not in
others. From 1925 to 1950 the labour force which was shaped by
British policy drew workers mainly from Blue Nile Province,
including immigrant groups settled within the scheme area and
along the Rahad, Dinder and upper Blue Nile Rivers. As late as
1950, two-thirds of the cotton picking labour in the Gezira
Scheme, and therefore a large proportion of the total
agricultural labour force, came from within the Blue Nile
Province.(75) These sources were supplemented by migrants from
the parts of central Kordofan adjacent to the railway line in
particular, and secondarily from Darfur and Kassala Provinces.
Within these principal labour supply areas various groups were
affected to different degrees by government policies and
participated in seasonal wage labour to different extents.
Western settlers provided the stable core of the labour force
from the beginning, although some of the immigrant groups which

settled in remoter parts of Blue Nile Province sought, more or less successfully, to replicate in their new homes self-contained village economies insulated as much as possible from external forces.(76) The indigenous inhabitants of the region responded in different ways.

Government taxation and other policies resulted in the widespread capitalist penetration of village production systems through stimulation and expansion of cash needs. Although these production systems were altered by the decline of traditional handicrafts, increased cultivation of cash crops and participation in wage labour, many of them remained basically self-sufficient peasant and/or pastoral communities in the limited sense that local production of subsistence and cash goods, irregularly supplemented by wage labour, generally was sufficient to reproduce the community from one year to the next. When local production was insufficient to meet all needs, seasonal wage labour was resorted to in order to make up the difference. The frequency with which this was necessary varied from community to community.

The wholesale disarticulation of domestic economies was not widespread in the colonial period and was mainly restricted to the core labour supply areas of Blue Nile Province and central Kordofan, but even in these areas it was not generalised. In this period such disruption seems to have affected nomads and recently settled former nomads more than others, especially in the drier northern and western parts of the region. As noted earlier, many nomads found the availability of dry season grazing and abundant water for their animals in the Gezira very attractive, and began from the start to work in cotton picking in order to gain access to these benefits.

Also, from an early date a process gained momentum in which unsuccessful nomads, unable to meet rising cash needs and maintain the minimum viable herding unit, settled in the northern parts of the Rahad/Dinder region and in the Managil area. For example, of 38 Arab villages between Sherif Ya'gub and Tineidba surveyed in the Rahad project area (east of the Blue Nile from Gezira) in 1974/5 and for which the date of establishment was ascertained, 28 were founded after 1925.(77) Many of these former pastoralists regarded heavy agricultural work as distasteful and had little interest in village self-sufficiency as such.(78) The practice which many of them adopted was to cultivate small plots sufficient to meet family needs for part of the year and then to spend the entire cotton picking season in the Gezira Scheme, where they were fed by the tenants. Not only did they thereby save the crops they had cultivated for consumption during the rainy season, but they used the cash wages they earned to buy meat and other food to supplement their diet and to meet other recurrent cash needs, such as for clothing. In addition, they were saved the rigours of digging dry season wells to supply themselves with water.

137

Sudan

As noted by Culwick and Abdel Hamid, the productivity of nomad and former nomad cotton pickers tended to be relatively low, since the food provided and the water which was easily accessible were the primary benefits they were interested in, and small amounts of cash were sufficient to meet other needs, particularly as in most cases several members of a family were working.(79) Such groups tended to bring with them to wage labour in the schemes a typical Chayanovian peasant's outlook on balancing drudgery and comfort.(80) They did not seek to maximise income from their available time and energy for work, but adjusted the duration and intensity of the working day to the conflicting requirements of their standards of dignity and desirable levels of consumption.(81)

An alternative response to the new and increasing cash needs deriving from colonial policies, particularly in higher rainfall areas further south, was increased effort in village production. Peasant cultivators could avoid migrating annually for seasonal wage labour by expanding household agricultural production and growing cash crops through extending and intensifying the working day, and the working season as a whole. This option was pursued by some peasant communities in which no stigma was attached to hard agricultural labour and a high value was placed on maintaining local autonomy. This was not simply a matter of sentimental attachment to peasant independence but involved fundamental questions of the maintenance of patriarchal authority within the peasant household and the ability of elders to continue to command the labour of juniors. In one such village on the Rahad River in Blue Nile Province, the normal working day in agriculture until the introduction of ploughing by hired tractors beginning in the mid-1960s was eleven to twelve hours, and villagers resorted to seasonal wage labour mainly in times of poor harvests.(82) Members of some unsuccessful units worked for wages more regularly.

Such an adaptation to the colonial political economy often required changes in food crops as well as the introduction of new cash crops. In particular, throughout much of central Sudan there was a general gradual shift away from labour-demanding millet crops to sorghum. Elsewhere, long-maturing sorghum varieties were replaced by quicker-maturing varieties in order to release labour earlier in the season for wage labour or work on cash crops. This kind of change was made by the Dinka cultivators in Renk District of Upper Nile Province after their traditional grazing lands were expropriated for Mechanised Farming Corporation schemes.(83) They were thereby able to replace their cattle-derived incomes by wage labour in weeding and sesame harvesting as well as in the later sorghum harvesting.

CONCLUSION

These alternative responses illustrate but do not exhaust the range of variation in responses to the colonial situation in Sudan by different communities, based on the internal characteristics and local conditions of those communities.(84) What is important in this context is the fact that the development of the colonial political economy, and the agricultural labour force in particular, proceeded in such a way that the manner and extent of incorporation of individual communities depended largely on their location and internal characteristics. Virtually all communities were penetrated, altered and partially incorporated into the expanding colonial markets, regardless of differences in internal characteristics. But complete disarticulation of village communities was not widespread, and where it did begin to happen it was not the inevitable outcome of irresistible forces unleased by colonialism, but was the result of the specific response of the community concerned to the pressures of incorporation into the colonial political economy.

This should not be surprising, for colonial labour policy in Sudan, as elsewhere in the continent, was specifically designed to avoid wholesale disarticulation of village economies. Colonial labour policy represented a departure from the historical process of primitive accumulation as it occurred in Europe, in which the disarticulation of village economies led to their dissolution and disappearance. Colonial capitalist expansion took place on the basis of absolute surplus value, preserving the production systems it found in operation and forcing them in various ways to provide surplus value through doing more work.(85) Instead of dissolving and replacing pre-capitalist productive systems, what was installed in the colonies were systems of semi-proletarianisation through extended primitive accumulation, in which the autonomy of the village economy was undermined and replaced by the new functions of reproducing the labour power of a cheap and flexible labour force. This requirement necessitated allowing village communities to respond to colonial development on the basis of the internal characteristics which were necessary to sustain them as sites of the reproduction of labour power. Members of these communities were to be incorporated into colonial markets as producers, but under conditions which entailed their exclusion from the market as consumers, except to the limited extent needed to ensure their participation as producers. The decisive requirement that the labour and cash crops they provided be cheap necessitated that they also produce most of their subsistence needs directly, outside the market. In this context then, the possibility of the wholesale disarticulation of village economies and the full proletarianisation of their agents was a threat to the colonial order. In fact, in Southern Africa, the area of greatest development of this form of self-reproducing labour force, disarticulation of village economies necessitated the institution of native reserves, pass laws and the other trappings of segregation and apartheid in order to halt the decay of community-based productive systems and to maintain this form of self-reproducing cheap labour force.(86)

A consequence of this condition of the colonial labour force was diversity of forms of incorporation which allowed continued reproduction of the organising social relations of specific communities. In Sudanese circumstances this meant a variety of patterns of labour migration. A number of patterns emerged to meet the demand for labour in the Gezira Scheme and the secondary irrigated schemes during the 1925-50 period. These patterns persisted after 1950 and other patterns emerged as new areas were incorporated into the labour market and new forms of capitalist agriculture developed and expanded.(87) In the colonial period and the first two decades following independence in 1956, the variety of patterns of incorporation of peasants and pastoralists into the agricultural wage labour force resulted in ethnically segmented markets. To the large extent that participation in labour markets was shaped by the traditional divisions of labour and related attitudes toward work of different communities, different tasks and patterns of work characterised different ethnic groups, and in turn came to be characterised by the ethnic identities of the groups participating most prominently in them. This pattern was deepened and reinforced in the 1950s and the first two decades of independence with the development of elaborate systems of wage labour recruitment in the rural areas.

This pattern of capitalist development based on the formation of a semi-proletarian agricultural labour force was effective in generating an important supply of cheap cotton to Britain during the colonial period and in maintaining an expanding apparatus of surplus value extraction well beyond independence. However, semi-proletarianisation is a contradictory and unstable process. In the long term, such a labour force is out-competed for good land by expanding capitalist production and increasingly loses its self-provisioning capacity as its fallow fields, grazing lands and forest sources of firewood and building materials disappear into capitalist farms. To maintain consumption levels, rural producers must turn to consumer markets - must become fully proletarianised - a transformation which requires increased wage incomes. Such a change of course threatens the cheap labour basis of an export-oriented economy and is not accepted by capital without a struggle.(88) The crisis which began to shake Sudanese agriculture - and the entire social order of the country - in the mid-1970s is a reflection of struggles over precisely this sort of transformation.

NOTES
1.   I have analysed the development of the agricultural labour force in Sudan from the British conquest through the 1970s in 'Agricultural Labour and Development in Sudan', unpublished PhD thesis, University of Connecticut, 1980 (hereafter, Thesis). For analyses of aspects of this development, see my 'The Formation of the Agricultural Labour Force in Sudan', Review of African Political Economy no.26 (1983); and Taisier Ali and Jay O'Brien, 'Labour, Community and Protest in Sudanese Agriculture', in J. Barker (ed.) The Politics of Agriculture in Tropical Africa (Sage Publications, Beverley Hills, California, 1984, in press). I have analysed capitalist agricultural development in Sudan in 'Sudan: An Arab Breadbasket?' MERIP Reports 99 (1981), pp. 20-6; 'The Political Economy of Capitalist Agriculture In the Central Rainlands of Sudan', Labour, Capital and Society vol.16, no.1 (1983); and, 'The Social Reproduction of Tenant Cultivators and Class Formation in the Gezira Scheme, Sudan' in B.Isaac (ed.), Research in Economic Anthropology, vol.6 (JAI Press, Greenwich, Connecticut, 1984, in press). The archival and field research upon which these analyses and the present paper are based was carried out in Sudan between 1974 and 1979 under grants from the Manpower Research Project of the Faculty of Economic and Social Studies, University of Khartoum (sponsored by Ford Foundation), and from the Economic and Social Research Council, National Council for Research, Khartoum.
2.   Tony Barnett, The Gezira Scheme: An Illusion of Development (Frank Cass, London, 1977), p. 4.
3.   Arthur Gaitskell, Gezira: A Story of Development in the Sudan (Faber and Faber, London, 1959); O'Brien, Thesis.
4.   P.M. Holt, The Mahdist State in the Sudan (Clarendon Press, Oxford, 1958); O'Brien, Thesis.
5.   The company which managed the first experimental station at Zeidab on the main Nile, the Sudan Plantations Syndicate (SPS), at one early point even went so far as to import Black Americans. See Gaitskell, Gezira.
6.   The government and the SPS renegotiated the original division of their combined shares between them to these proportions and extended the concession period to 25 years after the scheme had been operating several years. For details, see Gaitskell, Gezira.
7.   The actual distribution of tenancies was a good deal more complicated than can be indicated here. Gaitskell, Gezira, offers a general account. For greater detail and analysis, see G.M. Culwick, A Study of the Human Factor in the Gezira Scheme (Sudan Gezira Board, Barakat, Sudan, 1955; reprinted by SGB and Sudan Rural Television Project, 1975); O'Brien, Thesis.
8.   Gaitskell, Gezira, pp. 267-73; Adel Amin Beshai, Export Performance and Economic Development in Sudan 1900-1967 (Ithaca Press, London, 1976).

9.   Gaitskell, Gezira, p.270.

10. Barnett, Gezira Scheme, pp. 36-8.

11.   While the analysis here is primarily concerned with the formative 1925-50 period and its legacy for Sudan of British colonial labour policy, it should be noted that the development of the agricultural labour force in Sudan since 1898 has passed through three distinct phases, and by 1975 was entering a fourth phase. These phases are: 1) 1898-1925, when British strategic goals in occupying Sudan in order to defend British interests in Egypt and the Red Sea route to India dominated policy in all fields; 2) 1925-50, when securing a stable supply of labour to the Gezira Scheme, particularly in the context of a succession of crises due to cotton blights, the depression of the 1930s, and World War II, was the focus of all labour policy; 3) 1951-75, during which the expansion of large-scale agriculture was rapid and accompanied by the emergence of a highly segmented market for agricultural labour; and, 4) the present phase, dating from about 1975, characterised by the breakdown of barriers between segments of the labour market and consequent tendencies toward the equalisation of wage rates in agricultural labour. See O'Brien, Thesis; 'The Formation'.

12.   D.I./x/54166, dated 10 March 1928, for distribution to governors of provinces and all SPS Inspectors. Available in File 500-2 in the archives of the Sudan Gezira Board (SGB/A), Barakat, Sudan. The report includes brief 'historical and ethnological' descriptions of the main groups of immigrants.

13.   In this usage I follow Mark R. Duffield, 'Hausa and Fulani Settlement and the Development of Capitalism in Sudan: With Special Reference to Maiurno, Blue Nile Province', unpublished PhD thesis, University of Birmingham. Takari is a term by which these groups identify themselves. It derives from the name applied in the Hejaz to Black African pilgrims to Mecca. The term Fellata, from the Kanuri word for Fulani, is the name most commonly used for all people of West African origin by Arab Sudanese. In Sudan, however, the term has come to have pejorative connotations and is rejected by the people to whom it refers.

14. The alternative to wage labour was not starvation but temporary hardship. For discussion of traditional means of coping with famine and analysis of the impact on village economies of seasonal migration, see O'Brien, Thesis.

15.   Cf. Ahmed Abdel Hamid, The Agricultural Labour and the Gezira Scheme (Social Research Section, Social Development Department, Sudan Gezira Board, Musaad, Sudan, 1966, mimeographed).

16.   Report on the Finance. Administration and Condition of the Sudan (hereafter, GG/AR and year), submitted to the British Government by the Governor-General of Sudan, 1923, p. 19.

17. GG/AR 1922, p. 26.
18. These rates apply only to the northern and central parts of Sudan, the principal areas of development of labour markets. Rates in the far west and in the southern provinces were considerably lower. In the south, conscript labour - the main form of wage labour there until independence - was still paid only 1 to 2 pt per day throughout the 1940s and into the early 1950s. On this subject, and for additional information on wage rates for the colonial period, see Files C.S. SCR.C.1/1 and C.S. SCR./37.C.1/3 of the Civil Secretary's correspondence in the archives of the Department of Labour (DLA), Khartoum. Also, see DLA, File C.S. SCR/37.C.1. On wages in the south, see Conrad C. Reining, The Zande Scheme (Northwestern University Press, Evanston, Illinois, 1966).
19. SGB/A, File 124, 'Cotton Pickers "Labour"', GP/37/C/1.
20. Ibid. The SPS responded to this circular in characteristic fashion. A letter from the Manager to the Governor expressed alarm at the generosity of these terms, particularly for semi-skilled labour, and complained about the local labour recruiting activities of the military as a threat to the stability of wage rates and labour supply in the Gezira. See SGB/A, File 124, No. 5146, 5 November 1940.
21. See G.A. Balamoan, Migration Policies in the Anglo-Egyptian Sudan 1884-1956 (Harvard University Center for Population Studies, Cambridge, Massachusetts, 1976); J.S. Birks, Across the Savannas to Mecca: The Overland Pilgrimage Route from West Africa (Hurst, London, 1978); Culwick, Human Factor; Abdel Hamid, Agricultural Labour.
22. The only thorough and detailed studies of these important issues available are Duffield's PhD thesis, 'Hausa and Fulani Settlement', and his book based on it, Maiurno: Capitalism and Rural Life in Sudan (Ithaca Press, London, 1981). Duffield makes a complete break with previous interpretations and convincingly refutes the prevailing misconception of the nature of Takari settlement and socioeconomic integration in Sudan. Various aspects of Takari settlement in Sudan are treated by Duffield in 'Fulani Mahdism and Revisionism in Sudan: "Hijra" or Compromise with Colonialism' (Paper presented at the Third International Conference on the Bilad al-Sudan: Tradition and Adaptation, Khartoum, November, 1977); Peripheral Capitalism and the Social Relations of Agricultural Production in Maiurno near Sennar (Economic and Social Research Council, Khartoum, Bulletin 66, 1978); 'Threat or Scapegoat?' Sudanow, vol.4, no.3, (1979), pp. 40-2; 'Transformation and Contradictions: Hausa Settlement in the Towns of Northern Sudan' in V. Pons (ed.), Urbanization and Urban Life in the Sudan (Department of Sociology and Social Anthropology, University of Hull, 1980), pp. 209-46. The discussion of Takari settlement in this chapter relies heavily on Duffield's work, both published and unpublished.

23.   See 'Umar al-Naqar, The Pilgrimage Tradition in West
Africa (Khartoum University Press, Khartoum, 1972).
     24.   The information in the next three paragraphs is taken
from Duffield, 'Hausa and Fulani Settlement'.
     25.   See Duffield, 'Fulani Mahdism'.
     26.   See BNP, 1/31/244, in National Records Office (NRO),
Khartoum.
     27.   NRO, BNP, 1/25/175.
     28.   NRO, BNP, 1/25/177.
     29.   Dar, meaning homeland, was generally used in
combination with the name of a tribe in pre-colonial Sudan to
refer to the area in which the tribe lived, as in Dar Fur.
Under British rule, the system of Native Administration used
the vaguely defined traditional tribal dars as a basis for
sharply   demarcated   territories   which   became   units of
administration through government-appointed sheikhs.
     30.   NRO, CS, 66/8/57.
     31.   SGB/A, File 124, DC/SR/9.C.B., 12 February 1935.
     32.   See SGB/A, File 124.
     33.   Kadankas were used in indigenous Sudanese irrigated
agriculture along the Nile where the soils were heavy and
remained wet during weeding periods, but little seasonal labour
came to Gezira from this source. See Duffield, 'Hausa and
Fulani Settlement', chap. 3; O'Brien, Thesis.
     34.   The term 'Westerners' is used very imprecisely and
misleadingly in Sudan, sometimes to refer to people from
Sudan's western provinces in contrast to 'Fellata' who came
from the countries west of Sudan. Sometimes the term is
broadened   to include immigrants from what is now Chad,
reflecting similarities of patterns of migration and work. At
yet other times all these categories are lumped together under
the appellation of 'Westerners'. I use the term in this last
sense in contexts where it does not obscure important
differences between the groups thus classed together. Otherwise
I use the precise designations which are relevant to specific
cases.
     35.   SGB/A, File 142 (2 vols.), 'Settlement of
Westerners', C.G.A./SGR/91.C.10, 24 October 1933.
     36.   See SGB/A, File 142, vol. I.
     37.   See Ellen Gruenbaum, 'Health Services, Health and
Development in Sudan: The Impact of the Gezira Irrigated
Scheme', unpublished PhD thesis, University of Connecticut,
1982.
     38.   SGB/A, File 142, DCG/91.C.S., 27 March 1934.
     39.   SGB/A File 142, vol. I.
     40.   The chief inconsistency in ethnic identification was
one which is common in Sudan, and has to do with the variety of
terms used to refer to the Takari. 'Fellata', though properly
only used to refer to the Fulani, appears to have been used to
refer to all West African immigrants, including the Hausa and
sometimes even Chadians, in some cases in these returns,

especially for Turabi Group. On the other hand, since the majority of Fulani speak the Hausa language, they are sometimes identified ethnically as Hausa. Such an identification may also have been made in the census.

41. Culwick, Human Factor, p. 11.

42. SGB/A, File 142, 15 November 1933. The names used are proposed new sites for settler villages.

43. SGB/A, File 142, 15 November 1933.

44. Abdel Hamid, Agricultural Labour.

45. See Culwick, Human Factor; and, for the New Halfa Scheme, Gunnar M. Sorbo, How to Survive Development: The Story of New Halfa (Development Studies and Research Centre, University of Khartoum, Monograph 6, 1977).

46. Cf. Culwick, Human Factor.

47. See Barnett, Gezira Scheme.

48. Culwick, Human Factor, p. 12.

49. For an analysis of this problem and its solution, see O'Brien, 'Social Reproduction of Tenant Cultivators'.

50. For an analysis of the Nationality Act and its consequences for the Takari community in Sudan and their place in the labour force, see Duffield, 'Hausa and Fulani Settlement'. This law did not result in the immediate eviction of all Takari tenants. Rather, it was agreed that any Takari tenant who died or retired would not be replaced by a family member, but by a 'Sudanese'.

51. See The Laws of Sudan, in the Sudan Library (SLA) at the University of Khartoum.

52. World Bank, Sudan Agriculture Sector Review (Washington, D.C.: World Bank, 1978), Annex VIII.

53. GG/AR 1923.

54. Ibid., p. 47.

55. See O'Brien, Thesis.

56. Duffield, 'Hausa and Fulani Settlement', Chapter 1.

57. Abdel Ghaffar M. Ahmed, Shaykhs and Followers: Political Struggle in the Rufa'a al-Hoi Nazirate in the Sudan (Khartoum University Press, Khartoum, 1974), p. 57.

58. O'Brien, Thesis; 'Seasonal Labor Migration'.

59. These minutes and the minutes of other meetings of the Labour Board are available in an unnumbered file in SGB/A, hereafter referred to as MMLB.

60. MMLB, p. 2.

61. Ibid., p. 3.

62. See the correspondence between British Officials in the south and the central government in Khartoum dealing with the legal status and other aspects of the use of conscripted labour in the south in DLA, Files C.S. SCR.C.1/1 and C.S. SCR/37.C.1. I discuss this correspondence, the use of conscript labour in Sudan, and the British administration's attitudes toward the provisions of the ILC - including the emphasis on the notion of 'expediency' - in Thesis.

63.   In a letter to the Governor of Blue Nile Province dated 15 February 1932, the Manager of the SPS listed figures for drafted labour brought to Turabi Group which showed only 736 of 2088 imported still working one week after their arrival (SGB/A, File 124, No. 664). Experiences with conscripted labour were evaluated in a series of correspondence in 1931 and 1932 contained in File 124. In particular, see letters numbered 612, 664, and 4639 · from the Manager of the SPS to the Governor of Blue Nile Province.

64.   SGB/A, File 124, No. 4639, 12 December 1932.

65.   SGB/A, File 124, BNP/B/91.C.13., 19 January 1933.

66.   A government circular, SGB/A, File 124, TM/42/-2/4, dated 22 January 1933, announced a trial reduction of rail fares for picking labour from selected staions to the Gezira of one half the fourth class fare for the picking season.

67.   Cf. Barnett, Gezira Scheme.

68.   Gaitskell, Gezira, p. 229.

69.   See for example the statement by the Governor of Blue Nile Province in 1934, in which he states that the labour supply for that picking season was generally adequate and that no more than 300 'imported labourers' will be required (SGB/A, File 124, BNP/37.B.1, 11 January 1934). In the context of a labour supply which was largely migrant, including substantial numbers imported through government and SPS efforts, the term 'imported labourers' can only have a special esoteric meaning here.

70.   MMLB, p. 3. This practice was still in force in the 1970s. See Mohamed El Awad Galal-el-din, Population Dynamics and Socio-Economic Development in Rural Sudan (Development Studies and Research Centre, University of Khartoum, 1978, mimeographed).

71.   Gaitskell, Gezira.

72.   See Culwick, Human Factor; Abdel Hamid, Agricultural Labour.

73.   Culwick, Human Factor.

74.   O'Brien, Thesis, 'Capitalist Agriculture in the Central Rainlands'.

75.   Department of Statistics, Sudan Government, Survey of Labour Conditions in Gezira (Sudan Government, Khartoum, 1959). Until 1974 Blue Nile Province included the present White Nile and Gezira Provinces.

76.   See Duffield, 'Hausa and Fulani Settlement'; O'Brien, Thesis; Ali and O'Brien, 'Labor'.

77.   Mohamed El Awad Galal-el-din, The Human Factor in the Rahad Project Area: Phase I. Results of Population and Socio-Economic Survey (Ministry of Agriculture, Khartoum, 1975).

78.   See Jay L. Spaulding, 'Farmers, Herdsmen and the State in Rainland Sinnar', Journal of African History vol. 20, no. 3 (1979), pp. 329-47; O'Brien, Thesis.

79.   Culwick, Human Factor; Abdel Hamid, Agricultural Labour.

80.   Cf. A.V. Chayanov, The Theory of Peasant Economy (Dorsey Press, Homewood, Illinois, 1966).

81.   For examples, see O'Brien, Thesis.

82.   Ibid.; Ali and O'Brien, 'Labor'.

83.   See Khalil Abdalla el Medani, 'The Impact of Economic Development on the Ethnic Groups Inhabiting Al-Renk Region of the Upper Nile Province', unpublished MSc thesis, University of Khartoum, 1978.

84.   Greater detail about these different responses is provided for specific communities in the case studies discussed in O'Brien, Thesis, and summarised in Ali and O'Brien, 'Labor'.

85.   Cf. Karl Marx, Capital (International Publishers, New York, 1967), vol. 1.

86.   Cf. Harold Wolpe, 'Capitalism and Cheap Labour Power in South Africa', Economy and Society, vol.1, no.4 (1972).

87.   These various patterns and the segmentation of the agricultural labour force which resulted from their diversity are examined in detail in O'Brien, Thesis. For discussion of the crisis in this segmentation of the labour force, and in Sudanese agriculture generally, which emerged in the mid-1970s, see also O'Brien, 'Arab Breadbasket?'; 'The Formation'; Capitalist Agriculture'; Ali and O'Brien, 'Labor'.

88.   Cf. Alain de Janvry, The Agrarian Question and Reformism in Lain America (Johns Hopkins University Press, Baltimore, 1981).

Chapter Seven

POVERTY, PROLETARIANISATION AND THE PRODUCTION OF UNEVEN
DEVELOPMENT: A KENYAN VILLAGE

Phil O'Keefe

Soil erosion is a matter of general concern in Kenya. It is
expressed by everyone, from peasant farmers to the President,
and the widespread belief is that 'erosion removes soil
corresponding to one lorry-load from each acre every year'.
This loss has immense repercussions, not the least of these
being the need to purchase chemical nutrients to replace those
washed away. The process is not continuous, but in years of
extreme weather conditions, such as high rainfall after long
drought, the effects can become catastrophic.

The problem of soil erosion is not of course confined to
Kenya, and neither is it simply the result of climatic and
edaphic conditions. Around the world, natural processes wash
away about 9.3 billion tons of soil each year, but total soil
erosion (i.e not just from natural processes) is treble this
volume. People constantly intervene in nature and thereby
produce a new nature, new rates of erosion. Agriculture is an
obvious intervention that allows the controlled production of
food and non-food crops in settled arable communities, and
allows also the growth of urban settlements on the basis of
agricultural surpluses. But the new nature, produced by people
to permit agriculture, has additional implications; the removal
of vegetation and land clearance to permit cultivation
increases soil erosion to some 24 billion tons a year.(1)

The solution to soil erosion does not lie in the technical
design of conservation works, because there is no technical
difficulty in the construction of terraces. The problem is the
lack of labour time available. The FAO has calculated the
working time necessary to construct soil conservation measures:

On a terrace with a 30 per cent slope the construction of
a 3.5 metre-wide bench terrace implies the excavation and
refill of 483 cubic metres per hectare, the task
representing approximately 400 man-days, not including the
effort required for the construction of sheltered
evacuation canals, soil improvement and fertiliser.(2)

Over the past twenty years, the single most important lesson to be learnt about African peasant production systems is that they suffer a periodic, but critical, labour shortage. It is argued in this chapter that a main cause of this shortage, and of the deepening rural poverty that results, is the migration of male population and its incomplete or partial proletarianisation in urban areas.

SOIL EROSION - A VILLAGE PROBLEM?

In reviewing the social conditions that surround the issue of soil erosion in Kenya - specifically the serious lack of labour - the general tendencies of underdevelopment have been identified.(3) The first approximation of the cycles of underdevelopment is summarised by the interrelationships between (i) the high population density of the area (ii) the small size of landholdings (iii) the tendency towards land fragmentation, and (iv) the outmigration of males in search of wage employment. Such an approximation is, however, a gross over-simplification. A more detailed understanding is possible only by starting from an analysis of the material condition of the population.

In a village, which we may call Gakarara, in the Central Province of Kenya, the farm units were dispersed, with each male-headed household living on its own farmholding. These were on steep hillslopes, but the terracing on them was deteriorating and the lack of labour made it impossible to promote effective terracing. The material deprivation of the people may be judged by the nutritional status of its children. In Gakarara, 27 per cent of children under the age of three years were at or below 80 per cent of the median weight-for-age figure given as a basis for comparison by the World Health Organisation. Gakarara had a level of malnutrition that compared with the more arid areas of eastern Kenya. Such findings were clearly indicative of stress in an area of high agricultural potential. An understanding of the processes underlying this phenomenon clearly requires a more comprehensive interpretation.

The exploration of Gakarara's underdevelopment in the 1970s should begin with the advent of the cash economy during the colonial period. The imposition of tax on the pre-capitalist mode of production, originally by the colonial administration but continued after independence, required access to the monetary economy. This was only possible by selling cash crops or through male migration. As access to high value crop markets, especially coffee, was restricted, the only real option was male migration and integration into the metropolitan economy. By the early 1970s, over 30 per cent of male heads of household were permanently absent from the farms. In fact, very few males between the ages of 25-49 remained in the village.

Male migration for urban employment was essentially an aspect of the 'Dick Whittington' syndrome, a search for streets paved with gold. But if employment was found, wages were so low that only infrequent return visits were made to the rural area. Consequently, second households were frequently established in the urban areas severely increasing the demands on the low wage. The demands of the second households resulted in very low levels of remittances to the rural areas. Depressed urban wages resulted in a subsistence existence for male migrants in the city and exacerbated rural underdevelopment.

Three groups dominated the population in rural areas: old men, women and children. The old men did not make a significant contribution to the labour budget. More importantly, child labour decreased because of the growing availability of primary education. The burden of labour inevitably fell upon the women.

For historical reasons, especially the decline in ethnic warfare and the opportunities to open new land, the role of women in the social division of labour has expanded significantly since the 1940s. Male migration accelerated that expansion so much that, by the early 1970s, women were responsible for the whole range of production and reproduction activities: fields, animals and the home. In itself this was an onerous burden, further exacerbated by the disappearance of male and child labour and the maintenance of strong relics of patriarchal power structures governing decision making. Women were compelled to assume a major share of the labour burden in the peasant sector under increasingly constrained circumstances. Additionally, they faced the problems of limited market access, low prices for any cash crop they managed to produce, and the requirement to pay tax.

The lack of cash income for basic household requirements also forced women to seek wage employment. The only employment available in any proximity to the village was piece-rate agricultural work. This work on the large cash-crop 'European' farms required labour at precisely the times that labour was required for peasant farming activities. Consequently, labour was denied to the peasant sector at crucial periods, a denial that constrained effective cash cropping even when prices and market conditions were favourable. The labour squeeze even affected subsistence farming. This is illustrated by the fact that women perceived drought during years of average or above average rainfall. The drought resulted from late planting and thus low water availability for germination and early plant growth. The drought was labour-induced, not a meteorological event; it was certainly not a 'natural' disaster, unless one accepts capitalism as natural.(4) In addition, the lack of labour to maintain terrace soil increased the loss through erosion. Such a situation produced increasing pressure on the farmers in which not only the cash crop base but also the subsistence base was eroded. Food production declined requiring an increased reliance on commercial food. Such reliance required further cash, but cash was already a critical problem.

The result was the collapse of the production system.

It is worth considering soil erosion in more detail as it exemplifies these processes of heightened vulnerability. Terracing has been a traditional practice in Africa, not so much to control erosion but to create microcatchment areas to sustain production. Irrespective of enduse, soil erosion control is a technology well understood by the peasantry. However, the lack of labour, which forces the peasantry from cash cropping to subsistence and then to a deteriorating subsistence production system, has a severe impact on reproduction. Terraces are usually built and maintained during the 'slack' period between planting and harvesting. As more time is devoted to late planting efforts and horticultural 'rescue' operations to ensure minimal crop production, labour is withdrawn from this vital activity. Terraces collapse and the regenerative qualities of the soil are lost. Social reproduction is threatened by a 'man-made' process of desertification, a process that completes the spiral into underdevelopment.

The critical question is what strategies were available to the peasants to avoid the crisis? Ten years ago, the answer appeared to be that there were no options available to the peasantry, that the landscape would be destroyed. That answer was one-sided and assumed that capital had a rigid interest. Such a scenario is undoubtedly correct in instances where the peasantry is forcibly held to specific sites under the constraints outlined above. The environmental consequences of the Bantustan policy of the apartheid regime in South Africa clearly demonstrates this process. But, what of the Kenyan case, where capitalism does not require such rigid population control?

The peasants had one significant material asset besides their labour, and that asset was land. Land was alienable; it had changed from being a communally-held asset under customary control to being an individual possession under statutory law. The status of capitalism ensured that land could be bought, sold, and most significantly, accumulated. As a commodity, it could be used as a security against which to borrow money. Land entered the market at a rapid pace. Both the volume and velocity of land transactions, with land sometimes changing hands as frequently as twice a year, overwhelmed the bureaucracy. Land was used as security but, given the difficulties of sustainable production, it is not surprising that debt repayment schedules were not met. As more peasant households experienced the loss of their land, land ownership became more concentrated, and a landscape of larger farms rather than smallholdings was created. These mechanised farms, employing a small rural work force, represent the production of a new 'nature' under new relations of capitalist production.

What of the peasantry? They sought new holdings by expanding into the forest zone further up the environmental gradient or moved out to arid lands in the east of the Rift

Valley. This strategy, however, is only viable as long as the land frontier remains open. Even so, the problems of soil erosion and drought are both heightened in the high and low zones, respectively, of the environmental gradient. The process of human response places marginal people on marginal land.

For those households for which rural-to-rural migration is impossible there is the inexorable drift to the city, to the place where the male migrant resides. But there the final scene in this particular act unfolds. The urban wage which was insufficient to allow adequate remittances to the rural area cannot support the new migrants in the urban area. Besides the problem of supporting two households (the original urban household plus new migrants), there are structural reasons, under capitalism, why the wage level will not rise.

Consider the wage bundle. It should have four major elements to it in order to guarantee social production and reproduction. Firstly, the wage must support the subsistence of the worker, for without fit workers, capital is vulnerable to competition from other capitals by allowing its rate of profit to fall below the average rate. Secondly, the wage must cover the costs of social reproduction, or there will not be a new generation of workers for capital to exploit. Capital successfully uses partriarchal structures to avoid paying for household labour, i.e., to avoid the real costs of social reproduction, or patriarchal structures in a subordinate mode of production as in Gakarara. Thirdly, the wage bundle should include a sum of money that covers the replacement costs for workers' equipment which is consumed in the production process. And finally, the wage bundle contains an element that reflects the successful struggle of labour against capital, the historical-moral component that organised workers have won back from capital.

The urban wage in Kenya does not reflect these elements of the wage bundle. The historical-moral component is absent because there is no successful organisation of labour. In fact, as in most developing countries that follow a capitalist model of development, wage increases lag significantly behind reproduction costs. Moreover, there is no sum for the replacement cost of tools, for the Kenyan urban-industrial complex is built upon unskilled labour, not a tradition of craft. Thirdly, and most importantly, capital does not pay the costs of the reproduction of labour power. These costs are foisted on the rural population of Kenya. Until the peasant system collapses, as in Gakarara, capital can continue to exploit a system under which labour power is produced freely to capital. There is no wage bundle. All the worker receives is subsistence.

There are several questions that emerge from this discussion which require more analysis. It might first be asked why no militant labour organising has emerged from these conditions. Obviously there are many underlying and interconnected reasons, but the one which is most compelling is the fact that there are at least two million other households in the rural periphery beyond Gakarara that could enter the modern wage market. This potential exerts a downward pressure on wages. The current urban population is, in essence, a massive incipient proletariat always on the brink of being pushed back into the reserve army of labour. Under such conditions, and with no rural landholding to support them, it is not surprising that there is little labour militancy in Kenya; as there is little militancy among the Gastarbeiter, the 'guest workers', in developed countries. Secondly, are these conditions of downward pressure on wages attractive for capital accumulation? The answer is a qualified 'yes', reflecting the rate of profit attainable in a sub-metropolitan production centre, such as Kenya, and the growing need for capital to produce in low wage-rate areas. The qualification, however, reflects the uncertainty felt by transnationals as to how domestic capital may respond to opposition from nationalist and class fractions. Thirdly, what are the implications of these developments for the urbanisation process in Kenya? Frankly the prospects are bleak. Given the nature of transition to capitalism and the non-development of a working class, the process of urbanisation is uncontrolled. With the land frontier closing in the next decade, it would not be unreasonable to project Nairobi (current population 1 million) as a city of 4 million by the year 2000.

DEVELOPMENT IN KENYA

The low level of labour militancy, the comparative attraction of Kenya as an investment opportunity for international capital and the rapid growth of urbanisation have serious implications for development in Kenya. Despite a crescendo of statements that commit the Kenyan state to development, there has been increasing difficulty in matching the progress experienced in the decade after Independence. During 1964-73, real GDP grew at an average rate of 6.6 per cent per year, and per capita GDP rose at an average rate of nearly 3 per cent. More recently, Kenya's vulnerability to external events, lower levels of agricultural productivity and the political support for private accumulation and luxury consumption have combined to limit the access of wananchi (citizens) to economic benefits.

During the period 1974-80 the rate of growth of GDP fell to an average of 4.6 per cent annually, and to below 3 per cent in 1981. In five of the last eight years the growth of per capita income has in fact been negative. The level of per capita income, estimated at US $420 per annum, overstates average living standards because of the cumulative devaluation of the currency by 24 per cent in 1981 and a rate of increase of consumer prices of about 20 per cent. This is especially

Kenya

Table 7.1: Kenya: Gross Domestic Product By Sector, 1964-80

Sector	Share Of Total GDP* 1964	1974	1980**	Growth Rate *** 1964-73	1974-80
Total GDP*	100.0	100.0	100.0	6.6	4.7
Private	75.9	74.4	72.9	-	-
Public	24.1	25.6	27.1	-	-
Agriculture	39.8	35.4	32.6	4.7	4.2
Private	39.5	35.0	32.2	-	-
Public	0.3	0.4	0.4	-	-
Manufacturing	10.4	12.7	13.3	8.4	6.2
Private	8.8	10.6	10.5	-	-
Public	1.6	2.1	2.8	-	-
Mining and Quarrying	0.5	0.3	0.3	10.5	6.7
Construction	3.8	6.0	6.1	7.3	3.3
Electricity and Water	2.1	1.7	2.1	6.2	7.3
Government Services	12.9	14.6	14.7	9.8	6.2
Other	30.6	29.4	31.0	6.5	4.9

Notes: *   At factor cost and current prices.
         **   Preliminary.
         *** 1964-73 growth rates at constant 1964 prices;
              1974-80 growth rates at constant 1976 prices.

Source: Central Bureau of Statistics, Economic Survey 1975,
         1981; Statistical Abstract, 1980; National Accounts
         Companion Volume, 1979.

true for those in rural areas; in the larger urban areas, wage employees received percentage increases in average earnings that compared favourably with the rise of consumer prices. If GDP per capita figures were to be recalculated, using the IMF norms, the levels of recent years would be substantially reduced.(5)

The marked slowdown has occurred despite an increase in both internal and external resources that have become available since Independence. The overall increase in the share of investment in GDP has been made possible by a significant increase in the net inflow of resources from external sources. One quarter of Kenya's overall investment in the period 1974-80 has been financed by net external flows. Disbursements of development assistance have averaged nearly US $250 million per year, and the annual level of disbursement has been increasing by some 20 per cent per year. Private investment significantly exceeds public investment and, as much of this private investment is governed or supported by overseas capital, the vulnerability of the economy has to that extent increased.

Table 7.1 shows that every major sector of the economy has shared in the general slowdown of activity since the early 1970s. But some sectors have performed better than others and the economy has undergone a slow and steady structural transformation. The share of agriculture in GDP has declined from 39.8 per cent in 1964 to 32.6 per cent in 1980. Agriculture's share of wage employment (Table 7.2) declined more rapidly from 37.0 per cent to 23.0 per cent during the same period. Manufacturing has undergone a slow expansion since Independence from 13.3 per cent of GDP to 14 per cent in 1980. The public sector has increased its share of wage employment from 31.4 per cent of the total, in 1964, to 46.9 per cent, in 1980, but, over the same period, only increased its share of GDP by 3 percentage points. Kenya's foreign reserves which were comparatively healthy have fallen, and are now sufficient for only two months imports. With the declining contribution of agriculture, the inability to develop manufactured exports, the continued subsidisation of the urban areas, the rising foreign debt and the continuing balance of payments difficulties, Kenya faces a future of extreme uncertainty.

EMPLOYMENT

The reduced growth rate in the key sectors of the Kenyan economy has affected the overall growth rate of wage employment. Table 7.2 indicates that wage employment grew at an annual rate of 3.9 per cent during 1964-74, but only 3.3 per cent during 1974-80. Only 15.2 per cent of the estimated labour force was engaged in wage employment of any type in 1980.

Kenya's potential labour force is expected to rise from 6.1 million to 15.7 million by the end of the century. Only a

Table 7.2: Kenya: Wage Employment By Sector, 1964-80

Sector	Share Of Total Wage Employment			Growth Rate	
	1964	1974	1980*	1964-74	1974-80
Total	100.0	100.0	100.0	3.9	3.3
Private	68.7	60.0	53.1	2.5	1.2
Public	31.4	40.0	46.9	6.4	6.1
Agriculture	37.0	31.6	23.0	2.3	-2.0
Private	-	25.9	17.2	-	-3.6
Public	-	5.7	5.9	-	3.7
Manufacturing	-	12.3	14.0	-	5.7
Private	8.9	9.9	11.1	4.9	5.3
Public	-	2.4	3.0	-	7.3
Other	-	56.1	62.9	-	5.3
Private	-	24.3	24.9	-	3.7
Public	-	31.8	38.0	-	6.4
Male	86.1	85.3	82.4	4.0	2.7
Female	13.9	14.7	17.6	4.4	6.5
Total Wage Employment (000)	563.6	826.3	1,005.8	3.9	3.3
Potential Labour Force (000)**	3,675	5,176	6,601	3.5	4.1
Percent in Wage Employment	15.3	16.0	15.2	-	-

Notes: *   Preliminary.
         ** Estimate based on 85 per cent participation
             rate among those aged 15-59.

Source: Central Bureau of Statistics, Economic Survey 1968,
         1976, 1981. Statistical Abstract 1968, 1976, 1980.

small proportion of this population can expect to find employment in the modern sector. Even if the growth rate of employment in the modern sector rises to 6 per cent per annum, the remainder of the labour force, some 12 million people, will still be left to find employment. Given that the figures of employment in the modern sector include state employees, who contribute insignificantly at the margin to the growth of GDP, as well as personal servants and guards, it seems that the major opportunities will lie in the manufacturing sector. Much of the investment for this sector is expected to be external but such investment has certain consequences. Firstly, foreign enterprises are normally more profitable than indigenous enterprises because they are generally protected from and stifle local competition. Secondly, foreign enterprises, through the repatriation of profit, place an increasing burden on the balance of payments. Thirdly, foreign enterprises generate comparatively little employment, perhaps because they are capital intensive. Although there is considerable debate (6) about the last point, the conclusion which emerges is that foreign firms are not necessarily more capital intensive than local firms but, due to the supervisory skills in such transnational firms, they use semi-skilled labour more successfully than local firms. Clearly, however, this does not provide employment opportunity for 12 million people.

Major foreign companies have benefitted from the protectionist policies of the Kenyan government. But, more importantly, so have senior politicians and civil servants, both active and retired, who derive substantial personal gain from such enterprises. Among foreign companies with substantial local shareholdings, 80 per cent have relatively unconstrained access to their chosen markets; only 56 per cent of foreign companies without local shareholdings have such access. Although the foreign companies and the political managerial elite profit by such relationships, there is much documentary evidence to suggest that the Kenyan nation and even the local entrepreneurial class do not.

INCOME DISTRIBUTION

The most striking aspect of Kenyan income distribution is the urban-rural disparity. This is illustrated in Table 7.3. The urban sector is small (10 per cent of the total population) but extremely well rewarded (earning some 43 per cent of national income). The rural population, including the landless, account for 90 per cent of the population and about 57 per cent of national income.

This rural-urban disparity is not only found in respect of income but is true also of employment, education, nutrition and fertility. In 1972, it was estimated that 60 per cent of the wages paid in the formal sector, throughout the country, and

Kenya

Table 7.3: Kenya: Income Distribution and Poverty, 1974 (%)

Category	Population	Income	* % in Poverty	Poor Pop.
Rural	90.2	57.2	32.2	98.5
Smallholders	72.3	39.0	28.9	71.0
Large Farm Squatters	4.2	2.2	33.3	4.8
Landless With Poor Occupations	2.9	1.7	50.0	5.0
Landless With Good Occupations	1.7	6.5	-	-
'Gap' Farmers	1.9	5.0	-	-
Large Farmers	0.1	1.1	-	-
Pure Pastoralists	5.1	1.0	84.8	14.6
Pastoralists Who Farm	0.5	0.3	33.3	0.6
Migrants (To Semi-Arid Lands)	1.4	0.4	55.0	2.6
Urban	9.8	42.8	4.3	1.5
Nairobi	4.9	23.9	2.9	0.5
Other	4.9	18.9	5.7	1.0
Total (Percent)	100.0	100.0	29.4	100.0

Note: *   Percentage below household poverty line varies by
            household size and local living costs. Poverty is
            defined in terms of requirements to provide a minimum
            nutritional level with a small allowance for   other
            necessities.

Source: Adapted from Collier and Lal, Poverty and Growth in
         Kenya, IBRD, 1980. Livingstone, Rural Development,
         Employment and Incomes in Kenya, ILO, 1981.

probably a third of all personal income in Kenya, was paid in Nairobi and Mombasa. Over 80 per cent of men and 50 per cent of women in urban areas have wage employment, but only 15 and 3 per cent, respectively, in the rural areas. The disparities in educational opportunities are reflected in examination results, although this simple distinction between urban and rural is blurred by a gender bias - rural males do slightly better than urban females indicating a significant level of sexual discrimination in the quality of education. The urban areas have a greater proportion of children in the higher nutritional levels (as measured by weight for age), fewer stunted children (which would indicate long term nutritional deprivation) but, not surprisingly, a greater number of children in the wasted category which would suggest shorter term deprivation, especially when there were insufficient funds to buy food. Fertility declines rapidly with urbanisation but, as many women return to the rural areas, the overall demographic impact of this is unclear.

Table 7.3 also contains details of income distribution in Kenya. Existing data indicates that nearly one-third of the rural population falls beneath a poverty line based on expenditure required to maintain a minimum nutritional level. Rural areas contain 98 per cent of the poor under this definition. In the urban areas, those beneath the poverty line include the unemployed and the working poor. (There is much discussion on urban unemployment and underemployment: estimates vary from 6.4 to 10 per cent for males and 6.7 to 20 per cent for females). A disproportionately ranged share of these poor are represented by young, unskilled males seeking wage employment. With the acceleration of urbanisation, and a high rate of urban household formation, urban poverty will increase.

Within the rural areas, poverty exists for all but the large farmers and the wage employed, representing 2 and 1.7 per cent of the total population respectively. The highest proportions of the poverty stricken live in the arid and semi-arid areas where the pastoralists, who make up 5 per cent of the Kenyan population, are situated: 85 per cent of this population falls beneath the poverty line. But smallholders and squatters in the medium and high potential lands, who account for more than three-quarters of Kenya's population and a greater proportion of the poor, are the group who suffer most and have the greatest constraints. With details of current income distribution in mind, it is worth considering the 'resource base'. For, with the decline in manufacturing and limited opportunities for urban employment, that is where the majority of the population will be.

With details of current income distribution in mind, it is worth considering the 'resource base' of the Kenyan economy. The majority of Kenyans live in the rural areas and depend on some type of agricultural activity for income. Unfortunately, approximately 46 million of Kenya's 57 million hectares are unsuitable for agriculture or intensive animal husbandry; much of this area could be used as commercial rangeland but only if the peasants and pastoralists were removed. But to where? Of the remaining 20 per cent of land, much is already under cultivation by smallholders.

During the late 1960s and early 1970s, population growth was accommodated by heavy rural to rural migration towards the more marginal areas. The spatial limits of that migration have now been reached since it is impossible to farm areas where the probability of drought exceeds 40 per cent. In the more densely populated areas, available land per capita will fall from 0.35 of a hectare in 1979 to 0.24 of a hectare in 1989. By the end of the decade, only 0.5 hectares per person of medium potential land will be available. Only by cutting down forests, which have other uses, and massive irrigation, at a cost of some US $7,000 per hectare, will more land be made available. But even with more land available, what would be the lot of the small farmer?

SMALLHOLDER DEVELOPMENT - THE UNSECURED FUTURE

Smallholder farmers, the peasantry, are considered to be the development backbone of the Kenyan economy. To assess their viability, it is necessary to consider their political economy.(7) Firstly, as noted earlier, smallholders account for three-quarters of the Kenyan population. In most areas, however, low income smallholders (who account for 44 per cent of the smallholder population) depend on off-farm sources for more than half of their income. In many senses, therefore, it is wrong to address this group as 'farmers' because their production relations more clearly reflect those of a lumpen rural proletariat-cum-peasantry, functioning as a labour pool for more wealthy enterprises. Farming, for these people, could almost be viewed as a supplementary exercise - but this group is one-quarter of the total population. Moreover, access to off-farm income is increasingly limited because of the general economic recession and the consolidation of the informal sector into modern capitalised industry. Opportunities are limited therefore.

Secondly, depending where smallholders are placed on the ecological gradient, they have access to different cash crop production systems. On the higher slopes, tea and coffee predominate while cotton dominates the lower slopes. Tea and coffee provide a favourable return while cotton does not. Income, therefore, relates to ecological niche and it is the tea and coffee niches that are firmly occupied. Given that farmers in cotton production systems, with medium and large farms, are disadvantaged, then the smallholder population under stress is some 57 per cent (44 per cent who rely chiefly on off-farm income and the 13 per cent who, although they have large or medium farms, are located in the cotton belt).

Thirdly, there are significant differences between smallholders east of the Rift Valley and those to the west. Central Province, which is the most wealthy and has the highest level of consumption, dominates this picture irrespective of ecological zone. Infrastructure is more highly developed east of the Rift and this area remains the de facto seat of political influence. If, for the sake of argument, the medium and large tea and coffee zone producers west of the Rift Valley are taken as a disenfranchised group, in terms of their access to further agricultural development, then another 9 per cent of the smallholder population are not likely to back current government initiatives to revitalise the economy. Some 66 per cent of the smallholder population has questionable allegiance, under current conditions, to spear-heading development.

Fourthly, what land is available is increasingly consolidated. In Central Province, the core region of Kenya, small and medium landholders decreased their overall share of holdings by 30.3 and 6.2 per cent respectively while larger landholders increased their share by 22.3 per cent between 1961 and 1974. Even in the core region, such continued land accumulation will destroy the basis for the transition to a yeoman, smallholder farming system.

Fifthly, Kenyan history demonstrates strong links between levels of education and off-farm income through employment, between off-farm income and land accumulation, between land accumulation and access to agricultural inputs and between all these factors and material wellbeing. But, to begin to develop these links, the smallholding must first be productive. Without adequate access to technology or capital, the smallholders are forced to rely on their own labour, and their children's labour. Population continues to grow because peasants are making a 'market response' to the constraints of their own political economy; they are generating their own labour supply.

It is not very useful, at the present moment, to try to squeeze the complexity of this situation into a simple statement about imperialism, neocolonialism and the development of capitalist class relations in Kenya. Certainly, the use of such categories provides important polemic and, at a high level of abstraction, allows the beginnings of an argument about social change in Kenya.(8) But, unless the intent is to remain at an arid level of structural scholasticism, a more detailed level of analysis is necessary. This would focus on the dynamics of social reproduction in the family-based peasant mode of production. For, as the family-based peasant mode collapses, not least because off-farm employment opportunities are limited in the current form of Kenyan development, there does not seem to be much liklihood of the development of an urban proletariat. Too often, a facile assumption is made that urban employment signifies the development of a proletariat and mature capitalism when, in essence, it is based on off-farm income generation to support a family-based production system.

CONCLUSION

In the aftermath of the attempted coup in August 1982, led by the Kenyan Air Force, it is difficult to project probable developments. The Kenyan Air Force, like the people at the University who also participated, were educated and had an acute knowledge of problems in the rural area; after all, many of them came from those rural areas. But, despite the disbanding of the Kenyan Air Force and the continued closure of the University, major resources will continue to be devoted to further security, a non-productive activity. The impact of the coup on the elite urban population will probably produce a strengthening of the urban bias to the detriment of rural livelihood.

International agencies, especially the IMF, continue to back Kenya's development although, since the coup and with the impact of the current recession, they are asking for a different form of development - an end to import substitution, and growth led by agricultural exports. Surplus extraction from rural areas will continue but in a different form - it will be more rigourously backed by an increasingly repressive state apparatus. Contract farming on the Latin American model will emerge, focusing on the richer farmers. Already it is estimated that about 12 per cent of smallholders are producing cash crops on contract to agro-industries, amounting to some 30 per cent of total marketed output from smallholdings or one sixth of total agricultural marketed output in Kenya. The state controls labour and prices, and international capital has the relatively easy task of downstream manufacturing and marketing. International and national elites retain and consolidate power; some yeoman farmers are supported but most go to the wall.

It is not a model without opposition. During the early months of 1982, government efforts to raise the price of inputs to contract rice farmers produced protest strikes. Similar problems are rapidly emerging in the sugar areas. The rural population are not so much uninformed as unorganised. But with organisation, the political economy of Kenya after the next coup could be different. Opposition is also very strong in cultural terms.(9) Plays, poetry and pamphlets, capturing the plight of the peasantry, have emerged as an important focus of opposition. But cultural opposition is rarely strong enough to lead a movement for social change.

And Gakarara? Soil erosion is no longer a problem. Land has been consolidated; tractors do the terracing; the people have gone to the more marginal lands or the city. Gakarara itelf disappeared beneath a three-lane highway designed to bring tea, coffee and other produce rapidly to market and, by jumbo jet, to Europe. This transition was signalled by an incident in which 'four youngsters' were savaged by guard dogs on the new pineapple plantation, a fenced farm run by a multinational employing wage labour within which the dogs ran freely. But Gakarara is not simply a case study - it is one model from Central Province of a rolling process of capitalism that is now changing villages in Western, Rift and Eastern provinces: indeed in all of Kenya and of Africa.

NOTES
1.   M.W. Holdgate, M. Kassas and G.F. White. The World Environment, 1972-1982 (Tycooly International, Dun Laoghaire, 1982) p. 265.
2.   Food and Agriculture Organisation (FAO), Incentives for Community Involvement in Forestry and Conservation Programs (Rome, 1980).
3.   P. O'Keefe and B. Wisner. 'Development of Underdevelopment: A Kenyan Case Study', African Environment, vol. 2, nos. 1-2 (1976); P. O'Keefe et al., 'Kenyan Underdevelopment: A Case Study in Proletarianisation?', in P. O'Keefe and B. Wisner (eds.) Land Use and Development (International African Institute, London, 1979).
4.   K. Hewitt (ed.), Interpretations of Calamity from the Viewpoint of Human Ecology (Allen and Unwin, London, 1983).
5.   Much of the economic analysis in this section is owed to an unnamed USAID economist whose projections on development performance are used by Kenyan government planners.
6.   See R. Kaplinsky (ed.), Readings on Multinational Corporations in Kenya (Oxford University Press, Nairobi, 1978); S. Langdon, 'The State and Capitalism in Kenya', Review of African Political Economy, no. 8 (1977); C. Leys, 'Capital Accumulation and Dependency: The Kenyan Case', Socialist Register, 1978.
7.   For a discussion on the peasantry in Kenya see 'Kenya: The Agrarian Question', Review of African Political Economy, no. 20 (1981).
8.   See for example the following anonymous publications which contain detailed analysis and pertinent examples of recent Kenyan development: 'A Class Analysis of Colonial and Neocolonial Domination', IKWEZI, no. 21 (1982); In Dependent Kenya (Zed Press, London, 1982); and 'Kenya: The Politics of Repression', Race and Class, vol. 24, no. 3 (1983).
9.   See Ngugi wa Thong'o, Barrel of a Pen, (New Beacon Books, London, 1983).

Chapter Eight

PEASANTS OR PROLETARIANS? THE TRANSFORMATION OF AGRARIAN
PRODUCTION RELATIONS IN EGYPT

Elizabeth Taylor

Agriculture comprises the largest sector of the Egyptian
economy, accounting for one-third of GDP and employing over
half of Egypt's labour force. More than 90 per cent of
agricultural producers are peasants who cultivate small plots
of less than five feddans, primarily by means of household
labour.(1) At the end of the 1960s, and after the agrarian
reforms of the Nasser period, the stage seemed to be set for a
transformation of agrarian structure along classic lines laid
out by Lenin in The Development of Capitalism in Russia: an
increasing concentration of land in the hands of capitalist
farmers and a concomitant decline and eventual demise of the
peasantry.(2) In fact this has not taken place. The last decade
has witnessed not only the survival of the peasantry but a
reinforcement of their position in many respects. Since the
mid-1960s peasants have not only grown in number but so too has
their share of agricultural land. In 1965, peasants represented
89 per cent of Egyptian cultivators. Today their relative
numbers have increased to 94 per cent. From holding just over
half of Egypt's agricultural land in 1965, they now hold over
two-thirds. The majority of those cultivators who are not
peasants farm their land as capitalist enterprises; they
produce cash crops for the market solely by means of hired wage
labour and with the aim of capital accumulation. The increased
'peasantisation' of Egyptian agriculture in recent years has
been accompanied by a decline in the share of land now in the
hands of capitalist farmers. In this sense, a transformation of
capitalist to peasant production has taken place in the last
decade.
    This chapter attempts to identify some of the processes
involved in this transformation of agrarian production
relations. It begins with an outline of peasant production and
agrarian structure within the recent history of Egyptian
agriculture, and of the transformation processes at work at the
national level. It then proceeds to focus on the specific
mechanisms involved in the peasantisation of agriculture in one
Egyptian village.

STATE INTERVENTION, 1810-40

The conventional starting point for any discussion of modern Egyptian agrarian structure is the beginning of the nineteenth century, with the introduction of long staple cotton into Egyptian agriculture for export to Western markets. For it was at this point that a temporary coincidence of interest between the ambitions of the Egyptian state and the requirements of Western capital led to the total reorganisation of Egypt's economy. While the Egyptian state sought ways to gain control over, and increase, Egypt's agricultural surplus, Western industrial capital was searching for new suppliers of raw materials for expanding industrial production. Both of these interests were partially fulfilled, at least initially, but the coincidence of interests was to be short-lived.

The Egyptian state, which at this point was comprised almost entirely of the family of the new governor, Mohamed Ali, pursued its aims by assuming control over agricultural production and marketing, and by introducing into Egyptian agriculture high value, long staple cotton. Firstly, the tax collector class was forcibly eliminated from its pivotal position in the administration of agricultural land, most of which was appropriated as state property. Direct state control over production, marketing and organisation of labour was enforced through a bureaucratic apparatus, backed up by the army. Secondly, long staple cotton received on European markets two to four times the price of the short staple variety already cultivated in Egypt. The introduction of this new crop involved the reorganisation of Egypt's agriculture from one based on the production of subsistence crops to one which became centred around commodity production for export. The switch to long staple cotton also involved a major extension of the irrigation system to provide the additional water required by this variety of cotton in the summer months. New farming techniques had to be introduced to the peasant producers. Detailed instructions on the entire production process, from land preparation to the ginning of the cotton, were prepared by the state. Peasant labour was overseen by foreign experts, village sheikhs and state officials, and enforced by the whip and the army.

In the course of this massive and oppressive reorganisation of Egyptian agriculture peasant production was seriously undermined. Peasants lost control over cultivation and marketing to the state. They also lost land, confiscated by the state for default on increasingly heavy taxes. Peasant labour was forcibly appropriated by the state under the corvée system to work on the extension of the irrigation network and other public works. The peasantry responded by brigandry and sabotage, and by fleeing the land to escape conscription or taxation. By the beginning of the 1830s, an estimated 25 per cent of agricultural land was abandoned and lying fallow.(3) Egypt's economy was in serious difficulties.

Egypt

THE ESTABLISHMENT OF THE 'EZBA SYSTEM, 1840-1920

As a result of the failure of direct control over agriculture and peasant production, and under pressure from Western powers, the state retreated from its monopoly practices and a new system of agricultural organisation was gradually introduced. From the 1840s onwards a structure of agrarian relations began to take shape that predominated into the twentieth century and was only finally destroyed by the land reforms of the Nasser years. In place of state control over land, production and marketing, direct grants of land were made to state officials, members of the royal family and to foreigners involved in the cotton trade. Over time these lands gained the legal status of private property. A new class of landlords, based on the private ownership of large estates ('ezba) was thus created. These large landlords, who were now responsible for the production process, typically worked their estates under the 'ezba system whereby in return for their services on the estates peasants were granted a small subsistence plot of land for their own cultivation and possibly also a small wage in cash or kind. Often receiving loans advanced by the landlord as working capital, peasants were additionally 'bound' to the landlord by debt. By the mid-nineteenth century the estates of the large landlords incorporated most of the best agricultural land. It was on these estates that most of Egypt's cotton was cultivated.

Alongside the 'ezba of the landed aristocracy existed an independent peasantry which, whilst producing some cotton, continued to cultivate mainly subsistence crops. Although expanding in numbers, peasants were progressively confined to a smaller share of agricultural land, and on the whole to land not suitable for the cultivation of cotton. At the end of the eighteenth century, 90 per cent of Egypt's agricultural land had been worked by independent peasant households. By 1900, their share was reduced to 22 per cent.(4)

A further group in the countryside, who may be called, for want of a better term, the medium landlords, consolidated its power from the mid-nineteenth century onwards. This group mainly comprised supervisors of the large, and increasingly absentee, landlords' estates, and the village sheikhs. The powers of the estate supervisors and the sheikhs were greatly extended as they gradually were endowed with many of the functions previously performed by state officials. In return for their duties, they too received grants of land. As local medium landlords, performing a mediating role between the state and the landed aristocracy on the one hand, and the peasantry on the other, they became an increasingly powerful force in the countryside.

Increased differentiation of the rural population was a feature of this period. By 1900 large landlords, conventionally defined as those owning more than 50 feddans of land, were only

0.9 per cent of all landlords but owned 44 per cent of Egypt's agricultural land.(5) The peasants (identified as those owning less than 5 feddans), who were increasingly indebted to landlords and foreign merchants and, through their landlords, to foreign banks, formed in the same period 83 per cent of landowners but owned, as we have seen, only 22 per cent of the land.(6) As peasant land was expropriated, either seized for land grants or lost because of failure to pay taxes or debts, increasing numbers were made landless. By the turn of the century an estimated 25 per cent of agricultural households were landless.(7) However, the landless did not form the basis of agricultural production as wage labour for they were employed mainly as casual and supplementary labour on estates or as corvée labour on public works.

In fact the landless did not form a rural proletariat for they were essentially incorporated into pre-capitalist structures. It is true that the transformation of Egyptian agriculture over the course of the nineteenth century involved both the generalisation of private property relations in land and the transformation of subsistence agriculture into agricultural production centred around commodity production. By the 1880s most agricultural land was privately owned, and by 1900 cotton was grown on one-third of Egypt's land, which was the maximum land available under the then existing crop rotation system. Nonetheless, the agrarian structure that emerged was neither capitalist in its form of production relations nor in terms of its being shaped by the 'logic' of capital accumulation within the Egyptian economy. Egyptian attempts at local industrial development had failed by the mid-nineteenth century, blocked by the interests of the Western powers which insisted on a policy of free trade in industrial commodities, under which terms Egypt could not compete. Egyptian industrial development in this period was arguably capitalist in design.(8) There was little private investment within Egypt, except in land, and state investment was primarily in public works (notably the irrigation system and roads) and in the maintenance of a large standing army. In the rural sector the dominant form of production relations - the 'ezba system of the large estates and sharecropping or tenant farming on the lands of the medium landlords - remained pre-capitalist not only in form but also in substance. Capital accumulation took place, but outside the Egyptian economy, whose pre-capitalist structure it helped to sustain.

Over the course of the nineteenth century, therefore, Egyptian agrarian structure had undergone a radical transformation. In the struggle between peasantry, state and foreign capital, the balance of power shifted over time until by the end of the nineteenth century the interests of Western capital clearly predominated. From the 1840s, peasant production came to be controlled not directly by the bureaucratic and military power of the state but, on the large estates, by large landlords to whom peasants were bound as their chief suppliers of both land and credit. These large landlords on whose 'ezba most of Egypt's cotton was produced had interests closely or directly allied to foreign capital and the cotton trade. The direct penetration of foreign capital into Egyptian agriculture increased througout the nineteenth century, and was greatly extended after the establishment of the Mixed Courts in 1875 which both protected foreign interests in Egypt and guaranteed special privileges to foreigners. By 1914, 80 per cent of mortgages on land were provided by foreign capital and nearly 50 per cent of the large estates were held by foreigners involved in the cotton trade.(9)

THE 'EZBA SYSTEM UNDERMINED, 1920-52

At the beginning of the twentieth century a new process contributed to the dynamics of rural differentiation. The rate of growth of the peasant population began to exceed its access to land ownership. Peasant population pressure on scarce and unequally distributed land, exacerbated by the partitioning of land according to Moslem inheritance laws, set in motion a process of land fragmentation that remains a factor in rural differentiation today. Where it was impossible to rent additional land, peasants sold off their unviable plots, thus adding to the numbers of landless produced by land confiscation for default on taxes or debts. From 25 per cent of agricultural families in 1907, the percentage of landless agricultural households had risen to 60 per cent by 1950 (Table 8.1).

The rising numbers of rural landless and the fragmentation of land of the independent peasantry should be seen as important contributory factors in the undermining of the 'ezba system which was clearly evident by the beginning of the Second World War. For in the nineteenth century the scarcity or unreliability of a constant supply of peasant labour formed one of the rationales of the 'ezba system. By 'tying' the peasant to the estate a permanent labour supply was assured. In the twentieth century it was not labour but land that became the scarce factor. The peasants' need to secure additional land to maintain viable land holdings produced a ready supply of potential tenants. Increased landlessness produced also an abundant supply of wage labour, and indeed a rise in the use of wage labour, primarily on the lands of the medium landlords, seems to have taken place during this period. The major shift in production relations, however, occurred in the greatly increased amount of estate land leased out to tenant farmers, especially between 1939 and 1950. This dramatic shift in tenancy arrangements represented a serious undermining of the 'ezba system. During the same period an increase in absentee landlordism also occurred. From the beginning of the Second World War then, direct control of the labour process under the 'ezba system was giving way to independent peasant production.

Table 8.1:   Landless Households Engaged In Agriculture,
             Egypt, 1907-50

Year	No. Of Landless Households	% Landless To Rural Households
1907 (a)		25%
1929 (b)	697	37%
1939 (b)	1107	53%
1950 (b)	1469	60%

Sources: (a)   estimated   by   E.R.J.   Owen, Cotton in the
Egyptian   Economy,   1820-1914   (Oxford   University   Press,
London, 1969), p. 148.
           (b)   estimated by S. Radwan, Agrarian Reform and
Rural Poverty, Egypt, 1957-75 (ILO, Geneva, 1977), p. 23.

Table 8.2:   Land Owned And Land Farmed By Peasant
             Producers In Egypt, 1952-77/8

	1952	1961	1965	1977/8
% Land owned by Peasants	35	52	57	52
Average Size Of Peasant-Owned Land (Feddans)	0.8	1.1	1.2	0.9
% Land Farmed By Peasants	23	38	52	67
Average Size Of Land Farmed By Peasants (Feddans)	1.8	1.7	1.6	1.5

Sources: Data on land ownership for 1952-65 is taken from The
Statistical   Year   Book,   1978,   produced   by   the   Central
Organisation   for   Mobilisation   and   Statistics,   Cairo   (in
arabic);   and for the year 1977/8 from S. Radwan and B. Hansen,
'Employment   Opportunities   and   Equity   in   Egypt',   in   G.
Abdel-Khalek   and   R.   Tignor   (eds),   The Political Economy of
Income   Distribution   in   Egypt   (Holmes   and   Meier,   New York,
1982).   Data on land farmed in 1950 and 1961 is from National
Bank of Egypt, Economic Bulletin, vol. 31, no. 4 (1978); and
for 1965 and 1977/8 from the Agricultural Census Section of the
Ministry of Agriculture, Cairo.

This shift in tenancy arrangements coincided with a change in cropping patterns and the first large-scale government interference in agriculture since the mid-nineteenth century. Because of the severe grain shortage produced by the disruption of trade during the Second World War, the government organised compulsory deliveries of grain, and in effect nationalised the grain trade, to feed the British army. The shift in cropping patterns away from cotton to cereal production involved a shift to a lower value, less labour-intensive crop. It seems probable that the volume of permanent labour tied to the estates under the 'ezba system was thus in reduced demand, and the 'ezba system, based on the necessity to control a large and permanent supply of scarce labour, was far less crucial for cereal production. The cultivation of comparatively low value, less labour-intensive cereals therefore must have made the extraction of surplus through high rents more attractive economically to landlords than the continued control over labour and produce afforded by the 'ezba system. During the period 1939-50 there was a fivefold increase in rents.(10)

However, at the end of the war when cultivation again became centred around the production of cotton, there was no parallel reversal in tenancy arrangements. Richards suggests that by then the direct control of the labour process may not have seemed an entirely attractive proposition to large landlords.(11) Peasant unrest and protest against exorbitant rents mounted in intensity after the war.(12) So too did attacks on the landed aristocracy by the new urban bourgeoisie, who were, for example, beginning to press for land reforms, including the establishment of a ceiling on land ownership. Landlord insecurity in reponse to this double pressure may go some way towards explaining the continued retreat of most large landlords from the countryside and the maintenance of tenancy arrangements in favour of independent peasant production.

The landed aristocracy at this period was not only under some external pressures, but was also weakened by a split within its own ranks. For as industrialisation began to develop in the 1920s, so too some of this class began to invest in industry and to shift their economic base out of agriculture. Industrialisation in Egypt in the twentieth century was to a large extent successful because of the changing role of foreign capital within the Egyptian economy. Whereas in the nineteenth century the interests of foreign capital were opposed to Egypt's industrialisation, and were largely responsible for the blocking of local industrial development, in the early twentieth century, particularly from the 1920s onwards, industrialisation began to be actively encouraged.(13) As profit rates in Europe declined, industrial investment within Egypt was actively promoted by finance capital and by the British colonial administration, whose policy was to steer industrialisation along paths consistent with British interests. In 1922, when the Egyptian Federation

of Industry was established, eight out of its eleven directors
were non-Egyptian. By 1934, at least 35 per cent of all
industrial investment was in firms with foreign
participation.(14) As industrialisation within Egypt
progressed, so too there developed an Egyptian industrial
bourgeoisie drawn mainly from the merchant groups and a section
of the landed aristocracy who were moving into industrial
investment. Constrained not only by the traditional aristocracy
but also by the foreign domination of Egyptian industry, this
group attempted nationalist strategies to further its
interests, and developed a powerful nationalist ideology.

The major part of the landed aristocracy, however,
remained rooted in commerce and land. A significant impediment
to industrial development, they were increasingly attacked as
such by the industrial bourgeoisie.(15) Land reform bills
proposing limits on landownership were submitted to the
Egyptian parliament in 1945, 1948 and again in 1950, but each
time they were defeated by representatives of the landed
aristoracy.(16) The Egyptian ruling class was divided, but the
traditional landed aristocracy, closely allied to the Palace
and to the colonial government, retained its political
dominance. It was this group which formed the major source of
potential opposition to the new regime established by the Young
Officers' coup in 1952.

THE LAND REFORM YEARS, 1952-65

The achievement of agrarian reforms during the Nasser period
accelerated and completed processes that were already in motion
by finally eliminating the 'ezba system of debt peonage and
destroying the landed aristocracy as the dominant class in the
countryside. One of the first acts undertaken by the Young
Officers after assuming power was the implementation of the
first of a series of land reform measures. By so doing they
allied themselves with the interests of the industrial
bourgeoisie in its struggle with the landed aristocracy and in
its commitment to industrial development. The land reform
comprised a package of policies aimed at gaining control over
and increasing the agricultural surplus for the purpose of
national development, and at eliminating the landed
aristocracy; in fulfilment of these objectives, at least until
the economic crisis of the mid-1960s, the Nasser state was to a
large extent successful.

The first land reform laws in 1952 set the ceiling on
individual land ownership at 200 feddans, which subsequently
was reduced to 50 feddans. The power of the landed aristocracy
in the countryside was effectively destroyed after only minimal
resistance. Their lands were redistributed in plots of 3-5
feddans, primarily to tenant farmers on the confiscated
estates, and independent peasant production was thus

reinforced. As a result of the series of land reform acts enacted during the 1950s and 1960s the peasant share of agricultural land increased from 35 per cent in 1952 (prior to land reform) to 52 per cent in 1961, and to 57 per cent in 1965.(17) The position of the peasantry was further improved by the enactment of land tenure laws which covered tenant farmers not affected by land re-distribution. A relatively low annual rent was fixed and tenants were granted both security of tenure and inheritance rights over tenure. The peasant base of Egyptian agriculture was thus broadened and peasants acquired far greater security over the land they worked.

The destruction of the power of the large landlords in the countryside eliminated much of the feudal-type oppression, still vivid in many peasant memories. It did, however, leave a power vacuum which was filled both by the state and by those who prior to land reform had formed the group of medium landlords, who now took over, and indeed extended, many of the controls over peasants previously exercised by the large landlords. State control over agriculture at village level was effected primarily through a system of agricultural co-operatives, which were established in the early 1960s with the explicit aim of mobilising the agricultural surplus. By designating cropping areas and enforcing compulsory quota deliveries on certain crops, the state came to purchase a significant proportion of the agricultural output, at prices well below those on the international market. Through the co-operatives the state also became the major supplier of agricultural inputs and the main source of agricultural credit.

The personnel required to administer the co-operatives was largely drawn from the old group of medium landlords, whose historically dominant position had already been consolidated by the elimination of the landed aristocracy. Not only had they been the prime beneficiaries of 'distress sales' as land of the large estates was sold to avoid confiscation by the state; but in the role of state officials in the agricultural co-operatives and in the village and district level administrative councils, their power in the countryside was further extended. Within the co-operatives they were able to exercise a control over the distribution of subsidised agricultural inputs as well as over agricultural credit.(18) At the level of national policy too this group gained considerable influence. It has been convincingly argued that the state's 'squeeze' on agriculture would have been considerably greater had it not been for the medium landlords' successful protection of their own interests.(19) In the package of land reform measures introduced there was no attempt to eliminate the power of this dominant group. Rather the state incorporated the medium landlords into its machinery and thus consolidated their position at both the local and national level.

The structure of agrarian relations that emerged as a result of the land reforms was shaped by the struggle for control over the agricultural surplus of three forces: the state, capital and the peasantry. The reforms were not aimed at a revolutionary transformation of agrarian production relations, nor at encouraging the mobilisation of the peasantry or rural landless. When these groups did mobilise, in peasant movements involving land occupation for example, they were forcibly crushed by the army.(20) Nonetheless, although capitalist farming emerged as the predominant form of production on the lands of non-peasant producers, peasant production was greatly extended and revitalised.

The land reform measures only marginally and temporarily affected the landless agricultural labourers. The first beneficiaries of land redistribution were the peasant producers on the confiscated estate lands, and normally only thereafter was remaining land distributed to the landless. The numbers of landless agricultural labourers had been steadily increasing throughout the century, until by 1950 the households of landless agricultural labourers represented an estimated 60 per cent of agricultural families.(21) As permanent or casual agricultural labourers, who were also seasonally employed as contract labour on public works, they remained during the 1950s and 1960s non-unionised, lowly paid, and the most impoverished group in the countryside.(22) Although their numbers did fall after the first land reform laws were enacted, they began once more to increase after 1965. Indeed, their rising numbers in the late 1960s suggested to one Egyptian economist 'the spectre of a new agrarian crisis'.(23) By the end of the Nasser period the stage seemed to be set for differentiation of agrarian production relations according to the Leninist model of capitalist development. The predicted 'agrarian crisis' and the polarisation of production relations along classic capitalist lines, however, did not materialise.

'PEASANTISATION' SINCE THE AGRARIAN REFORMS

In response to the serious economic crisis of the mid-1960s, the final years of the Nasser period were marked by a realignment of economic policy. Towards the end of the decade a liberalisation of Egypt's economy began to take place, a process which was accelerated and made explicit in the 'infitah' or 'open-door' policy announced by Sadat in 1974. As a result of this, the balance in the agricultural sector between capital, peasantry and the state has changed. The state has continued to intervene, but it has loosened its tight control. Moreover, the divisions between the various elements that comprise the state have become more evident since the 1970s. The old landed aristocracy has made a limited come-back with, for example, the return of some previously sequestrated lands. The capitalist farmers, whose interests have always been well represented within the Ministry of Agriculture, have been able to promote these more fully by, for example, the extension of credit facilities and subsidies directed towards the larger farmers and agribusiness. In addition, the Ministry has continued to press for the lifting of price controls on agricultural produce in order to ensure a higher selling price to the farmer. Although not entirely unhindered by competing groups, the reinforcement of capitalist agriculture has continued into the 1970s. However, the anticipated large-scale investment of foreign and local capital in land reclamation and agribusiness has not materialised. Some of the few foreign firms that did invest in such ventures in the mid-1970s have since considerably reduced their investment or pulled out completely.(24) Nonetheless, although the injection of foreign capital into agriculture has been limited, local capitalist farming has without doubt been intensified.

In spite of this, rural differentiation in the last decade or so has not proceeded along the classic lines of capitalist transition. The processes giving rise to landlessness are still evident, but there are also countervailing tendencies. For within the rural sector the peasantry has not declined. In fact, the peasant base has continued to broaden, for since the mid-1960s the peasant share of land has increased by 15 per cent. From working just over half of Egypt's agricultural land in 1965, peasants now farm two-thirds of the total, a larger share than at any time over the last century. The main dynamics of change in agrarian structure in the 1970s has therefore produced an increasing 'peasantisation' of Egyptian agriculture and a corresponding decrease in the share of land under capitalist production. A limited transformation from capitalist to peasant production is thus a major feature of Egyptian agrarian structure in the 1970s.

Table 8.2 indicates the shares of land owned and land farmed by peasants before, during and after land reform. The figures for 1952 refer to the situation before the first land reform measures were passed later that year. The last effective land redistribution measures were taken following the 1961 Land Reform Law. The comparison of 1965 figures with those for 1977/8 therefore shows trends that have occurred since the completion of land reform.(25) In the table, as indeed throughout this chapter, peasant producers are defined as owners or holders of less than five feddans of land.(26) The residual category of farmers of five feddans and more are taken to be capitalist farmers after the first land reform in 1952. Prior to land reform this category would also have included the large landowners of estate lands. This crude identification of production relations based on farm size is made conventionally and is based on the 1961 agricultural census (the most recent published) which shows that farms of under five feddans are worked predominantly by household labour, and that the majority of farms of twenty feddans and more are worked by hired wage labour. According to the census, intermediate-sized farms of

five to less than twenty feddans include both peasant and
small-scale capitalist production units, but since wage labour
predominates on these farms, for the purpose of this discussion
they have been excluded from the category of 'peasant
producers'. The category 'land farmed' includes both land owned
and land rented; that is, it represents the total amount of
land held and worked.

The table demonstrates that many of the trends set in
motion by the land reform measures have been reversed since the
mid-1960s. More specifically, it is clear that the
redistribution of owned land accomplished by the land reform
laws represents a one-off gain to the peasantry rather than a
radical reshaping of structures inhibiting land fragmentation
and landlessness. For gains made by the peasantry as a result
of land reform were already being undermined from the mid-1960s
onwards. Due to land redistribution the peasants' share of
owned land increased from 35 per cent prior to the first land
reform law to 57 per cent in 1965. After 1965, however, the
peasants' share of owned land decreased. This reversal was not
merely the result of an increase in peasant numbers, but was
also due to an absolute decline in the amount of land owned by
peasant farmers.

Although the share of land owned by larger farmers
necessarily rose after 1965, this in fact did not represent an
equivalent gain in land area. During the period 1952-1977/8,
Egypt's total agricultural land area fluctuated in size between
5.5 and 6.5 million feddans, the increases being due to land
reclamation while about 0.9 million feddans was lost to urban
and rural sprawl. Peasants' land during this time decreased by
just over one million feddans. Since the larger farmers gained
only about 0.2 million feddans, most of the land lost to
peasants was sold mainly for real estate development. It did
not represent a net consolidation of small peasant plots into
larger capitalist enterprises.

During the period 1952-65, peasants owned more land than
they farmed; i.e., there was a net renting out of fragmented
peasant plots, and a consolidation of small plots into the
holdings of larger farmers. After 1965, this process was
reversed. Although owning in 1977/8 the same share of land as
in 1961, the peasants' share of farmed land had increased, so
that for the first time since 1952 (at least) peasants now
worked more land than they owned.(27) The process of a net
consolidation of peasant plots into larger farms has been
reversed to that of a net renting by peasant producers of land
owned by larger, mainly capitalist farmers. In this way, in
spite of fluctuations in their share of owned land, peasants
have maintained a remarkable relative stability in the average
size of land worked.

The transformation of Egyptian agrarian structure since
the mid-1960s has thus not taken the classic course of
capitalist transition. Land has not been increasingly

concentrated into the hands of capitalist farmers at the expense of small peasant producers, with the consequent expansion of a rural proletariat. Rather, in terms of access to land, the reverse has occurred. A transition from capitalist to peasant production relations has been one of the major processes in evidence. This is not to deny that processes giving rise to peasant impoverishment and landlessness are still underway. However, the landless since the mid-1970s have to a very large extent been absorbed outside agriculture, primarily into the construction sector within Egypt or, more significantly in terms of numbers, into the labour markets of the oil-rich Arab states. The predicted agrarian crisis has thus not occurred. Rather a new crisis has become apparent: that of a shortage of agricultural labour.

THE MIGRATION OF AGRICULTURAL LABOUR IN THE 1970s

The migration of Egyptian labour abroad was under tight government control during most of the Nasser period, and mainly comprised the secondment of professionals to Arab states. At the end of the 1960s there was a loosening of government restrictions on migration, and these were almost entirely lifted by the Sadat regime in the early 1970s as part of the accelerated liberalisation of the Egyptian economy. From the beginning of the 1970s onwards, Egypt has in effect pursued a policy to encourage the migration of labour. However, it was only after the rise in oil prices in 1973, and the subsequent implementation of large scale development programmes in the oil-rich Arab states, that the flow of Egyptian labour abroad began to take on the dimensions it has reached today. Estimates of the number of Egyptians working in Arab states in 1981 range from about 1.7 million to just under 3 million.(28) The special national council established by the Egyptian government to examine the question of labour migration estimated that 10-15 per cent of the labour force is at present working abroad.(29) This largely uncontrolled flow of labour abroad has led to distortions in the Egyptian labour market. Alongside unemployment there are pockets of serious labour shortage in certain sectors, notably in skilled construction work and in agriculture. The scarcity of labour has been accompanied by a steep and sustained rise in the real wage for male agricultural labour, from an index of 100 in 1973 to 174 in 1978.(30)

Whilst the volume of labour that has migrated out of agriculture is not known, what is clear is that the flow of labour abroad has not been evenly dispersed across the rural sector. In some villages most agricultural households have one or more male migrant abroad; in others, there has been little, if any migration. It is likely that a variety of factors account for this, such as variations between villages in the structure of landholding and in the viability of small scale peasant agriculture, as well as variations in the degree of incorporation of villages into the domestic and world markets.

Not only is there no uniform rate of migration out of villages, but the direction of the flow also varies. For example. in the governorate of Giza, which incorporates that part of the Nile valley immediately south of Cairo, the initial migration out of agriculture was to Libya and began at the end at the end of the 1960s. However, only villages lying to the west of the Nile were caught up in this movement. Here the Beduin, settled or partially settled on the semi-agricultural land on the fringe of the Western Desert, played a crucial role. Since they still maintain their trading and kinship links with the Libyan Beduin, they acted as labour contractors and as guides across the border for village migrants, most of whom at this period were travelling without passports or labour permits. There is no evidence of migration to Libya from villages in Giza to the east of the Nile. Migration here does not seem to have begun until 1973, and the direction of migration was to Saudi Arabia, which by the mid-1970s was attracting rural immigrants from throughout the Giza governorate and indeed the rest of Egypt. At present most Egyptian rural migration is to Saudi Arabia, but Libya, Jordan, Iraq and the Gulf States also absorb labour from the agricultural sector. Abroad, some rural migrants continue to work in agriculture, either as share croppers or wage labourers. The majority, however, are employed as wage labour in construction.

THE AGRICULTURAL LABOUR MARKET AND PRODUCTION RELATIONS IN ONE VILLAGE

The implications of an agricultural labour shortage for the labour market and for production relations may be analysed more closely by looking at the process in the context of one village.(31) The results obviously cannot be generalised for the rural sector as a whole, but since the case study illustrates the interaction of structures and processes which are characteristic of the sector to a greater or lesser extent, the study does have a significance beyond the purely local.

The village in question, Dahshur, lies in the governorate of Giza, 45 kms south of Cairo in the narrow strip of agricultural land that forms the Nile valley. Its houses are clustered together and surrounded by the village agricultural lands, which almost border the Western Desert. Of its 800 or so households, almost 60 per cent are engaged in agriculture. The major employer of non-agricultural labour is the state. Twenty per cent of village household heads are now employed either as unskilled workers in public sector industries in the nearby town of Helwan, or in government administration and services within the village. Both sectors are products of the Nasser period, during which the Helwan industrial complex was established, and increased state control over agriculture and an extension of the state's penetration into the rural areas were effected.

Prior to the 1970s, Dahshur was an important centre for the domestic production of textiles. Weaving and dyeing of carpets and materials formed the single major non-agricultural activity. With the growth of the national textile industry, some of whose materials are sold on the domestic market at subsidised prices, and with the flood of synthetic fabrics which had entered Egypt's 'open doors' in the 1970s, village textile production has severely declined. Today there remain only five households of weavers and three who are still engaged in dyeing.

Since 1968, the governorate of Giza has been released from growing the government-stipulated quota of cotton. Along with other areas surrounding Cairo, agricultural land in Giza has been transferred to fruit and vegetable production with the prime aim of feeding the ever-expanding capital. Village farmers now produce both subsistence crops and high value cash crops, including maize and clover for their own and their animals' consumption, and a variety of vegetables, such as cucumbers, tomatoes, courgettes, okra, peas, potatoes and broadbeans, primarily for the Cairo market. Vegetable production in the village is highly labour intensive, and cultivation is continuous throughout the year. On any one small plot of land, five or more crops at one time may be grown. Farming methods are mainly traditional, with only threshing and irrigation being in any significant degree mechanised. The demand for agricultural labour is therefore high, relative to areas where less labour intensive crops are cultivated or where agriculture is more fully mechanised.

Land in the village, like that throughout rural Egypt, is highly fragmented. Exactly half of village landholders, and 49 per cent of all Egypt's landholders, work less than one feddan of land.(32) However, land distribution in Dahshur, is less skewed than the national distribution pattern. The tip of the national distribution pyramid, the 2 per cent of landholders who farm 10-15 feddans of land, are not represented in the village, whose largest landholders work just under six feddans. Most village landholders (90 per cent, compared with 82 per cent nationally) farm plots of less than three feddans. However, in spite of the fragmentation of land and the fact that many agricultural households have one or more members employed in off-farm work, for the vast majority of Dahshur farmers the land is both their major source of revenue and the major consumer of household labour.

Peasant production forms the basis of village agriculture. Ninety per cent of Dahshur's landholders comprise a classic peasantry, working their land primarily by household labour and producing both for their own consumption and for the market. Two-thirds of Dahshur's peasant producers own some land, and half of these supplement their owned land by renting in additional land. The other one-third rent in all their land. The remaining village landholdings comprise owned land worked entirely by wage labour. These small-scale capitalist enterprises now account for only 10 per cent of village landholdings, compared with about 19 per cent in 1976.

In spite of the fragmentation of landholdings, and the fact that the majority of producers are peasants, hired agricultural labour is an essential component of village agricultural production. Only 12 per cent of Dahshur's peasant producers work their land solely by household labour. The rest rely considerably on hired labour, especially at peak seasons (which are numerous in this type of vegetable cultivation). Most peasant producers employ wage labour on a fairly regular basis, at least once or twice weekly. Hired non-household labour is therefore not marginal to peasant production in the village but rather an integral part of the production process. In the 1950s and 1960s landless wage labour was by all reports readily available in the village. Hired for the most part on a casual basis, labourers worked both on small capitalist farms and peasant holdings. Today, however, male landless agricultural labour has virtually disappeared. Peasant and capitalist farmers alike report a shortage of agricultural labour.

In Dahshur, as in the rural sector as a whole, the major factor contributing to the shortage has been the migration of agricultural labour. Migration began as a trickle in 1969, but by 1974 almost 10 per cent of village households had male members working abroad, and this level has been sustained and slightly increased in recent years. Prior to 1976, all migration was to Libya. Most migrants travelled and worked illegally, without passports or labour permits. This possibility of by-passing bureaucratic procedures, plus the fact that migration was relatively cheap, meant that migration was accessible even to the poor. Half the village migrants prior to 1976 comprised landless agricultural workers and peasants. As the relationship between the Sadat and Gadaffi regimes deteriorated in the mid-1970s, the Libyans announced their intention to deport illegal Egyptian migrants. Since 1976, illegal migration to Libya from the village has ceased and the main stream of migration has been diverted to Saudi Arabia. Authorised migration to Libya continues, but after the breaking off of diplomatic relations between Egypt and Libya in 1979, migration to Libya became more expensive and more cumbersome. The only route now is by air, and labour contracts are required before entering the country. Migration to Saudi Arabia is a much simpler process. Most migrants enter the country on pilgrims' visas and remain illegally if employment is found. Jordan and Iraq no longer require visas of Egyptian entrants, and in recent years both countries have begun to attract migrants from the village. At present just over 10 per cent of Dahshur households have members working abroad, most of whom are in Saudi Arabia or Libya.

Migration has not on the whole led to the 'proletarianisation' of village peasant migrants. Only temporarily moving out of the household production unit and entering the wage labour market, over 80 per cent of Dahshur peasant migrants are reabsorbed onto their land on their return to the village. Thus, the migration process does not in the main transform peasants into wage labourers. Neither does it release returning labour onto the agricultural labour market. Those peasants who do return to work as wage labour typically move out of agriculture into construction, which has boomed in the village since the mid-1970s and in which wages are higher and the work generally considered less laborious. The boom in this sector is a direct consequence itself of labour migration, as red brick housing is a major item of migrant investment. Labour migration thus acts, in Dahshur, to tighten the male agricultural labour market by absorbing agricultural labour; it does not replenish it by releasing returning migrants into the agricultural labour force.

Although all villagers are united in reporting an acute shortage of agricultural labour, it is clear that the implications of the shortage vary considerably for the different types of farming units. Whereas 78 per cent of all village farmers hire in male agricultural labour, only 14 per cent of these, who farm their land as small-scale capitalist enterprises, rely entirely on wage labour. For these capitalist farmers, the labour shortage means both an increase in labour costs which amounts to a profit squeeze, and an absolute dearth of labour. Labour is unobtainable in the required quantities, not only at peak seasons of agricultural activity but throughout the year. Peasant producers, however, experience the labour shortage almost exclusively in terms of a rise in agricultural wages. They report that hired labour, although less readily available than in the past, can always be found. For them the problem is increased labour costs. Peasants do not experience the absolute dearth of hired labour reported by the capitalist farmer.

The reasons for these different experiences of the labour shortage are not merely a function of the obvious fact that there is a greater dependency on wage labour on non-peasant, capitalist enterprises. As we have seen, hired wage labour is an integral part of peasant production as well. What has to be explained ·is how it is that wage labour is available for peasant but not for capitalist producers. A crucial factor here seems to be the manner in which the village agricultural labour market now functions. For whereas in the 1960s landless labour comprised a large section of male agricultural labour, today the male agricultural labour force is almost entirely composed of small peasants; but the agricultural labourer, who is also a small peasant, is not best characterised as a mere seller of individual labour. Rather, as a landholder as well, he is part of a separate production unit. This has its own production needs, which may, and often do, include the hiring of outside labour. The peasant agricultural labourer is thus often, at different stages of his production process or household life cycle, either a buyer or a seller of labour. As part of a production unit, he does not typically sell his individual labour in an anonymous labour market, but rather enters into specific exchange relations with certain other, often but not necessarily related, peasant households. In some cases these may take the form of the traditional peasant practice of direct labour exchange. In others, and now more commonly, a wage in cash and/or kind is also paid, but still the obligation to return (wage) labour remains with the hiring household. In relation to such a labour market, the capitalist farmer stands in a disadvantageous position. Having no household labour of his own to exchange, his is a weak bargaining position in a market determined by the needs of small peasant production. Since it is not now composed of 'doubly-free' labour, the market no longer functions according to the logic of capitalist production. The capitalist farmer thus experiences an absolute shortage of available labour.

The capitalist sector of village agriculture is at a further disadvantage compared with peasant producers, in its relationship to the international labour market. Whereas the peasant household can, and very often does, exercise some control over the flow of labour out of the production unit, the capitalist farmer can only compete with the international labour market by raising wages. The reproduction and production needs of the peasant household act as one set of constraints and determinants on the pattern of migration and re-absorption of household labour. The labour requirements of the farm often hold back essential or more useful household labour from migration. Household members nearing the age of marriage tend to assume priority for migration over those who are younger or already married. The departure of one family member is often delayed until the return of another, and so on. This is not to imply that there is perfect compatibility between the needs of the peasant household, the aspirations of individual household members and the 'pull' of the international market, but merely to suggest that the logic of peasant production and reproduction does have a determining role in the rate and manner of absorption of peasant labour into the international labour market.

The responses of the two sectors to the penetration of the international labour market have also been distinct. In order to minimise labour costs some peasants are planting a greater proportion of their land to less labour intensive but lower value crops. Agricultural tasks sometimes have to be delayed. However, neither of these adjustments have threatened the perpetuation of peasant production as a form. Small scale capitalist production has, however, been so threatened. The shortage of landless wage labour and the profit squeeze caused

by increased labour costs have forced capitalist farmers to
resort to alternative forms of production. Increasingly,
capitalist farmers are leasing out their land. The type of
rental arrangement takes one of two forms: either
sharecropping, or the leasing out of land for one crop and for
a cash rent in advance determined by the value of the crop to
be cultivated. In both cases the renting out is on a seasonal
basis, as a way of avoiding the relatively low annual rents
fixed by land reform law and also to avoid the possibility of
acquiring a sitting tenant. In both cases too the tenants are
peasant producers. In this way, capitalist enterprises are
increasingly being transformed into peasant production units.
Thus the functioning of village labour markets is at least a
contributory factor in the decline of capitalist production in
the village in recent years and in the major transformation now
in evidence: the peasantisation of village agriculture.

CONCLUSION

The specific context within which these observations have been
made is that of a village in which peasant agriculture is
thriving, high value vegetables form the major cash crops, and
production is for a market within direct reach of the
producers, many of whom can thus by-pass village-level
merchants. Small scale peasant production is thus more viable
in Dahshur than in villages less advantageously situated in
relation to their markets or which are in less lucrative
cropping zones. Moreover, the distribution of land in Dahshur
is not highly skewed. Peasants are not producing alongside
large scale capitalist farmers who dominate both production and
marketing, and who might have options open to them in a
situation of labour shortage (for example, mechanisation) which
are less readily available to the small scale capitalist farmer
in Dahshur. This is not to suggest that Dahshur is a 'special
case'. In terms both of its pattern of crops and of its land
distribution, it is clear that Dahshur is far from atypical; in
other types of village structure, however, other
transformations may well be underway, for example, the boosting
of capitalist farming through mechanisation in response to the
labour shortage.(33) From national data, it is clear that the
peasantisation of agriculture is a major process in evidence in
contemporary Egypt. The significance of this transformation in
agrarian structure is open to various interpretations. For
those who see peasant production as essentially a
pre-capitalist form, its increase can only indicate a reversal
of the transition process, i.e., a transformation back to
pre-capitalist production relations. For others the role of
peasant producers in Egypt after the agrarian reforms is to be
differently interpreted. Patrick Clawson, for example,
maintains that 'the final smashing of pre-capitalist production

relations in agriculture took place with the land reform proclaimed in 1952'.(34) Since then, he argues, peasant producers have 'in essence become an agricultural proletariat'.(35)

The first proposition, that peasant production is, in itself, a pre-capitalist form, can be usefully examined in the light of the nature of sharecropping arrangements increasingly being entered into by Dahshur farmers. In what sense are these a reversion to a previous form, and in what sense are they essentially pre-capitalist? In pre-land reform times, under the 'ezba system, where sharecropping existed both on the lands of the medium landlords and, to a lesser extent, on the large estates themselves, sharecroppers were primarily landless peasants, entirely dependent on the landlords' supply of land for their reproduction as peasant households. They were also most often tied to the landlord by indebtedness. The landlord's advance of credit as 'working capital' was certainly an essential part of the sharecropping relationship (and indeed of the maintenance of peasant production in general) at least by the last two decades of the nineteenth century. In this way the sharecropper was bound to the landlord in a form of debt peonage. In addition, the terms of the sharecropping arrangements were heavily tipped in favour of the landlord, unequal shares of both inputs and output being customary.

The substance of the sharecropping relationship in the village today more closely resembles a contract between two free agents mediated by the state. The peasant tenant is not landless, but is supplementing his landholding by sharecropping additional land. Neither is the peasant, under seasonal sharecropping arrangements, bound to the landlord by indebtedness. Moreover, the state's increased intervention in tenancy arrangements since land reform has been a crucial element in determining the form tenancy arrangements now take. Apart from seasonal sharecropping, to avoid the protection now available to tenants on annual leases, the division of input costs and shares in the produce are also constrained by state legislation. This stipulates that the costs of inputs are to be borne by the landlord, those of labour by the sharecropper, and that the crop is to be equally shared. This is not to suggest that landlord and tenant are equal partners, nor that the law operates in isolation from power relations. The way that the crop is divided and the costs shared in fact vary, generally in favour of the landlord, but still the constraints of state legislation are there and do set firm limits to the free exercise of landlord power. The formal category 'sharecropping' thus embodies a variety of types of relationship. It cannot therefore be treated as a single fixed category, indicative of one substantive type of production relations. Its revitalisation as a tenancy form in the village in recent years does not, in itself, indicate a reversion to a previous type of production relations. Sharecropping no more necessarily denotes a pre-capitalist form of production relations than does, for example, landless wage labour necessarily equal a proletariat and denote capitalism.

However, the recognition that tenancy arrangements, whilst retaining a common form, may in fact comprise a variety of substantive relationships, and that in Egypt today the production relations incorporated within seasonal sharecropping are more consistent with a capitalist mode of production than those for example, existing under the 'ezba system, does not necessarily imply agreement with those, such as Clawson, who equate the Egyptian peasantry since land reform with an agricultural proletariat. Clawson's argument rests on the proposition that peasants lost to the Nasserist state effective control of their land, labour and produce. This argument is elaborated in an examination of the role of the state-run agricultural co-operatives controlling peasant production. Clawson here makes three points: peasants are forced to purchase their inputs from the co-operatives; they are compelled to dispose of their produce through the co-operatives; and the co-operatives, in areas cultivating cotton, oversee the production process, determining crop mix and the timing of agricultural operations. On these grounds, Clawson concludes that due to agrarian reform measures 'the peasants lost control over the means of production, over the product and over the production process'.(36)

Although it is certainly the case that under the system of co-operatives, peasants have lost full control over their product, and to some extent of the production process (although this is less so in non-cotton producing areas which form over half of Egypt's agricultural area), the grounds on which Clawson maintains that peasants have lost effective control over the means of production are not elaborated. Indeed, in so far as peasants' rights to buy, sell and inherit land were not affected by land reform measures, this aspect of their control over land has remained intact. The amount of land owned by peasants was, moreover, extended by land reform measures. As we have seen, the peasants' share of land owned rose from 35 per cent in 1952 prior to land reform, to 57 per cent in 1965, which represented a gain of 1.5 million feddans. Peasant rights over land tenancies were also significantly secured by land reform. Rather than reduce peasants' control over the means of production, land reform measures increased both peasants' access to owned land and their security on leased land. It is hard to see how in terms of Clawson's argument the Egyptian peasantry have as a result of land reform become 'in essence' an agricultural proletariat.

Indeed, by Clawson's own admission at a later stage in his argument, in the 1960s small peasants were able to exercise sufficient control over their land as to successfully resist the state's attempt at crop consolidation. Clawson explains that crop consolidation (the organisation of small peasant plots within villages into large blocks within which one crop would be cultivated annually under a state-controlled system of crop rotation) had been successfully carried out on redistributed estate lands in some areas. Because of the improved yields on such consolidated lands, which were taken to be due to the increased efficiency of farming large areas under one crop, the state attempted to extend this system onto lands not distributed by land reform. According to Clawson, and indeed as is generally agreed, this system 'did not spread far because of the intense opposition from small landowners who were forced to get into debt to buy food during the years when their land was in a block devoted to cotton production'.(37) At this point Clawson has surely demonstrated that a significant degree of control over the means of production was in fact still retained by peasant producers under the Nasserist state. For if peasants' control over their land was effective enough to enable them to resist the attempts of the state to determine cropping patterns, then it is hardly convincing to dismiss their ownership of land as merely 'nominal'.(38) The point is not merely academic. The significant degree of control over land still maintained by the Egyptian peasantry differentiates them from the landless rural proletariat. This distinction is a crucial one to make in any consideration of future agricultural development and of the peasantry's actual and potential political alliances. What has then to be comprehended are both the processes weakening the peasantry's control over land, and those working against their final subsumption and full proletarianisation.

NOTES
    1.   One feddan = 1.038 acres. Throughout this chapter the term 'peasants' is used to refer to cultivators who farm their land (which may be either owned or rented) primarily by means of household labour, and who produce both for their own consumption and for the market. They are thus distinguished from capitalist farmers who work land, which they own, solely by means of wage labour. The lack (or at least the minimal role) of a wage component in peasant production, as well as the fact that the peasant enterprise is not only a production but also a reproduction unit, mean that the logic of production differs significantly from that of capitalist production. Peasant producers will continue to farm their land even when returns fall consistently below the average rate of profit.
    2.   V.I. Lenin, Collected Works (Lawrence and Wishart, London, 1977), vol. 3.
    3.   A. Richards, Egypt's Agricultural Development: Technical and Social Change, 1800-1980 (Westview Press, Boulder, Colorado, 1981).
    4.   K. Ikram, Egypt: Economic Management in a Period of Transition (John Hopkins University Press, Baltimore, 1980), p. 415.

5. Ikram, Economic Management, p. 415.

6. Ibid.

7. E.R.J. Owen, Cotton in the Egyptian Economy, 1820-1914 (Oxford University Press, London, 1969), p. 148.

8. See C. Bradley, 'State Capitalism in Egypt: a Critique of Patrick Clawson', Khamsin, no. 10 (1983), pp. 73-9. Bradley argues that Egyptian industry at this period was not intended to accumulate capital and was sustained by precapitalist dynamics.

9. P. Clawson, 'The Development of Capitalism in Egypt', Khamsin, no. 9 (1981), p. 84.

10. S. Radwan, Agrarian Reform and Rural Poverty, Egypt, 1957-75 (International Labour Organisation, Geneva, 1977), p. 7.

11. Richards, Egypt's Agricultural Development, p. 174.

12. Rents at this period equalled 75 per cent of net income. G Saab, The Egyptian Agrarian Reform 1952-1962 (Oxford University Press, London, 1967), p. 11.

13. This is convincingly argued by Patrick Clawson, who takes issue with those who have argued that foreign capital consistently opposed the development of local industry in Egypt. Clawson relates the changing role of foreign capital within the Egyptian economy to phases in the internationalisation of capital itself. See Clawson, 'Development of Capitalism'.

14. Ibid., p. 89.

15. Richards, Egypt's Agricultural Development, p. 174.

16. Ibid.

17. Data published by the Agricultural Census Section of the Ministry of Agriculture.

18. In 1966, for example, this group of medium landlords received 80 per cent of total agricultural credit: Fathy Abdel-Fattah, Al-Qariyya al-Masriyya 1952-1970 (Dar al-Thiqafa al-Jadida, Cairo, 1973), p. 27.

19. T.J. Byres, 'Agrarian Transition and the Agrarian Question', Journal of Peasant Studies, vol. 4 (1977), pp. 258-74. The main crops grown by this group, fruit and vegetables, were and indeed still are free from government price controls, and bills proposing the removal of land tax exemption from fruit orchards which were presented to parliamentary committees in 1972 and 1977 were rejected through the successful lobbying of this group: J. Waterbury, The Egypt of Nasser and Sadat (Princeton University Press, 1983), p. 293.

20. See A. Abdel-Malek, Egypt: Military Society (Vintage Books, New York, 1968), and G. Stauth, 'Subsistenzproduktion und Akkumulation', Bielefelder Studien zur Entwicklungssoziologie, no. 5, (1979) pp. 61-100.

21. Radwan, Agrarian Reform, p. 23.

22. Ibid, p. 31.

23. M. Abdel-Fadil, Development, Income Distribution and

Social Change in Rural Egypt, 1952-1972 (Cambridge University Press, 1975), p. 117.

24.   Eg. Pepsi-Cola and Coca-Cola. See A. Richards, 'Peasant Differentiation and Politics in Contemporary Egypt', Peasant Studies, vol. 9, no. 3, (1982), pp. 151-2.

25.   The final land reform law of September 1969 lowered the ownership ceiling for individuals from 100 to 50 feddans. No official statistics have been released on the resulting land redistribution, which is widely believed not in fact to have been enforced. It would anyhow have accounted for not more than about 30,000 feddans. See Waterbury, Egypt of Nasser and Sadat, p. 266.

26.   However the size brackets employed by the Ministry of Agriculture for land holdings changed in the mid-1970s. The figures for 1977/8 relate to the bracket which comprises landholdings of five feddans and less. (For other years and for land ownership, it comprises farms less than five feddans).

27.   Since, as already noted, the size brackets employed by the Ministry of Agriculture changed in the mid-1970s, there is an upward bias in the figures for landholding for 1977/8 compared with those for landholding in previous years and with the figures on land ownership. This however, does not affect the general argument which concerns trends.

28.   The estimates are from the Central Organisation for Mobilisation and Statistics, and the Ministry of Foreign Affairs, respectively; cited in Al-Ahram al Iqtisadi, 2 May 1983, p. 10.

29.   Ibid., p. 18.

30.   Alan Richards and Philip Martin, 'Rural Wages and Agricultural Planning: The Case of Egypt', Economics Working Paper, no. 31. Agricultural Development Systems Project, Egyptian Ministry of Agriculture and the University of California.

31.   This section is based on field work in the village of Dahshur between October 1981 and May 1983. The statistical data is based on a random sample of one hundred households and on records of the village agricultural co-operative. Dahshur is not a 'typical' village in the sense of its conforming to an average national type, for given the heterogeneity of villages in Egypt today, such an average type would indeed be meaningless. For a classification of different Egyptian 'village types', see N. Hopkins, 'Annotated Bibliography of Egyptian Village Studies', Economics Working Paper, no. 42, Agricultural Development Systems Project, Egyptian Ministry of Agriculture and the University of California.

32.   This and the following national level figures refer to the year 1977/8, the most recent year for which land holding data is available. Village data refers to the year 1981/2.

33.   An examination of modern Turkish agriculture has also suggested that the uneven penetration of the domestic and

foreign markets into different types of Turkish village structures has given rise not to a uniform transformation of agrarian production relations, but to alternative paths of transformation evidenced by different types of village structures: Caglar Keydar, 'Paths of Rural Transformation in Turkey', in T. Asad and R. Owen (eds.) Sociology of "Developing Societies": The Middle East (Macmillan, London, 1983), pp. 163-77.

34. Clawson, 'Development of Capitalism', p. 95.
35. Ibid., p. 96.
36. Ibid.
37. Ibid.
38. Ibid.

Chapter Nine

AGRO-INDUSTRY, STATE POLICY AND RURAL SOCIAL STRUCTURES: RECENT
ANALYSES OF PROLETARIANISATION IN BRAZILIAN AGRICULTURE

David Goodman, Bernardo Sorj and John Wilkinson

The profound transformation of rural social structures in
Brazil since the 1960s has prompted equally marked shifts in
the debate on the agrarian question. Three major formulations
of agrarian structures and their integration with industrial
capitalism can be distinguished. These are the articulation
approach, the classic internal proletarianisation process of
the 'Junker road', and formulations which posit the
subordination of modernised family producers to the
agro-industrial 'complex'. None of these perspectives has been
totally eclipsed despite the rapidly changing terrain of the
debate on the 'dominant tendency' in the social division of
labour in Brazilian agriculture. The evolution of this
discussion provides insights into the analysis and empirical
significance of the process of rural proletarianisation in
Brazil during the past twenty years.

A REVIEW OF THE BRAZILIAN AGRARIAN DEBATES

Our review focuses on recent formulations which regard
state-subsidised modernisation policies and the rise of
agro-industry as the critical determinants of change in
agrarian social structures in the 1970s. These policies, it is
argued, have promoted the capitalisation of the rural labour
process and the commoditisation of small-scale agriculture,
accelerating the rate of rural proletarianisation. It is
suggested that these tendencies reveal a fundamental
re-articulation of rural-urban relations, characterised by the
direct integration of agriculture in the reproduction of
industrial capitals. This so-called 'industrialisation' of
agriculture is presented as defining a new model of
accumulation, which represents a radical departure from the
articulation model proposed earlier by Oliveira and Sá. However
since these seminal contributions provide the starting point
for current formulations, we need to consider them, if only
briefly.(1)

189

Oliveira sought to demonstrate, contrary to dualist prognoses, that the persistence of 'backward' agrarian structures had not impeded rapid post-war industrialisation, whether by failing to mobilise the agricultural surplus or to constitute a 'home market' for capitalist industry. Oliveira argued that the extensive occupation of successive new agricultural frontiers by a 'primitive' agriculture was of primordial importance in the consolidation of an urban, industrial pattern of accumulation and growth. On the supply side, commodity surpluses for domestic consumption and export were achieved by frontier incorporation based on the reproduction of 'archaic', non-capitalist relations of labour exploitation embedded in the 'latifundio-minifundio complex'.(2) This historical process of frontier expansion or 'growth by the elaboration of peripheries' is characterised by Oliveira as one of permanent primitive accumulation.(3) Conditions for the permanent appropriation of the surplus by extra-economic means are created and reproduced by the transient access rural labour has to the land. These conditions are found both on the 'external frontier' of recent agricultural settlement and, via the rotation of uncultivated land, on the 'internal frontier' of latifundia in long-settled regions, such as the Northeast.

Frontier incorporation by non-capitalist forms of production enabled Brazilian agriculture to respond adequately to the demands of rapid industrial growth, releasing commodity and financial resource flows without provoking any sustained movement of the internal terms of trade against industry.(4) In Oliveira's model of inter-sectoral articulation, 'primitive' agriculture makes a direct contribution to urban capital accumulation by reducing the long-term reproduction cost of labour employed in urban capitalist sectors and commercial agriculture. The use-values produced by non-capitalist forms of production subsidise urban capital accumulation by depressing rural real wages, and hence the real prices of foodstuffs, the main urban wage goods,(5) and reducing the transfer price of rural migrants entering the urban reserve army of labour. These mechanisms were grounded in the existence of absolute surplus population and expanding agricultural frontiers which created the conditions for permanent primitive accumulation.

In his attack on the allegedly crude dualist models of the 'feudalism versus capitalism' controversy in Brazil, Oliveira thus emphasised that the reproduction of non-capitalist forms of rural production was functional, not inimical, to industrial capital accumulation. Moreover, the strong income concentration tendencies and the creation of an urban middle class market which characterised the import substitution pattern of industrial development in Brazil reduced the strategic significance of the rural sector as a 'home market' for manufactured goods. The articulation of the capitalist mode of production and non-capitalist forms of rural production established favourable conditions for urban capital formation, cementing the 'structural pact' between the urban bourgeoisie and the rural landed class. Despite the structural shift in the locus of accumulation from the primary export sector to industry, this articulation model 'permitted the system to leave the basis of agrarian production untouched, bypassing the problems of the distribution of land ownership which seemed critical at the end of the 1950s'.(6)

Following the coup of 1964, the authoritarian state upheld the pact between urban capital and landed rural property.(7) Rural labour movements were repressed and reformist, distributionist pretensions abandoned, despite their recurrence in policy rhetoric. Although the maintenance of conditions necessary for the expanded reproduction of urban industrial capital has imparted a fundamental continuity to post-war agricultural development policy in Brazil,(8) the focus of this strategy in the later 1960s moved gradually but decisively from frontier occupation to the capitalisation of the rural production process, via state-subsidised investment policies, principally rural credit programmes. The promotion of technological innovation and productivity growth within the inherited framework of highly concentrated landownership has aptly been described as 'conservative modernisation' since its purpose is to transform the latifundio, the symbol of 'primitive', 'feudal' agriculture into a large modern agricultural enterprise. This re-orientation of rural development strategy, supported by resource re-allocation on a massive scale, is regarded by many authors as a radical new stage in the capitalist penetration of rural social structures. The earlier articulation model, in which theoretical interest centred upon relations of exploitation within non-capitalist forms of production, is superceded in the literature by analyses of the extension of capitalist social relations to the countryside under the aegis of state modernisation policies.

Two moments can be discerned in the evolving analysis of the role of the state in the transformation of 'primitive' rural social structures. Initially, the wave of proletarianisation which accompanied such state interventions as the coffee tree eradication programme and rural labour and welfare legislation was seen as the response of latifundio owners to discriminatory, but isolated, policies.(9) Labour-intensive crops, such as coffee, were replaced by temporary short-cycle crops or permanent pastures and resident workers (colonos, agregados, moradores) were expelled in favour of temporary wage-labour (volantes), hired on a casual basis to circumvent the provisions of rural labour legislation.

Subsequently, however, it was recognised that the state was pursuing a deliberate, coherent strategy to transform the productive base in agriculture via its integration with the agro-industry complex. 'Conservative modernisation' was seen as an alternative to agrarian reform and analytical interest turned to the transformation of the labour process on large properties and the 'purification' of wage relations hitherto 'disguised' by non-monetary forms of remuneration. The 'mixed' labour control systems characteristic of large estates, particularly coffee and sugarcane plantations, received the coup de grâce from rural labour legislation and subsidised industrial inputs. The final collapse of these moribund systems, and the emergence of a rural proletariat, were hailed as the fullest expression of capitalist relations in agriculture. In this phase of the Brazilian debate, the classic Marxist treatments of social differentiation, particularly by Lenin and Kautsky, enjoyed a marked revival.

D'Incão e Mello presented a seminal statement of the 'Junker road' thesis in her study of changing social structures in the Alto Sorocabana region of São Paulo. She argued that the advance of capitalism, characterised by the concentration of land ownership, property speculation, and the rising capital-intensity of the rural labour process, was generalising the wage relation in agriculture. Rural workers, excluded from direct access to the production process, depressed wages in rural and urban labour markets, constituting an industrial reserve army as defined by Marx 'whether in terms of its structural causes or the form of its particular participation in the overall production process of the regional rural economy'.(10) The elimination of 'disguised wage workers', whether share-croppers, short-term tenants (arrendatarios) or resident workers, and their proletarianisation as non-resident, casual wage-labour, popularly called bóias-frias, is regarded as the 'historical affirmation' of the capitalist mode of production in agriculture.

Brant extended this formulation in his case-study of southwestern São Paulo, arguing that changes in land use, crop mix and the modernisation of the rural labour process have created a relative surplus population and so undermined the advantages of retaining a fixed, resident labour force, paving the way for the emergence of a capitalist labour market. The growing relative importance of temporary wage labour marks 'the transformation of agriculture into industry and the formation of an industrial reserve army'.(11) For Brant, the bóia-fria signifies the approaching unification of urban and rural labour markets which, by equalising conditions of accumulation, will unleash the capitalist forces of production in the 'industrialisation' of agriculture.

On this view, the state with its strategy of 'conservative modernisation' is the architect of a new model of accumulation characterised by the expansion and diversification of the agro-industrial complex and the rapid penetration of capitalist relations of production in agriculture. Inherited labour control systems on large properties, predicated on labour scarcity, would be superceded by the growth of a landless free labour force available for casual employment. The old latifundio structure, with its resident workers and 'internal minifundia' of share-croppers and tenants, would be replaced by the capitalised enterprise utilising temporary wage-labour as the new paradigm of Brazilian agriculture. The work of D'Incão e Mello and Brant stimulated a flood of case-studies of the bóia-fria phenomenon and its regional manifestations, which typically is taken as evidence of the consolidation of capitalist relations of production.(12)

The contribution of Graziano da Silva should be mentioned here as he straddles different stages of the debate.(13) Thus rural structures, and particularly the latifundio, remain as the focal point of his analysis of the state's modernisation policies. These are represented as an alternative to land reform in the context of rapidly expanding urban and international demand for agricultural products. However, Graziano draws attention to the singular nature of the new rural proletariat. Rather than the most advanced expression of capitalist relations, he suggests that it reflects the limited character of capitalist penetration, notably in harvest operations. Graziano da Silva also observes the increasing identity of interest between agro-industrial capitals and the state in extending the modernisation process. In this respect, he can be regarded as a precursor of current perspectives.

In the present stage of the debate, rural structures are no longer at the centre of theoretical discussion. The analytical focus now is firmly centred on the strategic importance assumed by agro-industrial capitals in determining rural social relations. The expansion of these capitals is treated as an integral part of the post-1964 industrialisation process and the concomitant internationalisation of the Brazilian economy. Three basic perspectives on rural social stuctures can be discerned within this general approach.

The first formulation, insofar as it focuses on agrarian social relations, tends to identify capitalism with modernisation. In the work of Geraldo Muller, for example, the modernised family farm becomes a small capitalist enterprise.(14) Muller defends the view that the dominant tendency in Brazilian agriculture is toward a generalised process of modernisation or capitalist penetration, both regionally and across different property size strata. This Leninist perspective is also advanced by Sandroni, for whom the modernised peasant is essentially bourgeois, and rural social structures are reducible to a capitalist/proletarian dichotomy.(15)

A second position, found in the work of Wanderley, is influenced by recent French contributions.(16) Affirming the strategic dominance of agro-industry in the dynamic of rural social structures, Wanderley discards the classical social differentiation thesis in favour of a conceptualisation of the modernised family farm as a specific form of the worker/capitalist relation.(17) This notion of subordination also receives support from Graziano da Silva, who accepts Wanderley's characterisation of the 'new peasant' on modernised, family-labour farms as 'a worker for capital'. Failure to appreciate that the peasant participates in the process of the expanded reproduction of capital leads to the adoption of an unnecessarily restrictive concept of proletarianisation, according to Graziano da Silva.(18)

Against these positions, a third formulation can be identified which applies certain Marxist propositions, recently re-stated by Dickinson and Mann, on the singularity of the production process in agriculture.(19) On this view, the marked divergence of labour time and production time and lower capital turnover rates depress the rate of profit in many sectors of rural activity, which effectively precludes the entry of large capitalist enterprises. This analysis has led several contributors to characterise the modernised family farm as the privileged partner of agro-industrial capitals. A variant of this argument, which also draws on the rate of profit hypothesis, contends that the conditions for the development of a capitalist agriculture have been undermined by the oligopolistic character of agro-industrial capitals.(20)

This brief exposition reveals that the Brazilian debate has evolved from the articulation model to perspectives which emphasise the generalisation of capitalist production relations and the instrumental role assumed by the state and agro-industrial capitals. Agro-industry now constitutes the point of departure for analysing the dynamic of rural social relations in Brazil.

CRITIQUE OF CURRENT THESES OF PROLETARIANISATION

While we would not dispute the centrality of agro-industry in identifying the main tendencies at work in Brazilian agriculture, the current literature is marred by several serious limitations. We would argue that these include (i) a false conceptualisation of the ' agro-industrial complex'; (ii) an incorrect characterisation of the rural labour process on modernised properties as constituting a specifically capitalist labour process, and (iii) the identification of one or other agrarian structure, whether 'worker for capital' or modernised family farm, as the privileged ally of agro-industry. This implies a functional, essentialist relation between the development of agro-industry and the consolidation of appropriate rural structures.

However, these limitations are not peculiar to the Brazilian literature. Indeed, as the review above suggested, the subordinate integration of Brazilian agriculture into the circuit of agro-industrial capitals has been accompanied by a growing approximation of Brazilian debates to those currently being conducted in Europe and the United States. This intellectual integration is not simply the product of imitation but reflects the increasingly similar pressures to which Brazilian agriculture is being subjected. Our critique thus extends beyond the Brazilian literature and can be understood as a contribution to the more unified debate now occurring on a world scale. In this paper, we will restrict our comments to those pertinent to the discussion of the main patterns which characterise the development of rural social structures in Brazil.(21)

Common to all current formulations in the Brazilian debate is the hypothesis of a dual alliance: that of agro-industrial capitals, as represented in the notion of the agro-industrial 'complex', and between the 'complex' and agrarian structure, with this alliance expressing a process of the 'industrialisation' of agriculture. Against the notion of the agro-industrial 'complex', with its implicit assumption of homogeneous, non-competing capitals, we would argue that, in their origin and subsequent development, agro-industrial capitals are essentially autonomous and the degree of their mutual integration is variable. The idea of the 'complex' derives from a misguided attempt to generalise the consolidation of a particular model based on the tractor/monoculture/hybrid seeds/fertiliser/herbicides. Yet the different agro-industrial branches make distinct demands on the agricultural sector and specific capital fractions have quite different growth prospects; consider, for example, the present crisis of the tractor industry, the alternative growth paths open to the inputs versus processing branches, or those of agro-chemical capitals given the prospect of nitrogen fixation based on biological processes.

State policies thus cannot be seen as uniformly representing or promoting the agro-industrial 'complex'. Furthermore, specific agro-industrial capitals clearly can have conflicting strategies of accumulation and growth, as in the case of the processing sectors and the food industry, with its increasing recourse to additives, synthetic compounds and alternative sources of protein. The emergence and conjunctural unification of different agro-industrial capitals is an uneven and successively re-defined process, dependent upon the rhythm of scientific advance and technological innovation. It is quite misleading to represent this process in terms of the formation of a static, consolidated 'complex'. To do so is to misinterpret both the dynamic of agro-industrial capitals and their integration with rural social structures.

A second limitation of the concept of the agro-industrial 'complex' is that it invokes the existence of a unified production process. This presumption is made explicit in the conceptualisation of the peasant or modernised family farmer as a 'worker for capital', that is, agro-industrial capital. Against this, we would argue that the emergence of these capitals demonstrates precisely the impossibility of establishing a unified capitalist labour process in the sphere of rural production. In the absence of these conditions, fractions of agro-industrial capital represent the successive but partial industrial appropriation of aspects of the rural production process. The direct rural producer is left to combine precisely those elements which have not yet been incorporated into industrial production. That is, he must coordinate or 'manage' the series of partial industrial appropriations represented by agro-industrial inputs: equipment, seeds, fertiliser, etc. Dramatic witness to the lack of integral responsibility for the rural labour process is given by the progressive destruction of its principal means of production, the land. This anarchic pattern of appropriation indicates the absence of a unified, capitalist labour process. It is the corollary of the predatory logic of fractions of agro-industrial capital which regard the rural sector merely as a market for their products.

The concept of the agro-industrial 'complex' also conveys the notion of a static division between 'agriculture' and 'industry'. Agro-industry is not constituted by the appropriation of those aspects of the agricultural labour process which are specifically 'industrial'. On the contrary, agro-industry embraces a constantly changing mix of capitals and represents the continuous attempt by industrial capitals to transform agriculture into an industrial process. As such, it has no static, pre-established limits: its terrain is determined by technical progress and innovation. In this respect, the agro-industrial 'complex' represents an incomplete, transitional phase in the industrial appropriation of agriculture.

As a corollary of this dynamic of capitalist growth, there is no basis for a privileged relation between agrarian structures and agro-industrial capitals. Such a notion completely misrepresents the movement of these capitals. They are constantly undermining the conditions of rural production, appropriating successively more elements of the labour process as advances in science and technology permit the industrialisation of previously 'rural' or natural activities. Nor should this development be seen from a unilinear perspective since a breakthrough in one area of science and technology may disrupt existing patterns of appropriation and create new directions for the expansion of agro-industry.

It is only in a negative sense, therefore, that agro-industry can be said to consolidate specific, privileged forms of rural production. The progressive appropriation of the rural production process by industrial capitals inhibits the development of large-scale, wage labour-based operations as a paradigm for agriculture. The existence of agro-industrial capitals, themselves products of the absence of a unified capitalist labour process, in turn thwarts its realisation in the form of large agricultural enterprises. The modern family labour unit can then be seen as the rural production structure most compatible with the process of industrial appropriation, but only to the extent that industrial capitals are unable to completely eliminate land and 'nature' as the basis of rural production.

In this context, it is important to emphasise that it is not rent which is the barrier to capital. Rent is simply the social expression of the domination of the agricultural production process by land as 'nature'. The family labour farm is not therefore an ally of capital, as Vergopoulos has suggested, arguing that it permits industrial capitals to appropriate rent. On the contrary, we would argue that the predominance of the family unit is the result of the progressive erosion of the conditions for the generation of rent due to the appropriation and transformation of agricultural activities into industrial production processes.

In conclusion, the Brazilian discussion suffers from a static, homogenising view of agro-industrial capitals, which in turn produces a static analysis of the relations between agro-industry and rural social structures. While one formulation reduces the modernised family farm to a transitional small capitalist enterprise in a revamped version of Leninist orthodoxy, the 'worker for capital' analysis erroneously assumes the existence of a unified, capitalist labour process and so is unable to capture the forms of representation and conflict peculiar to the modern farmer. Rather than the fullest expression and definitive form of capitalism's presence in agriculture, agro-industrial capitals are the protagonists of an unstable and constantly redefined alliance between rural, land-based or nature-based, processes and capitalist industrial production processes, with the former being successively undermined and appropriated by the latter. There can therefore be no permanently privileged alliance between agro-industry and agriculture. Rural production as dominated by land or 'nature' is intrinsically inimical to the capitalist industrial labour process, and the advance of agro-industry thus is necessarily at the expense of rural production, only reinforcing certain social structures conjuncturally.

AGRO-INDUSTRY AND BRAZILIAN RURAL STRUCTURES

This section presents a re-interpretation of the principal tendencies at work in Brazilian agriculture and attempts a schematic regionalisation of rural social structures. We begin, however, with some further observations on the development of agro-industry in Brazil. Prior to the 1960s, agro-industrial capitals were concentrated in crop processing and marketing, with imports as the major source of modern production inputs and agricultural equipment. This industrial structure was radically transformed by a series of vigorous state interventions in the later 1960s and 1970s, including import substitution programmes for modern inputs, rural infra-structural investment, the re-organisation of agricultural extension services and research and, above all, heavily-subsidised credit for investment in capital equipment and the purchase of modern inputs. Rural credit increased five-fold in real terms in the years 1968-78, and the interest rate subsidy was equivalent to roughly 30 per cent of the net value of agricultural production in 1978.(22) Through a bewildering array of official credit programmes covering production, marketing and investment activities, the state has mediated input-output relations between modernising agricultural sectors and agro-industrial capitals, subsidising markets and accelerating the diversification of agro-industry. This strategy also distinguishes Brazil from cases of partial incorporation of selected agricultural sectors by agro-industrial transnationals to establish export enclaves. In contrast, Brazilian agriculture as a whole is the object of modernisation, even though policy measures have been heavily selective by farm size, crop and region. Agro-industry in Brazil consequently has developed as an organic extension of the industrial structure and its domination by transnational corporations, as in other key sectors of the economy, is based primarily on the extension of the internal market.(23)

We would also suggest that the state's deliberate promotion of agro-industry as a strategy to resolve the 'agrarian question' in Brazil without undermining the latifundio-dominated agrarian structure does not imply that these two actors are privileged allies. In fact, since the growth of agro-industry represents the increasing appropriation of the rural production process, large wage-labour enterprises would be less likely a priori to establish conditions for their consolidation than owner-operator family units, as we argued in the preceding discussion. However, this general proposition abstracts from the rural social relations established prior to agro-industrial expansion in different social formations and, more specifically, the degree to which these relations are defended at the level of state policy. Access to state support may well compensate the erosive effect of agro-industry in progressively appropriating surplus. In such cases, and pre-eminently so in Brazil, agro-industrial expansion is compatible with the maintenance of a variety of rural social structures. In contrast to several of the formulations reviewed earlier, agro-industrialisation in Brazil has shown no tendency to impose a homogeneous pattern on the social division of labour. Rather, state policy in defence of existing agrarian structures has reinforced the heterogeneity of social relations in Brazilian agriculture.

In this respect, four basic structures can be discerned which broadly coincide with a regionalisation of Brazilian agriculture. The following analysis is highly schematic since all these social relations occur within each 'region'. Nevertheless, a specific social structure tends to predominate in each one, giving a particular 'regional' character to forms of representation and struggle.

Agro-industry and Large Properties: the Centre-South

Drawing on the analyses of D'Incão e Mello, Brant, and Graziano da Silva, we can summarise the modernisation process on large properties along the following lines. State subsidies for mechanical and chemical inputs have progressively transformed the labour-intensive production system, based primarily on permanent resident workers and 'internal' peasant tenants, complemented by casual wage labourers from nearby minifundia and seasonal migrants. This social division of labour has been superceded by production processes which are increasingly mechanised and dependent on industrialised inputs, and which simultaneously have replaced permanent by temporary labour and, within the permanent labour force, substituted semi-skilled machine operatives for unskilled workers. These trends have been exacerbated by the high concentration of land ownership and changes in land use, notably the process of pecuarização which involves the substitution of permanent pasture for annual arable crops, depriving 'external' family farm units of opportunities to rent in land on short-term, seasonal tenancies.

The character of the temporary rural labour force thus has changed radically, becoming increasingly urban-based in the sense that its reproduction costs are now derived entirely from wage labour. Lacking access to the land, the volante or bóia-fria foreshadows the unification of the urban and rural labour markets. Yet, while this proletarianisation process in the interior of large properties consolidates a permanent reserve army, it simultaneously eliminates the production of use-values by peasant families, the basis of the hitherto lower reproduction costs of rural labour. That is, it enhances the advantages of modernised labour processes.

According to this formulation, the rural proletariat of temporary urban-based volante labour is characteristic of the intensification of capitalist relations in the countryside. We would argue, however, that the true face of modernisation on these large properties is not this large impoverished rural proletariat but the relatively small number of permanent, semi-skilled machine operators. The volante proletariat, although the product of modernisation, exists only to the extent that this process is incomplete. The major demand for temporary rural labour occurs at harvest time, but recent advances suggest that there are no insuperable technological barriers to the mechanisation of harvesting operations. The maintenance of manual harvesting for such crops as coffee, sugarcane, cotton and oranges, which typically are produced on large properties, would thus seem to be a conjunctural phenomenon, determined by the rural labour surplus and the institutional context of repressive labour relations.

Other factors also cast doubt on the structural permanence of this large rural proletariat. First, increasing monoculture specialisation, notably in sugarcane, stimulated by the Brazilian Alcohol Programme (PROALCOOL), is reducing opportunities for year-round employment in rural activities.(24) Casual employment in the urban sectors also provides an alternative to rural wage labour. In addition, volante labour is gradually becoming more organised and attracting support from the leadership of the rural labour movement (CONTAG), although the high point of organisation and struggle of temporary rural workers is to be found outside the Centre-South in the sugarcane zone of Pernambuco.(25) Higher levels of labour organisation and the more favourable climate of the political abertura also have led to advances in the regulation of the conditions of temporary rural employment in recent years.(26) A marked accentuation of these trends, allied to a sustained recovery in urban employment and real wages, could significantly accelerate the mechanisation of harvest operations, which is primarily responsible for the mass character of volante wage labour.

A detailed assessment of the tendencies towards the consolidation or dissolution of the large casual rural proletariat remains crucial for an analysis of the dynamic of social relations and the character of rural struggles. Nevertheless, it is essential to recognise that the bóia-fria is not the rural variant of urban wage labour, whose condition will be consolidated by the development of capitalist relations in the countryside. The typical expression of modernisation on large properties is the replacement of large numbers of unskilled manual workers by a handful of semi-skilled labour. As we have suggested, harvest mechanisation would virtually eliminate volante or bóia-fria labour as a mass phenomenon. Large-scale production is not immutably associated with large-scale wage labour employment. The rural proletariat in the form of the volante or bóia-fria thus cannot be seen as a necessarily permanent feature of rural social relations.

This has important implications for the labour movement and future changes in the structure of agricultural production in the Centre-South region. In short, effective action in organising the bóias-frias, significantly increasing their bargaining power and coverage under official labour and welfare legislation, could lead to renewed efforts to mechanise the remaining phases of the agricultural cycle. This would produce a rapid and dramatic decline in the absolute size of the rural proletariat. On the other hand, the consolidation of such a highly mechanised, capital-intensive labour process would depend on the degree to which the state is able to maintain its traditionally privileged treatment of modernised large properties. In the present unsettled circumstances, it is difficult to predict where the final balance will lie. Brazil's current profound economic crisis already has brought a drastic reduction in levels of subsidy to the rural sector but it has also enhanced the priority of the PROALCOOL programme and export crops.

The Modernised Family Farm: The South

The modernisation of the family farm on a significant scale was first observed in the later 1950s and 1960s in the market gardening sector which developed in the 'green belt' surrounding metropolitan São Paulo. This phenomenon was analysed in a pioneering paper by Lopes and subsequently by Graziano da Silva.(27) Both explain this development in terms of a division of labour between capitalist and family farm sectors in which the latter survives by specialising in crops which require high and continuous labour inputs. The specificity of the labour process for particular crops thus may provide a special niche for the reproduction of modernised family farm units, permitting their co-existence with capitalist farm enterprises.

However, this analysis clearly is inadequate when we consider the predominance achieved by the modernised family farm in the 1960s and 1970s in the most dynamic and most highly mechanised sector of Brazilian agriculture, soybean production, in Rio Grande do Sul, Santa Catarina and Paraná. For example, in Ijuí, a major soybean-producing region of Rio Grande do Sul, 70 per cent of the cultivated area occurs on properties of under 100 hectares, and permanent and temporary wage labour together constitute only 5 per cent of the total labour force employed.(28) This modernisation of small family properties can be attributed in part to the institutional framework found in the South, including a relatively well-developed agro-industrial structure of input-supplying and processing firms, and a network of state agencies and cooperatives established earlier to promote wheat production. The world market boom in soybean prices of the early 1970s consolidated cooperatives as the preferred instrument of state modernisation policy, mediating between finance and agro-industrial capitals and their heterogeneous membership. The farming traditions inherited from the European immigrants who originally settled in the South also may explain the capacity of small family enterprises to respond to the new demands posed by agro-industrial capitals and integration with world markets.

In our earlier discussion of agro-industrial analyses, we advanced reasons for rejecting the 'new peasant-worker for capital' thesis. However, the alternative formulation given by Muller which regards the modernised family farm as a variant of the capitalist enterprise also is inadequate. First, the process of modernisation does not correspond to one of internal accumulation. Rather, this process is imposed from without by agro-industrial capitals, supported in the Brazilian case by institutional finance capital. For individual family units, the utilisation of mechanised equipment, selected seeds, fertilisers, pesticides and herbicides defines a technical 'threshold', which must be reached if the enterprise is to be incorporated into the agro-industrialised production process and achieve competitive levels of productivity. Moreover, access to this process requires systematic resort to credit, which carries the risk of cumulatively increasing indebtedness and foreclosure.(29) The 'technification' or 'capitalisation' of the labour process of the modernised family farm represents an accumulation of the means of production, not an accumulation of capital. Surplus value is appropriated by the different agro-industrial and finance capitals mediating the technification process, blocking the transformation of family labour units into capitalist enterprises.(30)

As 'technification' proceeds, traditional knowledge and skills are devalued as control over the production process increasingly becomes dictated by the norms of agro-industrial capitals. These norms have been enforced in the Brazilian case by making access to the official credit system conditional on technical agronomic criteria governing land preparation, use of modern inputs, and related practices. These criteria, moreover, are revised in line with the technical changes, and even conjunctural economic conditions, arising from the growth of the different agro-industrial capitals.

Integration into the circuit of agro-industrial capitals also involves a continuous struggle to maintain the minimum technological threshold, which is constantly being re-defined upwards in terms of the fixed assets and land area required to remain competitive. Farm families unable to accompany these technological transformations are progressively marginalised from the ongoing process of 'technification' or modernisation, constituting a relative surplus agrarian population. These marginalised or pauperised units arise from the continuous re-definition of relations between the modernising family farm and agro-industry. In the South, it is this layer which has provided the colonos to settle the new agricultural frontiers in Mato Grosso and Rondônia in the 1970s and early 1980s.

Integration with agro-industrial capitals and state institutions brings radical changes in the character of social representation and struggle. There is also a widening divergence of interest between the 'integrated' modernised family farmers and marginalised family producers. The privileged locus of the modernised family farm's insertion is through the cooperative movement, which was reinforced in the post-1964 period as a major element in the state's rationalisation of its modernisation strategy. The cooperatives facilitated the centralisation of credit, technical assistance and infra-structure services and thus provided an effective mechanism for the reconstruction of patterns of domination weakened by the rural mobilisations of the 1950s and early 1960s. Such incorporation both encourages the organised expression of interests at the same time as it structures demands within new parameters.

These demands are no longer primarily defined by antagonistic rural interests with land as the focus of conflict. Rather, the central issues arise from their subordinate integration into the structures of modernisation and involve credit, input costs, prices, and access to institutional mechanisms. The typical pattern of modernised family farmer mobilisations, such as the tractorcade through the state capital or strategic regional centre, graphically illustrates this shift from a rural to an urban definition of power relations. This can be sharply contrasted with the rural encampments, Ronda Alta providing an outstanding example, which characterise the mobilisations of marginalised peasants in the South whose struggle continues to centre on the classic demand for land.(31)

This is not to under-estimate the modernised farmer's capacity to organise nor deny that militancy may reach high levels, as shown by the protest movements in the 1980s in the states of Rio Grande do Sul, Paraná and Santa Catarina against low pig prices and the confiscation tax levied on soybean export earnings. However, the dominant demands of this category are losing their classic peasant content (agrarian reform) and assuming a more clearly corporativist and specific character. Land obviously remains a critical issue, particularly since modernisation continually increases the minimum efficient size of holding. However, with a developed land market and institutional mechanisms to facilitate purchase, access to land increasingly is perceived as an individual question, and less an object of collective struggle.

The Northeast

The continued heterogeneity of rural social structures in the Northeast owes less to any marked differences in the pace of modernisation or the vigour of state intervention than to its uneven spatial incidence. This unevenness is a direct consequence of the region's semi-arid climate and the poverty of its natural resources as the basis for productive rain-fed agriculture. The slower development of commodity production and the productive forces in turn has inhibited the expansion of markets for modern inputs and the related institutional network which would support a diversified industrial sector. Such factors, rather than any intrinsic backwardness on the part of large proprietors, explain the predominance of pecuarização as the general form of latifundio modernisation in the semi-arid agreste and sertão areas. Other modernised forms of production also are found, although from a regional perspective they constitute enclaves. This characterisation can even be stretched to include the agro-industrialised sugarcane plantation zone, as well as modernised large properties in recently settled areas, such as the newly-established coffee plantations in western Bahia.

Nevertheless, there are close parallels with the rest of Brazil, none more so than in the sugarcane plantation sector of the humid zona da mata, where the gradual purification of 'disguised wage relations' has been observed since the mid-1940s. The expulsion of moradores, permanent workers with rights of access to land within the plantation, and the recruitment of landless wage labour, intensified in the later 1960s and 1970s. The acceleration of this process of overt proletarianisation has been attributed to the introduction of rural labour legislation, plantation owners' easier access to subsidised working capital and, more recently, the expansion of sugarcane cultivation under the PROALCOOL programme.(32)

As in other regions, the ready availability of subsidised institutional credit, reinforced by the privileged access of large propietors to special lines of investment credit, has sharply increased land values and encouraged property speculation. In the transitional climatic zone of the agreste, pecuarização has emerged as the principal means of achieving centralised control of the production process on mixed, arable-livestock properties. This form of 'conservative modernisation' has dealt a decisive blow to the articulated reproduction of the 'latifundio-minifundio complex'. With the substitution of permanent artificial pasture for mixed farming systems, notably that of cattle-cotton, 'internal' peasantries have been deprived of access to the means of production. These small tenants, whose reproduction typically combines commercial share-cropping and the production of use-values, are no longer required as a subsidised source of on-farm labour.

The economy of 'external' peasant households also is undermined by the corresponding decline in seasonal wage employment and in arable land available for rent on short, annual tenancies. These diminishing opportunities for employment arising from changing land use on large properties reinforce the secular process of demographic pressure and fragmentation in areas of minifundia, accelerating out-migration and the subsequent re-concentration of the means of production. Pecuarização, by greatly reducing the labour requirements of the latifundio, previously met by internal and external minifundia, has removed the basis of the symbiotic reproduction of these forms of production. 'Proletarianisation, in this specific case, assumes the form of a rural exodus, since it is impossible for the small proprietor to survive with the output of his land'.(33)

Erosion of the conditions of existence of these minifundia is accelerating the immiseration of small family producers. This trend is supported empirically by 1975 Agricultural Census data which indicate that the value of production on 70 per cent of all rural establishments in the Northeast fell below the level of one minimum wage. In effect, these establishments, which numbered 1,636.3 thousand in 1975, are essentially consumption units, contributing only marginally, if at all, to the net marketed surplus of agricultural commodities.(34) Morever, given the adverse effect of modernisation on employment opportunities, minifundia have only a residual and declining role as a rural labour reserve. This mass of pauperised peasantry remains as a potential urban reserve army, but any specific 'regional' significance this may once have conferred on the Northeast is denied by the proletarianisation tendencies at work throughout Brazilian agriculture.(35)

The extremely low levels of gross output and output per hectare encountered on the vast majority of holdings in the Northeast emphasise the enclave characteristics of modernisation. This notion is particularly apposite for the production of high-value crops, such as citrus fruits and table grapes, in the capital-intensive irrigation programmes managed by the Sao Francisco River Valley Commission (CODEVASF) and the National Department of Works against the Drought. (DNOCS). Individual agro-industrial enterprises, attracted by regional credit subsidies and tax incentives, also have created enclaves of modernised family labour farms, as in the case of the fruit and tomato processing projects of Maguary and Cica. These isolated cases of 'technified' family establishments involve out-grower arrangements in which the direct producers typically retain formal ownership of the land but exercise only partial control over the technical basis of production and marketing. The special circumstances of subordination to institutional and agro-industrial capitals lend particular characteristics to peasant mobilisation. These struggles focus mainly on the terms of incorporation in public irrigation schemes, control of the immediate labour process, input costs, and monopsonistic marketing institutions.(36)

This enclave pattern also extends to the 'integrated rural development' strategy introduced in the mid-1970s. such programmes as POLONORDESTE and Projeto Sertanejo seek to intensify commodity relations in selected areas of small-scale agriculture and promote incipient trends toward specialised production. The strategy essentially involves the incorporation of small family producers into the network of subsidised institutional credit, thereby integrating modern, industrial inputs firmly into the labour process and subordinating producers to the technical norms of production established by state agencies and agro-industrial capitals.(37) The competitive pressure on less efficient units exerted by the higher yields of modernised producers and rising land values are accentuated by related state programmes, such as improved, all-weather roads, other infra-structure facilities, and special credit lines for investment in agro-industrial processing capacity.(38)

Although the process is more advanced in the South, the

differentiation of peasant production in the Northeast is creating a narrow stratum of 'technified' family farms closely integrated into the circuit of agro-industrial capitals. Its structural counterpart, more accentuated in absolute terms, is a huge contingent of impoverished family labour producers on minifundia whose proletarianisation is manifest as a continuing rural exodus or permanent seasonal migration.

Despite the specificities of modernisation in the Northeast, there are close parallels with the rest of Brazil in the mobilisation of rural wage labour and peasant struggles. Indeed, the organisation and militancy of sugarcane workers in Pernambuco and, more recently, Paraiba, place them in the vanguard of the rural labour movement. Thus in Pernambuco the state federation of rural trade unions (FETAPE) since 1979 has fought several successful campaigns for better wages, improved working conditions, and more rigorous observance of the provisions of labour legislation. Moreover, following the partial strike of 1979 and the general strike of 1980, the employers conceded the legal right of cane workers to have access to subsistence plots (sitios) of up to two hectares in the plantation. Some notable, though isolated, struggles have arisen from the expulsion of long-established tenant families, whether share-croppers, arrendatarios or posseiros. These mobilisations revolve around the question of land and the defence of peasants' perceived status as farmers or lavradores, although operationally the struggle is to secure the tenure and other legal rights conferred by the Land Statute and labour legislation. The famous case of the Alagamar ranch in Paraiba, where the state intervened to expropriate and re-distribute land, exemplifies the successful mobilisation of small tenants. Conversely, there are countless instances of the expulsion of posseiros and other tenants without due legal compensation by recourse to fraudulent practices (grilagem), intimidation, and violence. The advent of PROALCOOL and the expansion of sugarcane production into areas previously devoted to mixed agriculture has given new impetus to the proletarianisation of tenant farm families, heightening peasant militancy, and generating an increasing number of violent land conflicts.

Amazonia

As we have seen, growth by 'the elaboration of peripheries' and primitive accumulation, excluding labour from permanent access to the land, are central elements in Oliveira's analysis of the reproduction of latifundia on successive agricultural frontiers. From a different perspective, spontaneous frontier settlement by migrant posseiros has been seen, somewhat paradoxically, as a historical process which successively reconstitutes the conditions of existence of 'peasant economy'. For example, Velho characterises frontier expansion as the reproduction of a subordinate, 'peasant' mode of production.(39) The frontier has delayed the advance of capitalist relations in agriculture and maintained a relatively homogeneous peasantry which, denied property in the means of production, is subordinated to the capitalist mode in a permanent process of surplus appropriation. This 'closed' form of frontier occupation, in contrast to the bourgeois American path, creates an undifferentiated peasantry rather than land-owning pioneer 'farmers'. This type of frontier social structure is attributed by Velho to the authoritarian antecedents and contemporary character of the state and capitalism in Brazil.

A major difficulty with this formulation is that the historical development of social relations and productive forces under capitalism is not integrated into the analysis as the main determinant of changing forms of frontier settlement and their periodisation. In the case of Amazonia, Velho thus implies that the settlement process will follow traditional patterns, maintaining the articulation between an extensive agriculture and industrial development; frontier occupation will continue to be characterised mainly by the extension of 'primitive' agriculture by peasant settlers, whose output will represent an important source of cheap foodstuffs for the urban proletariat.(40)

The constancy of the internal dynamic of frontier settlement and its economic determinants also is defended by Foweraker.(40) Although capitalist forms of production may emerge on a restricted scale, as in certain parts of Amazonia today, the occupation of these new areas is more likely to involve the expansion of the 'sub-capitalist economic environment'. The reproduction of non-capitalist social relations on the pioneer frontier is explained by the continuity of primitive accumulation, and the significance of this process and the concomitant transfer of surplus in sustaining capitalist accumulation at the centre. In the Brazilian case, the cycle of frontier development and its characteristic process of accumulation is reproduced on successive frontiers, such that primitive accumulation is not a historical stage of capitalist development but a 'hybrid mode of accumulation' subordinated to capitalism.

In addition, Foweraker argues that the frontier cycle, marked by the transition from non-capitalist to capitalist social structures, is central to the reproduction of the conditions of accumulation of Brazilian agriculture. This transition, mediated by violence, the legal system and the state apparatus, culminates in the expulsion of posseiro families and the establishment of private property in land. The cycle of primitive accumulation having run its course, the monopoly structure of land ownership and the prevailing rural social relations, notably those of the 'latifundio-minifundio complex', are again consolidated.

While recognising the merit of Foweraker's framework in analysing the articulation of agriculture and industrial capital accumulation before the 1960s, Sorj and Pompermayer question its extension to the more recent period, and particularly in the case of Amazonia. These authors reject Foweraker's contention that the surpluses mobilised by small producers on the pioneer frontier and appropriated by merchant capitals are still of decisive importance to urban food supply. This view neglects the impact of recent modernisation strategies in raising levels of output and productivity on large rural properties and capitalised family farms in long-settled areas. With the consolidation of agro-industry and the concomitant modernisation of the rural labour process, intensive sources of aggregate output growth are rapidly displacing earlier extensive patterns based on the incorporation of new agricultural frontiers. This re-articulation of intersectoral rural-urban relations in turn has relegated primitive accumulation to a secondary and diminishing role in the process of capitalist accumulation in Brazil. For this reason, Foweraker's characterisation of rural social structures in terms of the binary latifundio-minifundio complex also is misplaced. It fails to recognise the heterogeneous social relations arising from the differentiated processes of subordination associated with agro-industrial expansion.

Moreover, Sorj and Pompermayer suggest that frontier settlement increasingly is determined by the dynamic of agro-industrial accumulation, and not merchant capitals, imparting new characteristics to this process. With state mediation, the privileged mode of settlement involves the direct establishment of large capitalist enterprises, by-passing the prior stage of occupation of the frontier by posseiros and petty commodity producers. For Pompermayer, the fiscal incentives introduced in the mid-1960s, reinforced by national integration infrastructure projects and regional development programmes during the 1970s, gave a 'new rhythm and specificity to the large agricultural undertaking in Amazonia' by attracting fractions of modern industrial and agro-industrial capital.(42)

These large corporate capitals, national and multinational, have used subsidised investment credits to acquire huge tracts of public land, often sold directly or auctioned at purely nominal prices, for cattle-ranching, private settlement schemes, and speculation.(43) The presence of posseiros is an unnecessary complication rather than an asset for such capitals, especially given the availability of heavy equipment for land clearance and pasture formation. In other words, primitive accumulation with its basis in violence and fraudulent grileiro land-grabbing strategems to secure legal title corresponds more typically, though not exclusively, to the imperatives of traditional merchant capitals. In contrast to this traditional pattern, the modern corporate capitals accumulated in the Centre-South, with access to subsidised state funds for land purchase, including the pre-emptive enclosure of hitherto unsettled land, do not have primitive accumulation as their modus vivendi.

The occupation of Amazonia must still be analysed within the process of capitalist accumulation, but this relation is no longer fully specified by permanent primitive accumulation, extension of the 'sub-capitalist economic environment', and reproduction of the latifundio-minifundio social structure. According to Pompermayer, previous extensive, 'horizontal' settlement patterns are being superceded by a simultaneous process of frontier settlement and 'vertical expansion'. With the state-mediated entry of large modern capitals, frontier settlement has become directly integrated into the expanded reproduction of agro-industry, providing sources of supply for meat-packing and food processing plants and markets for agricultural equipment and modern inputs.

The social structures which characterised the traditional 'pioneer' frontier and subordination to merchant capitals similarly are being transformed as modern capitals assume control of the settlement process. In this respect, major private settlement companies, such as Indeco and Sinop in northern Mato Grosso, recently have introduced out-grower arrangements with settlers or colonos as part of a strategy of internal vertical integration to supply their processing plants. Subordination of the rural labour process to institutional finance capital and its technical agronomic criteria also characterises public settlement programmes, as in Rondônia. More specialised commodity production, with food staples assuming secondary importance in terms of commercial interest, is actively encouraged by special credit programmes for selected products, including cocoa (Ceplac), manioc (PROALCOOL), and rubber (Proborracha).

The 'vertical expansion' associated with the direct participation of industrial, agro-industrial and finance capitals in the settlement process will bring changes in the forms of representation and struggle of rural workers. For example, the mobilisation in 1981-2 of capitalised family rice producers in northern Mato Grosso, which included an encampment in Brasília to press their demands to the federal authorities and Congress, was triggered by the unfavourable relations between production costs, credit terms for modern inputs, and official minimum prices. At present, however, rural conflicts focus pre-eminently upon the struggle of posseiros for permanent access to the land, which is fundamental to their reproduction.(44) Marginalised in their region of origin, these migrant families struggle desperately to avoid a similar fate in Amazonia lacking channels of representation and participation. Although their cause has been taken up by progressive sections of the Church, the organisation of

Brazil

posseiros and other rural workers remains incipient, localised, and sporadic. This inadequacy is accentuated by the sweeping, exceptional powers to intervene in land conflicts conferred on the state by National Security Legislation,(45) and the powerful corporativist representation of large capitals achieved through the Businessmen's Association of Amazonia.

CONCLUSION

This paper has presented a brief review of the recent literature on the 'agrarian question' in Brazil. Our discussion has been selective in that we have concentrated upon state modernisation policies and agro-industrial expansion as the prime movers in the re-definition of the role of agriculture in capitalist accumulation. Rather than any 'dominant tendency', these recent policies and agro-industrial appropriation have maintained, even accentuated, the diversity of rural social relations. Our critique of 'Junker road' proletarianisation and the various formulations which centre on the modernised family farm emerges from an alternative conceptualisation of agro-industrial development: that is, as the progressive appropriation by industrial capitals of the rural labour process. The dynamic of these capitals in the context of scientific and technological advance denies a permanent, privileged relation with any specific rural social structure.

While agro-industrial development, at the limit, eliminates rural production, family labour farms secularly have demonstrated greater resilience than large properties to industrial appropriation. However, and notably so in the Brazilian case of 'conservative modernisation', countervailing state intervention can create relatively favourable conditions for the integration of large rural properties with agro-industry. Conjuncturally, such intervention reinforces the heterogeneity of rural social relations; nevertheless, we suggest that the intrinsic tendency of agro-industrial appropriation is to reconstitute rural production as industry. The recent agro-industrialisation of poultry production in Brazil is especially instructive in this respect.(46) It warns against essentialist conceptions that certain forms of production and relations of labour exploitation are privileged partners of agro-industrial capitals.

The counterpart of the increasingly complex integration of Brazilian agriculture with agro-industrial and institutional finance capitals is the emergence of different forms of representation and struggle among direct rural producers. These processes of integration are rapidly differentiating the perceptions and demands of rural workers, militating against the unification of class struggle. Thus it is unlikely that a single key issue, notably access to land and agrarian reform, will unify and dominate the mobilisation of rural workers in the future. Over the past decade or so, it has been those workers tendentially excluded from the modernisation process, such as volante labourers and posseiros in Amazonia, who have been in the vanguard of rural labour movements. However although the conditions of reproduction of these marginalised groups will become progressively more precarious, their forms of representation and mobilisation probably will assume a less prominent role in rural labour organisation with the further agro-industrialisation of the rural production process and the 'enclosure' of Amazonia.

The crucial starting point for the analysis of future patterns of rural class struggle is defined by the terms and conditions of integration with agro-industry and the contradictions of its present and future development. In short, mobilisation and representation will take on an increasingly corporativist character, with the context of struggles being given by integration into the logic of agro-industrial and financial capital accumulation. Our analysis of the strategic importance of agro-industry in determining rural social relations suggests that rural struggles will focus on such issues as prices, financing, production costs and state agricultural policy, rather than global demands for sweeping social and institutional reforms. The volante, bóia-fria and posseiro therefore do not represent the future social relations of Brazilian agriculture so much as the painful transition toward a capitalised rural labour process subordinated to agro-industrial accumulation.

NOTES

1.   F. de Oliveira. 'A Economia Brasileira: Crítica A Razão Dualista', Estudos Cebrap, No. 2, (1972), pp. 5-82; F. Sá Jr., '0 Desenvolvimento da Agricultura Nordestina e a Função das Atividades de Subsistencia', Estudos Cebrap, No. 3, (1973), pp. 87-147. For a fuller discussion of this approach, see D.E. Goodman, 'Rural Structure, Surplus Mobilisation, and Modes of Production in a Peripheral Region: The Brazilian Northeast', The Journal of Peasant Studies, vol. 5, no. 1 (1977), pp. 3-32.

2.   'Latifundio-minifundio complex' refers to the interdependent, though unequal, relationships between the large estate (latifundio) and the small farm unit (minifundio). Small farm units may be located within the latifundio under various tenurial relations, paying rent to the landlord in crop shares, labour services, or money, or some combination thereof. Small farm units alternatively may be outside the latifundio but the employment provided by the large estate may be a crucial element in the reproduction of this 'external peasantry'.

3.   This concept, which occupies a significant place in the writings of Rosa Luxembourg, recently has been revised and extended by J. Foweraker, The Struggle for Land. A Political Economy of the Pioneer Frontier in Brazil from 1930 to the Present Day, (Cambridge University Press, Cambridge, 1981), in his analysis of frontier settlement in Paraná, southern Mato Grosso, and southern Pará.

Brazil

4.   Oliveira, 'A Economia Brasileira'. For further details, see D.E. Goodman and M.R. Redclift, From Peasant to Proletarian. Capitalist Development and Agrarian Transitions. (Basil Blackwell, Oxford, 1981), pp. 135-9.
5.   Oliveira, 'A Economia Brasileira', argued that '... the majority of vegetable food crops (such as rice, beans and corn) supplied to the great urban markets come from zones of recent settlement' (pp. 16-17).
6.   Oliveira, 'A Economia Brasileira', p. 18.
7.   The military coup of 1964 deposed the democratic nationalist regime of João 'Jango' Goulart, who had assumed the presidency in succession to the elected President, Janio Quadros, who resigned in 1962.
8.   The view is argued in Goodman and Redclift, From Peasant to Proletarian, pp. 128-50.
9.   The coffee tree eradication programme was introduced in the mid-1960s and provided financial incentives to induce coffee growers to diversify into other crops. Employment and welfare legislation for rural workers was enacted in the later 1960s, beginning with the Land Statute of 1964. These measures were introduced by the authoritarian military regime as the central element of a strategy to legitimate paternalistic state control of rural trade unions, which were required to administer the new provisions.
10.   M.C. D'Incão e Mello, O 'Bóia Fria' : Acumulação e Miseria, (Vozes, Petrópolis, 1975), p. 31.
11.   V.C. Brant, 'Do Colono ao Bóia-Fria', Estudos Cebrap, no. 19 (1977), p. 81.
12.   See the collection of annual conference papers published by the Department of Rural Economics, Botucatu, São Paulo, since 1975. Selected papers from these meetings can be found in CNPq/UNESP, A Mão-de-Obra Volante na Agricultura (São Paulo, Polis, 1982). The bóia-fria literature is reviewed in D.E. Goodman and M.R. Redclift, 'The "Bóias-Frias" : rural proletarianisation and urban marginality in Brazil', International Journal of Urban and Regional Research, vol. 1 no. 2 (1977), pp. 348-64, and W.S. Saint, 'The Wages of Modernisation : A Review of the Literature on Temporary Wage Arrangements in Brazilian Agriculture', Latin American Research Review, vol. 16, no. 3, (1981), pp. 91-110.
13.   J. Graziano da Silva, Progresso Técnico e Relações de Trabalho na Agricultura (HUCITEC, São Paulo, 1981).
14.   G. Muller, 'Agricultura e Industrialização do Campo no Brasil', Revista de Economia Política, vol. 2, no. 6 (1982), pp. 47-77.
15.   P. Sandroni, Questão Agraria e Campesinato (Polis, São Paulo, 1980).
16.   M. de N.B. Wanderley, 'O Campônes : um Trabalhador Para o Capital', Campinas, IFCH, 1979, mimeo. The influences are notably C. Faure, Agriculture et Capitalisme (Paris, Anthropos, 1978) and K. Vergopoulos, La Question Paysanne et le Capitalisme, (Paris, Anthropos, 1974), and 'Capitalism and

Peasant Productivity', The Journal of Peasant Studies, vol. 5 no. 4 (1978).

17. The reader will find echoes of the European debate in this position. See, for example, the work of J. Banaji, 'Modes of Production in a Materialist Conception of History', Capital and Class, vol 3, (1977), and H. Bernstein, 'Notes on Capital and Peasantry', Review of African Political Economy, no. 10, (1977).

18. Graziano da Silva, Progresso Técnico, pp. 130-2.

19. J.M. Dickinson and S.A. Mann, 'Obstacles to the Development of a Capitalist Agriculture', The Journal of Peasant Studies, vol. 5, no. 4 (1978).

20. Y. Nakano, 'A Destruição da Renda da Terra e da Taxa de Lucro na Agricultura', Revista de Economia Política, vol. 1, no. 3, (1981). This approach tends to ignore the basic question of the nature of the labour process in agriculture in favour of certain limited economic categories. It thus begs the question why oligopolisation has not occurred in agriculture.

21. A complete statement of our position is given in From Farming to Biotechnology : The Industrial Appropriation of Agriculture (Blackwells, Oxford, forthcoming 1984).

22. International Bank for Reconstruction and Development (I.B.R.D.) Capital Markets Study, (Washington, D.C., 1979), mimeo.

23. Analyses of recent agricultural modernisation policies include C.P.D.A., Evolução Recente e Situação Atual da Agricultura Brasileira, (BINAGRI, Brasília, 1979); I.B.R.D., Capital Markets Study; B. Sorj, Estado e Classes Sociais na Agricultura Brasileira (Zahar, Rio de Janeiro, 1980); Goodman and Redclift, From Peasant to Proletarian; and Graziano da Silva, Progresso Técnico.

24. Rural employment opportunities for volante workers would involve high levels of unemployment if calculated on an annual basis.

25. L. Sigaud, Greve Nos Engenhos, (Paz e Terra, Rio de Janeiro, 1980). The mobilisation of casual volante labour, and its priority in the overall strategy of rural labour organisation, has been a recurrent theme of the annual congress of the National Confederation of Agricultural Workers (CONTAG) since 1979. This is a thorny issue given CONTAG's heterogeneous membership of small proprietors, tenants, sharecroppers, and landless workers.

26. The term abertura ('opening') refers to the policy introduced in 1974 by the Geisel administration to conduct a gradual but controlled relaxation of the authoritarian military regime.

27. J.R.B. Lopes, 'Empresas e Pequenos Produtores no Desenvolvimento do Capitalismo Agrario em São Paulo, 1940-1970', Estudos Cebrap, no. 22 (1977); J. Graziano da Silva, A Modernização Dolorosa. Estrutura Agraria, Fronteira Agrícola e Trabalhadores Rurais no Brasil (Zahar, Rio de Janeiro, 1982).

28.   O.L. Coradini, Produtores, Cooperativismo Empresarial e Multinacionais : o Caso de Trigo e Soja (Zahar, Rio de Janeiro, 1981).

29.   The locus classicus on relationships between 'technification' and indebtedness is Vergopoulos, La Question Paysanne.

30.   For a recent account of this process, see R.J. Moreira, 'A Pequena Produção e A Composição Orgânica de Capital', Revista de Economia Política, vol. 1, no. 3 (1981), pp. 41-55.

31.   The Landless Movement (O Movimento dos Sem Terra) seeks to bridge this gulf between modernised and marginalised family farmers. Its members include many sons of modernised farmers for whom further division of the family holding would not create economically viable farms. On the significance of Ronda Alta in the context of recent rural mobilisation in southern Brazil, see C. Grzybowski, 'As Colonos Sem-Terra de Ronda Alta', Cadernos de CEAS, no. 82 (1982), pp. 51-9.

32.   M. Palmeira, 'Desmobilização e Conflito : Relações entre Trabalhadores e Patrões na Agro-industria Pernambucana', Revista de Cultura e Política, Year 1, no. 1 (1979).

33.   CPDA, Evolução Recente e Situação Atual da Agricultura Brasileira, 1930-1975 : Região Nordeste (Rio de Janeiro, EIAP/CPDA/FGV, 1978), p. 109.

34.   Indeed, the average value of production on establishments in this category was less than one-half of the minimum wage. See S. Silva, 'Sobre a Estrutura de Produção no Campo - II', Campinas, IFCH/UNICAMP, November 1982, ms.

35.   The labour reserve 'function' of the Northeast is emphasised in formulations of the articulation model by Oliveira, 'A Economia Brasileira', and J.R.B. Lopes, 'Desenvolvimento e Migrações: Uma Abordagem Histórico-Estrutural', Estudos Cebrap, no. 6 (1973).

36.   There are parallels here with certain categories of small family producers found in the South and their struggles with transnational capitals engaged in pork processing and the production of wine and tobacco.

37.   See J. Wilkinson, 'The State, Agro-Industry and Small Farmer Modernisation', unpublished Ph D thesis, University of Liverpool, 1982.

38.   The competitive pressures to which family producers are exposed are not confined to the supply-side effects of the higher yields and associated unit cost structures of 'technified' farms but can also be intensified by minimum pricing policies and related instruments.

39.   O.G. Velho, Capitalismo Autoritario e Campesinato (DIFEL, São Paulo, 1976).

40.   B. Sorj, and M.A. Pompermayer, 'Sociedade e Politica(s) na Fronteira Amazonica : Interpretações a Argumentos', Belo Horizonte, 1983, mimeo.

41. See Foweraker, The Struggle for Land.

42. M.J. Pompermayer, 'Estratégia do Grande Capital na Fronteira Amazónica Brasileira', Estudos Pecla, vol. 1, no. 3 (1982). The projects and programmes include the Trans-Amazonian highway and other long distance penetration roads, hydro-electric power projects, and the various regional development programmes, such as PRODOESTE, POLOCENTRO and POLAMAZONIA, implemented in the years 1972-9.

43. While the acquisition of land as a speculative asset by multinationals should not be minimised, this is far from being the most significant form of foreign penetration of Brazilian agriculture. Foreign investment is markedly more pronounced in agro-industry. Thus Central Bank data for 1975-9 indicate that annual direct foreign investment, including re-investment, in agriculture averaged US $50.2 million, compared to US $543.5 million in food processing alone.

44. For a recent discussion of these conflicts, including those between indigenous peoples, posseiros and land grabbers (grileiros), see J. de Souza Martins, Expropriação e Violencia : A Questão Política no Campo (HUCITEC, São Paulo, 1980), and Os Camponêses e A Política no Brasil. (Vozes, Petrópolis, 1981).

45. These powers currently are being used in huge areas of Amazonia following the creation by the federal government in 1980 of two Executive Groups, under the aegis of the National Information Service, to deal with conflicts in the Araguaia-Tocantins region (GETAT) and Lower Amazonia (GEBAM). These organs are now subordinated to the Extraordinary Ministry of Land Affairs, created in 1982, which has wide responsibility for land tenure questions and is an integral component of the national security system. On these recent institutional changes and the state's activities, see A.W.B. de Almeida, 'A Reforma Agrária Localizada e A Política Regional', Reforma Agrária, vol. 12, no. 1 (1982), pp. 22-34, and Comissão Pastoral de Terra, Denuncia : Caso Araguaia - Tocantins (CPT, Goiania, n.d.).

46. See the case-study of the transformation of this sector by B. Sorj, M.J. Pompermayer, and O.L. Coradini, Camponêses e Agroindustria : Transformação Social e Representação Política na Avicultura Brasileira (Zahar, Rio de Janeiro, 1982).

Chapter Ten

THE DEVELOPMENT OF CAPITALISM AND THE MAKING OF THE WORKING
CLASS IN COLONIAL INDOCHINA, 1870-1940

Martin J. Murray

INTRODUCTION

Peripheral Zones of the Capitalist World-Economy

The formation of the working class in colonial Indochina was a
heterogeneous process that did not really begin in earnest
until after World War I. The French colonisers shared similar
aims with other European colonial powers, namely, to force the
peripheral zones of the capitalist world-economy to produce,
among other things, those export commodities in high demand in
the metropolitan centre.(1) In particular, metropolitan
capital's dependence upon specific industrial raw materials and
tropical (or semi-tropical) foodstuffs required that
large-scale capitalist enterprises specialising in providing
these commodities should seek them wherever they could be
found. The establishment of formal colonial empires allowed
these giant agromineral syndicates considerable options
concerning how and where to invest, and gave them tremendous
leeway in organising directly the export production they
desired under the conditions that suited them.

In colonial Indochina, metropolitan capital was frequently
left with little or no choice but to organise production
directly. This requirement was particularly true in the case of
the existence of coal deposits and other mineral resources
available for extraction, and in the case of the commercialised
production of rubber, where long-term capital investments in
the crop itself and in somewhat sophisticated equipment and
machinery was an indispensible element of cultivation.
Metropolitan investments in agromineral extraction (coal,
rubber, tea, sugar cane, tin, phosphates, iron ore, and so
forth) assumed the form of large-scale estates where
considerable pools of low-cost wage-labour were a necessary
component of expanded output. Both plantation agriculture and
mining operations were dependent upon official state policies
designed to forcibly recruit labour-power and tie workers to
the point of production through a variety of coercive means. At
the same time, large-scale metropolitan investments in

agromineral extraction put into motion a wide array of ancillary investments that both complemented and spun off from the principal profitable activities. Further, in those areas of investment where metropolitan capital did not have the desire or inclination to accept risk, many local entrepreneurs advanced their capital in the hope of taking advantage of available - or creating new - profitable opportunities. Taken as a whole, these investment activities - metropolitan and indigenous alike - greatly expanded both the scope and the actual size of the proletariat.

Colonial Indochina and Migrant Labour

The metropolitan organisation of agromineral production along strict capitalist lines coincided with the emergence of the migrant labour system. The specific path of capitalist development in colonial Indochina was characterised ʋy three features. Firstly, the birth of the plantation zones (concentrated in western Cochinchina and southern Annam and inside Cambodia to the northwest of Saigon) and the mining zones (spread through the mountainous regions of Tonkin and Laos) went hand-in-hand with the transformation of vast areas of the countryside into virtual labour reserves. The process of centre/peripheral separation came about both as a result of state policies and of the process of class differentiation put into motion by capitalist penetration of the countryside. More specifically, the centuries of continuous habitation and partible inheritance (i.e. division and subdivision amongst male heirs) had left the overcrowded villages of the Red River delta region and the coastal lowlands of Annam with a mosaic of tiny dwarf holdings that were too small to sustain the household units attached to them. During the colonial period, the process of social differentiation in these villages - brought on by the spread and deepening of commodity relations - created a veritable surplus population. Tied both by custom, family connections, and kinship, and by the simple economic fact that no appreciable opportunities for betterment existed elsewhere, the poorest villagers eked out a livelihood by selling their labour-power, renting land, and/or venturing out of the village confines to seek wage-paid employment in the European mines, estates, plantations, and industrial undertakings that were clustered around the major urbanised centres of colonial rule. Thus surplus population - made up of the poorest landless villagers and hidden from sight within the myriad kinship networks inside the village bamboo walls - functioned as a reserve army of labour.

Secondly, the system of migrant labour that developed in colonial Indochina was characterised by what Burawoy has referred to as the 'institutional differentiation and physical separation of the process of [labour-force] maintenance and renewal'.(2) Namely, under colonial rule the costs of reproduction of labour-power were separated into two distinct processes. On the one hand, labour-force maintenance occurred exclusively at the point of production where wage-labourers exchanged the use of their labouring capacity for an historically-determined minimal day-to-day subsistence remuneration. More often than not, employers offered means of payment that took the form of a combination of money-wages and services (compound accommodations, meagre daily food rations, etc.). On the other hand, the renewal of the labour-force occurred through the recruitment of itinerant workers in order to fill vacancies created by the departure from or the expansion of the labour-force. In short, the social and political costs of labour-force renewal were externalised to the village reserve areas. The old, the sick, the young, the maimed, and the unemployed were forced back to the village subsistence communities for care and social security.

Thirdly, the rapid growth of the giant agromineral estates (as well as the other European industrial undertakings and the numerous ancillary operations associated with these) was accompanied by increased demands for unlimited supplies of low-cost labour-power and the institution of coercive types of labour recruitment that were reinforced by state repressive mechanisms. Itinerant workers thus ventured into wage-paid employment as seasonal, temporary, and marginal sojourners carrying the weight of colonial state power on their backs, where brute force served as a means of ensuring their docility, thrift and diligence.

THE DEVELOPMENT OF THE WORKING CLASS IN COLONIAL INDOCHINA

The Sites of Production and the Growth of Wage-Labour

The initial core of the working class in colonial Indochina emerged between 1890 and 1919 in mining, plantation agriculture, industrial undertakings (such as textiles, distilleries, tobacco and match factories, cement works, the railway yards, the docks, electrical plants, and tramways in the urban centres), and the hinterlands-to-town (river, rail and road) transport. By 1905, Tonkin alone had at least 85 separate European-owned industrial enterprises, concentrated in the Hanoi and Haiphong regions, which employed more than 12,000 workers, not including miners.(3) The number of wage-labourers employed by metropolitan mining undertakings quadrupled between 1904 and 1911, from 4,000 workers to 16,000 workers.(4) On the eve of the outbreak of World War I more than 200 European-owned establishments were in operation throughout Indochina and employed approximately 62,000 workers.(5)

The isolation of colonial Indochina during World War I generated some significant changes that greatly accelerated the growth of the working class. The inability of French expatriates and settlers to obtain commodities from metropolitan France precipitated expanded investments in local processing, manufacturing, and building materials industries. These 'import substitution' ventures opened new opportunities for wage-labour. In addition, the colonial authorities conscripted more than 43,000 Indochinese soldiers and an estimated 50,000 labourers for the war effort. These draftees received some training overseas and returned after World War I as the core of a semi-skilled labour force. Finally, metropolitan France demanded raw materials from Indochina as its 'contribution' to the Allied war effort. This expanded production required an increase in the absolute size of the working class.(6)

The greatest expansion of the working class took place between 1913 and 1929 (as the wage-paid labour force employed by the European-owned establishments increased fourfold to a figure of approximately 221,000 labourers).(7) These workers were distributed in three major fields of colonial economic activity: commercial and industrial undertakings, plantation agriculture, and mining operations. The largest number of workers were employed in commercial and industrial undertakings: 86,000 workers, or 39.2 per cent of the total. In this particular field, the most significant European enterprises were the railroads with over 10,000 workers (and expanding to 20,000 workers by 1940), and the Nam-Dinh cotton mills (La Cotonnière de Nam-Dinh) and the Portland cement factory in Tonkin with 4,000 to 5,000 workers each. In addition, Dumarest estimated that office employees for commercial and banking companies numbered 32,000 in Tonkin alone. Plantation agriculture employed 81,000 workers, or 36.8 per cent of the total. Finally, mining enterprises employed the remaining 53,000 workers, or 24.0 per cent of the total wage-paid labour force in European-owned establishments.(8)

Underestimation of the Size and Character of the Working Class

Taken at face value, these official colonial statistics would indicate that the wage-paid labour force in Indochina never represented more than approximately one per cent of the total indigenous population. Yet these figures fail to uncover both the absolute size of the working class and the processes of social differentiation that produced a rural proletariat in the countryside. In the first place, these official colonial statistics only listed indigenous workers employed by European-owned establishments, thus ignoring the very large number of workers employed by local capitalists. For example, Buttinger describes the numerous opportunities available for wage-labourers in small to medium-scale businesses owned by local Chinese and Vietnamese entrepreneurs:

> The Chinese owned many rice mills in Cochinchina and a considerable portion of all retail trade in Vietnam. The

> Chinese and Vietnamese also controlled all small river and road traffic. Printing presses, potteries, cabinet making, some sugar refining, soap factories, and other small establishments producing for the local market, were almost exclusively in Vietnamese and Chinese hands. Hundreds of Chinese and Vietnamese owned stores, restaurants, and repair shops. All cities had Chinese and Vietnamese tailors, pharmacists, butchers, and many other independent suppliers of goods and services, and most of them employed some people. There is no reason why the many tens of thousands working in Chinese mills or Vietnamese shops should not be regarded as members of the working class.(9)

In short, the thousands of local businesses employed large numbers of local residents in production, circulation, and distribution of services where employment was generally low-paid, working conditions were very poor, and turnover was high.(10)

Secondly, official colonial statistics disregarded the great mass of landless or virtually landless small-scale cultivators who were distributed throughout the countryside and were in continual search of casual, temporary, and seasonal wage-labour. In the Red River delta of Tonkin and the coastal lowlands of Annam, the process of social differentiation resulted in the concentration of arable lands in fewer and fewer hands. For example, Yves Henry (an economic geographer who conducted one of the two most detailed and comprehensive surveys of rural class relations) discovered that about 92 per cent of the total number of landowners in Tonkin were smallholders with 1.8 hectares of land or less in their possession. Equally important, he estimated that while slightly more than 960,000 rural households were in possession of some land, there were approximately 540,000 landless rural households in Tonkin, an estimated 36 per cent of the total rural population.(11) Pierre Gourou's 1939 study produced more or less the same results.(12) An official colonial study conducted for 1952-3 revealed that approximately 58 per cent of the rural households of Tonkin were landless. These household members were compelled to eke out a meagre existence on the gradually diminishing village communal lands, or were forced into exploitative tenancy, sharecropping, or wage-labour agreements with village or absentee landlords.(13) In Annam, the patterns of landownership and class differentiation were quite similar to those existing in Tonkin.(14) In the Mekong delta in particular and Cochinchina in general, the pattern of rural land distribution was substantially different from that which prevailed in Tonkin and Annam. In his survey of 1930-1, Henry estimated that in a rural population of approximately four million persons, only slightly more than 250,000 landowners, or one family household in every four, was in possession of at least some land.(15) In his 1939 survey,

Gourou reported that about 78 per cent of the total number of landholding households owned less than five hectares each, while 34 per cent of landholding households owned less than one hectare each. These small-scale owner-occupiers were thus forced to supplement their meagre incomes through part-time seasonal wage-labour or through fixed-rent tenancy agreements with larger landholders.(16) In the Red River delta and the coastal lowlands, the principal production relations were small scale owner-occupancy where the process of social differentiation was gradually separating the rural population into landlords with sufficient holdings to rent out land and hire wage-labour for specific tasks. In the Mekong delta of Cochinchina, the principal production relations were landlord/tenant relations where tenants paid a fixed rent in the form of surplus-product for the use of (generally) five hectares of land. The process of social differentiation was more pronounced in Cochinchina than elsewhere in colonial Indochina. Small and medium-scale landowners who leased portions of their land to tenant farmers also hired local landless or virtually landless villagers, generally on a part-time basis during planting and harvesting seasons. Large-scale landlords hired specialised work-gangs who migrated from place to place throughout the Mekong delta during the planting and harvesting seasons, generally along distinct pre-arranged routes.(17)

Seasonal-agricultural workers also shuttled back and forth between the main centres of European economic activity and the countryside. After World War I, seasonal migrations had gradually become a vital feature of rural class relations. The extent of this seasonal migration and its contribution to both rural and urban output cannot be reliably estimated. Nevertheless, it is evident that a sizeable proportion of the wage-labourers employed by large-scale European plantations and mining operations were never officially listed in colonial records. It was common practice for two or three employees to hold one labour-card (colonial records were based on estimates of the number of labour-cards issued). Family members, relatives,and friends often substituted for actual card-holding workers every couple of days in order to ease the gruelling burden demanded by European employers.(18) To cite one example, official colonial statistics for 1930 listed 49,000 workers engaged in rubber and other agricultural plantation labour. However, in an independent but reliable account, Bonout estimated that about 100,000 persons actually worked in the rubber plantations alone, if the supplementary labour of women and children was also included in work force participation statistics.(19)

Thirdly, official colonial statistics did not record the large numbers of indigenous workers drafted against their will to perform so-called 'public works' projects. Colonial authorities requisitioned villagers on a regular basis to complete various state infrastructural projects such as agricultural hydraulics (dykes, dams, and waterway dredging), road and bridge building, railway and harbour construction, and the erection of public buildings.

Fourthly, colonial statistics only listed wage-labourers employed at a given point in time and ignored the vast numbers actually mobilised for work. The combination of the high turnover and the part-time nature of substantial portions of wage-paid employment meant that a large reserve army of labour came into existence to supplement those actually working. This situation can be illustrated by the fact that European plantation managers found it necessary to recruit more than 75,000 workers between 1925 and 1930 in order to maintain the work force on the southern rubber plantations at a constant 22,000 workers.(20) Robequain reported that 'some mining companies have even had to recruit new workers each year because the coolies who left during the Tet holiday [the lunar new year] did not return'.(21)

THE WORKING CLASS AND THE WORKERS' MOVEMENT

The Rubber Plantations of Cochinchina

A brief descriptive account of the growth of the working class and the implantation of the workers' movement at the rubber plantations illustrates broader trends throughout Indochina. Rubber production only began in earnest in Cochinchina after the 1907 expansion of British rubber plantations in Malaya proved highly profitable. By 1910, the colonial administration had granted an estimated 61,268 hectares in Cochinchina for rubber cultivation. By 1929 (on the eve of the world depression), approximately 29,000 hectares in Cochinchina were actually planted. Production was slow to expand during the world depression. By the late 1930s, Indochina ranked fifth among world rubber producers as to acreage, fourth as to total output, and first among major producers as to the output per acre. By this time, most of the small-scale rubber entrepreneurs had either gone bankrupt or had their operations purchased by larger companies. By 1937, the total area planted to rubber was approximately 127,000 hectares.(22)

After 1925, the rubber plantations embarked on a systematic strategy designed to recruit able-bodied young men under three-year contracts from the over-crowded villages of Tonkin. By 1938, the General Labour Survey listed nearly 30,000 northern migrants under contract on the rubber plantations of Cochinchina and Cambodia. The plantations themselves were micro-societies; the land was rigidly divided between the working area and the living area (which was itself subdivided into European and 'native' areas). Needless to say, workers were housed in barrack-like compounds, forced to work long hours at a rapid pace, and hounded unmercifully by supervisors.(23)

Wage-labourers employed in the French-owned rubber plantations forged and created sophisticated responses to the dictatorship of metropolitan capital. The workers' strike represented an act of defiance against the prerogatives of capital, not merely a defensive measure to protect what the workers had previously accepted as part of the wage-bargain. Accounts of at least eight significant work stoppages on the rubber plantations between 1930 and 1937 can be found in official colonial records. Militants from the Revolutionary Youth League (and later the Indochinese Communist Party) had clandestinely infiltrated the plantations in order to organise workers into secret 'Red Unions'. The labour unrest that occurred on the rubber plantations involved different forms of struggle including the assassination of coercive labour supervisors, work stoppages, demonstrations and rallies, marches that involved the abandonment (termed 'desertion' by the colonial authorities) of the plantation grounds, and actual occupation and seizure of the plantations themselves.(24)

The Mining Estates and the Manufacturing/Commercial Enterprises

The officially listed number of Indochinese mine workers increased from 12,000 in 1920 to 53,000 in 1929. While the absolute number of mine workers declined during the world depression, the gradual expansion of production in the mid-1930s resulted in the growth of the number of workers to pre-depression levels by 1940.(25) Until the mid-1930s, the mining companies (mostly coal, but also tin, manganese, zinc, chromium and iron ore) relied upon a mobile labour force of temporary and seasonal wage-labourers. After that time, mining enterprises encouraged the formation of special villages in the proximity of the mines in order to ensure regular supplies of labour-power.(26)

The European manufacturing and commercial enterprises can be divided into a number of distinctive types. The agricultural processing industries included both European and Chinese-owned factories that specialised in the husking and polishing of rice for export. Rice processing plants varied in size from those which were hand-operated to large power-driven factories.(27) The principal milling centre was located in the Saigon-Cholon area with its easy access to both ocean-going traffic for easy exporting and the river-barge transport of the Mekong (leading to the rich rice-growing regions of the delta). By the late 1930s, there were 27 large-scale mechanised mills located in the Saigon-Cholon area, with others situated at Haiphong and other coastal ports. Hundreds of small-scale 'native' and Chinese rice mills were scattered throughout the rice-producing areas of Indochina where rice-processing activities were aimed at capturing the local market for necessary foodstuffs.(28) In addition, numerous alcohol distillation factories sprang up in the urban areas with the aim of taking advantage of marketing opportunities opened up by the removal of state restrictions (and the state monopoly) on private manufacture of alcohol in 1933. Finally, a number of sugar plantations and sugar refining factories developed in the Saigon region.(29)

Despite the strong opposition of French authorities to any forms of local industrialisation that would compete with metropolitan exports and would restrict opportunities for settler and metropolitan entrepreneurship, a number of manufacturing industries did emerge in Indochina, particularly during the 1930s. The principal causes for the growth of these light industries can be attributed to the distance from France, the abundance of low-cost labour, and the gradual development of a home market. These light industries included the manufacture of a variety of articles not competitive with French imports. These included such commodities as building materials, certain varieties of textiles, paper, matches, soap and cigarettes. In addition, electric power plants, breweries, and the like were established to meet the needs of urban communities, and the European settler-residents in particular.

Finally, the transportation industries included railroad maintenance and repair, harbour and dock facilities, and river navigation. Countless companies, large and small, sought profitable opportunities in the movement of commodities to and from the coast to the hinterlands. All in all, thousands upon thousands of wage-labourers were employed in the above-mentioned activities.(30)

The wage-labourers employed in European and indigenous manufacturing and transportation industries worked approximately ten to twelve hours per day. Barthel's description of Saigon's dock-workers in 1933 illustrates the deplorable working conditions of unskilled labourers: 'For twelve hours they carry rice bags on their naked sweating shoulders. Bearing their load, they come off the ship, over a precarious foot-bridge, cross the quay, and scorched by the heat of the sun, force their way to the warehouse, running up the swaying steps to throw off their load on a mountain of rice bags'.(31) Wage labourers were brutally treated, poorly paid, ill-housed, and taken advantage of at every opportunity. In Buttinger's words, 'no one protected them against humiliation, insults and physical mistreatment. If a foreman in a textile mill or a mine kicked a helpless man or a pregnant woman too hard and accidentally killed his victim, there was always a French judge who was willing to sympathise with the culprit and pronounce a mild, suspended sentence - that is, if the killer was brought to court at all'.(32)

During the 1920s, urbanised wage-labourers began collectively to embrace the anti-colonial sentiments that had succeeded in penetrating broad layers of the colonised population, especially the petty bourgeoisie of intellectuals, self-employed professionals, students, small businessmen, and salaried employees.(33) Until this time, the conjoined power of metropolitan capital and the colonial administration was able largely to contain the outbreak of overt collective industrial actions that were aimed at securing improvements in living conditions, wages, and working conditions for the labouring population. The first significant work stoppages occurred between 1922 and 1925. Workers also participated in the massive popular protests against the trial and imprisonment of the well-known nationalist leader, Phan Boi Chau, in 1925 and 1926.(34) For example, wage-labourers in 1924 at the cotton-weaving mills at Nam Dinh (in Tonkin) stopped work in order to demand higher wages and better working conditions. Strikes soon erupted at other factories in the Nam Dinh area, where a number of light industries had been established in the proximity of a working population of 50,000 persons.(35) In 1925, a clandestine labour union with some influence in the Saigon-Cholon industrial centre and with a loose membership of about 300 workers successfully promoted a strike at the Ba Son arsenal in support of the revolutionary activities taking place in China at the time.(36)

The formation of the Viet Nam Thanh Nien Cach Menh Dong Chi Hoi (Revolutionary Youth League of Vietnam) in 1925 signalled the first collective effort to implant communist ideas and Marxist analysis into the growing workers' movement. Trained in Canton, members of Thanh Nien filtered back to Vietnam where they aimed to establish regional committees in Tonkin, Annam, and Cochinchina, and to establish secret 'red unions' in commercial enterprises and factories, in the rubber plantations and mines, and in the schools: wherever popular discontent with the French colonial administration was expected to be greatest. Thanh Nien soon established regional organisations in addition to various city committees.(37)

Members of Thanh Nien were instrumental in providing organisational skills and leadership for the veritable 'strike wave' of 1928-9. In 1930, a number of significant strikes took place (the Phu-Rieng rubber plantation, the match factory in Ben Thuy, the textile plant at Nam Kinh, etc.) that helped to consolidate the burgeoning workers' consciousness of themselves as a collectivity with a class interest and class capacity. In 1930, a special unifying conference brought together various competing communist organisations (including Thanh Nien) in order to form a single communist party, the Indochinese Communist Party (ICP).(38) The ICP aimed to situate its activities in the industrial centres, encouraging the formation of illegal trade unions, especially amongst railroad workers, dockworkers and factory workers. As distinct from the past, striking workers began to advance political as well as strictly economic demands in their protests: wage increases, shortening of the working-day, abolition of fines arbitrarily imposed by supervisors, prohibition of corporal punishment for alleged infractions of work rules, social security for workers' families, social insurance to compensate for accidents on the job, an end to political repression of political dissidents, freedom of the press, and so forth.(39)

The widespread rural rebellion of 1930-1 that erupted principally in Ha-Tin and Nghe-An (the richest rice-growing provinces of Annam) awakened the propertyless agrarian masses. In the year that followed this rural upheaval, the French Surêté captured almost the entire leadership of the ICP, dispersed a large number of regional committees, and hence decimated the ranks of militants. Regroupment of the ICP and its popular committees took a number of years.(40) In 1932 alone, it was estimated that the French colonial authorities held more than 10,000 political prisoners.(41)

The May 1936 formation of the Front Populaire in France had an immediate impact in Indochina; the legal right to form political parties was extended to Cochinchina (considered a 'colony', unlike the legally distinct 'protectorate' status granted to Tonkin and Annam), large numbers of political prisoners were released, restrictions on the freedom of the press were eased, and a committee in France was appointed to review labour conditions in Indochina.(42) This political thaw provided all anti-colonial forces with renewed opportunities to agitate, organise, and function more openly. Work stoppages swept Indochina when the official labour inspection visit was cancelled in late 1936. During the course of 1936-7 the number and scope of strikes in the urban areas escalated. In particular, coal miners took an active role in the strike wave. By 1938-9, the fear of impending war in Europe led French authorities to repress the growing workers' movement through jailings, and restrictions on assembly and freedom of speech, in order to ensure a 'pacified' rear. With the Japanese occupation in 1940, the leadership of the workers' movement and the ICP were forced into a clandestine existence.

Agrarian Social Classes and the Class Struggle of Rural Masses

In colonial Indochina, the system of migrant labour was more than simply a conjunctural phenomenon linked to expanded demands for unlimited supplies of inexpensive labour-power. It was also a structural tendency characteristic of the growth of capitalist accumulation under colonial conditions. The evidence is far too sketchy to permit an identification of all migrant labour flows, and still less changes in their volume and direction. Nevertheless, it can be said that a sizeable number of strictly seasonal migrants were entangled in a dense web of both regular and irregular movements between one agricultural area and another during the planting and harvesting periods in search of part-time wage-labour. Thompson, for example, estimated that approximately two-thirds of the Tonkinese were engaged in wage-labour at least part of the year.(43) In Tonkin, these seasonal migrations were able to take place because the same harvests occurred at different moments and at different locations in the Red River delta. Generally, the tenth-month harvest was undertaken earlier in the Upper Delta than in the Lower Delta. Normally, migrant labourers could only obtain two or at most three months of secure wage-paid employment per year. Truong Chinh and Vo Nguyen Giap described the working conditions of rural wage-labourers:

> In Ha-dong, a reaper works from 5 a.m. to noon, stops just long enough to swallow a mouthful of rice, then works until nightfall. The paddy is carried to the house, he stops to eat, then back to work, threshing by beating or dragging a stone roller until 9 or 10 p.m. On an average harvest day, a reaper must work 15-16 hours . . . At harvest time an agricultural worker has work for a little more than a month; a work day is 12 hours long, and the landlord pays 3 piasters a month plus food. Earnings for the whole harvest season are 4.50 or 5.00 piasters at the most.(44)

In Cochinchina, the growth of capital/wage-labour production relations in the countryside was even more pronounced. Small and medium-scale landlords who both worked their own lands and leased portions to tenant farmers also hired local landless or virtually landless villagers, generally on a part-time basis during planting and harvesting seasons. Large-scale landlords who leased all their lands in discrete plots to tenant farmers hired specialised work-gangs. These work-gangs usually comprised 32 wage-labourers in addition to one labour supervisor. They migrated from place to place throughout the Mekong delta, generally along prearranged routes. While the landlords contracted for their labour-services, these wage-labourers were remunerated from a deduction from the surplus-product of fixed-rent tenants. In Cochinchina, a well-defined labour market with distinctive classifications ('worker-by-the-year', 'worker-by-the-month', 'worker-by-the-day', etc.) had come into existence by the 1920s.(45)

The cycle of rural violence escalated from the 1920s onward. Between May 1930 and June 1931, police records listed at least 54 separate incidents of mass demonstrations, marches, or assaults on colonial installations. Rural protestors demanded the abolition or reduction of colonial taxes, the elimination of rice hoarding, the end to arbitrary evictions from rental lands, and so forth. Often with the encouragement of the ICP, crowds of angry people plundered and destroyed civil registers, land survey records and tax rolls.(46)

In Tonkin and Annam, rural discontent in 1930 was largely confined, as it had been in Cochinchina, to large-scale petitioning and demonstrating at district or provincial offices. However, in the rural zones adjacent to Vinh (a growing industrial centre in Annam), villagers began systematically to destroy local land and tax records, to drive notables and French collaborators out of the villages, to assassinate wealthy mandarins, to burn colonial offices, and to seize hoarded rice stores. By mid-September 1930, the tempo and scale of the popular unrest had expanded to the extent that the colonial authorities had completely lost their administrative and military control over the rural population in Ha-Tin and Nghe-An provinces. The French authorities were unable to re-establish their rule until August 1931.

This heroic struggle of virtually unarmed dispossessed rural militants has been recounted in greater detail elsewhere.(47) The nascent 'Red Soviets' that were formed in the course of the rural uprising served as both a model for 'liberated zones' during the long wars of resistance against foreign invaders (French, Japanese, American) and as an inspiration for the national struggle for independence. For the ICP, the lesson of the 'Red Soviets' of Ha-Tin and Nghe-An did not go unnoticed. In the years following the rural insurrection, the ICP grappled with the most manageable means to integrate the rural and urban discontent into a broader mass movement. In 1939, the Sixth Congress of the Central Committee called for the shift of the centre of gravity of the anti-colonial struggle to the rural areas.(48) The ICP recognised, in the Peasant Question prepared by Truong Chinh and Vo Nguyen Giap, that the 'peasantry' did not constitute a homogeneous mass but was itself separated by class cleavages that pitted the propertied landlord/capitalist class against the propertyless (or virtually propertyless) tenants, sharecroppers, and wage-labourers.

CONCLUSIONS

'Peasantry' as a Social Category
In commonsense usage, the notion 'peasantry' has more often than not been employed in a sterile, ambiguous, and general fashion. To refer to the rural masses - propertied or propertyless and however differentiated through landholdings or degree of access to the market - generally glosses over and ignores not only the historical process of class differentiation occurring (no matter how slowly) in the countryside, but also the heterogeneous network of social-production relations and social-circulation relations that rural inhabitants enter into in order to reproduce their daily existence. While Truong Chinh and Vo Nguyen Giap (as representatives of the ICP) appreciated the manner in which capitalist penetration of the countryside produced class polarisation amongst agrarian social classes, many commentators in subsequent analyses refer to the 'worker/peasant alliances' as if its class composition was self-evident. During the colonial period in Indochina, rural inhabitants represented a varied collectivity of social categories and social classes

that could only be conceived of as existing in quite distinctive (and sometimes contradictory) relations of production and circulation. What was significant is that these social relations were increasingly capitalist relations.(49)

Understood in this manner, the formation of the proletariat as both an economic class of (virtually) propertyless wage-labourers exploited by capital and as a political force with the class capacity to act independently was a complex process that took place within the framework of an increasingly capitalist social division of labour and the expansion of the market for commodities. The development of capitalism in colonial Indochina involved the incorporation of the colonised territories into the capitalist world-economy (via metropolitan France). In particular, economic activities in colonial Indochina were increasingly integrated into this capitalist world economy via export production of agro-mineral commodities in demand elsewhere.(50)

Capitalist Production and the Working Class
Metropolitan capital took the form of large-scale agromineral estates (principally rubber, coal, tea, etc.), large and medium-scale manufacturing/commercial enterprises, and state-sponsored infrastructural projects (e.g. transport, including railroads, harbours and docking facilities, river dredging and canal building, etc.; colonial administrative office buildings; and prisons and military facilities). The enormous investment of foreign capital required the requisitioning of local wage-labour. During the colonial period, a numerically small but strategically placed industrial proletariat came into existence both in the urban areas (principally, Saigon/Cholon, Hanoi, Haiphong, Vinh/Ben Thuy, Hue, etc.) and on the agromineral estates. In addition, a numerically larger but more heterogeneous stratum of wage-labourers employed in small and medium-scale enterprises (principally manufacturing, construction and repair, and transport) encircled the concentrated core of industrial proletarians. Further, an even larger and still more heterogeneous collectivity of wage-labourers engaged in the circulation of commodities and so-called 'personal services' (e.g. wage-labourers employed by seemingly endless small and medium-scale firms/operations that catered to the privileged and wealthy) constituted the most numerous sector of the working class in the towns and peri-urban regions that came into existence as a consequence of capitalist development and colonial conquest.

Finally, the process of class differentiation in the countryside produced, on the one hand, an emergent landlord/capitalist class and, on the other, a propertyless (or virtually propertyless) rural proletariat. This rural proletariat itself was structurally divided between various gradations of permanent, semi-permanent, seasonal, and casual layers. This growth of the rural proletariat remained hidden from obvious view because its numerically largest sections were part-time seasonal migrants who remained attached to their native villages for both cultural identity and social security. The ICP forged a 'worker/peasant alliance' as the main force of the revolutionary movement. The dispossessed who permanently migrated to the towns during the colonial period began gradually to lose their rural roots. The 'peasant question' posed a more complex political problem. Capitalist penetration of the countryside increasingly compelled the poorest villagers to seek wage-paid employment in order to reproduce their conditions of existence. In the Red River delta and the coastal lowlands in particular, small-scale owner-occupancy remained the principal social relations of production where villagers were divided along a continuum of landlessness and abject poverty to ownership of sufficient lands where the landlords busied themselves with activities other than work. In the Mekong delta, the dominated classes of tenant farmers and landless wage-labourers were less attached to landownership yet aspired to hold title to the land they worked, as witnessed by the National Liberation Front's political programme of 'land-to-the-tiller' in the 1960-75 period.

NOTES
1.   See Martin J. Murray, The Development of Capitalism in Colonial Indochina, 1870-1940 (University of California Press, Berkeley, Los Angeles, and London, 1980), ch.5.
2.   Michael Burawoy, 'The Functions and Reproduction of Migrant Labour: Comparative Material from Southern Africa and the United States', American Journal of Sociology, vol.81, no.5 (March, 1976), p. 1050.
3.   Paul Isoart, Le Phénomène National Vietnamien: de l'Indépendance Unitaire a l'Indépendance Fractionnée (Libraire Général de Droit et de Jurisprudence, Paris, 1961), p. 264. See also J. Davallet, La Main-D'Oeuvre en Indochine (Universite de Paris, Faculte de Droit, Paris, 1905), pp. 25-76.
4.   André Dumarest, La Formation de Classes Sociales en Pays Annamite (Imprimerie P. Ferreol, Lyons, 1935), p. 62.
5.   Le Thanh Khoi, Le Viet-Nam: Histoire et Civilisation (Les Editions de Minuit, Paris, 1955), p. 427,
6.   See Dumarest, La Formation, p. 62.
7.   See Albert Sarraut, La Mise en Valeur des Colonies Françaises (Payot, Paris, 1923), pp. 44-52; Thomas Ennis, French Policy and Developments in Indochina (University of Chicago Press, Chicago, 1936), pp. 86-7; Jean Goudal, Labour Conditions in Indo-China, (League of Nations, International Labour Office, Geneva. Studies and Reports, Series B., No. 26, 1938), pp. 18-36; and Virginia Thompson, Labour Problems in Southeast Asia, (Yale University Press, New Haven, Connecticut, 1947), pp. 18-25.

8.   See Le Thanh Khoi, Le Viet-Nam, pp. 428-9; Dumarest, La Formation, p. 68; and Charles Robequain, The Economic Development of French Indo-China, (Oxford University Press, London and New York, 1944), pp. 76-85.

9.   Joseph Buttinger, Vietnam: A Dragon Embattled, Vol.I: From Colonialism to the Vietminh (Praeger, New York, 1967), p. 194.

10.   Ngo Vinh Long, Vietnamese Women in Society and Revolution, Vol.I: The French Colonial Period, (Vietnam Resource Center, Cambridge, Mass., 1974), pp. 13-15.

11.   Yves Henry, Economie Agricole de l'Indochine (Imprimerie d'Extrême-Orient, Hanoï, 1932), pp. 108-9, 144, 211.

12.   Pierre Gourou, Les Paysans du Delta Tonkinois (Editions d'Art d'Histoire, Paris, 1936).

13.   Michel Limborg, L'Economie Actuelle du Vietnam Démocratique (Editions en Languages Etrangères, Hanoï, 1959), p. 16.

14.   See Henry, Economie, p. 144; Pierre Gourou, Land Utilization in French Indochina (Institute of Pacific Relations, New York, 1945), pp. 280ff.

15.   Henry, Economie, pp. 144ff.

16.   Gourou, Land Utilization, pp. 272ff.

17.   See Rene Bunout, La Main-D'Oeuvre et la Législation du Travail en Indochine (Imprimerie-Librairie Delmas, Bordeaux, 1936), pp. 110-30.

18.   Ngo Vinh Long, Vietnamese Women, p. 14.

19.   Bunout, Main-D'Oeuvre, p. 112.

20.   Goudal, Labour, pp. 279, 300.

21.   Charles Robequain, Development, pp. 81-2.

22.   See, for example, Pierre Brocheux, 'Le Prolétariat des Plantations D'Heveas au Vietnam Méridional: aspects sociaux et politiques (1927-1937)', Le Mouvement Social, no. 90 (1975), pp. 55-86; Pierre Brocheux, 'Grands Propriétaires et Fermiers dans L'ouest de la Cochinchine Pendant le Période Coloniale', Revue Historique, vol. 246, no. 499 (1971), pp. 59-76; and Murray, The Development of Capitalism, ch. 6.

23.   Murray, The Development of Capitalism, ch. 6.

24.   Ibid.

25.   E. Willard Miller, 'Mineral Resources of Indo-China', Economic Geography, vol. 22, no. 4 (1946), pp. 268-79.

26.   See Robequain, Development, pp. 265-8. See also Jack Shephard, Industry in Southeast Asia (Institute of Pacific Relations, New York, 1942), pp. 18-24.

27.   V.D. Wickizer and M.K. Bennett, The Rice Economy of Monsoon Asia (Stanford University, Food Research Institute, Palo Alto, California, 1941), pp. 70-3.

28.   Kate Mitchell, Industrialization of the Western Pacific (Institute of Pacific Relations, New York, 1942), p. 156.

29.   See Shephard, Industry, p. 16; Robequain,

Development, p. 271; and Mitchell, Industrialization, p. 157.
    30. See Murray, The Development of Capitalism, ch. 7.
    31. J. Barthel, Regards sur l'Indochine: l'enquêtte d'une délégation ouvrière('Edition la défense', Paris, 1941), p. 5. See also 'Labour Conditions in French Indochina', Monthly Labour Review, vol. 59, no. 7 (1944), pp. 47-61; and 'Regulation of Labour in Indo-China', Monthly Labour Review, vol. 41, no. 1 (1940), pp. 78-87.
    32. Buttinger, Vietnam, p. 195.
    33. See David Marr, Vietnamese Tradition on Trial, University of California Press, Berkeley and Los Angeles, 1981), pp. 15-53; William Duiker, The Rise of Nationalism in Vietnam, 1900-1941 (Cornell University Press, Ithaca and London, 1976), pp. 103-199 and John McAlister, Vietnam: The Origins of Revolution (Anchor, New York, 1971).
    34. David Marr, Vietnamese Anticolonialism, 1885-1925, (University of California Press, Berkeley and Los Angeles, 1971), pp. 260-70. See also Cedric Allen Sampson, 'Nationalism and Communism in Vietnam, 1925-1931', unpublished PhD dissertation, University of California, Los Angeles, 1975.
    35. Duiker, Nationalism, p. 192.
    36. See Phan Than Son, 'Le Mouvement Ouvrier de 1920 à 1930', in Jean Chesneaux, et al., Tradition et Révolution au Vietnam, (Anthropos, Paris, 1971), pp. 169-71.
    37. Ibid., pp. 192-205.
    38. William Duiker, 'The Revolutionary Youth League: Cradle of Communism in Vietnam', China Quarterly, vol. 5, no. 1, pp. 475-99. See also Pierre Rousset, Le Parti Communiste Vietnamien (Maspero, Paris, 1973); and Robert Turner, Vietnamese Communism: Its Origins and Development (Hoover Institution Press, Stanford, California, 1975).
    39. Murray, The Development of Capitalism, p. 365.
    40. Jean Chesneaux, 'The Historical Background of Vietnamese Communism', Government and Opposition, vol. 4, no. 1, (1969), pp. 118-35.
    41. See Jean Chesneaux, 'Stages in the Development of the Vietnam National Movement, 1862-1940', Past and Present, vol. 7 (1965), pp. 63-75.
    42. See Daniel Hemery, Révolutionnaires Vietnamiens et Pouvoir Colonial en Indochine: Communistes, Trotskystes, Nationalistes à Saigon de 1932 à 1937 (Maspero, Paris, 1975), pp. 281-332.
    43. Thompson, Labour Problems, pp. 171-2.
    44. Truong Chinh and Vo Nguyen Giap, The Peasant Question, 1937-1938, (Southeast Asia Program, Department of Asian Studies, Cornell University, Ithaca, New York, 1974), p. 29.
    45. Bunout, Main D'Oeuvre, pp. 120-4.
    46. Murray, The Development of Capitalism, pp. 463-5.
    47. See Murray, The Development of Capitalism, p. 466, for references. For the most systematic account in English, see

Ngo Vinh Long, 'The Indochinese Communist Party and Peasant Rebellion in Central Vietnam, 1930-1931', Bulletin of Concerned Asian Scholars, vol. 10, no. 4 (1978), pp. 15-35.

48. Presentation of Ngo Vinh Long, 'Vietnamese Marxism in Comparative Perspective' Conference, Washington, D.C., October 28-9, 1979.

49. See Judith Ennew, Paul Hirst, and Keith Tribe, '"Peasantry" as an Economic Category', The Journal of Peasant Studies, vol. 4, no. 4, (1977), pp. 295-322.

50. See Martin Murray and Philip Picha, 'Why Make a Socialist Revolution? The Case of Vietnam', in Christopher Chase-Dunn (ed.), Socialist States in the World-System (Sage, Beverly Hills, California, 1982), pp. 253-70.

Chapter Eleven

PROLETARIANISATION IN THE WORLD ORDER: THE PERUVIAN EXPERIENCE

Nigel Haworth

The dominant processes of Peru's integration into the world economy commence with the conquest in 1533, and pass through a number of identifiable stages. Within each of these stages occur structural changes in sectoral production, social organisation and mobilisation, and state strategy. In particular, the export-orientation of Peru from conquest to the present day has had a dominant effect upon rural-urban and agriculture-industry-mining relationships, the creation of a labour force, and migration. In turn, these effects of Peru's world market status provide the framework within which the development of the labour movement and political parties has occurred. Furthermore, world market integration has impinged on the status and perceptions of gender, culture and ethnicity, at the levels of both production and ideology. This universe of changing relationships should not, however, be seen in terms of a classic base-superstructure model, in that each set of relationships conditions progressively the other sets, all encompassed within the stated dominant process. Hence the most accurate reflection of the interrelationships under consideration begins with a discussion of processes of market integration, pointing to the way in which the identified sets of consequences derive from these processes.

THE STAGES OF PERU'S INTERNATIONAL INTEGRATION

From Conquest to the World Market
The immediate consequences of the Spanish Conquest for the population of latter-day Peru were dramatic, as they were throughout Latin America. The most telling fact relates to population decline; between 1530 and 1560 the population may have slumped by as much as 75 per cent. Two features of this demographic collapse play a recurring role throughout the following centuries. Firstly, the degree of economic dislocation implied by the population slump indicates the extent to which contact with an international market destroyed substantial elements of pre-conquest production and society.

234

Secondly, the human consequence of this population decline were shattering in terms of disrupted social experience, aspirations and stability.(1) The cumulative effects of conquest recur in modern Peru, in terms of both the economic infrastructure and social/racial divisions. In particular, the establishment of a Spanish-dominated colony presumed an ethnic superiority on the conqueror's part, and a resulting belief in the availability of conquered labour on absolutely subordinate terms.(2) Population collapse, infrastructual dislocation and cultural subordination gave impetus and legitimacy to both semi-feudal and slave usage of labour once the conquest was consolidated. Forced labour in the agrarian sector was based on the encomienda; black slaves were imported from the sixteenth century until 1858. In the mining sector forced labour was organised through the mita.(3) Contemporary accounts point to atrocious working conditions, permitting only the most inefficient mechanisms of labour reproduction to continue. The long term implications of this for labour supply and the sexual division of roles have persisted to the present day.

During the early colonial period, wage labour systems were not developed, substantially obstructing the growth of a local labour market. This restriction on local market development was exacerbated by the importance of mining and agricultural production for export markets. This emphasis was both sanctioned and patrolled by the Spanish state, which initiated from the earliest days of the Conquest an export-orientation destined to become a structural feature of the Peruvian economy.(4) Post-conquest Peru was a world market economy, in which the predominance of primary exports curtailed any potential development of local manufacturing or infrastructure. Indeed the Spanish Crown legislated against indigenous artesanal production in obrajes (small-scale workshops serving local consumption) which rarely if ever were able to compete with imports.(5) It is thus not possible to talk of an industrial sector or workforce in any formal sense during the colonial period. Even state employment was very limited, again narrowing the potential basis of wage earning and free labour.

Parallel to the growth of mining enterprises, initially in silver and later in various non-ferrous metals, and large haciendas (estates) involved in various cash crops, there existed during the colonial period and after Independence large areas of agricultural production based on traditional, community-based land tenure.(6) Initially functioning mainly outside the market, though subject to increased integration over the centuries, these traditional communities maintained both their social coherence and their land rights despite repression, forced labour and general economic dislocation. The uneven distribution of haciendas and mining enterprises was partly responsible for the communities' resilience. Although the effects of mita and encomienda systems were widespread, they were concentrated round the location of their respective demands for labour, and many areas, especially in the sierra, were relatively unaffected by these labour recruitment patterns. The resilience of the traditional agricultural communities is an important factor in labour market formation in the nineteenth and twentieth centuries, when it obstructed the creation of a free labour market necessary for the growth of agricultural and mining production, and needed new labour supply strategies in these enterprises.(7)

The successful struggle against Spain for independence in the early nineteenth century did little to transform the structure of Peruvian production or its associated labour market patterns. Indeed, it may be argued that independence exacerbated problems in an already crisis-prone economy, in which both mining and agriculture were in decline, and what limited obraje production there was collapsed in the face of British and French exports into the newly independent market.(8) In agriculture particularly, quasi-feudal and slave production relations were maintained despite the crisis, with local terratenientes (landowners) receiving support from the military caudillos ('bosses') controlling the state. The background to the success of British and French exports lies in the relatively uncritical adoption of laissez faire economic policies by the new state, a feature of many Latin American countries in this period. Economic liberalism obstructed the creation of a strong intervenionist state which might have promoted industrialisation strategies.(9) In practice, Peru was to exhibit one of the weakest state structures in Latin America, initially adopting comparative advantage arguments in favour of primary product exports, later permitting massive intervention by foreign capital into export and commercial ventures, and eventually the mining, agricultural and manufacturing sectors. This state orientation, linked to the sectoral development discussed below, guaranteed that such proletarianisation as was to occur in Peru would originate in, on the one hand, the mining and capitalist agricultural complexes, and, on the other, relatively small-scale manufacturing enterprises, particularly in the Lima-Callao area.

1830-90: Guano, Nitrates, Cotton and Sugar

From the early 1830s exports of nitrate, and subsequently guano, were growing. The combination of these two export products gave rise to an export-led growth period which was to collapse in the mid-1870s and to terminate in the face of the War of the Pacific (1879-84). This growth brought with it a number of consequences. The commercial and financial sectors expanded as they came to service the growth sectors. The state's role in economic policy was strengthened, as was its capacity to maintain an ordered fiscal system. Infrastructual developments, especially the growth of a limited railway system, took place. Until the crisis brought this growth to a halt, guano and nitrate exports dynamised the Peruvian economy to previously unattained levels.(10)

This growth period had a number of consequences for labour market formation. The extraction of guano and nitrates required the formation of stable labour forces, as did the construction of railways and other infrastructual projects. The need to create an increasingly wage labour-based labour market was reinforced by a number of factors. Slavery was abolished in 1854, removing one form of forced labour. The import of Chinese indentured labour which began in 1849 and finally ended in 1874 was an inadequate solution to labour supply problems. Production of guano and nitrate was unsuited to labour supplies created on the basis of traditional tribute systems, a phenomenon which was to become increasingly important as the nineteenth century progressed. Had the guano and nitrate sectors been the only growth areas of the period, their labour supply requirements alone would have pushed substantial numbers of people into capitalist wage labour. However, this tendency was exacerbated by the expansion of cotton and sugar production for export in the same period, and the beginnings of the mining upturn which was to take off in the 1890-1930 period. This combination of factors emphasised the inelasticity of supply of labour in the Peruvian economy, especially the supply from the sierra. Hence the use of slaves until the mid-1850s, the indenturing of Chinese and later Japanese labour, and the use of criminals in wage labour, but only as inefficient and costly expedients. The particular problem of labour supply for agriculture was resolved by the creation of the enganche system of recruitment whereby money forwarded to workers had to be paid off by work in a given period on the plantation. Whilst it was designed to take labour from the traditional agricultural communities, and concentrated labour in centralised production centres, it was only a partial establishment of free wage labour as the basis of production, and depended on temporary labour migration which allowed the worker to return to the non-wage sector after the debt had been worked off. The growth period 1830-76 also had substantial effects upon the traditional agricultural sector. Increased consumption created by the growth in the economy tended to increase the integration of traditional agricultural sectors into market relationships. Ensuing peasant differentiation gave rise to further wage labour in agriculture, already developing in the export-orientated cash crop sectors.(11)

In the 1830-90 period, therefore, export-led growth caused a major restructuring of labour supply in order to create stable workforces. Manufacturing was of marginal importance in this period; urban production continued primarily on an artesanal, small-scale basis. Proletarianisation as such could only be described as incipient. Autonomous organisation and political debate within this incipient proletariat was limited, although present. For in addition to mutinies amongst the indentured Chinese labour, and disputes caused by the enganche system, some politicisation did occur due to the importation of ideas from Chile, mainly carried by Chilean railway workers.(12) More importantly, the orientation towards the world market was consolidated in this period. The solutions sought for labour supply problems were produced by the need to establish that integration on a firmly competitive basis.

1890-1930: The Take-off of Proletarianisation

This period has been described by the pre-eminent analysts of modern Peruvian economic history as the rise and fall of a local development effort. Thorp and Bertram convincingly argue that at the beginning of this period, especially in the 1890s, national capital was able to carve out a substantial role for itself across the range of sectors.(13) However, this potential basis for a national economic strategy collapsed, due primarily to a combination of unfavourable movements of relative prices in the world market, the financial power of foreign capital and, on occasion, foreign monopoly of natural resource production. An initial boost to industrialisation was confounded by an export-orientated anti-protectionism, and a failure to build a pro-industrialisation lobby within the state. Instead of an autonomous economic strategy, Peru found itself by the 1920s enmeshed in the world market more firmly than ever before. Simultaneously the power of foreign capital was greatly increased.

The sectors which were either foreign controlled, or orientated towards export markets, were also those in which labour supply issues were most important. In mining, 1889 saw Backus and Johnson begin the displacement of Peruvian capital in the central sierra. In 1901, the Cerro de Pasco Corporation entered the race, precipitating the demise of small-scale mineral producers. This restructuring of mining (extended to the northern sierra by the Northern Peru Mining Company in 1921) induced major changes in local markets for food and consumer goods. The sugar industry became further concentrated in agro-industrial complexes located on the northern coast. Small and medium haciendas were swallowed by monopoly concerns, which came to control local commerce. The enganche system was used to maintain labour supplies at an adequate level, though in the early years of this century a more stable non-migratory workforce began to make its appearance in these agro-export concerns.(14) Cotton production was export-orientated, controlled primarily through foreign-owned export houses, and based upon a mixture of big landholdings and sharecropping (yanaconaje). Meanwhile, the International Petroleum Company extended its production in the north, again becoming an important factor in local commerce. The Peruvian economy had by the 1920s become a classic enclave-based system orientated towards the world market.

It is useful to establish at this stage the size of the waged workforce in the period up to 1930. Sulmont argues that approximately 80 per cent of the national population remained outside the 'modern' capitalist sector, being located in the traditional rural sector and blocking the formation of free wage labour in classic terms, whilst simultaneously failing to create a 'reserve army of labour' sufficient to resolve the problems of labour supply inelasticity noted above. It is not surprising, therefore, that relatively few people can be found working in the urban manufacturing and service sectors. Sources from the period point to the small number of factories in operation at the time of the First World War, and it is likely that only 115,000 people out of a national population of 4.5 million were engaged in waged capitalist production in the whole Peruvian economy at that time. Much of the manufacturing capacity which did exist was in the Lima-Callao district, with the regions offering few examples of industrial growth.(15)

1930-48: The Depression and its Consequences

Thorp and Bertram identify in the period 1930-42 a trend towards increased economic autonomy in Peru, as a result of the effects of the international downturn on the linkages binding national production into the world market. Local entrepreneurial activity expanded as foreign investment faltered, and, as control over export industries fell under the sway of local capitalists, a degree of sectoral integration between export production and the internal market was achieved. The 1930-42 period is marked by increased state intervention, import substitution, exchange and import controls, and legislative support for local manufacturing enterprise. However, what is remarkable is less the trend towards increased economic autonomy than the poor performance put up by Peru in its attempt to take advantage of international market dislocation. Whilst there is argument as to how poor this performance was, it is difficult not to agree that economic diversification was limited, that only minor displacement of the dominant foreign-owned export firms was achieved, and that the state strategy foundered badly on ineffective protectionist controls, rapid inflation and a chronic balance of payments problem, the result of which was the 1948 coup replacing the Bustamante government with the Odría regime.

The reasons for this poor performance are various. It has already been noted that the social base for an industrialisation model was fragmented and unable to dominate state policy. Thus throughout the period those dominant class groups involved in the agro-export and extractive industries remained pre-eminent in the economy, supported by the particular advantages offered by a high level of export product diversity (a wide range of minerals and agricultural products). This continuing orientation towards the world market perpetuated not only the obstruction of internal market formation, but also an anti-industrialisation sentiment in the dominant class and, consequently, the coherence of that class. Unlike other cases in Latin America, it maintained its integrity relatively unscathed.(16) As a result, manufacturing development was limited, providing few opportunities for a large-scale increase in free labour employment in urban centres; the agro-export and mining enclaves remained the key centres round which wage labour formation continued, but there the effects of the international downturn resulted in a drop in labour recruitment, increased unemployment and substantial wage decreases. Such expansion of wage labour in the economy as there was remained relatively limited. Factory-based wage labour did increase fourfold over the period 1925 (21,000) to 1945 (88,000) but non-factory artesanal production continued at a substantially higher level throughout the period (298,000 to 320,000 over the same period). Mining employment fluctuated sharply from a dramatic slump in the early 1930s to a growth phase in the late 1930s and early 1940s. In agriculture, cotton fluctuated similarly, as it began to lose its importance in the economy.

Since 1948: The Era of Total Integration

The failure to grasp the opportunities of the previous period led after 1948 to a massive integration of the Peruvian economy into the world market, but this time on the basis of substantial foreign investment in all sectors including manufacturing.

> The economy from 1948 until the end of the 1960s was the example par excellence in Latin America of that dream of orthodox development economists: an export-led system in which cyclical balance of payments difficulties were handled by domestic demand restraint and exchange devaluation, in which the entry of foreign capital and the repatriation of profits were virtually unrestricted and in which government intervention and participation were kept to a minimum.(17)

The opening-up of the economy to the international market resulted in growth across all sectors until the late 1950s, whereupon a declining export performance, limited internal market development, and the continuing weakness of the national 'industrial' bourgeoisie provoked the series of crises which marked the Peruvian economy up to (and indeed after) the 1968 military coup. The crises tended to affect national enterprises more dramatically than their international counterparts, enhancing the latter's dominance in the economy.(18)
Thus the economy and the process of proletarianisation remained trapped in the dominant framework of world market integration which had taken on its modern form after 1830. The

1948-68 period saw this reach an extreme by the major role of
foreign enterprises in the economy, supported by an explicitly
pro-integration state policy. However, what Fitzgerald has
interpreted as a dualism continued in the economic structure;
two-thirds of the population existed outside the formally
economically-active population (9 million of a population of 13
million) and of the remainder very many were active in marginal
enterprises which at best were only partially in the 'modern'
sector.(19) If this indicates a tremendously heterogeneous work
and social experience, it also suggests that the
classically-defined basis for proletarian action (i.e. class
action as a conscious political process) was remarkably small
and fragmented as a direct consequence of the continuing degree
of world market integration.

PROLETARIANISATION IN THE ENCLAVES

The origins of proletarianisation in Peru lie primarily in the
export-orientated enclave sectors. The example of the sugar
industry illustrates the dilemmas of the enclave economy.(20)
Albert's chapter in this volume analyses the problems of labour
force creation in the Peruvian sugar industry. The sugar (and
also cotton) hacendados were constantly attempting to reconcile
a number of pressures upon their enterprises in the interests
of maintaining their world market position. These pressures
comprised the provision of adequate levels of manning (both
stable and seasonal); the adaptation of technical inputs to
production such that productivity benefits might be gained; the
stability of price levels of the finished crop; and, finally,
the potential for political opposition and trade union
organisation within the labour force. The hacendados juggled
with these factors constantly, particularly as world price and
market changes exogenously disrupted the search for stable
production relations in the industry.

To meet the increasing demand for labour, the enganche
system was employed to hire sierra workers for the coastal
estates. Two points are of importance when considering
enganche. Firstly, although initially providing a source of
seasonal migrant labour, the tendency was for greater levels of
permanent migration to develop, both to the original
destination of migration (the estates) and on into other urban
centres. Enganche promoted the development of a rural
proletariat on the coast and therefore played an important role
in the overall process of proletarianisation. Secondly, it has
been argued by some that this process of proletarianisation was
perceived by the migrant labourer as a means of protecting the
peasant economy of the sierra from its destruction by sierra
hacendados and market expansion. In other words enganche may be
seen as the nexus of a contradiction between coastal rural
proletarianisation and a peasant defence strategy in the
sierra.(21)

Enganche was not the only means of resolving the crisis of coastal rural labour supply. In the coastal cotton-producing sector, yanaconaje appeared as a means of resolving the problems posed by world market demands. Yanaconaje was a form of share-cropping, through which firms like Grace and Fox might maintain their supply of cotton without consolidating production in extensive haciendas. However, some large-scale landowning did develop, displacing many yanaconas and non-yanacona land-holders, and promoting the proletarianisation of the displaced.(22)

Sulmont traces the effects of coastal agricultural proletarianisation in terms of the development of two types of proletariat - the mixed and the transitional.(23) The former would in any one year work on its own land yet also work within the capitalist wage sector; the latter would extend its waged labour over a number of years before returning to the land, thus promoting the stability of the wage-labour sector. This consolidation is considered by Sulmont to have become better established from the 1920s onwards, with the mixed and transitional semi-proletariat giving way to a full proletariat especially after the Second World War, in line with the processes of world market integration discussed above. It has been argued that this consolidation is in part a result of increased workforce stability over the period, wherein changing technological and work conditions confirmed the need for larger numbers of full-time labourers, to be complemented by seasonal labour during harvest. Parallel to this, the rural areas providing this seasonal labour were in themselves confronting tendencies towards the creation of further wage labour-based production as peasant differentiation increased the incidence of rural wage-labour.

The mining sector exhibits similar characteristics to those found in the rural agricultural sectors.(24) The focal point of mining was the massive growth of the Cerro de Pasco Corporation (C de P) in the Central Sierra. The monopolisation of this area began in 1901, with over 730 metal mines and 108 coal mines falling into C de P's hands by the end of 1902.(25) Railway expansion permitted the infrastructural development of the region, and an ore refinery was constructed at Oroya by 1922. In the process of monopolising the mining sector, substantial land-holdings fell into C de P's hands, and the consequences of the building of the Oroya refinery included massive pollution of the region. As a direct consequence, C de P bought out the polluted land from surrounding comunidades. This 'smoking-out' of the highland peasantry forced local labour into Oroya and the mines, partially displacing the enganche system which had previously provided much labour, both for the mines and the construction of the refinery.(26) Further benefits also accrued to the firm. The acquisition of local land allowed wage levels to be depressed through the subsidising of wage-labour by produce from the firm's land, whilst the firm came to monopolise local trade, permitting it to influence local price levels and introduce 'scrip' payment into its payments systems. Laite argues that there were three proletarianising tendencies in operation around the C de P monopoly, all deriving from the efforts of the C de P management to treat labour as a homogeneous commodity. Firstly, the expansion of skill and productivity-orientated payment systems established a wage-based 'free' labour market offering flexibility to management's employment and production plans. Secondly, a process of urbanisation took place in Oroya, its construction financed by deductions from wages. Thirdly, management attempted a commoditisation of labour based upon its world market requirements. Thus the demand for labour has fluctuated as a consequence of world demand, world prices and the state of investment and expansion of the enterprise. These three processes lead Laite to conclude that a properly constituted industrial labour force was created in the mining sector, albeit with a substantial migrant element due to the fluctuations in the company's world market position.

However, this conclusion obscures a continuing debate about the relationship of the mining workforce and the surrounding rural communities. Laite argues that, rather than being an evolutionary transitional process creating a stable mining workforce, migration was both a strategic defence of the rural base from which the labour came, and merely one option amongst many which rurally-based labour kept open. Laite's argument stresses the rational, calculated basis upon which the perception of options existed, whereas Taylor and Favre reflect more the sense of imperatives imposed on the rural population by encroaching labour demands and market forces, but both interpretations view migration and wage labour as a strategic question confronting rural workers. Once again, the resilience of the rural sector is highlighted by this confrontation, emphasising the potential (and often realised) asymmetry between the demands of the wage labour sectors and the putative workforce. However, despite such resilience, it is difficult to disagree with Sulmont's argument that the dominant processes observed in the mining regions tended towards the long-term creation of a stable, urbanised/enclave waged labour force. In other words, Laite's contention that rural options remained relatively open and in equilibrium with urban opportunities underestimates the overall historical trend of migration and workforce creation. Empirically, evidence for this trend may be found in the migration from rural base to enclave and on to urban centres; in the direct rural base-urban centre movement; and in the massive growth of marginal barrios (districts) round Lima in particular in this period.(27)

THE GROWTH OF MANUFACTURING AND THE ESTABLISHMENT OF AN URBAN INDUSTRIAL WORKFORCE

The cities of Lima and Callao, considered as a unit, developed as the biggest centre of manufacturing, with Arequipa, Trujillo and Chiclayo having much less importance. The dominance of Lima-Callao was enhanced by its exceptional population growth and its qualitatively greater degree of political and economic sophistication in manufacturing, state and service sectors. However, it is as the cradle of working class political and trade union organisation that Lima-Callao now attracts attention. Despite the relatively small numbers of manufacturing workers nationally, their organisation in Lima, and exposure to radical intellectual currents, caused political reverberations beyond the immediate vicinity, linking with enclave and rural populations.(28)

Sulmont traces four early stages in the process of urban worker organisation.(29) Prior to 1850, the predominant artesanal organisation of production precluded collective action beyond guild protection of crafts and markets. Between 1850 and 1883, the consequences of the guano and nitrates boom led to an expansion of the construction, service, white-collar and manufacturing sectors (especially in glass, beer, paper, textiles and food). Worker organisation grew in these sectors based on the legacy of the guilds, with friendly societies blossoming. In this second period, artesanal production was still important, and its organisation could be readily adapted to the demands of the growth sectors. However, this relationship tied the new organisations to the relatively limited demands of the guilds. Within the growing mutualista (co-operative) movement political discussion took place and numbers of militant actions developed, especially in the 1890s. However, these actions tended to be sporadic and short-lived, reflecting in part the tradition of the 'rabble' which existed in Peru as elsewhere, as well as the fragmented, limited and politically-accommodative nature of urban worker organisation up to 1900.(30)

In Sulmont's third stage (1900-14) a manufacturing workforce was increasingly consolidated as expansion in the textile, food and general consumer goods sectors continued. However, factory size was still very small, and total numbers involved were equally restricted. Yepes, however, has argued that new currents were present in the nascent workers movement after the 1901 'Congreso Obrero', qualifying the mutualista tradition. Simultaneously with the growth of non-mutualista political publications, socialist ideas current in Trujillo and Arequipa were given a place in Lima's political ambience, accompanied by the development of anarchist ideas. This post-1900 transformation of the terms of political debate found a focus in the struggle for the eight-hour day, linked to wider issues of wages and conditions of work. The eight-hour day was achieved in 1919, giving a boost to trade-union organisation, and, in turn, the Leguía government gave further impetus to worker organisation, as a result of its interventionist pro-growth policies. It was this period, from 1919 to 1930, which can be seen as a fourth stage in the development of working class organisation in the urban sector.

However, perhaps the defining distinction between the third and fourth periods lies in the dominance of anarcho-syndicalism as the organisational politics of the former, and the success of socialist alternatives in the latter, although this success came to be qualified by the growth of Aprista populism as the fourth stage progressed.(31) It is indeed the debate between Alianza Popular Revolucionaria Americana (APRA) populism and the socialist/communist alternative which has dominated Peruvian working class politics up to the present. The debate was founded on shifting power bases, with APRA nonetheless tending to maintain its strength in the so-called 'solid north', and in certain manufacturing sectors, whilst other sectors, for example, mining, printing and brewing, became the site of conflicts between APRA and the Peruvian Communist Party.(32) The consequences which derive from this historical experience of labour organisation may be seen in terms of three related characteristics of Peruvian worker organisation which have been present from the initial post-1850 stirrings - problems of fragmentation and dispersion; the problem of political and organisational inertia; and the issue of collective class experience, that is, the appearance or not of a collective conscience within the Peruvian working class.(33)

Fragmentation and dispersion have been constant themes in the formation of the Peruvian labour movement.(34) Spatially, centres of worker concentration have been widely dispersed, a phenomenon much exacerbated by the enclave nature of the Peruvian economy. Thus, the sugar workers of the northern coast were many hundreds of miles from the areas of cotton-worker organisation around Ica; mining centres in the central sierra were internally dispersed, and were many miles from both northern and southern mining areas; in parallel, the manufacturing centres of Lima-Callao, Chiclayo, Trujillo and Arequipa were spatially remote from each other.(35) The point is not so much that distance restricted political debate; rather, the issue is one of political and organisational coherence. National and even regional collective responses were almost impossible to organise, a problem both exacerbated by and exacerbating the relatively limited bases from which such a response might be expected given optimum conditions. Dispersion facilitated state and company responses against worker activity; the mines and agro-export enclaves could be isolated with relative ease, and similarly the urban centres could be readily patrolled and controlled. Under certain circumstances the spatial problem might rebound on the state, as indeed is the present case in Andahuaylas where a peasant-based movement is not proving amenable to military strategy, but this is an exceptional case, and, importantly, is not occurring in a centre of wage-labour employment.

The problems of spatial diversity are minor compared with the dilemmas posed by political fragmentation. A list of factors creating this fragmentation misses the sense in which they are interrelated, and in which they in turn reflect the spatial issues noted above. However, fragmentation has five key aspects - ideological, sectoral, spatial, organisational and temporal. All workers' movements face these same problems, and their relative success is to be measured in the extent to which they overcome the blockages to action thus created. On balance, it must be argued that the Peruvian movement has remained sectionalised and disunited in contrast to, for example, the labour movements of Chile and Argentina.(36) Ideologically, the fragmentation has occurred on classical lines, with the limited potential resource base for group organisation weakened by competing political tendencies. Two have transcended the achievements of the others - APRA and the Peruvian Communist Party (PCP) - but in neither case have they consolidated themselves across the nation, or comprehensively vis-a-vis the potential recruitment base. APRA lost its power base in the workers' movement in the 1960s, in the face of a PCP-led challenge, which in turn succumbed partially to a left-wing challenge in the 1970s. Perhaps the 'solid north' is the only area where an ideology united a regional workers' movement to any great degree over time, a success reflected in the studies of APRA's organisational base in that area.(37) The reasons for the general ideological incoherence lie in a combination of factors: a traditional 'vanguardist' approach towards the bases, which in many cases led to party decision-making taking place remote from the issues concerning the constituencies; a resultant non-coincidence of local-base issues with the national-regional programmes being put forward; and the effects of repression by the state and the management of political debate from the earliest days of worker organisation.

Ideological incoherence has been reinforced by organisational as well as spatial conflicts within political debates. It has always been the case that there have been five potential bases upon which worker organisations might be built. Apart from the sectoral base, there are the plant, the community, the region, and the nation. It is not impossible for a worker to be represented at all these levels, but to find at each level a different complex of political processes and tendencies in motion.(38) If this multi-levelled basis of organisation is compounded by the ideological incoherence noted above, then the potential confusion is immense. The resolution of such complexity is not a function simply of achieving political and/or organisational coherence, because the multi-level basis of organisation permits a worker to adopt a complex set of identities vis-a-vis each level, their discrete political and organisational affiliations, their perceived relevance to particular issues affecting the individual and his/her work group, and so on.

Whilst the issue of sectoral organisation is integral to the complexity noted above, it also takes on a peculiar importance due to characteristics often attributed to workers on the basis of their sectoral location. Sectoral organisation has always been a crucial aspect of Peruvian labour activity. It is a logical consequence of plant-level union activity, rather than cross-plant skill-based or general union organisation. Where each plant maintains its own white and blue-collar unions, they in turn look to alliances in plants based in the same industrial sector. This is seen in virtually all the principal activities in all three broad categories of employment (primary, secondary and tertiary sectors). Furthermore, sectoral organisation is promoted by two further circumstances: firstly, in some key cases, as in mining, sectoral organisation also coincides with relatively discrete spatial and political debates; secondly, the growth of collective bargaining has given some support to sectoral negotiation, often with state connivance. The second point is important, because sectoral negotiation implies the lumping together of plants with very different characteristics (size, location, profitability, technology, managerial strategy, union density) into one group, homogeneous in the eyes of the broad negotiation. This may benefit workers, particularly in the lower-paid plants, as it might also give management a basis for sectoral organisation of representation to both state and managerial agencies. For these and other reasons, sectoral union organisation is important in Peru, but it is a double-edged weapon in union hands. On the one hand, it is the basis of some degree of historically-coherent organisation; on the other, it suffers a number of weaknesses. The sector itself may be small and of relatively little weight in the national economy; it might be spatially diverse; it may become the parameter for political faction fights; it may suffer secular growth or contraction in comparison with other sectors of the economy; it can lend itself to a skewed balance of power between constituent unions, based on economic power, tradition, history and so on. Despite these many potential problems, sectoral organisation has in many ways been a bulwark against encroaching fragmentation, primarily because the sector provides the basis of identity which workers may appeal to.(39)

Temporal fragmentation may be seen in two contexts; those of continuity and coincidence. Organisational unity is dependent upon the capacity of many disparate groups and contexts to coincide over an extended period. As such a practice is impossible to achieve perfectly, the success of a labour movement will depend upon the degree of temporal coherence maintained. In this as in other contexts, the Peruvian labour movement has displayed a chequered history. Two indicators exemplify the problems faced since the turn of the century in this context. General strikes have rarely been successful, because of the lack of temporal coincidence between

discrete organisational, political and spatial elements. Labour
movement organisation around election campaigns has rarely been
coherent, with, perhaps, the 1980 elections an exception
proving the rule.(40)

The degree of organisational coherence which has been
achieved in the face of these divisive factors suggests a
necessary resilience on the part of Peruvian workers as they
strive to unite and organise. But in this display of resilience
appears the second of the three main characteristics noted
above - that of inertia. Whilst the use of the term inertia is
intended to carry with it no mechanistic overtones, it does
capture in a social sense the idea of the qualitative and
quantitative change needed to turn a fragmented and relatively
incoherent organisational base into a powerful, united and
effective force for change. This has quantitative aspects in
terms of the relatively weak numerical position of wage labour
in Peru vis-a-vis other large and significant sectors.(41) But
there are also qualitative aspects. Political will,
determination, and consciousness, are required to translate the
potential power of the labour movement into effective action
when faced with difficulties which are both internal and
external. Internally, there are problems of fragmentation, but
also those of vision, planning and foresight, responsiveness of
institutions, and of timing in particular. Externally, besides
the obvious issues of state and managerial responses to action,
in which the unknown consequences of repression loom large,
there is the 'negative response' syndrome, which plagues all
labour movements seeking change in circumstances defined by
dominant capitalist social relations. It is as if the terrain
for action is pre-defined by the power of the state, causing
workers' organisations to respond to a situation already
offering the opposition disproportionate advantages.(42)

However, the internal factors are more important and are
the conditioning circumstances over which labour has most
power. The Peruvian labour movement has had the benefit of
numbers of thinkers within both populist and socialist
traditions, Haya de la Torre and Mariátegui being the most
obvious.(43) However, their vision, and their capacity to
promote thinking about alternative ways of organising
production and the wider civil society, have failed to take
root in any consistently effective sense in the labour
movement. Fragmentation and economism have caused the labour
movement to stand effectively apart from the organisations of
the political left. In a formal sense they are linked in the
alliances of APRA with the Confederacion de Trabajadores
Peruanos (CTP), and of the PCP with the Confederacion General
de Trabajadores del Peru (CGTP), but the politics of these
fusions have rarely come to dominate or even consistently
impinge upon the priorities of labour movement organisations.
This is most obviously seen in the way ultra-left groups have
been universally on the margins of organised labour's

activities. Groups like the Comité de Coordinación y Unificación Sindical Clasista (CCUSC) have come and gone, without threatening the parochialism and economism of the labour movement.(44) In turn, this has reinforced the unresponsiveness of generally bureaucratic institutions within workers' organisations. It is generally the case that workers' organisations are conservative in their practice, and often conduct their internal deliberations on the basis of restrictive formality, on the one hand, and alienating power politics, on the other. Finally, the temporal discontinuities discussed above have combined to minimise the occasions propitious for transcending the existing organisational and political context. These factors have jointly inhibited the qualitative development of the Peruvian labour movement, and have acted as a historical brake on activity, a reinforcement of the inertia which must be overcome for change to take place. Of course, there have been occasions when such inertia has been threatened. The reformation of the CGTP in 1967-9, and the consequent threat to the CTP, was such a moment, and led to the post-1968 military government having to seek an accommodation of a new kind with waged labour. However, such occasions have been few and far between.(45)

Further, there is a general issue which may contribute to the failure of a challenge to inertia, and to the partial nature of the collective consciousness discussed below. The Peruvian labour movement is a predominantly male tradition. Despite the numbers of women who work in domestic employment, waged agriculture, and, increasingly, manufacturing and services, they are marginalised institutionally and politically. Though nothing new in relation to the experience of women elsewhere in the world, this marginalisation brings with it crucial consequences in Peru in particular. The overcoming of fragmentation and inertia may rest on the welding of traditional areas of conflict on to wider community-based mobilisation. This has happened elsewhere (for example, Chile in the 1970-3 period) and was recognised explicitly by the strategists of Sistema Nacional de Apoyo a la Movilisación Social (Sinamos) in the 1968-80 period in Peru. Quite simply, the requirement that production-based organisation may need to integrate with wider-based activity means that women, both as value-creators and as domestic labour, must be integrated into a broader institutional and political framework, beyond the limits of the present labour movement, and probably with different foci of action. However, there is little evidence available on Peru to pursue this point.

If we take to heart Thompson's admonition that class is not a thing but a process, the friction and movement between the parts that make up capitalist society, it is clear that the notion of a collective class experience must be in turn dynamic.(46) The key question becomes the achievement of circumstances wherein the political, ideological,

organisational, spatial, gender and temporal aspects of the
constituent parts of class action coincide most effectively. At
this point, both fragmentation and inertia may be overcome, and
the process of 'class for itself' may emerge. In other words
proletarian action occurs on a general basis. In Peru, whilst
partial manifestations of such action have taken place since
the early decades of this century (as discussed above), such a
general basis of collective class action as described has never
been created. Besides fragmentation and inertia, a number of
other explanatory factors may be pointed to, underlying this
historical characteristic. Primarily, the diversity of social
differentiation and cleavage within both urban and rural
contexts has posed major problems for the growth of collective
class action. Such differentiation has led political and
organisational activity into a parochialism based on social
units such as the plant, community, and village. The dynamic
needed to transcend this parochialism has usually been lacking
and has further been hindered by problems of gender, ethnicity,
religion and age which reflect back on the issue of
fragmentation and disparity discussed above. Despite the
dominance of capitalist social relations, Peru is a most
diverse society in which any individual or collective action
must confront challenges on many levels. The narrowness of
traditional political thinking, both within and outside the
formal labour movement, has failed to grasp this diversity
which, incidentally, is recognised constantly throughout
Mariategui's writings. The orthodoxy of concentration on
workers at the point of production as the central (and, often,
only) concern of political and union organisation has
reinforced a process whereby other centres of organisation -
community, region, rural area and so on - are perceived as
discrete and often diversionary. There is a strong sense of
repetition in the way the Peruvian labour movement has
reorganised itself in its various phases of growth since the
1920s. This repetition, in its failure to extend beyond a
narrow orthodoxy, owes much to the circumstances created by the
insertion of Peru into the world economy, and its consequences
for forms of organisation and political practice. It is to this
determining context that the Peruvian working class must look
when considering its history and its potential for collective
class action.

CONCLUSIONS

Peru has endured a particularly comprehensive involvement in
the world economy across almost all its productive sectors. The
range of products, regions, work-forces and state relations
created or affected by this process is arguably one of the
widest found in the Third World, with perhaps the 1950s seeing
the conditioning effect at its maximum. Despite the attempt to

reverse the process after 1968, it would appear that the post-1980 Belaunde government is returning to policies which reproduce this same degree of international definition of Peru's political economy. It is important to grasp that it is not merely the productive sectors which have been thus conditioned; the nature of the Peruvian state has been so defined, with the result that Peru is exceptional in the degree that its socio-economic structure responds to international pressure. As a consequence of this, Peruvian proletarianisation has been peculiarly responsive to the pressures of the world market. The fragmentation noted above has been a direct consequence of these pressures, to be understood in the following way: whilst the conditioning factors behind proletarianisation have been externally defined, albeit mediated through the national and regional state apparatus, the weakness of national economic integration, and its concomitant spatial, organisational and temporal aspects, has caused the incipient Peruvian labour movement to rely upon a narrow organisational orthodoxy, essentially parochial and economistic in nature. It is as if two interrelated processes have occurred, the one (determination) determining the other (internal labour movement formation/proletarianisation), on terms so disadvantageous to the labour movement that fragmented, dispersed political and organisational responses have been the only effective basis for action. The problem for Peru's national labour movement is that, of itself, it cannot hope to confront the international process on equal and effective terms, precisely because, even if the problems identified above were resolved, a new international response from labour would be required to counter-balance capital's international structure. And, furthermore, even tentative steps towards a new, more effective labour response would seem to be dependent upon a widening of political and organisational perception of class action beyond the existing orthodoxy. Of course, in confronting this dilemma, radical thought in Peru is not alone.

NOTES
   1.   For an account of the experience of conquest, see N. Wachtal, The Vision of the Vanquished (Harvester, Brighton, 1977).
   2.   See Wachtal, Vision; and F. Bourricaud, Power and Society in Contemporary Peru (Praeger, New York, 1970).
   3.   The mita was a form of periodic personal service, originally levied by the Inca state, and taken over post-conquest by the Spanish. The encomienda was a land-holding, and associated rights to labour, appropriated by the Spanish conquerors after the defeat of Inca power. Wachtal's Vision shows how the encomienda division often failed to grasp how complex pre-conquest land divisions and production relations were, with the result that the encomienda often

tended towards inefficiency and irrational resource usage.

4.　　See, for example, A. Flores, <u>Arequipa y el Sur Andino</u> (CISEPA, Lima, 1976).

5.　　Ibid.

6.　　　　There is an extensive literature on sierra land-holding during the colony and thereafter. Of particular relevance to this paper are H. Favre, 'The Dynamics of Indian Peasant Society and Migration to Coastal Plantations in Central Peru', in K. Duncan and I. Rutledge (eds), <u>Land and Labour in Latin America</u> (Cambridge University Press, Cambridge, 1977), and L. Taylor, 'Main Trends in Agrarian Capitalist Development: Cajamarca 1880-1976' (unpublished PhD thesis, University of Liverpool, 1979).

7.　　This is a theme taken up later in the context of the growth of the C de P company in the central sierra.

8.　　See D. Sulmont, <u>Historia del Movimiento Obrera en el Peru 1890-1977</u> (Lima, 1977).

9.　　　See J. Roddick and N. Haworth, <u>Chile 1924 and 1979: Labour Policy and Industrial Relations through Two Revolutions</u> (mimeo, Glasgow, 1982).

10.　　See E. Yepes, <u>Peru 1820-1920: un Siglo de Desarrollo Capitalista</u> (Lima, 1972).

11.　　See Sulmont, <u>Historia</u>.

12.　　See N. Haworth, 'The Industrial Community in Arequipa: the Failure of a New Unitarism' (unpublished PhD thesis, University of Liverpool, 1982).

13.　　See R. Thorp and G. Bertram, <u>Peru 1890-1977: Growth and Policy in an Open Economy</u> (Macmillan, London, 1978).

14.　　See B. Albert, <u>The Labour Force in Peru's Sugar Plantation 1820-1930: A Survey</u> (mimeo, Norwich, 1982).

15.　　This data is compiled from Yepes, <u>Peru 1820-1920</u>; Sulmont, <u>Historia</u>; Thorp and Bertram, <u>Peru 1890-1977</u>.

16.　　This argument is put forward nationally by Thorp and Bertram, <u>Peru 1890-1977</u>; A. Ferner, 'The Industrial Bourgeoisie in the Peruvian Development Model' (unpublished DPhil thesis, University of Sussex, 1977), and locally, Haworth, 'The Industrial Community'.

17.　　Thorp and Bertram, <u>Peru 1890-1977</u>, p.205.

18.　　This was despite the consequences of the 1959 Industrial Promotion Law, designed to give a boost to industrialisation and national enterprise.

19.　　See E.V.K. Fitzgerald, <u>The Political Economy of Peru 1956-78</u> (Cambridge University Press, Cambridge, 1979).

20.　　A number of studies of the sugar industry in this period exist. See, for example, Albert, <u>The Labour Force</u>; B. Albert, <u>An Essay on the Peruvian Sugar Industry</u>, (Norwich, 1976); M. Gonzales, 'Cayaltí; The Formation of a Rural Proletariat on a Peruvian Sugar Cane Plantation 1875-1933' (unpublished PhD thesis, University of California at Berkeley, 1978).

21.　　See Taylor, 'Main Trends'; Albert, The Labour Force; and Favre, 'The Dynamics', for various arguments in this tradition.

22.　　For more detail on the labour market effects of yanaconaje, see Sulmont, Historia.

23.　　See Sulmont, Historia.

24.　　For accounts of the mining sector see, for example, J. Laite, Industrial Development and Migrant Labour (Manchester University Press, 1981); J. de Wind, 'From Peasants to Miners: The Background to Strikes in the Mines of Peru', in R. Cohen et al., Peasants and Proletarians (Hutchinson, London, 1979); and D. Kruijt and M. Vellinga, Labour Relations and Multinational Corporations: The Cerro de Pasco Corporation in Peru 1902-1947 (Van Gorcum, Assen, 1979).

25.　　See Laite, Industrial Development, p. 47.

26.　　There are a number of contemporary accounts of the 'smoking-out'. See N. Haworth, Miners' Political Action in Peru and Chile (mimeo, Glasgow, 1980).

27.　　A discussion of data and bibliographical sources on barrio formation may be found in A. Lowenthal (ed.), The Peruvian Experiment: Continuity and Change under Military Rule (Princeton University Press, Princeton, 1975); and D. Chaplin (ed), Peruvian Nationalism: A Corporatist Revolution (Transaction, New Brunswick, N.J., 1976).

28.　　Jorge del Prado, the PCP leader, is classically in the mould of the activist who spent much of his youth moving from Lima to the mining areas and elsewhere, creating these reverberations. This is a tradition maintained despite the pressure for centralisation on Lima.

29.　　See Sulmont, Historia.

30.　　See Yepes, Peru 1820-1920.

31.　　See Sulmont, Historia.

32.　　An extensive literature on the growth of Aprismo exists. See, for example, R. Alexander, Aprismo; The Ideas and Doctrines of Victor Raul Haya de la Torre (Kent State, Kent, Ohio, 1973); G. Hilliker, The Politics of Reform in Peru: The Aprista and Other Mass Parties in Latin America (Johns Hopkins Press, Baltimore, 1971); H. Kantor, The Ideology and Program of the Peruvian Aprista Movement (Savile Books, Washington, 1966); P. Klarén, Modernisation, Dislocation and Aprismo: Origins of the Peruvian Aprista Party 1870-1932 (University of Texas Press, Austin, 1973).

33.　　The idea of collective conscience in this sense is borrowed from Robin Murray.

34.　　Sulmont's work illustrates this well; in the 1910s and 1920s the disputes between and within anarcho-syndicalism and socialism are followed by similar confrontations between and within populist and socialist/communist movements up to the present day.

35.　　See Haworth, 'The Industrial Community'.

36.   See, for example, A.Angell, Politics and the Labour Movement in Chile (Oxford University Press, London, 1972); J. Godio, Sindicalismo y Politica en America Latina (ILDIS, 1983).

37.   See the references in note 32 above.

38.   It should also be borne in mind that this complexity may be reinforced by non-labour movement factors. For example, during the post-1968 period, workers in complex organisational structures were also involved in various levels of industrial community activity, patrolled by Sinamos and other state institutions. Each of these levels could display different political priorities and presences - reinforcing the sense of potential fragmentation which is so particularly evident in Peru.

39.   In passing, it is notable that there are no comprehensive sectoral studies of Peru, apart from those related to mining, construction and agriculture in general. At the level of labour relations, no comprehensive studies appear to exist.

40.   See N. Haworth, 'Conflict or Incorporation: the Dilemma of the Peruvian Working Class 1968-80', in D. Booth and B. Sorj, Military Reformism and Social Classes; The Peruvian Experience (Macmillan, London, 1983).

41.   See A. Angell, The Peruvian Labour Movement (mimeo, London, 1980).

42.   See Haworth, Miners' Political Action, for a discussion of the notion of predefinition of terrain.

43.   See José Carlos Mariátegui, Seven Interpretive Essays on Peruvian Reality (University of Texas Press, Austin, 1971); and note 32 above.

44.   See Angell, The Peruvian Labour Movement, and Haworth, 'Conflict or Incorporation'.

45.   Possibly the electoral alliances of 1979-80 were another example of a move through the barrier of inertia, but the outcome of current disputes will decide.

46.   See E.P. Thompson, 'Peculiarities of the English', in The Poverty of Theory (Merlin Press, London, 1978).

Chapter Twelve

THE FORMATION AND DEVELOPMENT OF THE WORKING CLASS IN ARGENTINA, 1857-1919

Ronaldo Munck

Compared with the rest of Latin America, the trade union movement in Argentina has traditionally been strong. Moreover, Peronism, a populist political movement based on the urban masses, has been a major force in the political life of the country for almost four decades. There is, therefore, great significance in an attempt to establish the factors which conditioned the formation of the proletariat in Argentina and shaped its political aspirations and expression. This is particularly the case in view of the fact that, perhaps not surprisingly, current political controversies in Argentina have always been an important influence on the historiography of the labour movement, and the disputes of the present have often been read back into the history of the movement. This chapter analyses the formative period of the Argentine working class movement, with particular reference to the period between the introduction of early forms of factory production in the 1890s and the events of 1919 which profoundly affected the nature of the future political integration of the working class.

LABOUR'S PRE-HISTORY, 1857-90

It was only after the battle of Caseros in 1852 that an Argentine nation-state began to take definitive shape, thus ending a long period of civil wars which had torn the country apart since the achievement of independence in 1810. The consolidation of national state hegemony embodied in the constitution of 1853 coincided with the incorporation of the fertile pampa region into the international circuit of capital accumulation. This dual economic and political process was to be largely completed by 1890, opening up the 'golden era' of agrarian-based development in Argentina which was to last until 1930.(1) This dynamic agrarian capitalism was based largely on wage labour - the various forms of payment in kind (the vale de proveduría, for example, which was not formally abolished until 1923) only constituting feudalism in a most forced analogy. But

255

of course the organisational form of the capitalist mode of production - the factory - was not present in the early stages. From the colonial period onwards there was an important presence of artisans and craft-workers (based largely on slaves and ex-slaves) but the industrial proletariat itself was to emerge more slowly.

The 1853 municipal census for Buenos Aires indicated the presence of 700 workshops and 100 'factories' employing some 2,000 workers.(2) The export of wool since the 1840s had begun to transform the semi-nomad herdsmen, the gauchos, into agricultural labourers, a process which found in Juan Manuel de Rosas ('populist' dictator from 1829 to 1852) its main promoter. It also stimulated the development of urban artisans (involved in the fabrication of wood and leather products, metal-working, etc) who replaced the largely slave-based artisan sector squeezed by British manufacturing competition after independence.(3) Agrarian expansion brought in its wake a subsidiary sector of manufacturing. In 1845 the first primitive steam-engine had made its appearance, and by 1857 the first locomotive had arrived. Significantly, this was also the year in which the Buenos Aires printworkers formed their mutual aid society - the Sociedad Tipográfica Bonaerense.

Immigration made a major contribution to the rapid rate of growth of Argentina's population (Table 12.1). The share of Argentina in total world immigration during this period was considerable - rising from 5 per cent in 1860 to 8 per cent between 1870 and 1885, and to 17 per cent between 1885 and 1890. Though the share dropped to 7 per cent during the Baring crisis (4) it again rose to 15 per cent between 1895 and 1920. It was immigration and not the dispossession of the peasantry which formed the basis of the working class in Argentina. If the volume of immigration was important, so too was the political impact of the refugees fleeing from the repression of the 1848 revolutions in Europe and later in the aftermath of the 1871 Paris Commune.(5)

The 1870s were a period of transition in the formation of the working class. Mutual-aid societies were giving way to unions and the first 'modern' strike took place in 1878. The printers union won a wage increase, a reduction of the working week and the abolition of child labour after a month-long strike. But the establishment of a section of the First International in 1872 was in many ways out of phase with the predominantly artisan status of the working class. This was still the age of the caudillos (rural populist leaders) who rallied the masses of the deprived provinces with the cry of 'religion or death'. The conservative/revolutionary nature of pre-industrial protest should not cause surprise. In the same way that Hobsbawm speaks of 'collective bargaining by riot', for the Luddite period in Britain, Astesano makes an analogous argument when he refers to the early montonera (rural popular militia) as a federación a cuchillo (literally a union based on

Table 12.1: Gross and Net Immigration to Argentina,
            1857-1920 (000)

	Entries	Exits	Net Immigration
1857-1860	20	9	11
1861-1870	160	83	77
1871-1880	261	176	85
1881-1890	841	203	638
1891-1900	648	328	320
1901-1910	1,746	626	1,120
1911-1920	1,205	936	269

Source: Guy Bourde, Urbanisation et Immigration en Amérique
         Latine: Buenos Aires (XIX et XX siècles) (Aubier,
         Paris, 1974), p. 163.

Table 12.2: Argentina: Characteristics of Manufacturing
             Industry, 1895 and 1914

	Number of Establishments		Number of Workers		Horse-power	
	1895	1914	1895	1914	1895	1914
Food	4,082	18,983	27,071	134,842	7,373	164,786
Clothing	5,713	7,081	32,599	57,764	1,686	5,784
Construction	3,955	8,582	30,519	87,312	10,486	44,570
Furniture	2,259	4,441	12,721	29,007	696	9,026
Ornament	949	996	2,560	4,297	25	442
Metallurgy	3,163	3,275	14,631	29,327	2,122	17,935
Chemical	317	567	4,712	9,986	1,850	4,915
Graphic Arts	427	1,439	5,080	13,286	459	3,058
Others	1,339	3,415	15,757	44,375	2,530	428,241
TOTAL	22,204	48,779	145,650	410,196	27,227	678,757

Source: J.Godio, El Movimiento Obrero y la Cuestión Nacional
         (Erasmo, Buenos Aires, 1972), p. 30.

the knife).(6) That is to say, the non-proletarian nature of their demands (such as industrial protectionism which could only benefit the provincial elites) should not blind us to their fundamentally plebeian class composition. Not really understanding this, Raymond Wilmart (a leader of the First International in Argentina) wrote bluntly to Marx that without the influence of foreigners no progress was possible in Argentina, and that 'they would not know how to do anything but ride horses'.(7) The immigrant's confidence in the capitalist development of the new country did not predispose him to sympathise with the death-throes of a confused popular provincial rebellion. And apart from the statements of Felipe Varela on the need for Latin American unity against imperialist intervention, there was nothing in the ideology of the caudillos to attract the rising urban proletariat.

During the 1880s there was a significant increase in the level of industrialisation. At the beginning of the decade the province of Buenos Aires could boast 12 meat salting plants (saladeros) employing 7,740 people; 57 flour mills with 500 workers; 400 carpentry and metal workshops employing 1,800; 80 brick factories with 900 workers and more than 60 soap, cheese and clothing factories employing 580 people.(8) With the exception of the saladeros these figures testify to the semi-artisanal level of production with generally fewer than ten workers per factory or workshop.

A further characteristic of early industry was the predominant role of immigrant enterprise and labour. The 1887 Industrial Census found that 92 per cent of industrial workshops and factories were owned by foreigners, and 84 per cent of the workers were immigrants.(9) More often than not, labour associations were divided by nationality and workers' publications were often directed to individual nationalities. At this stage also the immigrants still saw real prospects of upward social mobility. There was a genuine duality in their consciousness between their condition as workers and as immigrants - a type of 'contradictory class location'.

Labour in its early and not quite crystallised form was already organising and protesting. The printing workers established the first genuine trade union in 1876. The bakers and the carpenters organised themselves in 1886. The skilled railworkers union, La Fraternidad, was formed in 1887 and won important gains. Strike statistics in general are unreliable for this period but Julio Godio has estimated that some 48 strikes took place during the 1880s, of which 21 were won, 21 were lost, and 6 were inconclusive.(10) Of these, 40 were concerned with wages and 34 occurred in Buenos Aires alone.

Finally, the 1880s saw the beginning of a fundamental shift from artisan labour to manufacturing, with the appearance of the first meat packing plants (frigoríficos) between 1883 and 1886. Unlike the worker-artisans in the metal or textile workshops, the workers in the frigoríficos were mainly of national origin, the descendants of the gauchos driven to the saladeros by Rosas and the more recent flow of internal migrants to the capital after the definitive collapse of the provincial rebellions in the 1880s.

THE WATERSHED, 1890-1901

The year 1890 is an important turning point in the economic and political history of Argentina. For Di Tella and Zymelman, 'the crisis of 1890 is one of the most important in Argentine economic history, by virtue of its magnitude and because of the political, social and economic repercussions which accompanied it'.(11) The crisis of Barings in London and the subsequent financial and trade dislocations provided a boost to industrialisation in Argentina. The 1895 census indicated the presence of 22,204 industrial establishments with 174,782 workers. Nevertheless, it is estimated that 70 per cent of the establishments and 60 per cent of the employees were still in the artisan or domestic industry category.

This was a prosperous period for Argentina's ruling elite. President Roca had at the end of the 1870s launched the conquista del desierto (literally the conquest of the desert) wiping out the remaining indigenous peoples and securing the extension of the latifundios. Domingo F. Sarmiento (president 1864-74) had already stressed the need to exterminate the gaucho and bring in more 'civilised' European immigrants. The generación del '80 (the 1880s generation) brought to power an organised fraction of the ruling classes which launched a coherent capitalist growth project. Between 1887 and 1895 the number of industrial establishments rose from 6,128 to 8,439 and the number of wage earners doubled. With Argentina's import capacity reduced by the lack of new foreign loans after 1890 local industry boomed, labour being provided by the masses of unemployed driven off the land in the impoverished provinces. The second half of the 1890s saw a stagnation in the global figures for industry and a slight decline in the numbers employed. These figures, however, mask a real change in the structure of industry after 1895. Whereas the 'traditional' sectors (furniture, food, etc) continued to dominate the process of industrial growth, the 'dynamic' industries (metallurgical, chemical, etc) significantly increased their role also. As mechanisation progressed, so too did the concentration of workers in bigger plants. Table 12.2 shows the overall evolution of this process between 1895 and 1914.

This pattern of capital accumulation marked an important shift in the configuration of the working class. Three main fractions can be identified: the trades (bakers, carpenters, bricklayers, etc), who though not highly concentrated were still the main pole of attraction for the labour movement; the highly concentrated and strategic sectors within the

Argentina

agro-export economy, the railworkers and the dockers, sometimes
considered a labour aristocracy; and finally, the meat-packing
workers in the frigorificos and others already under the real
(as against formal) subordination to capital. Between 1891 and
1896, there were 58 strikes, which were just about evenly lost
and won, but significantly nearly half were for causes other
than wage demands (especially the eight hour day). In 1896 the
first general strike across an industrial sector paralysed the
railways.(12) That year there were also sympathy strikes for
the first time, and class solidarity began to displace the
vague appeals to 'justice' of the early labour organisations.
In 1897 an important movement of the unemployed materialised
for the first time. As José Ratzer noted,

> the proletarian protests were no longer relatively
> spontaneous and isolated outbreaks. The resistance
> movement was raised to a higher plane, it was generalised,
> it drew in numerous organised unions. The notable
> struggles of the rail proletariat formed part of a much
> broader current. There were strike actions, meetings and
> demands by workers in various metallurgical
> establishments, by carpentry workers, at a hat factory,
> amongst cobblers . . . New unions were formed and others
> were transformed . . . The class as a whole was beginning
> to act. (13)

SYNDICALISM, ANARCHISM AND SOCIALISM 1904-14

The shared experience of the working population in the 1880s
and 1890s and the growth of solidarity led to a remarkable
explosion of the Argentine labour movement in the first seven
years of the twentieth century. Between 1897 and 1899 there was
a relative calm in industrial relations, the product of a
severe cyclical crisis which created a high level of
unemployment. Then in 1901, a series of strikes and labour
conflicts swept across the country. A strike of seamen was
followed by a port-workers strike in Buenos Aires, which
rapidly spread to other ports. In June, a major strike by the
bakery workers succeeded in preventing a cut in wages and
working conditions. An attempt by the anarchists to move
towards a general strike was unsuccessful; but with anarchists
and socialists working closely together in this wave of
strikes, it was possible to form in 1901 a unified labour
organisation, the Federación Obrera Argentina (Argentine
Workers Federation).
  The anarchists had provided the main ideological impetus
to the working class movement since the 1880s, having had the
benefit of such notable visitors as the Italian, Errico
Malatesta, who was resident in Argentina from 1885 to 1889.
Malatesta encouraged anarchist involvement in the unions and

was himself active in the first bakers' strike in 1888 and attempted to set up a trades union federation open to all ideological currents.(14) After his departure, the 'anti-organisers', or individualists, gained the upper hand in the anarchist movement. This, and the serious effects of the 1890 crisis, led to a decline of labour agitation until about 1896. By then the anarchists had accepted the French syndicalist Pelloutier's strategy of making the unions 'a practical school for anarchism'. The journal La Protesta Humana, formed in 1897, was the voice of this new turn towards the unions. As a result, in 1901 the two tendencies came together and reinforced each other.

In 1902 there were again strikes in the ports of Buenos Aires, Rosario and Bahia Blanca, and an important strike by workers in the Central Fruit Market. The government passed a Residence Law aimed at immigrant anarchists, which led to a general strike, and the government, in its turn, declared a state of siege. The workers' quarters in Buenos Aires had effectively become armed camps, when government forces occupied the central parts of the city for fear of an 'invasion'. As Howard Spalding notes, during 1903 and 1904 around half of all strikes occurred outside the capital, a trend reversed by 1907-9 when strikes in Buenos Aires accounted for nearly three quarters of the total.(15) Although the general strike of 1905 may be seen as the high point of the anarchist influence in the Argentine labour movement, massive 'political' strikes nonetheless continued.

In 1907, however, there were more factory stoppages than 'political' strikes as repression intensified, and as a sign of changed attitudes the Departamento Nacional de Trabajo (National Labour Department) was set up. In 1905, the first labour law was passed, establishing the Sunday rest day; in 1907, the work of women and minors was brought under legislative control; and in 1915, an important law on accidents at work was ratified. The tide seemed to be turning towards order and regularity in industrial relations. The printing workers (who formed the first union in 1876 and carried out the first strike in 1878) in 1906 pioneered the first collective agreement with employers and set up the comisiones paritarias (collective bargaining bodies) which were to institutionalise wage bargaining thereafter. However, this was still only an undercurrent as events in 1909 were to show. On the 1st of May of that year, anarchists and socialists held their separate commemorations of international workers day in the midst of a transport strike. A cavalry charge against the anarchist rally resulted in a dozen deaths and over a hundred injured. The following day the anarchist, socialist and independent unions called a general strike to free the imprisoned workers and ensure the reopening of the union offices. After a week, the transport workers dispute was settled and the other demands were granted. By 1910, when the independence centenary celebrations were held, Buenos Aires was under a state of siege and the city resembled a military camp with the jails full of workers.

The dominance of the anarchists in the labour movement up to this time deserves some comment. Syndicalist (Marotta), socialist (Oddone) and communist (Iscaro) authors,(16) are agreed in their appraisal of anarchism - it appealed to the immigrant independent artisan on a 'low political level', it 'ignored the state' and was unable to articulate the 'true' interests of the proletariat. However, anarchism did seem to correspond to the real conditions and aspirations of a heterogeneous mass of independent workers only just emerging into industrial capitalism. Its decline cannot be related in a deterministic manner to the development of the economy but is tied closely to the Russian Revolution in 1917 and the rise of a new international pole of attraction for workers.(17) For a long time the anarcho-syndicalist theory did fit closely with the reality of a bourgeois state impervious to workers' demands, but in which the possibility existed of gaining real victories through 'direct action', because of a certain degree of employer disorganisation. This was all to change with the Saenz Peña Law granting universal male suffrage in 1912 and the subsequent victory of the Radicals in 1916. The bourgeois state was coming of age, and repression was to be blended with cooption.

The Socialist Party had been formed in 1896, under Juan B. Justo's leadership. It soon broke with the revolutionary marxism of those such as German Lallemant who had pioneered the early socialist groupings. Imperialism, the national and agrarian questions, all disappeared from a basically liberal and evolutionary socialist discourse. The proletariat was required to trust the 'rules of the game' established by parliamentary democracy. As Spalding concludes, on the role of the Socialist Party between 1890 and 1912, 'its non-revolutionary character served to soften the eruption of social problems onto the national scene'.(18) Syndicalism for its part emerged in 1906 ostensibly as a revolutionary opponent of socialist revisionism. However, its economism outbalanced its genuine affirmation of the need to unify the labour movement. It soon lost its radical thrust, and as David Rock notes, 'it stressed continuously the value of tactics, and the virtues of coordination, timing and planning (which) quickly overshadowed the lip-service the movement paid to the goal of class revolution'.(19) Not surprisingly, this current was to produce the labour bureaucrats who paved the way for Peron's hegemony over the working class, when the Socialist and Communist parties paid the price for their anti-national liberalism.

In the conflict between anarchist and socialist tendencies, the unity of the labour movement was bound to be the loser. The labour history of the period is marked by endless congresses, talks and resolutions producing little of any substance. On balance, the anarchists had a sectarian attitude towards workers' unity, but the growing evidence of socialist reformism provided a ready excuse for this. The evolution of the major union confederations is represented in Figure 12.1. A previous organisation, the Federación de Trabajadores Regional Argentina (1891), failed to establish itself. The unity of the first solid organisation, Federación Obrera Argentina, was short-lived, as the socialists broke away after the second congress in 1902 and later formed the UGT with ten associations and 1,780 members. The anarchists remained with fifteen associations and 7,360 members, building up FOA until, in 1904, they formed FORA, on an anarcho-syndicalist platform. A government report of 1910 showed that barely one-fifth of the 240,000 industrial workers in Buenos Aires were unionised, and these were divided more or less equally between the FORA, CORA, and independent unions.(20)

Though unionisation levels were low, strikes usually drew into action much greater numbers - for example, the general strike of 1907 mobilised 93,000 workers of whom 31,000 were involved in union work and only 10,000 were paid-up members.(21) In 1905 the fifth Congress of FORA took the unprecedented step of committing a trade union movement to the 'anarcho-communist' philosophy ('from each according to his ability, to each according to his need' to be implemented immediately). Then in 1906, the UGT passed into the hands of the 'pure' syndicalists. These two currents merged briefly in 1914-15, but the syndicalist reluctance to endorse general strikes led to a new split - a minority FORA V held to the principles of the Fifth Congress, whereas the majority FORA IX adopted the syndicalist pattern and grew rapidly from 20,000 members in 1915 to 70,000 in 1920.

CONDITIONS OF THE WORKING CLASS

What is known of the living conditions of the working class at the turn of the century? A remarkable source is the enquiry into labour conditions by Bialet Massé in 1904, which was commissioned by the government in a bid to dampen political unrest in the provinces. Bialet Massé's uncompromisingly objective report makes it a striking document. In examining a recent sugar strike in Tucuman the conditions of the workers were frankly exposed:

> exploitation was fierce and absorbed the whole product of the workers' labour, which was paid with vouchers [to use at the company's store] . . . the state of the workers on the ingenio [mill] where the strike began was miserable and disastrous; exploitation was iniquitous and the work brutal.(22)

Argentina

Figure 12.1: Union Confederations in Argentina, 1901-22

1901 Federación Obrera Argentina

1904 - Federación Obrera Regional Argentina (anarcho-syndicalist)

1903 Unión General de Trabajadores (socialist)

1909 Confederación Obrera Regional Argentina

1915 - Federación Obrera Regional Argentina V (anarcho-communist)

1915 - Federación Obrera Regional Argentina IX (syndicalist)

Independent Unions (eg La Fraternidad, and Federación Gráfica)

1922 - Unión Sindical Argentina

Source:
Adapted from David Tamarin 'The Argentine Labor Movement in an Age of Transition, 1930-1945', unpublished PhD dissertation, University of Washington, 1977, p. 85.

264

The latest rural strike was imputed to the 'lack of consideration towards the personnel and the inhuman work imposed on them'.(23) The workers of La Rioja were said to be 'in a deplorable state [due to] the effect of insufficient food which will unfortunately lead to a lack of 'hands' for the mining industry'.(24) The super exploitation of women in the domestic industries is also eloquently detailed.

If the conditions of the working class in the provinces were bad, those in the capital were not much better, as a survey by the newspaper La Prensa in 1901 testified.(25) Of 235,000 wage-earners, 46,500 (20 per cent) were classified as unemployed. For those in work, wages did not cover the officially estimated minimum expenditure needed to maintain a 'normal and modest' living standard. In the previous two years, wages had dropped by 30-40 per cent in the crowded immigrant quarters such as La Boca. Accommodation accounted for 30-40 per cent of the workers' budget. Immigrants, who at this stage comprised nearly half of the total population, suffered particularly severely in the conventillos (working class tenements). Overcrowded, insanitary and expensive, these quarters brought the immigrants' aspirations into sharp conflict with the reality.(26)

In 1907, the conventillo tenants launched a rent strike to achieve a 30 per cent reduction in rents, guarantees against arbitrary eviction, and improvement in sanitary conditions. The movement, during which armed self-defence was widely practised, spread throughout Buenos Aires and even to Rosario, and a long struggle (with anarchist support) was at least partially victorious. In this type of action, the large number of home-workers could join with their factory counterparts. As one popular labour history puts it, 'the conventillo was the bitter site of a new cultural synthesis'.(27) Immigrants and Argentine-born workers were united in their proletarian condition. Heterogeneity persisted but it was no longer to be a block to concerted working class action. The working class communities were rapidly developing a distinctive class culture. There was a dense social and cultural network established within the working class and the wider popular masses, which was to become a powerful bulwark against repression. By the 1920s the conventillos were dispersed to new outlying suburbs.

The development of capitalism between 1890 and 1910 had brought together a heterogeneous group of immigrants, craftworkers and artisans, established local workers, internal rural migrants and others, who were gradually formed into a proletariat. But can we say, as Kuczynski does in his classic account of the rise of the working class, that 'the factory fused these various groups, these men (and women) who came from such different strata of society, into one unit'?(28) It has been suggested that given the conditions of industrialisation in Latin America, 'the capitalist factory has not been able to operate as the principle of economic unification'.(29) In the case of the conventillo it is clear that unification operated outside the factory, and certainly there has always been a strong community element in the class solidarity forged by the Argentine workers' movement. The general strikes - those great schools for anarchism or socialism, depending on the particular writer's point of view - certainly played an immense role in crystallising a proletariat. Not until Peronism did organisation in the workplace - the comisiones internas (factory committees) - become a prime element in this process. Openly political struggles, such as against the deportation of anarchist militants, helped to forge a remarkably advanced labour movement for the period, comparable to the American IWW and the French CGT.

THE SEMANA TRAGICA

The oligarchic hegemony of the generación del '80 had lost some of its vigour by the time of the 1912 electoral reform law which enfranchised the native but not the foreign-born workers. This cooptation strategy may be judged, on balance, to have been successful. For President Saenz Peña, there was no 'labour question' in Argentina because wealth was attainable for all, but he still feared the 'dangerous classes'. The Saenz Peña Law was designed to incorporate the growing middle layers through the Radical Party and allow the Socialist Party to become the voice of the 'respectable' working class which could now be weaned from anarchism. The electoral advances of the Socialist Party under the new secret ballot were significant - its poll in Buenos Aires totalled 5,000 in 1908, 7,400 in 1910, 27,000 in 1912 (two deputies elected), and 48,000 in 1913 (one senator elected).(30) This led to limited legislative measures in favour of the working class. If anarchist influence in the labour movement was on the wane after the tremendous exertions of the first decade, the beneficiaries were to be the syndicalists who had now settled down to a tame trade unionism far removed from the original doctrines of revolutionary syndicalism in France. The syndicalists' heyday lasted approximately from 1916 to 1920, in which period they helped consolidate stable industrial relations amongst key sections of the working class, such as the port and railway workers. Significantly, they paid less attention to the meat packers in the frigoríficos and the metallurgical workers, two areas where Peronism was later to achieve widespread support.(31) Ultimately they owed their new position of influence to the unresolved conflict between anarchist idealism and the socialist reformism.

During the First World War strike activity declined slightly compared with the pre-war years. By 1917, however, industrial unrest was increasing and in spite of growing unemployment there was a steady rise in the number of strikes, with 138 occurring in 1917, 196 in 1918 and 367 in 1919. A significant difference between this strike 'explosion' and that of 1907 is that then the most affected sector was small scale industry, whereas in 1917 some 70 per cent of the strikers were involved in transport activities.(32) Of particular importance were the strikes organised by the powerful maritime union, the Federación Marítima, in 1916 and 1917. With Yrigoyen in the presidency, the syndicalist leadership was able to negotiate a favourable settlement; the state was beginning to play the role of 'honest broker' between labour and capital. On the other hand, when the refuse collectors of Buenos Aires went on strike - a group which was neither economically nor politically strategic - the government did not hesitate to use the big stick. There were a number of strikes on the railways during 1917 and 1918, including a general strike which served to expose the division between the syndicalist-led La Fraternidad of the footplatemen, and the workshop personnel's Federación Obrera Ferroviaria in which the anarchists maintained significance amongst the rank and file. Strikes also took place in 1917-18 in the frigoríficos, concentrations of a thousand or more workers labouring under atrocious conditions. The Radical government's ultimate dependence on the landed oligarchy (who in turn sold their livestock to the frigorífico companies) led to them sending in the marines to repress the strikes.

By 1919, unemployment had declined to perhaps 8 per cent of the labour force, but real wages had dropped by about 30 per cent since 1915, as post-war inflation reduced working class living standards.(33) The syndicalists were on the ascendancy, particularly given their 'understanding' with the Radical government, while the influence of the anarchists began to wane. In December 1918, the workers of a large metallurgical plant in Buenos Aires went on strike soon after forming a union. Clashes between strikers and the police led to four deaths and a general strike was called in protest. The union leadership was opposed to prolonged or militant action but a semi-spontaneous rising in the workers' quarters of Buenos Aires occurred. The 'white guards' of the Liga Patriótica Argentina lent their support to the repressive forces of the state in an orgy of anti-worker violence. The syndicalists FORA IX decided to lift the general strike when the original strike was settled, and the Socialist and fledgling Communist parties agreed. Only the anarchist FORA V called for a revolutionary strike for an indefinite period. As Belloni concludes, 'disunity, anarchy and the conciliatory tendencies of the reformists withdrew all cohesion from the working masses who fought desperately for a week in a mad fury of fire and blood'.(34) The Semana Trágica, as it became known, left a balance sheet of nearly 500 workers dead and thousands injured. The political significance of the Semana Trágica remains a matter of conflicting interpretation. In the political tradition of the left it was a spontaneous popular uprising bordering on an insurrection.(35) However, Rock has concluded that 'in broad terms the general strike of 1919 was more a series of unarticulated riots than a genuine working class rebellion'.(36) Rock emphasised the participation of non-unionised groups in the strike, which itself promoted the organisation of these sectors. Certainly the strike was ephemeral, limited geographically and in terms of support, and above all it did not receive any realistic revolutionary leadership. But was it just 'a chaotic outburst of mass emotion', in which 'there was nothing . . . to suggest either an attack on the state or an assault on the capitalist system'?(37) Demystification of traditions may be generally healthy, but there is a danger of reducing an important historical conjuncture to its discrete, and often 'ordinary' elements. Certainly the Semana Trágica has significance in terms of the working class perception of events, and the militant reaction against the subsequent anti-union laws proposed by the government testifies to its impact on worker consciousness.

THE RURAL SECTOR

Though the focus of this analysis has been the urban working class, it is necessary to consider briefly developments in the rural sector. The predominance of cottage industries and artisan work in the provinces after independence lasted until the 1870s. With the rise of a modern sugar industry in Tucumán after 1875, along with the forestry industry of the north-east, a rural proletariat began to emerge. The status of the immigrant colonos (tenant farmers) in the wheat economy was more ambiguous - they were exploited but nevertheless not proletarians. It was this sector, however, which launched the first large-scale rural strike - the Grito de Alcorta in 1912 - which resulted in the formation of the Federación Agraria Argentina. The syndicalist CORA intervened in this small farmers' revolt but its economism did not allow it to advance any ideas of a 'worker-peasant alliance'. During World War I, rural labour unions began to form as a result of anarcho-syndicalist agitation, and the demands of the labourers (braceros) for increased wages, improved conditions and a reduction of working hours brought them into conflict in 1919 with the farmers. As Solberg notes,

> now that the tenant farmers were subjected to a bracero strike, their fundamental conservatism became apparent. When their interests had been at stake, colonists had generated sustained agitation and had indignantly denounced government policy. But the farmers, whose support for agrarian reform hardly envisaged social

democracy in the countryside, vigorously applauded the government's use of force to end the bracero strike.(38)

This was the year of the Semana Trágica, and its rural equivalent was to come in 1921. The labourers on the big estancias of the Patagonia region, who had sought improvements in vain since 1912, finally launched a strike, occupied the estancias, and organised their armed defence against the police. The army moved in and murdered some 1,500 workers, many of them Chilean immigrants.(39) However, this was no longer the heyday of anarchism as in 1909, but the beginning of a new era in the relations between capital and labour, so these events found little response in the city.

CONCLUSION

The year 1920 was a turning point in the history of the Argentine working class. It marks the end of an era of revolutionary mass strikes and a turn towards reformism.(40) Government suppression of city and rural workers during the Semana Trágica and the Patagonia Tragedy left the Radical party unable to forge a stable alliance with the working class. The political integration of the working class would have to await Peron, who was also able to stifle ruling class resistance to this reformist strategy. If the period from 1890 to 1910 had seen the failure of the anarchists to translate their combativity into a political strategy, the 'era of proletarian revolution' after 1917 was marked by the failure of the communists to translate their international political capital into consistent national politics. The socialists operated on the basis of a radical divide between strike action and parliamentary activity. In sum, the level of organisation and combativity of the Argentine industrial working class in this period was never extended into a broad popular movement capable of articulating an anti-imperialist perspective, even though it had become during 1880-1919, 'the most developed and prestigious (labour movement) within Latin America'.(41)

NOTES
    1.   A classic study of this period is R.Cortés Conde and E. Gallo, La Formación de la Argentina Moderna (Paidos, Buenos Aires, 1967). See also Marcelo Cavarozzi, 'Elementos para una Caracterización del Capitalismo Oligárquico', Documento CEDES No 12, Buenos Aires, 1978.
    2.   Adolfo Dorfman, Historia de la Industria Argentina (Solar-Hachette, Buenos Aires, 1970), pp. 72-4.
    3.   See Lyman Johnson, 'The Impact of Racial Discrimination on Black Artisans in Colonial Buenos Aires', Social History, vol. 6, no. 3 (1981). For the decline of the female cottage industry of the provinces after 1870, see Donna

Guy, 'Women, Peonage and Industrialization: Argentina 1810-1914', Latin American Research Review, vol. XVI, no. 3 (1981).

4. For an analysis of the Baring crisis, see A.G.Ford, 'Argentina and the Baring Crisis of 1890', Oxford Economic Papers, vol. VIII (1956).

5. See Marcelo Segall, 'En Amérique Latine: Développement du Mouvement Ouvrier et Proscription', International Review of Social History, no. 17 (1972). Also Ricardo Falcón, 'La Primera Internacional y los Origenes del Movimiento Obrero en Argentina (1857-1879)', CEHSAL Cuaderno, no. 2, Paris, (1980).

6. Eduardo Astesano, La Lucha de Clases en la Historia Argentina (Editorial Pampa y Cielo, Buenos Aires, 1964), p. 29.

7. Quoted by Falcón, 'La Primera Internacional', p. 37.

8. Dorfman, Industria Argentina, p. 73. See also Ricardo Ortiz, Historia Económica de la Argentina (Editorial Plus Ultra, Buenos Aires, 1970).

9. Guy Bourde, Urbanisation et Immigration en Amérique Latine: Buenos Aires (XIX et XX Siècles) (Aubier, Paris, 1974), p. 163.

10. Julio Godio, Historia del Movimiento Obrero Latinoamericano (Nueva Imagen, Mexico, 1980), p. 165.

11. Guido di Tella and Manuel Zymelman, Los Ciclos Económicos Argentinos (Paidos, Buenos Aires, 1973), p. 32.

12. Classic studies of the history of Argentine labour, on which the following account of strikes is partly based, are Sebastián Marotta, El Movimiento Sindical Argentino (Libera, Buenos Aires, 1960); Jacinto Oddone, Gremialismo Proletario Argentino (Libera, Buenos Aires, 1949); Rubens Iscaro, Origen y Desarrollo del Movimiento Sindical Argentino (Editorial Anteo, Buenos Aires, 1958).

13. José Ratzer, Los Marxistas Argentinos del 90 (Pasado y Presente, Cordoba, 1970), p. 62.

14. See G. Zaragoza Ruvira, 'Anarchisme et Mouvement Ouvrier en Argentine à la Fin du XIX Siècle', Le Mouvement Social, no. 103 (1978).

15. H. Spalding, Organized Labor in Latin America (Harper and Row, New York, 1977), p. 25. See also Spalding's introduction to La Clase Trabajadora Argentina (Documentos para su Historia - 1890/1912 (Buenos Aires, 1970).

16. For full references to these authors, see note 12.

17. The Brazilian case, where anarchists provided the cadres for the Communist Party, is a contrasting experience. See Boris Fausto, Trabalho Urbano e Conflito Social, 1890-1920, (DIFEL, São Paulo, 1976).

18. Spalding, La Clase Trabajadora Argentina. p. 76.

19. David Rock, Politics in Argentina 1890-1930: the rise and fall of Radicalism (Cambridge University Press, Cambridge, 1975), p. 85.

20. Cited by Peter de Shazo, 'The Failure of

Revolutionary Labour Syndicates in Argentina, 1900-1930', mimeo, (1973), p. 7.

21. Spalding, Organized Labor, p. 14.

22. Juan Bialet Massé, Los Obreros a Principios de Siglo (Centro Editor de América Latina, Buenos Aires, 1971), p. 103.

23. Ibid, p. 97.

24. Ibid, p. 74.

25. Cited by Iaacov Oved, El Anarquismo y el Movimiento Obrero en Argentina (Siglo XXI, Mexico, 1978), pp. 127-8.

26. See José Panettieri, Los Trabajadores(Jorge Alvarez, Buenos Aires, 1967), ch. 3.

27. Guillermo Gutierrez, La Clase Trabajadora Nacional (Cuadernos de Crisis, Buenos Aires, 1975), p. 37.

28. Jurgen Kuczynski, The Rise of the Working Class (Weidenfeld and Nicolson), London, 1967), p. 76.

29. Silvia Sigal and Juan Carlos Torre, 'Una Reflexión en Torno a los Movimientos Laborales en América Latina', in R. Katzman and S.L. Reyna (eds.), Fuerza de Trabajo y Movimientos Laborales en América Latina (El Colegio de Mexico, Mexico, 1979), p. 142.

30. See Richard Walter, The Socialist Party of Argentina 1890-1930 (University of Texas, Texas, 1977).

31. Rock, Politics in Argentina, p. 270.

32. Ibid., p. 166. The rest of this paragraph draws substantially on Rock's meticulous account.

33. Di Tella and Zymelman, Ciclos Económicos, p. 174.

34. A. Belloni, Del Anarquismo al Peronismo - Historia del Movimiento Obrero Argentino (Pena Lillo, Buenos Aires, 1960), p. 33.

35. See for example Julio Godio, La Semana Trágica de Enero de 1919 (Gránica, Buenos Aires, 1972), and Rock's critical review 'La Semana Trágica y los Usos de la Historia', Desarrollo Económico, vol. 12, no. 45 (1972).

36. Rock, Politics in Argentina, p. 168.

37. Ibid., pp. 162-8.

38. C. Solberg 'Agrarian Unrest and Agrarian Policy in Argentina', Journal of Interamerican Studies and World Affairs, vol. 13 (1971), p. 42.

39. See Osvaldo Bayer, La Patagonia Rebelde (Nueva Imagen, Mexico, 1980).

40. See Ruben Rotondaro, Realidad y Cambio en el Sindicalismo (Pleamar, Buenos Aires, 1971), p. 101.

41. Godio, Historia del Movimiento, p. 219.

Chapter Thirteen

VANGUARD OF THE PROLETARIAT? COMMUNISTS AND UNIONS IN SHANGHAI
AND BOMBAY, 1927-1929

Richard Newman

Few episodes in the history of Asian trade unionism have had
such a profound effect upon the subsequent development of
labour organisation as the Shanghai insurrection of 1927 and
the Bombay strikes of 1928-9. The Shanghai insurrection was, as
the name suggests, an armed uprising, one of many working-class
demonstrations that were linked with the northward march of the
Kuomintang armies as they fought to rid China of its factious
warlords and unite the country under a truly nationalist
government. The crushing of the insurrection was a shattering
blow to trade unionism in Shanghai and the political status of
the Communist Party throughout China. The strikes in Bombay
were more industrial in origin and economic in character, the
outcome of a long period of decline in the cotton textile
industry and growing militancy among the workers. Here also
communists were able to seize control of the trade union
movement and dominate local politics for a time. Here, too,
their success was short-lived; the actions of government and
employers led to the arrest of the union leaders, the collapse
of the strikes and the apparent evaporation of union support.
Though separated by distance and by different contexts, the two
episodes can be linked through London and Moscow: on the one
hand, through the policies and attitudes of the British
government and its intelligence services and, on the other,
through the Communist International and the instructions issued
by Moscow to the colonial labour movements. At this level, and
especially concerning the Comintern, the events in Shanghai and
Bombay have already been the subject of much discussion.(1) The
purpose of the present chapter is to examine the relationship
between the working class and local, rather than international,
forces, and to suggest that the meteoric career of the early
trade unions was to some extent inherent in the nature of their
organisation at the grass roots.
    By the mid-1920s Shanghai and Bombay were large,
cosmopolitan cities with a world-wide reputation for trade and
manufacturing. Shanghai was the larger of the two, with
approximately 2.5 million people to Bombay's 1.3 million.

Shanghai's industry was also more varied, ranging from cotton mills and silk filatures, printing and machine shops, shipbuilding and power plants to food, tobacco and match factories and a multitude of handicrafts.(2) On the other hand, a large number of these industries only dated from after 1895, when foreigners obtained the right to build and operate factories in China - many, in fact, had been founded as recently as the period of the First World War - and many of these establishments were small, often scarcely more than a family workshop in one room of a dwelling. Bombay's industrial landscape was dominated both physically and economically by the cotton mills, where the workforce was numbered in thousands and the traditions of industrial employment went back to the mid-nineteenth century. Although Bombay had to share the industrial leadership of India with Calcutta, while Shanghai was pre-eminent among the manufacturing centres of China, Bombay's millhands were the largest concentrated workforce in India and, superficially at least, the one most likely to be receptive to proletarian aspirations.

These facts alone would have made the two cities into tempting constituencies for trade unionism and left-wing politicians, but there were, in addition, the leading roles which both cities played in the political life of their nations. Political organisation and competition had been an established part of Bombay life for fifty years or more; in Shanghai, the administrative division of the city between the foreign powers and the Chinese authorities made formal political organisation more difficult, but the city was still a hotbed of radical ideas and a haven for dissidents. Bombay and Shanghai were centres of communication by railway, river-boat or the printed word, and both drew a large part of their population from the country areas, so that an urban politician could speak through his immediate audience to a wider public in the surrounding provinces. These factors gave the urban working classes an influence out of all proportion to their numbers and presented trade union leaders with an irresistible challenge and opportunity.

THE SHANGHAI INSURRECTION

In the middle of 1926 the National Revolutionary Army of the Kuomintang, led by General Chiang Kai-shek, set out northwards and eastwards from Canton. By October the northward thrust had conquered the province of Hunan and captured Hankow and the other important cities in the central Yangtze valley. The eastward march through the coastal provinces was less rapid. Sun Ch'uan-fang, the local warlord, handled his troops and allies effectively at first; he put up a fierce fight for northern Kiangsi, crushed a provincialist movement in Chekiang during October and then, as pressure on him mounted, brought in aid from the great Manchurian warlord Chang Tso-lin. Before long, however, Sun's luck ran out and a series of defections and defeats allowed Chiang Kai-shek to push eastwards towards Nanking while the nationalist general Pai Ch'ung-hsi drove Sun's troops northwards out of Chekiang. In Shanghai city the military situation deteriorated rapidly. Sun's army commanders openly sought an opportunity to defect and by the third week of March, when the first nationalist units began to filter into Shanghai's outer suburbs, Sun and his northern allies had decided to abandon the city and retreat to more defensible positions north of the Yangtze.(3)

A feature of the Kuomintang advance was the response of the labouring classes. Instead of melting away, as they had learned to do when other armies passed over the countryside, they stayed to sell food to the nationalists or take jobs as porters or scouts. In some areas, chiefly in Hunan, they mounted strikes against the warlords, held up supplies of munitions, sabotaged railways and even attempted uprisings in a few cities to coincide with the arrival of the Southern forces. Trade unions mushroomed in the wake of the victorious armies, especially in the heavy industries of cities like Hankow and in communications services like the post office, but also among a variety of non-industrial workers like hand-cart coolies. Strikes multiplied and union membership tripled in a few months. In some places the trade unions became a significant economic and political force in the absence of credible government institutions. They negotiated and supervised the introduction of better wages and conditions for their members and occasionally took a share in the management of certain enterprises. They set up their own militia - not, in the circumstances, a surprising development, given the prevailing militarisation of Chinese society - and played a leading role in the demonstrations that forced the British out of their concessions in Kiukiang and Hankow.(4) These events were an example to the workers of Shanghai and to some of the city's communist leaders who had been active in the war zones elsewhere before returning to Shanghai in the early weeks of 1927.

Trade union initiatives exacerbated the tension that existed between the left and right wings of the Kuomintang. This tension had been latent since 1923 when the communists became members of the Kuomintang and thus established a coalition between the Communist Party and the nationalists. In a sense, the tension can be traced back to the Second Congress of the Communist International in 1920 when Lenin and the Comintern urged contradictory policies on colonial labour movements: to form 'temporary agreements or even alliances' with national liberation movements while at the same time pressing ahead with the independent organisation of the proletariat.(5) From the end of 1923 Russian advice and assistance was channelled into the Kuomintang. Mikhail Borodin, the chief Comintern agent in China, helped the nationalists to redraft their political programme, reorganise their party along Bolshevik lines and establish a military academy to train their new army, while the small Chinese Communist Party put itself and its labour organisations at the service of the nationalists.

The partnership had advantages for everyone, but the benefits to the communists and left-wingers were more obvious and the right-wing faction in the Kuomintang began to fret and then to plot. Borodin rose to this challenge and the changes which he initiated during the party congress of January 1926 apparently put the communists and their left-wing allies more firmly in control of the Kuomintang than before. Military power, on the other hand, remained with Chiang Kai-shek and his fellow officers in the academy. In March 1926 Chiang put Canton under martial law, arrested a number of Russian and Chinese communists and closed down some of the local trade unions. He followed this up with changes in the constitution of the Kuomintang which limited the access of communists to party offices and committees. Unfortunately for Chiang the political balance began to swing away from him again as large areas of China were liberated by the Northern Expedition and some political and governmental organs of the Kuomintang were moved from Canton to the more central location of Hankow. Here, in a city of great strategic significance and in a region where labour and peasant organisations were unusually strong, the communists began to recover their influence and the Kuomintang its radical complexion. As the advantages of Hankow accrued to the communists, so Chiang began to press the claims of an alternative centre of government, first at Nanchang, in Kiangsi province, where he was then campaigning, and later at Nanking. During the first months of 1927 the rivalry within the Kuomintang was often expressed in geographical terms as each faction called meetings at the venue of its choice. Hostile resolutions were passed and quickly followed by denials that any showdown was intended. In the case of the communists, these denials carried some conviction, restrained as they were by their own military weakness and by the Comintern strategy of an alliance with the nationalists. Chiang, on the other hand, had fewer inhibitions about dealing with his opponents. During February and March 1927 he systematically liquidated the students' and workers' organisations in Nanchang, Hangchow and other southeastern cities, using gangsters and soldiers in plain clothes to murder labour leaders, ransack union offices and establish rival unions that were firmly under army control.(6)

The city of Shanghai was therefore crucial, both to the power struggle in the Kuomintang and to the continuation of the Northern Expedition itself. Chiang's operations were running out of money, as was the left-wing government in Hankow, which found that the civil war and the separation of Shanghai from its hinterland were ruinous to the regional economy. Shanghai's bankers, taxpayers and customs houses were a vast potential source of revenue and loans and a necessary element in the economic control of the whole Yangtze valley. Neither of the Kuomintang factions could afford to ignore its supporters in Shanghai. As the largest industrial centre in China, the home of many trade unions and the scene of recent strikes and demonstrations, Shanghai seemed to have the makings of a power base for the communists. Chiang Kai-shek, on the other hand, needed the support of the Shanghai bourgeoisie and the Kuomintang right-wingers who were living in the sanctuary and semi-exile of the foreign concessions. The foreigners themselves were an element in everybody's calculations. Shanghai was the site of the wealthiest and most populous of the foreign settlements in China and was very heavily defended. Any method of capturing the Chinese districts of the city, whether by frontal assault or by civil insurrection, might be threatened by foreign intervention on the side of the warlords.

There was no doubt that as the nationalist armies neared Shanghai the city's labour organisations would try to seize the initiative and launch an uprising against the remnants of Sun Ch'uan-fang's forces. Two attempts had already been made to bring this about. The first, in October 1926, had been intended to coincide with the Chekiang rebellion against Sun. The plans were coordinated by the Kuomintang branch office in Shanghai and the uprising went ahead on 24 October even though the Chekiang rebels were already in retreat. Small bands of workers led by communists attacked police stations in various parts of the city and were easily picked off by Sun's police and troops.(7) The second uprising was precipitated by the fall of Hangchow on 17 February and the apparent removal of the last obstacle that lay between Pai Ch'ung-hsi's army and Shanghai. Once again the nationalist forces failed to appear and the Shanghai insurgents were left to fight alone.(8)

The February uprising was launched and led by the General Labour Union (GLU). The GLU had been organised by the communists in May 1925 during an outburst of anti-foreign agitation and was intended, in the first instance, to be the means of bringing the working classes into a nationalist coalition with other sections of the Chinese community. In the longer term the GLU became the central organisation of Shanghai labour. By the end of 1926 it had extended its influence into most areas of the city's working life through nearly 200 affiliated unions, covering workers in industry, commerce and transport as well as those in a range of other occupations such as building and handicrafts. The GLU was therefore the logical command structure for a communist-led insurrection. It called a general strike at very short notice for Saturday 19 February, and by the afternoon of that day about 70,000 employees had stopped work. By the following Monday more than 100,000 were involved. The strike was particularly well supported in the tram sheds, the post office, the Japanese cotton mills, the tobacco factories and the large department stores. Electricity and water supplies were maintained with reduced staff and work continued on the wharves, although crews deserted some of the ships.

The GLU attached a list of demands to its announcement of the strike, including a call for better wages, greater job security and improved conditions of work, but the union's main objectives were two: the removal of Sun and his forces from Shanghai and the withdrawal of the 'imperialistic' British troops that were coming in by sea to defend the International Settlement.(9) Most labour leaders seem to have rated the opposition to Sun as their major concern. Despite an undisguised hostility to the foreign powers and their position in Shanghai, the GLU insisted that there should be no assaults on foreigners or damage to their property and these instructions were generally obeyed. Some leaders of the affiliated unions preferred to stress economic issues. This may account for the swift response from groups of workers who had recently been in dispute with their employers and for the fact that the weight of the strike fell on Chinese and Japanese, rather than British, concerns. Other workers responded to the simplest idea in the union's propaganda which suggested that the strike should be observed as a three-day holiday to celebrate the Kuomintang advance.

It was a celebration that rapidly soured. Sun's commander in Shanghai, General Li Pao-chang, promptly carried out his threat to execute anyone who prejudiced Sun's campaign. Squads of soldiers armed with broadswords roamed through the Chinese districts of the city, seizing agitators, executing them on the spot and hanging their severed heads in cages above the street as an example to others. As many as 200 people may have been done to death in this way and some of the hundreds arrested probably suffered a similar fate. On 21 February the same punishment was threatened against the men and women in the silk filatures after the president of the Silk Guild had complained to Li about the loss of contracts that would follow a strike. On 23 February the return to work was widespread and by 25 February, the day when the GLU formally called off the strike, there were only about 10,000 workers absent from their jobs.

During the last two days of the strike the GLU attempted, somewhat irresolutely, to convert its demonstrations into an armed uprising with attacks on police stations in the working class district of Chapei. Some members of the union appear to have been emboldened by a wave of popular revulsion against Li's executions and the prospect of a mutiny in two of Sun's warships at anchor alongside the city.(10) Union leaders were encouraged by the favourable course of negotiations with the Chinese merchants and shop-keepers which were aimed at bringing these classes into a nationalist alliance with labour.(11) In the event, the merchants and shopkeepers backed away from an alliance, the naval mutiny went awry and the nationalist army under Pai Ch'ung-hsi refused to advance from its forward positions only 25 miles away. The GLU did not feel strong enough to attempt an insurrection on its own.

Within a month, however, the political and military situation had changed considerably. Tensions within the Kuomintang had become more acute and the communists needed more than ever to assert themselves in Shanghai. Sun's forces were in retreat, so much so that the Chinese areas of the city were practically devoid of troops that could oppose the union militias. The nationalist armies were advancing again at last and Lunghua, on the southern outskirts of Shanghai, was reached by forward parties of Pai Ch'ung-hsi's army on the night of 20 March.

On 21 March the GLU launched a strike and an armed insurrection simultaneously. The strike was effective at once, involved a much larger number of workers than the previous uprisings and paralysed all industries and shops, large and small, as well as the public utilities.(12) The insurrection took the form of attacks on police stations by gangs of workers and students wearing Kuomintang armbands and armed with pistols, bayonets and iron bars. Some of the police defected or surrendered readily in the hope of clemency, while others put up more of a fight, and in a few instances there were lengthy fusilades ending in the destruction of the building and the slaughter of the occupants.(13) Arms were captured and handed out to a growing number of union volunteers. Within a day the GLU was the effective civil authority in the southern and western districts of the Chinese city. Only in the northern industrial suburb of Chapei did the union have difficulty in establishing its supremacy. Rearguard units of the warlord army clung tenaciously to one major building after another and a squad of White Russian mercenaries, trapped in an armoured train in the North Shanghai Railway Station, answered the snipers' bullets with a stream of shells which started a huge fire and destroyed hundreds of dwellings. Chapei was not finally subdued until the arrival of units of Pai's army on the evening of 22 March.

The scale and speed of the union's success would not have been possible without detailed planning and organisation in advance of events. Ever since the February uprising the GLU had worked hard to extend its membership and influence. It had backed a number of strikes, formulated demands for higher wages and better conditions in various industries and elaborated the rules governing the relationship between itself and its affiliated institutions so that the loyalty and discipline of the whole workforce could be relied upon.(14) It had persisted with the difficult negotiations between itself and the merchants and shopkeepers and had brought them, on the eve of the insurrection, to what appeared to be a successful conclusion. On 20 March a delegate conference of middle-class and working-class associations set up a Provisional Committee of the Nationalist government to work for a number of common objectives, such as the elimination of warlord rule and the establishment of an autonomous popular government. In reaching this conclusion, the GLU had skillfully played upon the merchants' antipathy to the northern allies of Sun Ch'uan-fang, the desire of the Chekiangese businessmen for a measure of provincial autonomy, and the determination of all classes to have the foreign concessions returned to Chinese rule. Unfortunately, support for the agreement was very far from unqualified, and a section of the Chinese Chamber of Commerce broke away almost immediately to form a new merchants' association.(15)

Shortly after the insurrection had succeeded the Provisional Committee was reconstituted as a Provisional Government for Shanghai. Its executive of 19 members included Wang Shao-hua, the secretary of the GLU, and four other unionists and communists, together with a prominent journalist, a Chinese woman lawyer, the head of the local branch of the Kuomintang and a number of bankers and businessmen, among them Yu Hsia-ch'ing, the influential former chairman of the Chamber of Commerce.(16) All of this was in clear contradiction of an order from Chiang Kai-shek that no administration should be formed until the military situation had been stabilised. Because of this, and because of their extreme hesitation about the Provisional Government in the first place, many of the middle-class members found excuses for not attending. The Provisional Government did, however, take the important steps of lifting the official ban on the GLU and endorsing much of its political and economic programme. On 24 March the GLU felt able to end the strike because it had 'evidently proved a success' and the Provisional Government had 'recognised our 22 Demands and consented to enforce them as soon as possible'.(17) The union's new freedom of action had unprecedented results. Existing organisations were reconstituted and regrouped, new unions were established among workers that had never been organised before, such as hawkers, wheel-barrow coolies and night-soil carriers, as well as workers in small industries, and new demands were handed in to the employers although the GLU was careful not to threaten strike action unless an existing economic grievance was involved.(18) By the end of March the GLU was claiming a total of 821,000 members in 499 affiliated organisations.(19)

Throughout the heady days of liberation a new struggle was developing. General Pai was determined to stamp Chiang Kai-shek's authority on the whole of the Chinese city and as soon as his occupation of Shanghai was completed he met representatives of the GLU and told them to end their strike and submit to his orders. During the following days his troops attempted to disarm the union militias. The workers, however, resisted vigorously and furious battles were fought for the control of police stations and other buildings.(20) Captured workers were marched off and shot. When Chiang Kai-shek arrived in Shanghai on 26 March the preparations for a counter-coup gathered pace. Businessmen hurried to ingratiate themselves and the new Federation of Commerce and Industry offered financial backing for any measures that Chiang might take against the unions. Right-wing Kuomintang politicians came out of the foreign settlements to help tilt the balance of power away from Hankow and the communists. The British and French authorities were cooperative. Most ominous of all were Chiang's consultations with the Green Gang, one of the largest secret societies in Shanghai and probably the only intelligence network and armed force that could operate with equal facility in all areas of the city. Through his friends in the Gang, Chiang had access to a vast range of supporters and contacts, from wealthy and influential Chinese in all walks of life - in one case, the chief detective of the police force in the French Concession - through the lower strata of trade and industry to the mobsters and racketeers of the underworld.(21) Chiang covered these preparations with a screen of conciliatory communiques and declarations of harmony with Hankow. The Kuomintang left-wingers, and even to some extent the communists, associated themselves with these announcements even though they cannot have been in any doubt about Chiang's real intentions.(22)

The blow fell on 12 April. Early that morning hundreds of armed men, dressed as labour organisers, but under orders from the Green Gang and supported by plain-clothes soldiers from Chiang's army, attacked union offices throughout the city. In most places the defenders were quickly overwhelmed. Even in buildings where they managed to regroup the fighting was over in a few hours. Once captured, the union men were stripped of their weapons, lashed together and led away to their execution.(23) Wang Shao-hua was already dead, having been enticed to the house of one of the Green Gang leaders and kidnapped at the gate. Next morning a crowd of union activists descended on army headquarters in Chapei to demand the return of their weapons, but they were fired on by the soldiers, even though women and children were in the front of the crowd, and many were killed.(24) The same day the GLU's surviving leaders called a general strike. Most of the major industries were affected immediately and 111,000 workers left their jobs, but the protest rapidly subsided and by 22 April there were only 10,000 still out of work, mainly as a result of lock-outs in individual plants.(25) Meanwhile mopping up continued at union offices with raids on the headquarters of unions affiliated with the GLU and the daily arrest and execution of leaders.

The final outcome of the Shanghai insurrection was therefore a victory for Chiang Kai-shek and his faction in the Kuomintang. The communist position was completely destroyed in the very city where the industrial structure and the development of working-class organisations offered China's best hope of a proletarian revolution. It was a few months yet before the disintegration of the Hankow government, the separation of the non-communist left wing from their communist allies and the revision of Comintern policy in the light of these changes, but Chiang's coup in Shanghai was a turning point in events. The GLU leadership was decimated, driven underground and replaced, not by a new generation of working-class leaders, but by members of the Green Gang and puppet unions such as the Committee for the Reorganisation of the Shanghai Labour Unions which the Political Bureau of Pai's army established in GLU headquarters the day after the coup.(26) The quiescence of the Shanghai working class during the next two decades is an indication of the influence which Chiang and his allies could exert, as well as an indication of the limits of GLU success in developing a class-conscious leadership cadre during its days of power.

THE BOMBAY STRIKES

During the months when the Shanghai communists were being deserted and then crushed by their Kuomintang partners, the communists in Bombay were laying the foundations for an alliance with middle and working-class radicals. Founded in 1925, the Communist Party of India was insignificant in comparison with its Chinese counterpart; its membership around the sub-continent was numbered in ones and twos rather than hundreds or thousands, and the activities of the British police severely limited its contacts with Moscow. Like their Chinese comrades, the Indian communists were members in an individual capacity of the country's leading nationalist organisation, in this case the Indian National Congress. In fact, considering their intellectual and political background, there is good reason to describe them as nationalists first and communists second. A few of them had achieved quite high positions in the Congress hierarchy, but nowhere, not even in the ward committees of the industrial cities, were they sufficiently numerous or influential to dictate policy.

In 1927 three emissaries of the Communist Party of Great Britain evaded the police and entered India to help the local communists develop a more effective strategy. On the political front this involved the founding of a Workers' and Peasants' Party in each of the Indian regions. The new party was intended not to replace the Congress but to work within it; the aim was to push Congress policy constantly to the left and provide a forum in which communists could meet non-communist allies and build a working relationship with them. In particular, it was hoped that the Workers' and Peasants' Party would function as the progenitor and mentor of trade unions. With the assistance of their British advisers, the communists in Bombay set out to form unions in those industries that currently lacked them - municipal transport and services, printing and dock labouring - and draw into the Workers' and Peasants' Party the leaders of existing unions, the most important of which were in the cotton mills.(27)

By 1927 the Bombay cotton textile industry was well into a period of economic decline. Its difficulties stemmed in part from the unhealthy prosperity of the years immediately after the First World War and the speculative attitudes that were engendered by it. More important, however, was the loss of markets; Bombay lost its substantial export trade with East Asia to the mills of Osaka and Shanghai, and customers in the Indian hinterland turned instead to the new local mills, which specialised in catering for regional tastes and operated at much lower costs than mills in the metropolis. By the end of 1927 most of the Bombay mills were shedding labour or cutting wages, and a few of the larger companies were experimenting with comprehensive rationalisation schemes designed to raise the efficiency of labour and shift production towards varieties of yarn and cloth that were less affected by competition.(28)

All of these changes had repercussions on the workforce. In 1919, for the first time in the industry's history, and again in 1920, the millhands mounted a general strike for higher wages to compensate for the sharp rise in prices.(29) On both occasions they won quick and substantial victories, since the mill companies could well afford to pay. In 1924, soon after the onset of the depression, the millhands went on strike against the loss of their annual bonus, but were beaten. In 1925 they struck again to resist a general cut in wages. This time the government intervened and removed an excise duty so that the employers could restore wages to their former level. Each of these strikes was spontaneous and unplanned. Strike committees and trade unions emerged only after the strikes had become accomplished facts and it was not until 1924 and 1925 that any of these organisations put down sufficiently deep roots to survive and grow. Even then, the unions depended to a greater or lesser extent on outside help and they never achieved a membership of more than a few thousand. One, the Bombay Textile Labour Union, was founded and controlled by a group of social workers who had run a relief service during the 1925 strike. The other, the Girni Kamgar Mahamandal, made its first appearance during the strike of 1924. It operated a policy of excluding outsiders from the millhands' affairs, but in practice it had to depend on the advice and encouragement of senior and influential employees, such as time-keepers and clerks, and, through them, of the lower middle-class members of Congress committees in the mill area. It was thus that the communists acquired their first foothold in the city's major industry.

During the last months of 1927 and the early months of 1928 everyone in the textile industry was preoccupied with rationalisation. The communists argued from the beginning that this was an issue that exemplified the opposing interests of capital and labour; in their view, nothing but a general strike could remove the danger to the millhands. Most of the social workers and radical Congressmen took a more equivocal position and the communists were therefore able to recruit the more determined of the union leaders to their side. There was no doubting the hostility of the ordinary millhands to particular aspects of rationalisation - a wage cut here, redundancies there, new machinery and redeployments somewhere else - and strikes in individual mills were fought with a vigour that surprised even the communists, but the inter-relationship of these grievances was difficult to appreciate. In the end, however, rationalisation proved to be the ideal issue on which to build a general strike and an industrial union, requiring, as it did, a detailed understanding of the effects of rationalisation on each process, a wider perspective on the consequences for the industry as a whole, and a corresponding attention to the needs of the millhands both as individuals and as an inter-related workforce.

A new general mill strike developed out of a convergence of local disputes. The stoppage began on 16 April 1928 and was essentially complete within a week. The communists urged on the strike with speeches and processions, but their contribution to the unfolding of events was probably no greater than that of the police, who shot a striker during a demonstration and caused a surge of public feeling, or of the employers, who were in such a hurry to cut costs that there was no time for them to break strikes mill by mill.

The strike of 1928 was one of the longest and largest in India's industrial history. It involved nearly 80 mills and 140,000 workers and it lasted for six months, causing a loss of 22 million working days. A large proportion of the millhands sat out the strike in their native villages, sometimes hundreds of miles from Bombay; the remainder survived precariously in the city with the help of casual labour and rations of grain supplied by the trade unions. By October, when the strike ended, some sections of the workforce, notably the Muslims, were right at the end of their tether, but there was never any doubt of their determination or their solidarity with the rest of the workforce.

The strike made possible collaboration between the communists and the social workers, which was institutionalised by a Joint Strike Committee, since, once the strike was a reality, the social workers could put their ideological hesitations aside and work wholeheartedly for the millhands on humanitarian grounds. The social workers had access to money for relief supplies and the communists played a prominent part in distributing these rations each week to the most impoverished of the strikers. The social workers also had some standing with the government and the employers and were therefore able to promote negotiations in which the communists eventually became equal partners. One communist in particular, S.A. Dange, soon mastered the technicalities of the textile industry and won the respect of the millowners for his intelligence and ability. In various other ways, such as their control of picketing and their prominence as public speakers and pamphleteers, the communists were transformed into something like popular heroes in the working-class districts of the city. When the strike was called off, pending the report of an official committee of enquiry but with the main issues essentially unresolved, the communists were riding the very crest of a continuing wave of discontent.

Another consequence of the strike was the disappearance of the millhands' distrust of outsiders in the running of union affairs. A new textile union, called the Girni Kamgar Union (GKU), was launched during the strike. Dange was its secretary and communists and millhands shared the other important offices. During the months after the strike, the communists devoted themselves to the millhands' interests, settling conflicts in individual mills, negotiating grievances, examining the everyday problems of ordinary workers, explaining the economic position of the industry and encouraging the millhands to organise themselves. The response was 'magical'; thousands of workers flocked to join the GKU and by January 1929 the union had at least 65,000 paying members and probably more.(30) Ironically enough, it was at this point that the echoes of events in Shanghai, having reverberated for months in Moscow, finally reached Bombay in the form of a new Comintern directive. Just when the Bombay comrades were beginning to reap the political rewards of collaboration, colonial communist parties were instructed to avoid alliances with bourgeois nationalists and work alone for revolution.

The explosive growth of the GKU made it vital for the union to elaborate its administrative structure and pass over the day to day conduct of industrial relations to mill committees elected from the ordinary workers. The communists had always intended to introduce a participatory system of this kind but they had been reluctant to set up the committees immediately because of fears that caste and other divisive factors in the workforce would destroy the developing class consciousness of the union members. The millhands had to be given real control over their own affairs if they were ever to increase their new-found solidarity, but at the same time there was a danger that the union's strength might be dissipated in sectional strikes, called by the mill committees in furtherance of some local dispute, when larger interests required these resources to be conserved or applied elsewhere. For several months the communists managed to reconcile these needs. Local strikes were successfully negotiated and union hotheads held in check, while the GKU and its branches won general acceptance from the employers and a regular place in collective bargaining. By March 1929, however, this policy was becoming increasingly difficult to follow; more and more mill committees were forcing the union into untenable positions. At this point, as part of an anti-communist campaign that had been under consideration for nearly a year, the government arrested most of the GKU leaders, including almost all of the men whose reputation and experience were the union's best hope of continuing unity and development. The younger communists who replaced them were much less experienced and relied much more, when they got into difficulties, on the militant strategy of the Comintern's new line. The employers, for their part, had decided that the time had come to crush the mill committees, whatever the cost. A new strike was therefore inevitable.

The general mill strike of 1929, which began on 26 April, was the first strike in the Bombay textile industry to be called by a union, launched at an advertised time and fought in defence of a union's interests. It never won total support from the millhands, though at the outset it affected about three-quarters of the mills and about two-thirds of the workforce. From the beginning of June the numbers returning to work rose steadily and by mid-September, when the strike was called off, the solidarity of the workforce had been shattered completely. Most of the strikers were simply too weary to continue; their savings were eaten up, their credit with moneylenders exhausted and their families too poor to support them any longer. Muslims and untouchables capitulated first, encouraged by their communal leaders; then confidence in the communists was undermined by politicians in the non-Brahman movement, playing on the high-caste background of the communists; and finally, some sections of the workforce, seeing that the owners were determined to put up a fight, calculated that the support of the millowners was likely to serve their interests better than loyalty to the union. Nevertheless, the defeat of the GKU was not as complete as the defeat of the GLU in Shanghai. The aims and methods of trade unionism were sufficiently well-established to survive the departure of the communist leaders. Genuinely working-class cadres existed to provide the basis for organisational growth, even if this growth was to be distorted by competing political movements in the decades ahead.

PROBLEMS OF ORGANISATION

If the non-Brahmans of Bombay lacked the machine guns of Chiang Kai-shek and the flashing broadswords of Li Pao-chung were a rougher form of justice than the long-winded trial of the Indian communists at Meerut, the political environments of the two communist movements still had strong similarities. Both were shaped by a nationalist struggle and both were heavily affected by the complex character of the nationalist movements, in which regional and sectional interests were often as much concerned with competition among themselves as they were with opposition to the imperialists and their collaborators.(31) The struggle between the left and right wings of the Kuomintang was only the most obvious of the tensions between fellow nationalists. The problem for labour organisers was to avoid those issues and interest groups that were likely to pull the working class apart and concentrate on those that would unite it.

In Shanghai the administration of the city and its services was the issue that most readily united all sections of Chinese opinion. The city was divided between the areas under Chinese rule, the French Concession and the International Settlement, in which the British were the dominant community. The Shanghai Municipal Council was elected by a few thousand foreign ratepayers to run the Settlement, together with its police force and its municipal undertakings; the 700,000 Chinese who also lived there were unenfranchised. Moreover, the influence of the foreigners reached well outside Settlement limits in the form of roads that were under municipal control and the substantial number of foreign-owned factories and warehouses that were located in Chinese territory. For Chinese in general the situation in Shanghai was a deep affront to national pride, and for the workers the poor conditions and harsh discipline that existed in the foreign-owned factories were a daily reminder of their inferior status. The working class came to share the resentments felt by the intellectuals and the bourgeoisie and it was natural that the communists should have tried to build an anti-foreign alliance between these classes as part of the preparation for their bid for power.

In Bombay, on the other hand, the devolution of administrative control into Indian hands was already far advanced. The Bombay presidency had a legislative council containing representatives of the Millowners' Association and other employers, as well as three representatives of labour, and in Bombay city there was an elected Municipal Corporation with an Indian majority. British businessmen played only a small part in the ownership and management of the cotton mills. Paradoxically, since China was nominally independent while India was not, the British occupied a less autocratic position in Bombay than they did in Shanghai. It was therefore logical and appropriate for the Bombay communists to emphasise industrial unionism and class interests.

The position of trade unions in the two cities differed correspondingly. Trade unions were legal in India and the Bombay communists were entitled to hold office in them; then, as properly elected union leaders, they came under the protective eye of the British Labour party and the international trade union movement. No such protection existed for Chinese unions; they were officially dissolved by

government order in 1913 and the penal code prescribed harsh
punishments for anyone leading strikes or making wage demands.
Labour law was liberalised to some extent under the Kuomintang
government in Canton, but the limits of union action were still
extremely unclear, especially in Shanghai, where Chinese law
was nominally in force but the municipal authorities did not
necessarily apply it. If a strike broke out in Shanghai it was
extremely difficult to stop; foreign consuls were often
involved and they might have to agree among themselves before
concessions could be offered to the strikers, while Chinese
officials took part in negotiations reluctantly and on their
own responsibility, realising that their actions had no backing
in law and might be repudiated by their superiors.(32) Force
was often the only arbiter in Shanghai's labour relations,
whether the force was exercised by army execution squads or
union pickets. In Bombay, on the other hand, there was a
government Labour Office to monitor wages and conditions and
government officials, both British and Indian, with
responsibility for intervening in serious disputes. There were
precedents for handing disputes to a committee of enquiry, as
happened in 1928, and it was customary for such committees to
act in a judicial manner, with representatives of labour being
summoned to present evidence and argue a case. The
administrative system in Bombay therefore encouraged the formal
development of labour organisation, whereas the system in
Shanghai actively discouraged it.

Strikes in Bombay were almost entirely economic in
character. Anti-British sentiments were sometimes detectable,
as in strikes on the railways and in the post office, where the
employers were exclusively British, but even here the real
issues in dispute were economic. Industrial workers were hardly
involved in any of the mass campaigns of the Indian National
Congress between 1918 and 1922. There were a few occasions when
the millhands were absent from work because of riots or as a
protest against the arrest of local politicians; there were
also a few occasions when millhands were gathered into crowds
to serve the political purposes of others; and there was a
small number of millhands who were inspired to become Congress
members by Gandhi and his methods. However, there was no
tradition of mass political action for the millhands as a body.
The most potent examples of united action were the general mill
strikes. Each of these shows a greater degree of solidarity,
but this development was a product of the pursuit of economic
goals.

Economic issues were also of great importance in Shanghai.
There was a rash of strikes in 1919-21 caused, as in Bombay, by
a rapid rise in prices, and wage demands continued to be the
major cause of disputes in later years, as they were in Bombay
also.(33) A rise in food prices in the second half of 1926
undoubtedly contributed to the militancy that found expression
in the insurrections of 1927.(34) Shanghai workers were more

concerned than their Bombay counterparts with questions of hours and conditions, these being less well regulated by government than they were in India, and with ill-treatment by supervisors, especially in Japanese establishments where discipline tended to be rather severe. On the whole, there was no lack of incentive for strike action, yet stoppages, when they occurred, seem to have taken place trade by trade or factory by factory, sometimes linked together by proximity or by the nationality of the employers. General strikes in any one of the factory industries seem to have been rare. In any case, no industry in Shanghai dominated the economic life of the city as much as the cotton mills did in Bombay and there were therefore no strikes to equal the Bombay mill strikes as examples to a whole urban proletariat.

The great formative influences on working-class action in Shanghai were nationalistic: the May Fourth Movement of 1919 and the May Thirtieth Movement of 1925. The first of these began with a violent protest by students in Peking against the extension of Japanese interests in China as proposed by the Peace Conference in Versailles. The movement in Shanghai was also initiated by students, to be followed by a boycott of Japanese goods and a general closure of shops and factories. Industrial workers undoubtedly shared the sense of national humiliation displayed by the students and merchants and some of their reactions were spontaneous: for example, one of the first groups of workers to strike were the Chinese employees of the Japanese-owned Naigai Wata Kaisha mills. Many other workers, however, were slow to join in the protests and were eventually mobilised for action 'by organizations that despite their influential position among the working class were primarily representative of other social classes':(35) student propagandists, craft guilds, associations for 'industrial advance' and secret societies such as the Green Gang, which came out early in favour of a strike and maintained strict discipline over its members and clients.(36) The workers were only part of the supporting cast in a drama enacted by nationalists of other classes.

In the May Thirtieth Movement the workers moved to the centre of the stage. A new wave of strikes began in the Japanese cotton mills in February 1925 and brought to the surface a broader groundswell of discontent with rising prices and other economic factors. At the same time the merchants, shopkeepers and students were becoming incensed by proposals from the Municipal Council, such as an increase in wharfage dues and control of the press, which inflamed anti-foreign feeling and touched the pockets of the bourgeoisie. When, on 30 May, ten Chinese demonstrators were killed by Settlement police under the orders of a British officer, the nationalist coalition of 1919 was quickly reconstructed and its wrath turned on the British. A general strike began on 1 June and a Shanghai Workers', Merchants' and Students' Federation was formed soon afterwards to promote a common political programme which demanded the involvement of Chinese in the government of the Settlement and also touched on such matters as trade union rights. Communists had been active in the strike wave from February onwards and on 31 May they founded the GLU to link the existing unions in the city and control their participation in the general strike. For the next month the GLU's endeavours had the support of the Chamber of Commerce and its devious chairman Yu Hsia-ch'ing. Yu calculated that the strike was the best way of putting pressure on the municipality and damaging some of his business competitors at the same time, but his colleagues were never happy about their association with labour's political demands and a few small concessions from the municipality, combined with the disconnection of their power supply from the Settlement's generators, were enough to pull them out of the coalition after a few weeks. From then until the end of September the GLU kept the strike going in various industries on the strength of economic demands.(37)

In the first month of the May Thirtieth Movement the GLU had captured the leadership of the Shanghai working class by emphasising its nationalist credentials; in the next 18 months it had to try to reconstruct its position on an anti-capitalist foundation. This was no simple matter. In some industries, such as cotton textiles, support for the trade unions declined; in others, such as public utilities, the unions disappeared completely and were replaced by others of differing size; and in some industries, such as the Chinese-owned silk factories, the GLU and its affiliated unions had virtually no influence even at the height of the May Thirtieth Movement. Although the total membership claimed by the GLU in June 1926 was almost the same as the membership in June 1925, the composition of this membership had radically altered.(38) The status of the GLU had also changed. Instead of being the undisputed leader of the city's workers, the GLU soon found itself in competition with the guilds, the various welfare bodies and the industrial associations that represented the employers' ideas of partnership between capital and labour. The collapse of the nationalist coalition can be illustrated by a dramatic incident. In June 1925 the GLU offices were protected by gangs of men described as the Merchants' Volunteer Protection Corps,(39) but only two months later the offices were attacked by several car-loads of well-armed coolies, who drove up under the eyes of the Chinese military authorities, ransacked the building and left a number of union helpers badly wounded - an attack that was attributed to the industrial associations.(40) On 19 September the Chinese police dissolved the GLU and the main unions affiliated with it and forced the communists to operate from headquarters underground. When Sun Ch'uan-fang took control of Shanghai later in the year he chose to interpret trade union law in a way that continued to outlaw the GLU but permitted combinations at the plant level where industrial associations and other divisive agents had the greatest effect.

Shanghai and Bombay

All of this was in sharp contrast with the situation in Bombay where the formal development of trade unions was a desirable element in the government's policy on industrial relations. It may also be doubted whether the bureaucratic structure of the union movement in Shanghai was as appropriate to the task of industrial unionism as the structure of the GKU in Bombay. In Shanghai the GLU was at the apex of a pyramid of organisations reaching down through district federations and industrial federations to individual unions and ultimately to branches on the factory floor. The communists and other activists who were trying to stimulate union growth were therefore at some distance from their potential members and supporters. The success of the whole movement depended on the quality of the leaders at intermediate levels. Who these leaders were is not known precisely. In June 1925, when the urgent need was to expand the protest movement as quickly as possible, the GLU probably accepted help from anyone with an influence over the workforce - impeccable nationalists, no doubt, but dubious proletarians, whose involvement in labour affairs may well have been a liability in later months. There is evidence that the communists were willing to accept help from various quarters in making contact with groups of workers for the first time. At the very beginning of their work in Shanghai, for example, the communists used the help of the Green Gang in establishing links with workers in the tobacco and silk factories,(41) and it is likely that the secret societies, the guilds and the industrial associations were used again in 1925. Having entered into a partnership with these bodies, the GLU's problem was to supplant them. This is probably what lies behind the union's obsession with structure and discipline; time after time the GLU found it necessary to bring in reforms to strengthen the ties between its affiliates, improve the representation of ordinary workers and clarify the lines of command that ran down from the centre to the branches. The unanimity of the workers' responses in March and April 1927 was a tribute to what had been accomplished, yet the impression still persists of a rather cumbersome organisation, sufficient for the needs of a nationalist demonstration but decidedly ramshackle for other purposes, in which the leaders were often remote from the members.

In Bombay the communists did not attempt to build a general union for the whole city; they concentrated on the organisation of separate industries and therefore worked closer to the union members than their comrades in Shanghai. The Bombay GKU was founded in circumstances that encouraged a close relationship between the communists and the millhands: the communists had to collect detailed information from the workers in each mill department if they were to argue effectively against the rationalisation scheme; they had to know the social background and family circumstances of individual millhands if they were to distribute relief supplies fairly and wisely

during the 1928 strike; and the communists' allies in Bombay -
the social workers and the moderate trade unionists - were far
more cooperative and far more committed to at least the
short-term interests of the strikers than their counterparts in
Shanghai. When the GKU mill committees were proliferating in
the period between the strikes of 1928 and 1929, the Bombay
communists were much more in control of the process than the
leaders of the GLU. They were present at gatherings when mill
committee members were elected - in fact, they often coaxed the
more intelligent and self-confident workers to come forward
after they had felt the pulse of a meeting and seen which
millhands were generally respected - and they took delegates
from the mill committees into the higher levels of union
decision-making where they could be trained and controlled. The
Bombay communists drew genuinely working-class leaders into
partnership with themselves to a much greater extent than in
Shanghai. If, in spite of this, the relations between the GKU's
central office and its branches eventually proved to be the
union's undoing, the size of the same problem in Shanghai can
readily be appreciated.

The problem of organisational unity, of overcoming
pre-existing divisions within the workforce, was a consequence
of the social composition of the workforce itself. Here too
there are important parallels between Bombay and Shanghai. Both
were cities of migrants; in each case the workforce was largely
of peasant origin, retained many links with the countryside and
was divided into distinctive social groups based upon dialect,
district of origin and so forth. Indian society was more
stratified than Chinese, owing to the pervasive influence of
the caste system, but the Bombay workforce had had two or three
generations in which to accommodate its social traditions to an
industrial system. In Shanghai, on the other hand, the
workforce was newer and younger than its Bombay counterpart and
it brought with it to the city's industry a much richer
tradition of apprenticeship and guild exclusiveness. On the
whole, the Chinese workforce probably offered a better
long-term prospect to trade unionists, but in the circumstances
of the 1920s the task of creating class consciousness and
labour unity was more daunting than it was in Bombay.

In both cities the social divisions of the workforce were
transmitted into industry by the system of recruitment. In
Shanghai many industries - such as the cotton mills, the docks
and the Municipal Public Works Department - recruited through
labour contractors, sometimes even through a hierarchy of
contractors, who went out into the countryside to find
recruits, paid them out of a lump sum which they received from
the employers and controlled most aspects of working and
living. Even those industries which ostensibly operated in the
free labour market depended on foremen for choosing their
workers and the foremen, like the contractors, were susceptible
to bribes or the recommendations of kinsfolk and other

intermediaries.(42) There was, in any case, a tendency for workers to come together into clubs to give themselves protection and companionship in the strange environment of the city and to improve their bargaining power in the various networks of urban life. It was at this level that informal labour organisations, secret societies and other groups with economic and political influence could interprenetrate. 'In our factory', said one worker, 'all the powerful workers are members of the gangs. The reason is that if they join the gangs they are sure of their jobs'.(43)

In the Bombay cotton mills recruiting was done by a person known as a jobber. He was not a true contractor, since both he and his workers were on the company's payroll and paid at rates determined by the employers, but he was responsible for selecting recruits, deploying them around the machines and imposing discipline. He negotiated with management when the men had complaints to make and arranged housing, credit and other services outside the mills for new recruits. It seems probable that a jobber's gang was socially homogeneous, or at least socially compatible, and its solidarity and loyalty to its leader was born out of a desire for comradeship and patronage.(44)

The jobbers played a crucial role in the Bombay mill strikes.(45) Although they had a duty to their employers, this had to be weighed against their obligations to their men. If the men's demands were really insistent, as they were, for example, over rising prices in 1919, the jobbers could not stand out against them without running the risk of repudiation by their followers and a consequent loss of influence inside and outside the mills. The jobbers' attitude to trade unions was equally equivocal. For the most part the jobbers were hostile to them because the unions stood for a formal unity that contradicted the jobbers' informal style and undermined their local influence, but there were occasions when the unions could offer the kind of resistance to the employers that the jobbers could not offer on their own. The battle against rationalisation was just such an occasion. The communists and the GKU were a threat to the jobbers because they offered qualities of leadership which the jobbers could not match, but the rationalisation scheme, with its wholesale redundancies and redeployments, threatened an even more far-reaching disruption of the jobbers' position. From July 1928, when the rationalisation scheme became known in all its details, the jobbers decided to back the general strike and the trade unions. The communists were very relieved by this development. They needed the jobbers' knowledge to combat rationalisation effectively and later, when the strike was over, to bring their gangs of workers into the GKU and build the union up rapidly to a point where it could act for the workforce as a whole. Once the GKU was firmly established and the mill committees were ready to provide the members with an alternative leadership on the factory floor, the jobbers could be dispensed with. 'Our aim', said Dange, the GKU's secretary, 'was to neutralise them by a temporary alliance'.(46) The months from October 1928 to April 1929 were therefore an extremely turbulent period in the Bombay mills as two forms of leadership struggled for supremacy. Mill committees usurped the jobbers' functions, jobbers' were set upon and beaten in the streets and discipline broke down so completely in some mills that the GKU even had to intervene against its own members.

By the time that the next general strike broke out in April 1929 the jobbers' were ready to switch their support back to the employers. There were probably many other reasons for this change beside a reaction against the GKU: the manifest determination of the millowners to recruit a new workforce with new jobbers if this was necessary to break the strike; pressure from the jobbers' own patrons, such as moneylenders and grain dealers, who wanted the commercial life of the mill area brought back to normal; and encouragement from political interests such as the non-Brahman movement, which resented the communists' popularity among workers from the non-Brahman castes and was able to offer the jobbers' an alternative political alliance.(47)

Information about grass-roots politics in Shanghai is extremely difficult to find but there is some evidence to suggest that the GLU became trapped in the same kind of political web as the GKU in Bombay. The GLU was not able to subsume the existing, intermediate leadership as easily as the GKU; there was no possibility of a tactical alliance for industrial purposes between the union and the informal leaders such as the contractors and foremen because the latter were too sharply differentiated from the ordinary workers and much more unpopular than the jobbers' in Bombay. Left-wing unions in Hunan and Hupeh prohibited the admission of foremen and high-ranking employees as members and it is probable that unions in Shanghai followed the same principle. There was no alternative, therefore, to a head-on collision between the GLU and the informal leaders and networks. The violence that marked the growth of the GKU in Bombay was far surpassed in Shanghai; murders were common and foremen were a particular target in the weeks leading up to the 1927 insurrections. Complaints about the behaviour of overseers were regularly included in strikers' demands and attempts were made to have the contractor system replaced, sometimes successfully.(48) The GLU and its affiliated unions took every opportunity of insisting on their recognition by the employers and often tried to win the right to collect subscriptions in the factories, exercise a veto over dismissals and generally develop a role in the day-to-day conduct of industry. By March and April 1927 the GLU was organising craftsmen such as the carpenters and masons and encroaching on the membership of the guilds and the provincial associations that were so important among these classes of workers. The turning point in this process seems to have come with the near success of the GLU in extending its influence to the shopkeepers and street unions of petty traders. One of the leaders of the Green Gang played a prominent part in dissuading the shopkeepers from any involvement with the communists and it is not difficult to imagine how the GLU might have impinged upon the protection rackets and other commercial ventures that brought the underworld so much of its profits.(49) By April 1927 the GLU had made an impressive array of enemies. Chiang's coup was their counter-attack.

CONCLUSION

Lenin and the Comintern were right to raise the problems of an alliance between colonial labour movements and local politicians, but discussion of these problems was focussed on larger issues such as the ideological and organisational relationship between communism and nationalism. The Comintern did not give any detailed guidance on local tactics - indeed, it would have been impossible to do so, given the complex character and rapidly changing alignments of the communities that made up the working classes in cities like Bombay and Shanghai. Trade unions had to make use of these alignments if they were to get a foothold in industry; the industrial labour force was not a discrete entity and its organisation inside the workplace could not be started without involving the various networks that operated across the workers' lives. These networks could be allies or competitors. In the circumstances of 1925 in Shanghai they were allies, as they were in Bombay in 1928, and the unions were able to grow rapidly as a result. Before long they began to see the communists as a danger and their hostility was a major factor in the unions' demise. On the whole, the Bombay communists seem to have been able to handle their local industrial and political environment more successfully than their counterparts in Shanghai: the issues in Bombay were more clearly economic, the administrative system was more favourable to the emergence of formal trade unions and the intermediate leadership in the workforce, the jobbers, were easier to bend to the unions' purpose. As a result, the trade union movement that existed in Bombay in the 1930s and 1940s was much more vigorous than the union movement in Shanghai, even though it was still deeply divided. The underlying problem in both cities was the lack of a united and fully self-conscious proletariat.(50) In these circumstances the communists were less like the vanguard of a revolution and more like the brokers and patrons in the shifting alliances that surrounded them.

NOTES
1.   R.C.North, Moscow and Chinese Communists, 2nd edn
(Stanford University Press, Stanford, 1963); H.R. Isaacs, The
Tragedy of the Chinese Revolution, 2nd edn (Stanford University
Press, Stanford, 1961); G.D. Overstreet and M. Windmiller,
Communism in India (Perennial Press, Bombay, 1960); J.P.
Haithcox, Communism and Nationalism in India: M.N. Roy and
Comintern Policy 1920-1939 (Princeton University Press,
Princeton, 1971); Intelligence Bureau, Communism in India,
1924-1927 (Government of India Press, Calcutta, 1927).
2.   D.K. Lieu, The Growth and Industrialisation of
Shanghai (China Institute of Pacific Relations, Shanghai,
1936). The statistics provided by Lieu and others are discussed
by R.Murphey, Shanghai: Key to Modern China (Harvard University
Press, Cambridge, Mass., 1953), pp. 165ff.
3.   D.A. Jordan, The Northern Expedition: China's
National Revolution of 1926-28 (University of Hawaii Press,
Honolulu, 1976).
4.   J. Chesneaux, The Chinese Labour Movement 1919-1927
(Stanford University Press, Stanford, 1968), pp. 319-32.
Jordan, Northern Expedition, chs.19-20, offers important
modifications of Chesneaux's account.
5.   Quoted by C. Brandt, Stalin's Failure in China
1924-1927 (Harvard University Press, Cambridge, Mass., 1958),
p.3.
6.   Isaacs, Chinese Revolution, pp. 143-4 and 152-3.
7.   Isaacs, Chinese Revolution, p. 131, and Chesneaux,
Chinese Labour Movement, p. 341, imply that the Kuomintang
deliberately left the union activists to their fate. Jordan,
Northern Expedition, p. 209, says that the communists decided
to go ahead with the attacks, despite the weakness of their
position.
8.   Isaacs, Chinese Revolution, p. 135, and Chesneaux,
Chinese Labour Movement, p. 335, claim that the Kuomintang
forces deliberately held back to allow the defenders to
liquidate the communists. Jordan, however, emphasises the
difficulty of a frontal attack on Shanghai and says that the
Kuomintang intention was to undermine the warlord defence of
the city by negotiating the defection of its commanders
(Northern Expedition, p. 115). The two interpretations are not,
of course, mutually exclusive.
9.   North China Daily News (Shanghai; hereinafter NCDN),
21 February 1927.
10.   Manchester Guardian, 22 February 1927; S. Barton,
British Consul-General in Shanghai, to British Legation,
Peking, 28 February 1927, FO/228/3020.
11.   NCDN, 24 February 1927.
12.   Chesneaux, Chinese Labour Movement, p. 357; NCDN, 22
March 1927. Most estimates of the number of workers involved
range between 600,000 and 800,000. NCDN gave a figure of
150,000 but admitted that thousands of small establishments had
been left out of this total (23 March 1927).

13.   NCDN, 22 March 1927.
14.   Chesneaux, Chinese Labour Movement, pp. 355-6; NCDN, 2 April 1927; Barton to British Legation, Peking, 16 March 1927, FO/228/3021.
15.   Barton to British Legation, Peking, 28 March 1927, FO/228/3161.
16.   NCDN, 25 March 1927; Chesneaux, Chinese Labour Movement, pp. 356 and 362.
17.   NCDN, 25 March 1927.
18.   NCDN, 31 March 1927 and 2 April 1927. Chesneaux, Chinese Labour Movement, p. 359, says that 75 new unions were formed between 21 March and 12 April.
19.   Chesneaux, Chinese Labour Movement, p. 360.
20.   NCDN, 25 March 1927, 26 March 1927 and 4 April 1927; Shanghai Defence Force to War Office, London, 2 April 1927, WO/191/2.
21.   Y.C. Wang, 'Tu Yueh-sheng (1888-1951): A Tentative Political Biography', Journal of Asian Studies, vol. XXVI, no. 3 (May 1961), pp. 433-55. Tu was the Green Gang leader most involved in the subverting of the trade unions. According to one set of legends, the Green Gang emerged in the early 18th century as an association of boatmen on the Grand Canal which linked north China with the Yangtze delta. Around 1900, when cargo began to travel in large quantities by coastal shipping, many of the boatmen lost their jobs and the Green Gang reorganised itself, moved into other economic activities, such as the opium traffic, and began to adopt a more political role. The Gang was originally organised into twenty-four 'generations' or ranks, but by the 1920s this hierarchy had apparently been overlayed by a series of interlocking circles of patronage. Thus Tu, who was officially a member of one of the lowest generations, was nevertheless one of the Gang's most important leaders. The membership had also become more diverse and reached from top to bottom of Chinese society in Shanghai. In the 1930s it was possible to distinguish cliques that were identified particularly with mill workers, seamen, gamblers and shopkeepers. Chiang Kai-shek is said to have been a member of the Gang during his early career as a share broker in Shanghai. Isaacs, Chinese Revolution, pp. 142-3; J. Chesneaux, Secret Societies in China in the Nineteenth and Twentieth Centuries (University of Michigan Press, Ann Arbor, 1971), pp. 47-51 and 162-9; A Note on Chinese Secret Societies and Political Organisation by Major J. Gwyn, General Staff (Intelligence), Shanghai, 18 March 1937, WO/106/5375.
22.   For a discussion of this, and an indictment of the communists for not alerting the union members to their impending fate, see Isaacs, Chinese Revolution, ch. 10.
23.   NCDN, 13 April 1927; Isaacs, Chinese Revolution, pp. 175-7.
24.   NCDN, 14 April 1927.

25.   NCDN, 14 April 1927; Shanghai Political Report for the Quarter Ending 30 June 1927, FO/228/3640.

26.   W.E. Gourlay, '"Yellow" Unionism in Shanghai: A Study of Kuomintang Technique in Labor Control, 1927-1937', Papers on China, VII (1953), pp. 103-135.

27.   Haithcox, Communism and Nationalism, pp. 46-57 and 96-102; R.K. Newman, Workers and Unions in Bombay 1918-1929: A Study of Organisation in the Cotton Mills (Australian National University Press, Canberra, 1981), pp. 103-110.

28.   Indian Tariff Board (Cotton Textile Industry Enquiry) 1927, Report of the Indian Tariff Board (Cotton Textile Industry Enquiry) 1927, 4 vols (Government Central Press, Bombay, 1927); Bombay Strike Enquiry Committee, Report of the Bombay Strike Enquiry Committee, 1928-29 (Government Central Press, Bombay, 1929).

29.   A full account of these strikes, as well as others that took place up to 1929, is given in Newman, Workers and Unions.

30.   The description was Dange's in his Statement (p. 2507) during the Meerut Communist Conspiracy Case. The figure of 65,000 was given by the government's Labour Office, but income from monthly subscriptions indicates a membership of more than 100,000.

31.   Jordan, Northern Expedition, passim; R.W. Rigby, The May 30 Movement: Events and Themes (Australian National University Press, Canberra, 1980); G. Omvedt, 'Non-Brahmans and Communists in Bombay', Economic and Political Weekly, vol. VIII, no. 16 (21 April 1973), pp. 749-59 and 17 (28 April 1973), pp. 800-5; I. Rothermund, 'Gandhi and Maharashtra: Nationalism and the Provincial Response', South Asia, 1 (1971),pp. 56-73.

32.   Report by Acting Consul-General Moss on the organisation and development of trade unions in Shanghai, enclosed with despatch of 16 August 1924, FO/228/3140.

33.   Chesneaux, Chinese Labour Movement, pp. 374-82; Newman, Workers and Unions, ch. III.

34.   Chesneaux, Chinese Labour Movement, p. 339.

35.   Ibid., p. 153.

36.   Ibid.; J. Chen, The May Fourth Movement in Shanghai (Brill, Leiden, 1971), pp. 151 and 176.

37.   Rigby, May 30 Movement, passim; Chesneaux, Chinese Labour Movement,pp. 262-72.

38.   Chesneaux, Chinese Labour Movement, pp. 280-1.

39.   Report by Municipal Police annexed to minutes of the Diplomatic Delegation to Shanghai, 10 June 1925, FO/228/3143.

40.   Chesneaux, Chinese Labour Movement, p. 269; Barton to British Legation, Peking, 31 August 1925, FO/228/3149.

41.   Chesneaux, Chinese Labour Movement, p. 171.

42.   Ibid., pp. 54-64.

43.   Quoted by Gourlay, '"Yellow" Unionism', p. 121.

44.   Newman, Workers and Unions, ch. II; R.K. Newman, 'Social Factors in the Recruitment of the Bombay Millhands' in K.N. Chaudhuri and C.J. Dewey (eds), Economy and Society: Essays in Indian Economic and Social History (Oxford University Press, Delhi, 1979), pp. 277-95.
45.   The role of jobbers in strikes and unions is discussed at length in Newman, Workers and Unions.
46.   Interview, 5 July 1969.
47.   For a description of the shifting position of jobbers, neighbourhood bosses and others in the politics of the Bombay mill area, see R. Chandavarkar, 'Workers' Politics and the Mill Districts in Bombay between the Wars', Modern Asian Studies, vol. XV, no. 3 (1981), pp. 603-47.
48.   Chesneaux, Chinese Labour Movement, p. 272; NCDN,8 April 1927.
49.   NCDN, 24 February 1927.
50.   Chesneaux repeatedly claims in Chinese Labour Movement that the Chinese workers were a developed proletariat when his own evidence shows clearly that they were not. See, for example, the contradictory statements on p. 142.

FURTHER READING

Alba, V. Politics and the Labor Movement in Latin America
    (Stanford University Press, Stanford, California, 1968)
Alexander, R.J. Organized Labor in Latin America (The Free
    Press, New York, 1965)
Allen, V.L. 'The Meaning of the Working Class in Africa',
    Journal of Modern African Studies, vol. 10, no. 2 (1972)
Amin, S. Modern Migrations in West Africa (Oxford University
    Press, London, 1974)
Ananaba, W. The Trade Union Movement in Africa (Hurst, London,
    1979)
Anderson, R.D. Outcasts in Their Own Land: Mexican Industrial
    Workers, 1906-1911 (Northern Illinois University Press,
    DeKalb, Illinois, 1976)
Angell, A. Politics and the Labour Movement in Chile (Oxford
    University Press, London, 1972)
Anker, R. (ed.) Sex Segregation in Urban Labour Markets of the
    Third World (International Labour Organization, Geneva,
    1984)
Arizpe, L. and Aranda, J. 'The "Comparative Advantages" of
    Women's Disadvantages: Women Workers in the Strawberry
    Export Agribusiness in Mexico', Signs, vol. 7, no. 2
    (1981)
Aronson, R.L. 'Labour Commitment Among Jamaican Bauxite
    Workers', Social and Economic Studies, vol. 10 (1961)
Arrighi, G. 'Labor Supplies in Historical Perspective: A Study
    of the Proletarianisation of the African Peasantry in
    Rhodesia' Journal of Development Studies, vol. 6, no. 3
    (1970)
Arrigo, L. 'The Industrial Workforce of Young Women in Taiwan',
    Bulletin of Concerned Asian Scholars, vol. 12, no. 2
    (1980)
Aziz Allouni, A. 'The Labor Movement in Syria', Middle East
    Journal, vol. 13, no. 1 (1959)
Baily, S.L. 'The Italians and the Development of Organised
    Labor in Argentina, Brazil, and the United States, 1880-
    1914, Journal of Social History, vol. 3 (1969)

Further Reading

——Labor, Nationalism and Politics in Argentina (Rutgers University Press, New Brunswick, N.J., 1967)

Banaji, J. 'Modes of Production in a Materialist Conception of History', Capital and Class, no. 3 (1977)

Bauer, A. 'Chilean Rural Labor in the Nineteenth Century', American Historical Review, vol. 76, no. 4 (1971)

Beinin, J. 'Formation of the Egyptian Working Class', MERIP Reports, no. 94 (1981)

Beling, W.A. Modernization and African Labor: A Tunisian Case Study (Praeger, New York, 1965)

Bennvune, M. 'Origins of the Algerian Proletariat', MERIP Reports, no. 94 (1981)

Berg, E.J. 'The Development of a Labor Force in Sub-Saharan Africa', Economic Development and Cultural Change, vol. 13, no. 4 (1965)

Bergad, L.W. 'Coffee and Rural Proletarianization in Puerto Rico, 1840-1898', Journal of Latin American Studies, vol. 15, part 1 (1983)

Bergquist, C. 'What Is Being Done? Some Recent Studies on the Urban Working Class and Organized Labor in Latin America', Latin American Research Review, vol. 16, no. 2 (1981)

Berman, B.J. and Lonsdale, J.M. 'Crises of Accumulation, Coercion, and the Colonial State: The Development of the Labor Control System in Kenya', Canadian Journal of African Studies, vol. 14, no. 1 (1980)

Bernstein, H. 'Notes on Capital and Peasantry', Review of African Political Economy, no. 10 (1977)

Béteille, A. Caste, Class and Power: Changing Patterns of Stratification in a Tanjore Village (University of California Press, Berkeley and Los Angeles, 1965)

Blanchard, P. 'The Recruitment of Workers in the Peruvian Sierra at the Turn of the Century: The Enganche System', Inter-American Economic Affairs, vol. 33, no. 3 (1980)

——The Origins of the Peruvian Labor Movement, 1883-1919 (University of Pittsburgh Press, Pittsburgh, 1982)

Bolton, D. Nationalization: A Road to Socialism? The Case of Tanzania (Zed Press, London, 1983)

Bondestan, L. 'People and Capitalism in the North-Eastern Lowlands of Ethiopia', Journal of Modern African Studies, vol. 12, no. 3 (1974)

Bonner, P. Strikes in South Africa (Ravan Press, Johannesburg, 1980)

Bozzoli, B. (ed.) Labour, Townships and Protest (Ravan Press, Johannesburg, 1979)

Breman. J. 'Seasonal Migration and Cooperative Capitalism; The Crushing of Cane and Labour by the Sugar Factories of Bardoli, South Gujarat', Journal of Peasant Studies, vol. 6, no. 1 (1978)

Brow, J. 'Class Formation and Ideological Practice: A Case From Sri Lanka', Journal of Asian Studies, vol. 40, no. 4 (1981)

Bryceson, D. 'The Proletarianization of Women in Tanzania',
    Review of African Political Economy, no. 17 (1980)
Buch-Hansen, M. and Marcussen, H.S. 'Contract Farming and the
    Peasantry: Cases From Western Kenya', Review of African
    Political Economy, no. 23 (1982)
Bujra, J. 'Proletarianization and the "Informal Economy": A
    Case-Study From Nairobi', African Urban Studies, no. 47
    (1978)
Burawoy, M. The Colour of Class in the Copper Mines (Manchester
    University Press, Manchester, 1972)
Bush, A.C. Organized Labor in Guatemala 1944-1949 (Colgate
    University Press, New York, 1950)
Byres, T.J. 'Agrarian Transition and the Agrarian Question',
    Journal of Peasant Studies, vol. 4, no. 3 (1977)
Cadbury, W.A. Labour in Portuguese West Africa (Routledge,
    London, 1910)
Carmi, S. and Rosenfield, H. 'The Origins of the Process of
    Proletarianization and Urbanization of Arab Peasants in
    Palestine', Annals of the New York Academy of Science,
    vol. 220 (1974)
Chan, M.K. Historiography of the Chinese Labor Movement
    (Hoover Institution Press, Stanford, California, 1981)
Chandavarkvar, R. 'Workers' Politics and the Mill Districts in
    Bombay Between the Wars', Modern Asian Studies, vol. 15,
    no. 3 (1981)
Chapkis, W. and Enloe, C. (eds.) Of Common Cloth: Women in the
    Global Textile Industry (Transnational Institute,
    Amsterdam, 1983)
Chaplin, D. The Peruvian Industrial Labor Force (Princeton
    University Press, Princeton, N.J., 1967)
Chattopadhyay, P. 'Labour and Development', Labour Capital and
    Society, vol. 13, no. 1 (1980)
Chaudhuri, K.N. and Dewey, C.J. (eds.) Economy and Society:
    Essays in Indian Economic and Social History (Oxford
    University Press, Delhi, 1979)
Chesneaux, J. The Chinese Labor Movement 1919-1927 (Stanford
    University Press, Stanford, California, 1968)
Cho, U. and Hagen, K. 'Economic Development and Women's Work in
    a Newly Industrialising Country: The Case of Korea',
    Development and Change, vol. 14, no. 4 (1983)
Clarence-Smith, W.G. Slaves, Peasants and Capitalists in
    Southern Angola, 1840-1926 (Cambridge University Press,
    Cambridge, 1979)
Clark, D.G. Contract Workers and Underdevelopment in Rhodesia
    (Mambo Press, Gwelo, 1976)
—— Agricultural and Plantation Workers in Rhodesia (Mambo
    Press, Gwelo, 1977)
Clark, M.R. Organized Labor in Mexico (University of North
    Carolina Press, Chapel Hill, 1934; reissued Russell and
    Russell, New York, 1973)
Clayton, A. and Savage, D.C. Government and Labour in Kenya

1895-1963 (Frank Cass, London, 1963)

Clegg, I. Workers' Self-Management in Algeria (Allen Lane The
    Penguin Press, London, 1971)

Cock, J. Maids and Madams (Ravan Press, Johannesburg, 1980)

Cohen, R. Labour and Politics in Nigeria, 1945-71 (Heinemann,
    London, 1974)

———'From Peasants to Workers in Africa', in P.C.W.Gutkind and
    I.Wallerstein (eds.) The Political Economy of Contemporary
    Africa (Sage Publications, Beverly Hills, 1976,

———'The Making of a West African Working Class', in T.Shaw
    and K.Heard (eds.) Africa: The Politics of Dependence
    (Africana Publishing, New York, 1979)

———'Resistance and Hidden Forms of Consciousness Amongst
    African Workers', Review of African Political Economy, no.
    19 (1980)

———and Hughes, A. Towards the Emergence of a Nigerian
    Working Class: The Social Identity of the Lagos Labour
    Force, 1897-1939, Occasional Paper D7, Faculty of Commerce
    and Social Science, University of Birmingham, 1971

———, Gutkind, P.C.W., and Brazier, P. Peasants and
    Proletarians: The Struggles of Third World Workers
    (Hutchinson, London, 1979)

Conway, H.E. 'Labour Protest Activity in Sierra Leone During
    the Early Part of the Twentieth Century', Labour History,
    vol. 15 (1968)

Cooper, F. From Slaves to Squatters: Plantation Labor and
    Agriculture in Zanzibar and Coastal Kenya 1890-1925 (Yale
    University Press, New Haven, Conn., 1980)

Crisp, J. The Story of an African Working Class: Ghanaian
    Miners' Struggles 1870-1980 (Zed Press, London, 1984)

Cronje, G. and Cronje, S. The Workers of Namibia (International
    Defence and Aid Fund, London, 1979)

Davies, I. African Trade Unions (Penguin, Harmondsworth, 1966)

———and de Miranda, S. 'The Working Class in Latin America',
    Socialist Register 1967 (Merlin Press, London)

Davies, R. Capital, State and White Labour in South Africa
    1900-60 (Harvester Press, Hassocks, Sussex, 1979)

Davis, S.M. and Goodman, L.W. (eds.) Workers and Managers in
    Latin America (Heath, Lexington, Mass., 1972)

De Clercq, F. 'Apartheid and the Organised Labour Movement',
    Review of African Political Economy, no. 14 (1979)

Deeb, M. 'Labour and Politics in Egypt, 1919-1939',
    International Journal of Middle East Studies, vol. 10
    (1979)

Deere, C.D. 'Rural Women's Subsistence Production in the
    Capitalist Periphery', Review of Radical Political
    Economics, vol. 8, no. 1 (1976)

———and León de Leal, M. 'Peasant Production,
    Proletarianization, and the Sexual Division of Labour in
    the Andes', Signs, vol. 7, no. 2 (1981)

De Janvry, A. and Garramón, C. 'The Dynamics of Rural Poverty in Latin America', Journal of Peasant Studies, vol. 4, no. 3 (1977)

DeShazo, P. Urban Workers and Labor Unions in Chile 1902-1927 (University of Wisconsin Press, Madison, 1983)

De Vylder, S. Agriculture in Chains: Bangladesh - A Case Study in Constraints and Contradictions (Zed Press, London, 1982)

DeWind, J. 'From Peasants to Miners: The Background to Strikes in the Mines of Peru', Science and Society, vol. 39, no. 1 (1975)

Di Tella, T. 'Working Class Organization and Politics in Argentina', Latin American Research Review, vol. 16, no. 2 (1981)

Du Toit, D. Capital and Labour in South Africa: Class Struggle in the 1970s (Kegan Paul International, London, 1981)

Duncan, K. and Rutledge, I. (eds.) Land and Labour in Latin America (Cambridge University Press, Cambridge, 1977)

Elkan, W. Migrants and Proletarians: Urban Labour in the Economic Development of Uganda (Oxford University Press, London, 1960)

Elkan, W. 'Is a Proletariat Emerging in Nairobi?', Economic Development and Cultural Change, vol. 24, no. 4 (1976)

Elson, D. and Pearson, R. '"Nimble Fingers Make Cheap Workers": An Analysis of Women's Employment in Third World Export Manufacturing', Feminist Review, no. 7 (1981)

Erickson, K.P. et al. 'Research on the Urban Working Class and Organized Labor in Argentina, Brazil and Chile: What Is Left To Be Done?', Latin American Research Review, vol. 9, no. 2 (1974)

———The Brazilian Corporative State and Working Class Politics (University of California Press, Berkeley, 1977)

Feder, E. 'Agribusiness and the Elimination of Latin America's Rural Proletariat', World Development, vol. 5, nos. 5-7 (1977)

Freund, W. Capital and Labour in the Nigerian Tin Mines (Longman, London, 1981)

———'Labor and Labor History in Africa: A Review of the Literature', African Studies Review (forthcoming)

Friedland, W.H. Vuta Kamba: The Development of Trade Unions in Tanganyika (Hoover Institution Press, Stanford, California 1969)

Fröbel, F., Heinrichs, J. and Kreye, O. The New International Division of Labour: Structural Unemployment in Industrialised Countries and Industrialisation in Developing Countries (Cambridge University Press, Cambridge, 1980)

Frucht, R. 'A Caribbean Social Type: Neither "Peasant" Nor "Proletarian"', Social and Economic Studies, vol. 16, no. 3 (1967)

Fuenter, A. and Ehrenreich, B. Women in the Global Factory (Institute for New Communications, New York, 1983)

Gale, R.P. 'Industrial Development and the Blue Collar Worker in Argentina', International Journal of Comparative Sociology, vol. 10 (1969)

Galvin, M. The Organized Labor Movement in Puerto Rico (Associated University Presses, London, 1979)

Gates, H. 'Dependency and the Part-Time Proletariat in Taiwan', Modern China, vol. 5, no. 3 (1979)

Gonzales, M.J. 'Capitalist Agriculture and Labour Contracting in Northern Peru, 1880-1905', Journal of Latin American Studies, vol. 12, part 2 (1980)

Goodey, C. 'Workers' Councils in Iranian Factories', MERIP Reports, no. 88 (1980)

Goodman, D.E. and Redclift M.R. 'The "Bóias-Frias": Rural Proletarianisation and Urban Marginality in Brazil', International Journal of Urban and Regional Research, vol. 1, no. 2 (1977)

———and ——— From Peasant to Proletarian: Capitalist Development and Agrarian Transitions (Blackwell, Oxford, 1981)

Gordon, R.J. Miners, Masters and Migrants: Life in a Namibian Mine Compound (Ravan Press, Johannesburg, 1977)

Grillo, R.D. African Railwaymen: Solidarity and Opposition in an East African Labour Force (Cambridge University Press, Cambridge, 1973)

Grobart, F. 'The Cuban Working Class Movement From 1925 to 1933', Science and Society, vol. 39, no. 1 (1975)

Grossman, R. 'Women's Place in the Integrated Circuit', Pacific Research, vol. 9, nos. 5-6 (1978)

Gutkind, P. The Emergent African Proletariat, Occasional Paper Series no. 8, Centre for Developing Area Studies, McGill University, Montreal, 1974

———, Cohen, R. and Copans, J. (eds.) African Labor History (Sage Publications, Beverly Hills, California, 1978)

Halliday, F. 'Iran: Trade Unions and the Working Class Opposition', MERIP Reports, no. 71 (1978)

Hammam, M. 'Egypt's Working Women: Textile Workers of Chubra-el-Kheima', MERIP Reports, no. 82 (1979)

Harding, T. 'The Politics of Labor and Dependency in Brazil: An Historical Approach', International Socialist Review, vol. 33, no. 7 (1973)

Harris, P. 'Industrial Workers in Rhodesia 1946-72', Journal of Southern African Studies, vol. 1 (1975)

Harriss, J. (ed.) Rural Development: Theories of Peasant Economy and Agrarian Change (Hutchinson, London, 1982)

Hart, J.M. Anarchism and the Mexican Working Class 1860-1931 (University of Texas Press, Austin, 1978)

Hemson, D. 'Dock Workers, Labour Circulation and Class Struggles in Durban, 1940-59', Journal of Southern African Studies, vol. 4 (1977)

——— 'Trade Unionism and the Struggle for Liberation in South Africa', Capital and Class, no. 6 (1978)

Hinchcliffe, K. 'Labour Aristocracy - A Northern Nigerian Case

Study', Journal of Modern African Studies, vol. 12, no. 1
(1974)
Hirschman, C. 'Industrial and Occupational Change in Peninsular
Malaya, 1947-70', Journal of Southeast Asian Studies, vol.
13, no. 1 (1982)
———and Aghajanian, A. 'Women's Labour Force Participation
and Socioeconomic Development in Peninsular Malaysia,
1957-1970', Journal of Southeast Asian Studies, vol. 11,
no. 1 (1980)
Hodgkin, T. Vietnam: The Revolutionary Path (St Martins Press,
New York, 1981)
Holmstrom, M. South Indian Factory Workers: Their Life and
Their World (Cambridge University Press, Cambridge, 1976)
Hopkins, A.G. 'The Lagos Strike of 1897: An Exploration in
Nigerian Labour History', Past and Present, no. 35 (1966)
Horowitz, J. 'The Impact of Pre-1943 Labour Union Traditions on
Peronism', Journal of Latin American Studies, vol. 15,
part 1 (1983)
Hoyt, E.E. 'The Indian Laborer on Guatemalan Coffee Fincas',
Inter-American Economic Affairs, vol. 9, no. 1 (1955)
Hüsken, F. 'Landlords, Sharecroppers and Agricultural Labour-
ers: Changing Labour Relations in Rural Java', Journal of
Contemporary Asia, vol. 9, no. 2 (1979)
Hussein, M. Class Conflict in Egypt 1945-1970 (Monthly Review
Press, New York, 1973)
Ibrahim, B. 'Family Strategies: A Perspective on Women's Entry
to the Labour Force in Egypt', International Journal of
the Sociology of the Family, vol. 11, no. 2 (1981)
Ibrahim, Z. 'Malay Peasants and Proletarian Consciousness',
Bulletin of Concerned Asian Scholars, vol. 15, no. 4
(1983)
Ingleson, J. 'Workers' Consciousness and Labour Unions in
Colonial Java', Pacific Affairs, vol. 54, no. 3 (1981)
———'Life and Work in Colonial Cities: Harbour Workers in
Java in the 1910s and 1920s', Modern Asian Studies, vol.
17, part 3 (1983)
Institute of Development Studies, 'Women and Development',
Development Research Digest, no. 7, IDS, University of
Sussex
Jackson, R.N. Immigrant Labour and the Development of Malaya
1786-1920 (University of Malaya Press, Kuala Lumpur, 1961)
Jayawardena, V.K. The Rise of the Labor Movement in Ceylon
(Duke University Press, Durham, North Carolina, 1972)
Jeeves, A. 'The Control of Migratory Labour on the Southern
African Gold Mines in the Era of Kruger and Milner',
Journal of Southern African Studies, vol. 2, no. 1 (1975)
Jeffries, R. 'The Labour Aristocracy? Ghana Case Study',
Review of African Political Economy, no. 3 (1975)
———Class, Power and Ideology in Ghana: The Railwaymen of
Sekondi (Cambridge University Press, Cambridge, 1978)

Further Reading

Johnson, D.L. 'Industrialization, Social Mobility and Class
    Formation in Chile', Studies in Comparative International
    Development, vol. 3, no. 7 (1968)
——'Observations on Rural Class Relations', Latin American
    Perspectives, vol. 9, no. 3 (1982)
——'Class Formation and Struggle in Latin America', Latin
    American Perspectives, vol. 10, nos. 2-3 (1983)
Johnson, F.A. Class, Race and Gold: A Study of Class Relations
    and Racial Discrimination in South Africa (Routledge and
    Kegan Paul, London, 1976)
Johnson, H. and Bernstein, H. (eds.) Third World Lives of
    Struggle (Heinemann, London, 1982)
Johnson, R.E. Peasant and Proletarian: The Working Class of
    Moscow in the Late Nineteenth Century (Rutgers University
    Press, New Brunswick, N.J., 1979)
Kapferer, B. Strategy and Transaction in an African Factory:
    African Workers and Indian Management in a Zambian Town
    (Manchester University Press, Manchester, 1972)
Karnik, V.B. Indian Trade Unions: A Survey, 2nd edn
    (Manaktalas, Bombay, 1966)
Kearney, R.N. Trade Unions and Politics in Ceylon
    (University of California Press, Berkeley, 1971)
Kennedy, P. 'Workers in Petty Production, Accra, Ghana: Towards
    Proletarianization?', Labour Capital and Society, vol. 16,
    no. 1 (1983)
King, L. 'Factory Work and Women in Taiwan', Signs, vol. 2, no.
    1 (1976)
Knight, G.R. 'From Plantation to Padi-Field: The Origins of the
    Nineteenth Century Transformation of Java's Sugar
    Industry', Modern Asian Studies, vol. 14, no. 2 (1980)
Lacey, M. Working for Boroko: The Origins of a Coercive Labour
    System in South Africa (Ravan Press, Johannesburg, 1981)
Laite, J. Industrial Development and Migrant Labour (Manchester
    University Press, Manchester, 1981)
Lambert, R.D. Workers, Factories and Social Change in India
    (Princeton University Press, Princeton, N.J., 1981)
Landsberger, H.A. 'The Labor Elite: Is It Revolutionary?', in
    S.M.Lipset and A.Solari (eds.) Elites in Latin America
    (Oxford University Press, New York, 1967)
Leitner, K. 'The Situation of Agricultural Workers in Kenya',
    Review of African Political Economy, no. 6 (1976)
Lim, L. Women Workers in Multinational Corporations in
    Developing Countries: The Case of the Electronics Industry
    in Malaysia and Singapore, Occasional Paper no. 9,
    Women's Study Program, University of Michigan, 1978
Lin, T-B., Rance, P.L. and Udo-Ernst, S. (eds.) Hong Kong:
    Economic, Social and Political Studies in Development
    (M.E.Sharpe, White Plains, N.Y., 1979)
Little, W. 'Popular Origins of Peronism', in D.Rock (ed.)
    Argentina in the Twentieth Century (Duckworth, London,
    1975)

Lloyd, P. A Third World Proletariat? (Allen and Unwin, London, 1982)

Lomnitz, L. Networks and Marginality: Life in a Mexican Shanty Town (Academic Press, New York, 1977)

Long, N.V. Before the Revolution: The Vietnamese Peasants Under the French (MIT Press, Cambridge, Mass., 1973)

Longuenesse, E. 'A History of the Syrian Labor Movement' MERIP Reports, no. 110 (1982)

Lourdes, B. (ed.) Women and Employment (Praeger, New York, 1983)

Lubeck, P. 'Labour in Kano Since the Petroleum Boom', Review of African Political Economy, no. 13 (1978)

—————— 'The Value of Multiple Methods of Researching Third World Strikes: A Nigerian Example', Development and Change, vol. 10 (1979)

Luckhardt, K. and Wall, B. Organize ... Or Starve: A History of the South African Congress of Trade Unions (Lawrence and Wishart, London, 1980)

Magill, J.H. Labor Unions and Political Socialization: A Case Study of Bolivian Workers (Praeger, New York, 1974)

Magubane, B. and Ntalaja, N. (eds.) Proletarianisation and Class Struggle in Africa (Synthesis Publications, San Francisco, 1983)

Mann, S.A. and Dickinson, J.M. 'Obstacles to the Development of a Capitalist Agriculture', Journal of Peasant Studies, vol. 5, no. 4 (1978)

Maram, S.L. 'The Immigrant and the Brazilian Labor Movement 1890-1920', in D.Alden and W.Dean (eds.) Essays Concerning the Socioeconomic History of Brazil and Portuguese India (University Presses of Florida, Gainesville, 1977)

Martinez-Alier, J. 'Peasants and Labourers in Southern Spain, Cuba and Highland Peru', Journal of Peasant Studies, vol. 1, no. 2 (1974)

Mazumdar, D. The Urban Labor Market and Income Distribution: A Study of Malaysia (Oxford University Press, New York, 1981)

Meer, Y.S. et al. Documents of Indentured Labour, Natal 1851-1917 (Zed Press, London, 1983)

Mehmet, O. (ed.) Poverty and Social Change in Southeast Asia: Selections from the Proceedings, Canadian Council for Southeast Asian Studies (University of Ottawa Press, Ottawa. 1979)

Mennoune, M. 'Origins of the Algerian Proletariat', MERIP Reports, no. 94 (1981)

MERIP Reports, 'Women and Work in the Middle East', MERIP Reports, no. 95 (1981)

Meyer, E. 'Between Village and Plantation: Sinhalese Estate Labour in British Ceylon', European Conference on Modern South Asian Studies, Sèvres (Editions du Centre National de la Recherche Scientifique, Paris, 1979)

Mhlongo, S. 'Black Workers' Strikes in South Africa', New Left

Further Reading

Review, no. 83 (1974)
Michie, A.N. 'Agricultural Mechanization and Economic
    Inequality: The Indian Experience', Social Science
    Quarterly, vol. 59 (1978)
Middleton, A. 'Division and Cohesion in the Working Class:
    Artisans and Wage Labourers in Ecuador', Journal of Latin
    American Studies, vol. 14. part 1 (1982)
Mihyo, P. 'The Struggle for Workers' Control in Tanzania',
    Review of African Political Economy, no. 4 (1975)
Mintz, S.W. 'Labor and Sugar in Puerto Rico and in Jamaica,
    1800-1850', Comparative Studies in Society and History,
    vol. 1, no. 3 (1959)
———'The Rural Proletariat and the Problem of Rural Prolet-
    arian Consciousness', Journal of Peasant Studies, vol. 1,
    no. 3 (1974)
Mitra, M. and Vijayendra, T. 'Agricultural Labourers and
    Peasant Politics: Rural Proletarianisation in Purnea,
    Bihar', Journal of Peasant Studies, vol. 9, no. 3 (1982)
Moorsom, R. 'Underdevelopment, Contract Labour and Worker
    Consciousness in Namibia, 1915-72', Journal of Southern
    African Studies, vol. 4, no. 1 (1977)
———'Labour Consciousness and the 1971-72 Contract
    Workers' Strike in Namibia', Development and Change, vol.
    10 (1979)
Morley, M. Labour Markets and Inequitable Growth: The Case of
    Authoritarian Capitalism in Brazil (Cambridge University
    Press, Cambridge, 1982)
Morris, M.D. The Emergence of an Industrial Labour Force in
    India: A Study of the Bombay Cotton Mills 1854-1947
    (University of California Press, Berkeley and Los Angeles,
    1965)
Munson, F.C. Indian Trade Unions: Structure and Functions
    (University of Michigan Press, Ann Arbor, 1970)
Murphy, E.D. Unions in Conflict: A Comparative Study of Four
    South Indian Textile Centres 1918-1939 (Manohar, New
    Delhi, 1981)
Murray, M.J. The Development of Capitalism in Colonial Indo-
    china: 1870-1940 (University of California Press, Berkeley
    and Los Angeles, 1980)
Myers, C.A. Labor Problems in the Industrialization of India
    (Harvard University Press, Cambridge, Mass., 1958)
Nakhleh, E.A. 'Labor Markets and Citizenship in Bahrayn and
    Qatar', Middle East Journal, vol. 31 (1977)
Nash, J. 'We Eat the Mines and the Mines Eat Us': Dependency
    and Exploitation in Bolivian Tin Mines (Columbia
    University Press, New York, 1979)
———and Fernández-Kelly, M.P. (eds.) Women, Men, and the
    International Division of Labor (State University of New
    York Press, Albany, N.Y., 1983)
Nevadomsky, J.-J. and Li, A. The Chinese in Southeast Asia: A
    Selected Bibliography of Publications in Western Languages

(University of California Press, Berkeley, 1970)

Newman, R.K. Workers and Unions in Bombay 1918-1929: A Study of Organization in the Cotton Mills (Australian National University Press, Canberra, 1981)

Niehoff, A. Factory Workers in India (The Public Museum, Milwaukee, Wisconsin, 1959)

Nore, P. and Turner, T. (eds.) Oil and Class Struggle (Zed Press, London, 1979)

Norman, J. Labor and Politics in Libya and Arab Africa (Bookman Associates, New York, 1965)

Nzula, A.T., Potekhin, I.I. and Zusmanovich, A.Z. Forced Labour in Colonial Africa (Zed Press, London, 1979)

O'Brien, J. 'The Formation of the Agricultural Labour Force in Sudan', Review of African Political Economy, no. 26 (1983)

O'Meara, D. 'The 1946 Mine Workers' Strike and the Political Economy of South Africa', Journal of Commonwealth and Comparative Politics, vol. 13, no. 2 (1975)

Omvedt, G. 'Revolution and the Rural Proletariat in Contemporary Western India', Journal of Contemporary Asia, vol. 3, no. 3 (1973)

Orde-Browne, G.St.J. The African Labourer (Oxford University Press, London, 1933; reissued Frank Cass, London, 1967)

Ornati, O.A. Jobs and Workers in India (Cornell University Press, Ithaca, N.Y., 1955)

Orr, C.A. 'Trade Unionism in Colonial Africa', Journal of Modern African Studies, vol. 4, no. 1 (1966)

Owen, E.R.J. (ed.) Studies in the Economic and Social History of Palestine in the Nineteenth and Twentieth Centuries (Macmillan, London, 1982)

Parpart, J. Capital and Labor on the African Copperbelt (Philadelphia, 1983)

Payne, T. Labour and Politics in Peru (Yale University Press, New Haven, Conn., 1965)

Peace, A. Choice, Class and Conflict: A Study of Southern Nigerian Factory Workers (London, 1979)

Perrings, C. Black Mineworkers in Central Africa: Industrial Strategies and the Evolution of an African Proletariat in the Copperbelt 1911-41 (Heinemann, London, 1979)

Phimister, I.R. and Van Onselen, C. Studies in the History of African Mine Labour in Colonial Zimbabwe (Mambo Press, Gwelo, 1976)

Phizacklea, A. One Way Ticket: Migration and Female Labour (Routledge and Kegan Paul, London, 1983)

Poblete Troncoso, M. and Burnett, B.G. The Rise of the Latin American Labor Movement (Bookman Associates, New York, 1960)

Popkin, S. The Rational Peasant: The Political Economy of Rural Society in Vietnam (University of California Press, Berkeley and Los Angeles, 1979)

Quijano, A. 'Imperialism and Marginality in Latin America', Latin American Perspectives, vol. 10, nos. 2-3 (1983)

309

Further Reading

Quintero-Rivera, A.G. 'Socialist and Cigarmaker: The Artisans'
    Proletarianization in the Making of the Puerto Rican
    Working Class', Latin American Perspectives, vol. 10, nos.
    2-3 (1983)
Rains, P. 'The Workers and the State in Latin America: Patterns
    of Dominance and Subordination', Civilisations, vol. 29,
    nos. 1-2 (1979)
Ramaswamy, E.A. The Worker and His Union: A Study in South
    India (Allied Publishers, New Delhi, 1977)
Richardson, P. Chinese Mine Labour in Transvaal (Macmillan,
    London, 1982)
Rodney, W. A History of the Guayanese Working People 1881-1905
    (Heinemann, Kingston and London, 1981)
Roper, J. Labour Problems in West Africa (Penguin,
    Harmondsworth, 1950)
Roseberry, W. 'From Peasant Studies to Proletarianization
    Studies', Studies in Comparative International Development
    vol. 18, nos. 1-2 (1983)
Royal Commission on Labour in India, Report, Cmd. 3883 (HMSO,
    London, 1931)
Safa, H.I. 'The Changing Class Composition of the Female Labor
    Force in Latin America', Latin American Perspectives, vol.
    4, no. 4 (1977)
———'Runaway Shops and Female Employment: The Search for
    Cheap Labour', Signs, vol. 7, no. 2 (1981)
Saffioti, H.I.B. Women in Class Society (Monthly Review Press,
    New York, 1978) [Brazil]
Saint, W.S. 'The Wages of Modernisation: A Review of the
    Literature on Temporary Labour Arrangements in Brazilian
    Agriculture', Latin American Research Review, vol. 16, no.
    3 (1981)
Salaff, J. Working Daughters of Hong Kong (Cambridge University
    Press, Cambridge, 1981)
Samaraweera, V. 'Land, Labour, Capital and Sectional Interests
    in the National Politics of Sri Lanka', Modern Asian
    Studies, vol. 15, no. 1 (1981)
Sandbrook, R. 'The Working Class in the Future of the Third
    World', World Politics, vol. 15, no. 3 (1973)
———Proletarians and African Capitalism: The Kenyan Case
    1960-1972 (Cambridge University Press, Cambridge, 1975)
———and Cohen, R. The Development of an African Working
    Class: Studies in Class Formation and Action (Longman,
    London, 1975)
Sandhu, K.S. Indians in Malaya: Some Aspects of Their
    Immigration and Settlement 1786-1957 (Cambridge University
    Press, Cambridge, 1969)
Sau, R. 'Rural Work Force in India: Proletarianization or
    Immiserization of the Peasantry?', Labour Capital and
    Society, vol. 12, no. 1 (1979)
Scott, C.D. 'Peasants, Proletarianization and the Articulation
    of Modes of Production: The Case of Sugar-Cane Cutters in

Northern Peru, 1940-69', Journal of Peasant Studies, vol. 3, no. 3 (1976)

Sen, S. Working Class of India: History of Emergence and Movement, 1830-1970 (K.P.Bagchi, Calcutta, 1977)

Serageldin, I. et al. Manpower and International Labour Migration in the Middle East and North Africa (Oxford University Press, London, 1983)

Sheth, N.R. The Social Framework of an Indian Factory (Manchester University Press, Manchester, 1968)

Shivji, I. Class Struggle in Tanzania (Tanzania Publishing House, Dar es Salaam, 1975)

Silver, J. 'Class Struggle in Ghana's Mining Industry', Review of African Political Economy, no. 12 (1978)

Simons, H.J. and Simons, R.E. Class and Colour in South Africa 1850-1950 (Penguin, Harmondsworth, 1969; reissued International Defence and Aid Fund, London, 1983)

Sketchley, P. Casting New Moulds (Institute for Food and Development Policy, San Francisco, 1980)

Soekarno, A. Marhaen and Proletarian (Cornell University Press, Ithaca, N.Y., 1960)

Sofer, E.F. 'Recent Trends in Latin American Labor Historiography', Latin American Research Review, vol. 15, no. 1 (1980)

Spalding, H.A. 'Recent Labor Studies: Old Assumptions and New Approaches', Latin American Research Review, vol. 10, no. 2 (1975)

——Organized Labor in Latin America (Harper and Row, New York, 1977)

Stichter, S. Migrant Labor in Kenya: Capitalism and African Response 1895-1975 (Longman, London, 1982)

Swanson, J.C. 'Some Consequences of Emigration for Rural Economic Development in the Yemen Arab Republic', Middle East Journal, vol. 33 (1979)

Takaki, R. '"An Entering Wedge": The Origins of the Sugar Plantation and a Multiethnic Working Class in Hawaii', Labor History, vol. 23, no. 1 (1982)

Tedjasuknana, I. The Political Character of the Indonesian Trade Union Movement (Cornell University Press, Ithaca, N.Y., 1958)

Tharamangalam, J. Agrarian Class Conflict: The Political Mobilization of Agricultural Labourers in Kuttanad, South India (University of British Columbia Press, Vancouver, 1981)

Thaxton, R. 'Land Rent, Peasant Migration, and Political Power in Yao Cun, 1911-1937', Modern Asian Studies, vol. 16, no. 1 (1982)

Tibi, B. 'Trade Unions as an Organisational Form of Political Opposition in Tunisia', Orient, vol. 20, no. 4 (1979)

Torre, J.C. 'Workers' Struggle and Consciousness', Latin American Perspectives, vol. 1, no. 1 (1974)

Touraine, A. and Pécaut, D. 'Working Class Consciousness and

Economic Development in Latin America', in I.L.Horowitz
    (ed.) Masses in Latin America (Oxford University Press,
    New York, 1970)
Trejo Delarbe, R.T. 'The Mexican Labor Movement 1917-75',
    Latin American Perspectives, vol. 3, no. 1 (1976)
Tuan-Wleh Mayson, D. and Sawyer, A. 'Labour in Liberia', Review
    of African Political Economy, no. 14 (1979)
Turner, H.A. with Fosh, P. et al. The Last Colony: But Whose?
    A Study of the Labor Movement, Labor Market and Labor
    Relations in Hong Kong (Cambridge University Press, New
    York, 1980)
United Nations Industrial Development Organization. Women in
    the Redeployment of Manufacturing Industry to Developing
    Countries, UNIDO Working Paper on Structural Changes, no.
    18 (1980)
Urrutia, M. The Development of the Colombian Labor Movement
    (Yale University Press, New Haven, Conn., 1969)
Van Niel, R. 'The Effect of Export Cultivations in Nineteenth
    Century Java', Modern Asian Studies, vol. 15, no. 1 (1981)
Van Onselen, C. Chibaro. African Mine Labour in Southern
    Rhodesia 1900-1933 (Pluto Press, London, 1976)
——Studies in the Social and Economic History of the
    Witwatersrand, 1886-1914 (2 vols., Longman, London, 1982)
Van Zwanenberg, R.M.A. Colonial Capitalism and Labour in Kenya
    1919-1939 (East African Literature Bureau, Nairobi, 1975)
Vergopoulos, K. 'Capitalism and Peasant Productivity', Journal
    of Peasant Studies, vol. 5, no. 4 (1978)
Volk, S.S. 'Class, Union, Party: The Development of a
    Revolutionary Union Movement in Bolivia (1905-1952)',
    Science and Society, vol. 39, nos. 1-2 (1975)
Wales, N. The Chinese Labor Movement (John Day, New York, 1945)
Walgama, S. A History of the Trade Union Movement in the
    Plantations in Sri Lanka (Centre for Society and Religion,
    Colombo, 1979)
Wallerstein, I. (ed.) Labor in the World Social Structure
    (Sage Publications, London, 1983)
Waterman, P. 'The Labor Aristocracy in Africa: Introduction to
    a Debate', Development and Change, vol. 6, no. 3 (1975)
——'Workers in the Third World', Monthly Review, vol. 29,
    (1977)
——'Consciousness, Organisation and Action Among Lagos
    Portworkers', Review of African Political Economy, no. 13
    (1978)
——Division and Unity Amongst Nigerian Workers. Lagos Port
    Unionism, 1940s-1960s (Institute of Social Studies, The
    Hague, 1982)
Watt, D.C. 'Labor Relations and Trades Unionism in Aden, 1952-
    1960', Middle East Journal, vol. 16, no. 3 (1962)
Werlhof, C.v. and Neuhoff, H.-P. 'The Combination of Different
    Production Relations on the Basis of Nonproletarian-
    ization: Agrarian Production in Yaracuy, Venezuela', Latin

American Perspectives, vol. 9, no. 3 (1982)
White, L.T. 'Shanghai's Contract Proletariat', *Comparative Urban Research*, vol. 3, no. 3 (1976)
————'Workers' Politics in Shanghai', *Journal of Asian Studies*, vol. 36, no. 1 (1976)
Wilson, F. *Labour in the South African Gold Mines 1911-1969* (Cambridge University Press, Cambridge, 1972)
Winn, P. 'Loosing the Chains: Labor and the Chilean Revolutionary Process, 1970-1973', *Latin American Perspectives*, vol. 3, no. 1 (1976)
Wolpe, H. 'Capitalism and Cheap Labour Power in South Africa: From Segregation to Apartheid', *Economy and Society*, vol. 1, no. 4 (1972)
————(ed.) *The Articulation of Modes of Production* (Routledge and Kegan Paul, London, 1980)
Young, K. (ed.) *Serving Two Masters* (Routledge and Kegan Paul, London, 1984)
————, Wolkowitz, C. and McCullagh, R. (eds.) *Of Marriage and the Market: Women's Subordination in International Perspective* (Routledge and Kegan Paul, London, 1981)
Zeitlin, M. *Revolutionary Politics and the Cuban Working Class* (Princeton University Press, Princeton, N.J., 1967)

resistance 2, 8, 11, 12,
14, 34, 36, 87, 90, 94
'worker-peasants 5, 79
see also labour, prolet-
ariat
world market 7, 123, 240-3

World Health Organisation 149

Young Officers' coup (Egypt)
171

Zimbabwe 5

For Product Safety Concerns and Information please contact our EU
representative GPSR@taylorandfrancis.com
Taylor & Francis Verlag GmbH, Kaufingerstraße 24, 80331 München, Germany

www.ingramcontent.com/pod-product-compliance
Lightning Source LLC
Chambersburg PA
CBHW070554270326
41926CB00013B/2305